THE PASSIONS OF MODERNISM

THE PASSIONS
OF MODERNISM

ELIOT, YEATS, WOOLF, AND MANN

ANTHONY CUDA

The University of South Carolina Press

© 2010 University of South Carolina

Published by the University of South Carolina Press
Columbia, South Carolina 29208

www.sc.edu/uscpress

Manufactured in the United States of America

19 18 17 16 15 14 13 12 11 10   10 9 8 7 6 5 4 3 2 1

Library of Congress Cataloging-in-Publication Data

Cuda, Anthony.
   The passions of modernism : Eliot, Yeats, Woolf, and Mann / Anthony
Cuda.
      p. cm.
   Includes bibliographical references and index.
   ISBN 978-1-57003-862-4 (cloth : alk. paper)
   1. Modernism (Literature) I. Title.
   PN56.M54C83 2010
   809'.9112—dc22

                                    2009043339

This book was printed on Glatfelter Natures, a recycled paper with
30 percent postconsumer waste content.

For Gabriel

CONTENTS

ACKNOWLEDGMENTS

"Books are indeed awful things," Lytton Strachey wrote to T. S. Eliot in July 1920, in reply to Eliot's recent letter about the "colossal" task of finishing his first book of essays, *The Sacred Wood.* "But, somehow or other," Strachey assured him, "they do get done." I suspect that—even in cases less colossal than Eliot's or Strachey's— the phrase "somehow or other" always gestures toward the names of the many friends and colleagues who help us to finish these awful things. My thanks go to the following individuals for their conversations and criticism on portions of this project at its various stages, early and late: Charles Altieri, Denise Baker, Bruce Barnhart, Marshall Brown, Giuliana Carugati, David Chinitz, Kevin Corrigan, Keith Cushman, Mary Gage Davidson, Frances Dickey, Gavin Drummond, Mary Ellis Gibson, Nancy Gish, Jennifer Grotz, Anne Hartle, Geraldine Higgins, Christopher Hodgkins, Walter Kalaidjian, Brian McGrath, Frank Meaux, James Morey, Patrick Query, James Matthew Wilson, and Lee Zimmerman. Thanks are also owed to Jim Denton and my readers from the University of South Carolina Press for their constructive comments and inquiries. I would like to extend a special thanks to the members of the Eliot Society, who listened and responded generously to early versions of this material, as did members of the Modernist Studies Association.

I am very grateful to Anne Wallace and the English Department, the College of Arts and Sciences, and the Office of Research and Public/Private Sector Partnerships at the University of North Carolina at Greensboro for research and travel grants and course-load reductions that helped to finish this project, as well as to the Graduate School of Arts and Sciences and the Center for Humanistic Inquiry at Emory University for the time and resources to sketch out its beginnings. Early versions of some sections first appeared in *Modern Language Quarterly, Twentieth-Century Literature,* and the *Yeats Annual,* and I thank the respective editors for their permission to reprint the material, all of which has been revised and expanded.

Ronald Schuchard has been an adviser, colleague, and friend of boundless generosity and invaluable guidance, and I thank him heartily for both. Whenever I try to thank Katherine Skinner for her candor and intelligence as a critic and her love and patience as my wife, I invariably fall short of the mark, and I am afraid that this time is no exception.

Excerpt from "Burnt Norton" in *Four Quartets* by T. S. Eliot, copyright © 1936 by Harcourt, Inc., and renewed 1964 by T. S. Eliot, reprinted by permission of Houghton Mifflin Harcourt Publishing Company.

Excerpts from "East Coker" in *Four Quartets,* copyright © 1940 by T. S. Eliot and renewed 1968 by Esme Valerie Eliot, reprinted by permission of Houghton Mifflin Harcourt Publishing Company.

Excerpt from "The Dry Salvages" in *Four Quartets,* copyright © 1941 T. S. Eliot and renewed 1969 by Esme Valerie Eliot, reprinted by permission of Houghton Mifflin Harcourt Publishing Company.

Excerpts from *Inventions of the March Hare: Poems 1909–1917* by T. S. Eliot, text copyright © 1996 by Valerie Eliot, reprinted by permission of Houghton Mifflin Harcourt Publishing Company.

Excerpts from *The Family Reunion: A Play,* copyright © 1939 by T. S. Eliot and renewed 1967 by Esme Valerie Eliot, reprinted by permission of Houghton Mifflin Harcourt Publishing Company.

Excerpt from *The Cocktail Party,* copyright © 1950 by T. S. Eliot and renewed 1978 by Esme Valerie Eliot, reprinted by permission of Houghton Mifflin Harcourt Publishing Company.

Excerpt from *The Letters of T. S. Eliot, 1898–1922,* copyright © 1988 by SET Copyrights Limited, reprinted by permission of Houghton Mifflin Harcourt Publishing Company.

Excerpt from *The Confidential Clerk,* copyright © 1954 by T. S. Eliot and renewed 1982 by Esme Valerie Eliot, reprinted by permission of Houghton Mifflin Harcourt Publishing Company.

Excerpt from *The Waves* by Virginia Woolf, copyright © 1931 by Harcourt, Inc., and renewed 1959 by Leonard Woolf, reprinted by permission of the publisher.

Excerpt from "Modern Novels" in *The Essays of Virginia Woolf,* vol. 3, *1919–1924,* copyright © 1988 by Quentin Bell and Angelica Garnett, reprinted by permission of Houghton Mifflin Harcourt Publishing Company.

Excerpt from "The Moment: Summer's Night" in *The Moment and Other Essays* by Virginia Woolf, copyright © 1948 by Harcourt, Inc., and renewed 1976 by Marjorie T. Parsons, reprinted by permission of the publisher.

Excerpts from "Street Haunting" and "A Letter to a Young Poet" in *The Death of the Moth and Other Essays* by Virginia Woolf, copyright © 1942 by Houghton Mifflin Harcourt Publishing Company and renewed 1970 by Marjorie T. Parsons, Executrix, reprinted by permission of the publisher.

Excerpts from "Appendix II: 'The Plumage Bill,'" in *The Diary of Virginia Woolf,* vol. 2, *1920–1924,* copyright © 1978 by Quentin Bell and Angelica Garnett, reprinted by permission of Houghton Mifflin Harcourt Publishing Company.

Excerpts from *the Collected Works of W. B. Yeats,* vol. 1, *The Poems, Revised* edited by Richard J. Finneran. Copyright © 1940 by Georgie Yeats. Copyright renewed © 1968 by

Bertha Georgie Yeats, Michael Bulter Yeats & Anne Yeats, reprinted with the permission of Scribner, a Division of Simon and Schuster, Inc. All rights reserved.

Excerpts from *The Variorum Edition of the Plays of W. B. Yeats* edited by Russell K. Alspach. Copyright © 1965 by Macmillan Publishing Company. Copyright © 1966 by Russell K. Alpach and Bertha Georgie Yeats, reprinted with the permission of Scribner, a Division of Simon and Schuster, Inc. All rights reserved.

Excerpts from *Autobiographies: Collected Works of W. B. Yeats,* vol. 3, by William Butler Yeats. Copyright © 1916, 1936 by Macmillan Publishing Company. Copyright renewed © 1944, 1964 by Anne Yeats, reprinted with the permission of Scribner, a Division of Simon and Schuster, Inc. All rights reserved.

Various excerpts from the prose of W. B. Yeats reprinted with the permission of A P Watt Ltd on behalf of Gráinne Yeats.

Excerpts from *The Magic Mountain* by Thomas Mann, translated by H. T. Lowe-Porter, translation copyright © 1927 and renewed 1955 by Alfred A. Knopf. Copyright © 1952 by Thomas Mann. Used by permission of Alfred A. Knopf, a division of Random House, Inc.

"Who Stood over Eliot's Shoulder? Passions of Recognition in His Later Work" first appeared in *Modern Language Quarterly* 66 (September 2005): 329–64.

"T. S. Eliot's Etherized Patient" first appeared in *Twentieth-Century Literature* 50 (Winter 2004).

"The Turbulent Lives of Painted Horses" first appeared in *Yeats Annual* 17 (2007).

ABBREVIATIONS

Principal editions of works cited frequently

T. S. ELIOT

CPP	*The Complete Poems and Plays, 1909–1950*
IMH	*Inventions of the March Hare: Poems 1909–1917*
KE	*Knowledge and Experience in the Philosophy of F. H. Bradley*
Letters	*The Letters of T. S. Eliot. Vol. 1: 1898–1922*
Plays	*The Complete Plays of T. S. Eliot*
PWEY	*Poems Written in Early Youth*
SE	*Selected Essays*
TVP	*The Three Voices of Poetry*

W. B. YEATS

Au	*Autobiographies*
CL1, 2, 3, 4	*The Collected Letters of W. B. Yeats,* Clarendon Press edition
CL InteLex	*The Collected Letters of W. B. Yeats,* InteLex edition
EE	*Early Essays*
E&I	*Essays and Introductions*
Ex	*Explorations*
IDM	*The Irish Dramatic Movement*
LE	*Later Essays*
Mem	*Memoirs*
VP	*The Variorum Edition of the Poems of W. B. Yeats*
VPl	*The Variorum Edition of the Plays of W. B. Yeats*
Vision	*A Vision*
Wade	*The Letters of W. B. Yeats*

VIRGINIA WOOLF

CR2	*The Second Common Reader, Annotated Edition*
Diary 1–5	*The Diary of Virginia Woolf*
Essays 1–4	*The Essays of Virginia Woolf*
Lighthouse	*To the Lighthouse*

Moments   *Moments of Being*
Moth   *The Death of the Moth, and Other Essays*
The Moment   *The Moment, and Other Essays*
Waves   *The Waves*

THOMAS MANN

Diaries   *Diaries, 1918–1939*
Essays   *Essays of Three Decades*
Faustus   *Doctor Faustus: The Life of the German Composer Adrian Leverkühn*
               as Told by a Friend
Letters   *Letters of Thomas Mann, 1889–1955*
Mountain   *The Magic Mountain*
Order   *Order of the Day: Political Essays and Speeches of Two Decades*
Stories   *Collected Stories*

THE PASSIONS OF MODERNISM

INTRODUCTION

Poets frequently, if not always, borrow from other poets;
we need to be reminded to what extent they do, and must,
borrow from themselves.

T. S. Eliot, "Poets' Borrowings" (1928)

SHELLEY AND THE TYPIST

This study takes its bearings from of one of W. B. Yeats's most compelling insights into the precocious character of the imagination, the ways in which its nimble, intuitive discoveries always surprise and surpass the intellect and its slow, awkward deliberations. In his illuminating early essay "The Philosophy of Shelley's Poetry" (1903), Yeats borrows a scene from his Romantic master's work to conjure a gothic vision of Shelley himself wandering through an abandoned, dimly lit temple to kneel in devotion at the altar of the Muses. He draws the scene not merely from one of Shelley's poems, he explains, but from *all* of them; it is a composite of the symbols and scenes that dominated Shelley's imagination throughout his career, returning time and again at crucial moments to help him to resolve the riddles of his own "half-understood visions" (*E&I* 87). Stepping into Shelley's place, Yeats imagines what he would have heard in that supremely receptive, meditative posture amid the sacred ruins: "I think too that as he knelt before an altar where a thin flame burnt in a lamp made of green agate, a single vision would have come to him again and again . . . and that voices would have told him how there is for every man some one scene, some one adventure, some one picture that is the image of his secret life, for wisdom first speaks in images, and that this one image, if he would but brood over it his life long, would lead his soul, disentangled from unmeaning circumstance and the ebb and flow of the world, into that far household where the undying gods await all those whose souls have become simple as flame, whose bodies have become quiet as an agate lamp" (*E&I* 95).

The meandering syntax and chantlike rhythms of this passage nearly seduce us away from its sense, as if Yeats (who was deeply committed to the initiations and ceremonies of the occult at this time) were intent on protecting a secret, on burying his hermetic treasure so that only the literary initiate might uncover it. There are two important elements here that Yeats's ideal literary apprentice would not fail to discern. First, his paradigm of the artist obsessively returning to a single image or scene is less a symbolic, mystical account of Shelley's verse than a nearly literal description of Yeats's own creative tendencies, of the way that his own imagination circled and circled in widening gyres around a distinct group of salient and ambiguous tropes over the course of his career, his own motley band of "circus animals," as he calls them in his final volume (*VP* 629). But more important, what Yeats calls the artist's "brooding" seems not so much a conscious, deliberate pattern of return and revision—especially in his own case—as an imaginative compulsion, an inward dictum that refuses to be ignored, or the result of a hidden mechanism of the mind that compels it to revisit certain scenes much as the trauma victim relives a traumatic event over and again until its psychological turbulence reaches equilibrium. It is as if the flame in the agate lamp burned a powerful intoxicant, irresistibly luring its worshipper time and again through the same labyrinthine ruins of the temple to gaze at its mysteries. What Yeats describes here, in short, is the passion of the artistic imagination, the process by which the creating mind assumes the character of *the moved*—without or even against its conscious awareness—rather than that of *the mover*.

This paradigm of creative return and revision is not unique to modernism. But what distinguishes it in writers like Yeats, T. S. Eliot, Virginia Woolf, and Thomas Mann—the primary objects of attention here—is that the image or scenario to which the modern artist is compulsively drawn is often itself a depiction of compulsion and passivity, a moment when the imagination is overwhelmed by its own creative energies, or when the mind succumbs to its own powerful affective forces. What most consistently moves the modern imagination is not a stately pleasure-dome, a vision of the Muse or the Deity, but the mind itself being moved, the processes by which it is acted upon and the ways in which it responds.

To put this claim to the test right away, I want to begin by offering an instance from *The Waste Land*, precisely because it seems such an unpromising place for us to begin a book about passion in literary modernism, a study of the ways that several modern writers situate passion—in several senses—at the foundations of psychological and creative activity. In fact, it is difficult to imagine a poem more barren of the telltale trappings of ardor and emotional intensity typically associated with passion. It possesses none of the fiery revelations that blaze through D. H. Lawrence's novels; none of the liberating cries of William Carlos Williams's poetry; and none of the visionary flames that smolder behind the eyes of Virginia Woolf's most memorable protagonists. In fact, if this most quintessentially modernist work of art may be said to approach a passion, it could only be Eliot's zealous desire to erase the possibility of passion entirely, to transform its dazzling flames into infernal tortures, its outbursts of freedom and self-possession into nightmarish shrieks of imprisonment and voices crying out of empty cisterns. Or as one reviewer of his earlier work remarked, perhaps it is simply that "Mr. Eliot . . . has forgotten his emotions."[1] Eliot was, after all, the poet who famously insisted that poetry is an escape from emotion. And is not *The Waste Land* his grand escape, his personal instrument of "relief"?[2] In its broken lines, even passion's brief, still moments of contented fullness and vibrancy become merely the low-humming throbs of a human engine, or the aching, paralyzed murmurs of an intimacy gone awry.

In a scene so familiar that it hardly needs retelling, Tiresias is witness to the arrival of the infamous "young man carbuncular"—a feeble, arrogant clerk with pretensions to high society—to his afternoon rendezvous at the typist's flat (*CPP* 44). In her boredom, the typist acquiesces to the young man's graceless sexual advances. After their brief, anticlimactic tryst, the clerk fumbles his way down the darkened stairwell and (in the draft) pauses to urinate in the street; the typist reassembles the room, grateful for his hasty removal. When last we see her, she is setting a record on the gramophone to begin the music—or perhaps to continue the haunting music that has already begun in a different key—that accompanies us into the poem's next section. As the sole witness to such a distinctly passionless affair intimates—"I Tiresias have foresuffered all"—there is much more to this scene than the apathy of its participants or the sneering irony that so many readers initially discerned in its retelling (*CPP* 44). Something about the typist passage has, in fact, sparked a disproportionate degree of critical debate, and in part it is this disproportion, the unlikely magnetism of the scene, that makes it so intriguing. For earlier scholars, it captured in miniature what they understood to be the poem's central concern: Eliot's sardonic critique of modernity, his invective against society's emotional emptiness and moral depravity. For others, it performed the sexual ambivalence and misogyny with which Eliot's earlier poems had carelessly toyed as well, from Saint Sebastian's brutal sexual fantasies to Sweeney's close encounters with ravenous female pursuers and traitorous adulterers.[3] More recent scholars have gravitated toward the uncanny automatism of the typist's final gesture, sensing in it a powerlessness beyond the mere unthinking routine of apathy, a helplessness that seems crucial to Eliot's vision of human relationships and especially to a scene so "intimate with suffering."[4] As Tiresias hints, suffering is in fact central to this moment, and I argue that a more wide-reaching and paradoxical sort of suffering is central to Eliot's thought about passion and poetics.

This scene so acutely traces in miniature the broader contours of *The Waste Land* because the typist's suffering registers a concern that had haunted Eliot's imagination for long before, from the writhing, tormented protagonists of "The Love Song of St. Sebastian" (1914) and "The Death of Saint Narcissus" (1915) to the anesthetized patient that opens his later, more famous "Love Song." Yeats would surely have recognized the emotions that accompany it; they are akin to those that he dramatizes in his own "Leda and the Swan" and in the late "Cuchulain Comforted." The scene is one of those rich and complex moments to which the artist is drawn throughout his entire career, one which promises (according to Yeats) to lead the imagination from meaningless ebb and flow of creative self-dispersion toward the hard, gemlike simplicity of a unified vision. It captures, in a kind of shorthand, the experience of suffering without acting, of being possessed by a force that the conscious will cannot resist or overcome, and of enduring a "passion" (in the broadest sense of the word, something which "moves" us or causes us to suffer) that transforms the autonomous mind into something like an automatic object; the typist's "automatic hand" sets the gramophone playing.

The emotional upheaval associated with this experience returns, even more thoroughly charged with the ambivalence of attraction and repulsion, in the final stanzas of *The Waste Land,* when the speaker imagines the "awful daring" of willfully surrendering oneself to this condition—both the excitement and the terror of suffering without resistance or escape (*CPP* 49). The passion of *The Waste Land* begins precisely here, I believe, in the emotional turmoil provoked by the awful, daring realizations of powerlessness and vulnerability—"awe-filled" because the mind typically resists losing control with all of its might, and "daring" because the loss of control, or the surrender of the ego's vigilance, can promise imaginative discoveries beyond what the mind's self-possession would have otherwise allowed. If the typist scene has attracted a degree of critical attention disproportionate to its seemingly minor place in the poem, I believe that this is because its implications reach far beyond *The Waste Land,* beyond any of Eliot's poems, and into concerns central to the way that a particular strand of modernism defines itself and its most ambitious projects. In short, I believe that following it will lead us deep into the same ruined temple where Yeats's Shelley kneels in silence, rapt in a vision of his own rapt imagination.

PASSION AND PATIENTS

This book explores how four modern writers engage with passion, how they learn to dramatize its upheavals and illuminations, and how this engagement changes the way that they think about creativity and literary composition. Each chapter offers a self-contained narrative, which can be consulted on its own, though here and in the conclusion I discuss how those narratives overlap and intertwine and where they challenge the prevailing scholarly consensus. I begin by resuscitating a classical meaning of the word "passion," the contemporary usage of which—as a vehement or powerful emotion—is a relatively late development. Historically the word derives from the Latin *passio,* meaning "to suffer" or "to be moved," an etymology from which we also derive "patient," which is the object of a passion, as well as "patience," which actually refers to the state of suffering. When I say that I will exercise patience, I am saying, in effect, that I will allow myself to be acted upon. As I discuss below in more detail, the classical definition of "passion" relies upon the distinction between the entity that acts and the entity that is acted upon, between what Aristotle calls the mover and the moved. In this sense, then, passion refers to suffering in general—anything that moves us, either with or without our intention—as well as to the particular instantiations of suffering, whether these be physical pain, emotional turmoil, the psychological movements compelled by what we call the unconscious, or those mysterious creative forces that we refer to as "inspiration." It is with passion in this broader, philosophical sense that the following pages will be concerned. I argue that many of the well-known hallmarks of literary modernism—its experimental forms, its radical poetic theories, and its innovative ideas about emotion and personality—arise in part from an urgent desire among modern writers to meaningfully encounter powerlessness, to both know and feel what it means to be *the moved* instead of *the mover.*

My claims run counter to a number of surprisingly intransigent assumptions about this school or strand of modernism, including those that underlie Peter Nicholls's claims in his relatively recent *Modernisms: A Literary Guide* (1995), a desperately needed and yet deeply flawed polemic in favor of expanding the conventional modernist canon. With an eye toward what he calls canonical modernism's "defensive" ironies and the "ubiquitous trope of mastery," Nicholls contrasts several marginalized or neglected strands of modernism with the masculinist aesthetics and ideology of Ezra Pound, Wyndham Lewis, and the "Men of 1914," among whose later ranks he includes Eliot and Yeats.[5] For him, this domineering modernism relentlessly privileges "intellect over emotion" and aggressively enforces "strong and authoritative versions of the self."[6] Poets like Eliot and Yeats undertake "the task of stabilizing the self, closing it to the turbulent movements of desire," Nicholls argues: "One of the first moves of this Modernism had been to reconstitute the self as closed, autonomous, and antagonistic." Poets such as H.D. and Gertrude Stein, he concludes, aimed instead to destroy the autonomy "which is so much prized by the 'Men of 1914,'" and in doing so successfully "*open* the self to what is outside it."[7] I agree with Nicholls's assessment of H.D., but I believe that he is profoundly wrong about Eliot and others, that they are the wrong straw men for this line of argument. To be fair, Nicholls is only building upon the similar claims in the first volume of Gilbert and Gubar's *No Man's Land* (1988), another polemic that made its much-needed corrections to the canon at the expense of canonical modern writers, whose complexity they were similarly forced to elide. "The Eliotian theory," Gilbert and Gubar argue, "that poetry involves 'an escape from emotion' and 'an escape from personality' constructs an implicitly masculine aesthetic of hard, abstract learned verse that is opposed to the aesthetic of soft, effusive, personal verse supposedly written by women and Romantics."[8] There is a kind of critical metonymy at work in statements like this one, a familiar tendency to focus upon one aspect of modernist aesthetic theory and allow it to eclipse the complexity and ambivalence of the whole, which often provides ample evidence to the contrary as well. In fact, the very essay under consideration, Eliot's over-determined "Tradition and the Individual Talent" (1919), also describes the poet in terms of passivity and emotional sensitivity; its rhetoric, in other words—as well as the rhetoric of Eliot's nearly contemporaneous lecture for the Arts League of Service, "Modern Tendencies in Poetry" (delivered in 1919 but not published until 1920)—is deeply divided between what Gilbert and Gubar would characterize as masculine and feminine aesthetics. I believe that scholars of modernism like Nicholls continue to misunderstand the modernist preoccupation with tropes of control and mastery because they are too quick, ultimately, to succumb to the temptation of this critical metonymy, to rely upon reductive and incomplete readings of canonical authors whose profound misgivings about the possibility of self-sovereignty and self-transparency would otherwise threaten to render the conventional critical shorthand no longer useful. This failure is symptomatic of a wide range of critical attitudes about canonical or mainstream modernism that I address, both implicitly and explicitly, in the following chapters.

The modernist writers whom I address here, to the contrary, deeply valued the destabilizations of passion and the intensities of affect and were frequently sus-picious of the illusions of a "stabilized," autonomous self. Modernism is, for the majority of scholars, renowned for its theoretical and imaginative assaults on uni-fied subjectivity and consciousness, but the purpose and valence of these assaults as well as the roles of passivity and affective experience in dramatizing them have been, I believe, simplified and elided by our tendency to conflate them with the linguistic critiques of subjectivity proper to postmodernism. In this vein, my assumptions are largely in accord with the findings of scholars like Charles Altieri, Richard Sheppard, Tim Dean, and others who discern a post-Enlightenment cri-tique of "exaggerated human self-valuation" (yet not a wholesale critique of En-lightenment rationality) at the foundation of modernist aesthetics.[9] Especially for Yeats and Eliot, a "closed" self is not merely an obstacle to artistic creativity but a psychological impossibility, a fantasy undercut at every step by the turbulent pas-sions to which the self succumbs and upon which it depends for its vitality.

I have made Eliot the central figure of this study not only because his render-ings of passion strike me as richly complex and compelling but also because his work is a magnet for the kinds of critical misconceptions about modernism that I seek to correct. Yeats is my counterpoint because he seems diametrically opposed to Eliot on the topics of emotion, passivity, and suffering, and yet he too sought to situate passion at the foundations of intellectual and creative activity while simultaneously refusing to dismiss the value of active, rational thought. Their two drastically different ways of envisioning a productive response to passion—Eliot attempts to bring the conscious mind into a consonant meditative state, Yeats attempts to heighten its activity to a fever pitch—represent the boundary conditions of mental activity and thus circumscribe the space of artistic experiment and affective modulation that their modern contemporaries also inhabit. I include Mann and Woolf not because they are alone among modern novelists who share these concerns but because their means of addressing them—the repeated dramatization of certain dominant or touchstone tropes—so closely correspond to Yeats's and Eliot's methods that the resemblance seems to indicate a widespread imaginative mode rather than an isolated stylistic strategy. The four writers whom I have chosen to address in this book, I realize, are canonical, and especially in light of recent scholarship on formerly marginalized figures and movements, I do not assume their modernism to be the only modernism. My goal is to say something meaningful and compelling about each of them, often with the help of evidence from the archives and from neglected texts. If another corner of modernism's enormous room becomes a bit more familiar to us in the process, then I will have accomplished much.

PASSION AND INSPIRATION

Rethinking these four well-known writers in terms of passion will demand that I revisit the distinctively modernist *topoi* that have become attached to their names, like the dissolution of the self, the doctrine of impersonality, and the autonomy of art. Each of these contested and overdetermined *topos* began, however, not in pure mind but amid the rags and bones of the artist's workshop. And if questions about subjectivity, impersonality, and autonomy all derive from the process of creative composition, then I believe that I can best address them and others by focusing more directly upon modernist ideas about inspiration and creativity. In the pages that follow, the process of creative composition—and the innovative theories about creativity that each writer explores—will become the conceptual backdrop against which other modernist commonplaces and conventions will appear in new and perhaps unexpected forms.

Several contemporary scholars have explored the recent rehabilitation of inspiration as a conceptual category, remarking its surprising centrality to the philosophies of language and subjectivity in twentieth-century poetry and in poststructuralist theory in France and America.[10] But for most scholars of literary modernism, it remains the vestige of Platonic metaphysics. Contemporary scholarship often considers inspiration an ideological device aimed at establishing authority and control.[11] If we talk about inspiration at all, we do so with either irony or suspicion. The contemporary mistrust of metaphysics, however, need not be an obstacle if our primary concern is to address the experience of artistic creation solely from within the immanent, phenomenological circumference of the artist's awareness. If we restrict the conversation to the domain of the "moved," the "patient" or recipient of the divine *afflatus,* then the concept of inspiration gestures not toward transcendence (the ostensible agent or origin of the utterance) but solely toward a certain incompleteness or insufficiency proper to the creative mind. It presents the artist with a vision of his or her own mind that is partial, half-darkened, and deeply ambivalent in its foreignness. In the finished work of art, the mind is confronted with a task that it did not accomplish alone, a work whose origin and ultimate meaning it cannot decipher, and the evidence of a seemingly intentional agent that is, however, not identical with the conscious agent that we identify as the self. The artist writes; the text is written. And although these two actions occur simultaneously, they are not identical.

Were this anxious sense of mental foreignness merely part of the preparatory work of the artist, the deliberate receptivity that the mind cultivates before composition begins, the modern view of inspiration would remain squarely within Romantic parameters, like those that Shelley sets when he suggests that inspiration is already on the decline when composition begins. The act of writing would be yet another way of reasserting the ascendancy of the conscious will, a way to recuperate whatever mastery the artist might temporarily abandon beforehand. Writing would be, in short, a tranquil recollection that neutralizes the dangers and risks of emotional upheaval. But the writers whom I address all hold that passivity can be—and in some cases must be—simultaneous with artistic creation, that the creative act fuses action and passion together in an impossible simultaneity. Each refuses to submit to the conventional dichotomy whereby passion and action—in this case, inspiration and composition—remain opposing, mutually exclusive states. Once we cede the possibility that the mind can *sometimes* be moved without our conscious awareness—that is, once we fully register the more disturbing possibilities implicit in this artistic "possession"—we must also admit the possibility that the mind is *always* moved, that no conscious agent is free from a motivating energy unknown to it. In short, because passion need not abide by and often obscures the faculties that allow us to recognize it, we can never be certain of its absence.

In terms strikingly reminiscent of literary and philosophical discussions of inspiration since Plato—and that distinctly recall Freud's early descriptions of the unconscious, a parallel that will become important later—contemporary philosopher Michel Meyer contends that passion is "in fact *the other* in us, without whom we would not exist, but with whom it is difficult and dangerous to be."[12] To adopt a turn of phrase from Eliot, the apparently impenetrable walls of the artist's psyche have been breached. Somewhere in the basement, a door has been left ajar, and no amount of fumbling through the dark will suffice to find it and secure its latch. Although they receive little critical attention, the affective implications of this open door—the sense of anxiety and passivity that it tends to provoke—cannot be overstated. In a way, modernism discovers its theories of both poetics and passion in the very act of confronting this door and grappling with the disturbing realization that it will not be—nor perhaps was it ever—safely closed.

The emotional and psychological ramifications of this version of inspiration are what most interest me here, the ways that modern writers' theories of creative "possession"—which arise explicitly from their experiences of being spoken through, or unconsciously moved—lead them toward the same confrontation with vulnerability and powerlessness that they discover in their other spheres of interest, from Yeats's experiments with trance mediumship and Mann's infatuation with infectious diseases to Woolf's and Eliot's fascination with surrender and impersonality. In this way, the theory of inspiration becomes a metonym for psychological processes more generally; rather than a rare, aberrant occurrence from which the mind returns to its normative state of control and activity, it becomes the standard against which all mental acts are measured.

METHOD: THE PASSION SCENE

I am interested in how modern writers think about passion and passivity, but I am equally interested in how passivity informs and underwrites the process of composition for those same writers. Eliot says, for instance, that writing demands a tremendous degree of surrender and passivity, and yet for years scholars have considered him a master of deliberate craftsmanship, intense self-consciousness, and aesthetic control. In "Adam's Curse," Yeats admits that a single line of verse often takes hours of concentrated attention to compose, and yet elsewhere he proposes that the poet is no more than a vessel or passive medium for the daemonic spirit of inspiration. If we want to avoid simply dismissing these claims as self-contradictory, as poetic ideals never realized in the poetry itself, we must find a way to account for their strange simultaneity. In other words, my method must address both theory and praxis, how each writer imagines passivity and how passivity affects the way that he or she writes. But what sort of analysis will offer evidence of the writer's compositional process? How can one hope to determine if the writer practices what he or she preaches?

The examination of a single text and the implications of its verbal strategies might reveal the writer's thoughts about passivity at a single point in time, or how those thoughts inform the text's figurative operations. But it will not tell us whether a particular scene or trope exerted an unusual pressure on the writer's imagination; whether he or she felt compelled to revisit it repeatedly, as if to dress a reopened wound or consult an oracle; whether it was, in short, one of those intensely magnetized scenes toward which, as Yeats believes, the compass needle of the poet's imagination invariably snaps. Admittedly no method can promise certainty about the degree of passivity that a writer did or did not experience during composition. But I might offer some fruitful speculations if I begin by tracing, diachronically, how certain tropes and scenes recur throughout the writer's career, how they seem significant enough to be invoked (consciously or unconsciously) in a wide variety of contexts and genres. At the very least, directing our attention toward such insistent repetitions and recurrences will provide the basis, in each individual chapter, for a micronarrative of creative self-revision and imaginative continuity. These narratives do not shy away from biography or intentionality, which I consider to be valid and illuminating—if always contingent—tools of interpretation. As Yeats argues, a poet's biography and intentions must always inform but can never exhaust the text's possibilities of meaning.

Primarily for the purposes of shorthand—but also in order to distinguish them from the symbol and the image—I refer to these recurrent tropes and scenarios in the chapters that follow as "passion scenes," and I choose that term for two reasons: First, they typically portray passive suffering, vulnerability, and powerlessness; passion in its several senses is their subject matter. Second, they seem to exert an unusual psychological force upon the creative mind that conjures them, an autonomous energy that may very well trump conscious intention and deliberation; passion is somehow part of their method. In short, I have taken the passage from Yeats with which this book began as both a thematic prompt and a methodological blueprint.

I begin by identifying a trope or scenario that occurs regularly over some segment of the writer's career, one which tends to appear at key moments of intellectual or emotional discovery and which extends laterally through multiple genres of poetry, fiction, nonfiction, even letters and autobiography. With the salient structural features of this scene in mind, I then attempt to think through the imaginative situation at the text's origin, the questions and quandaries that the author was facing each time that the scene offered itself as mode of aesthetic exploration or resolution. In this vein, I find it useful to recall that medieval thinkers like Augustine and Aquinas wrote of the imagination as a "storehouse" of forms or shapes (*thesaurus formarum*), a vast mental warehouse in which the mind accumulates images, impressions, and composite arrangements of sensory experience. My assumption is that the items stockpiled in a writer's imaginative storehouse tend to form idiosyncratic groupings associated with certain intellectual and emotional problems, so that when the mind confronts one of these problems, it cannot help but draw upon (consciously or unconsciously) the particular stores of images attached to it. Over time, these groupings shift, alter, and intermingle; new, more useful chains of association assemble, while others lose their urgency and usefulness. So with each reappearance of a particular passion scene, I ask: What intellectual and affective problems are now at stake? What new creative demands does it attempt to meet? And how does its current manifestation alter the dramatic landscape of the work in which it appears?

Eliot's etherized patient lying upon a table or his startled narrator glancing over his shoulder; Yeats's white horses descending from their painted surface; Mann's microscopic agents of infection invading an unsuspecting victim; and Woolf's portrayals of the naked eyeball threatened by the razor-sharp objects of perception— these are all vivid, intense tropes toward which each writer repeatedly gravitates in the attempt to address a constantly changing yet remarkably constant set of questions. My aim is not to assemble these scenes in the hopes of discovering an all-encompassing psychological, symbolic, or mythological system into which they all might fit. The urgent pressure exerted by the scenes, in fact, derives from the impossibility of such a system, from the frustrating ways in which they simultaneously seem to offer and refuse resolution and fulfillment. Nor do I want to claim for them a reconciling unity consistent with Frank Kermode's "Romantic Image" or with what another scholar calls the "erotics of the image," both of which imply a self-perpetuating symbolic system aimed at containing and resolving polarities.[13]

Though I insist on using the term "passion scene" primarily as a critical expedient and not as a new aesthetic or theoretical category, it is important to distinguish between it and the similar conventions of the symbol or the image. In standard modernist discourse, the crucial element of the symbol or the image is its apparent atemporality, the way in which it ostensibly unifies the verbal elements of the poem and the disparate elements of experience by tapping into an originary, ahistorial phantasmagoria. On the contrary, the passion scene relies entirely upon a set of changing, conflicted valences and is contingent upon the context and circumstance of its latest appearance. Its critical usefulness, in fact, derives from the way that its unpredictable shifts and modulations register the artist's shifting and modulating concerns. If the symbol hovers or glides over change and tension, one might say that the passion scene falters and lurches with each altered, renewed appearance. In each chapter, I trace the constantly changing valences of such a scene over the course of a single artist's career, and I attempt to show how the tensions that arise also indicate important tensions in his or her thinking about passion and creativity. If the discrete verbal units of an individual poem offer us a stylized chart of mental conflict and change, then the many works that comprise a single artistic corpus—alongside the published and unpublished archival records that complicate and illuminate them—promise to sketch for us the wildly uneven contours of a lifelong emotional and intellectual engagement, complete with all of its false starts, circularities, and paradoxes.

The method that I am suggesting will offer, in short, a series of narratives of creative struggle and development, each of which traces what Yeats memorably called the poet's quarrel with himself. It is predicated upon the possibility that an artist's career is influenced by persistent and not altogether conscious sets of metaphors, and it implies that the artist's imagination is not always the prime mover in its universe of created forms.

If there is another discourse that is equipped to gauge the complex implications of Yeats's formulation—creativity as a quarrel with oneself, with the internal foreignness and opacities of one's own mind—it is psychoanalysis. The four authors whom I consider here were all, to varying degrees and with varying levels of commitment, aware of the developments in the emergent fields of psychology and psychoanalysis in the early decades of the twentieth century. Eliot regarded Freud with suspicion but was influenced by the empiricist psychology of James, whose work he studied ardently at Harvard. Yeats was more strongly moved by Jungian psychology, though he arrived there by way of the occult and the symbolic. Both Woolf and Mann knew and appreciated Freudian psychoanalysis, but both harbored profound misgivings about its effects on art and the imagination. To do justice to the varied and heterogeneous psychological discourses that inform modernism's passions—including not only Freud and Jung but the "new psychologists" of the late nineteenth century, like James, Mach, and Brentano—would itself require a book-length study, one that would explore, for instance, how texts as different as Mach's *Analysis of Sensations* (1886) and Freud's "The Unconscious" (1915) come together in Yeats's psychosomatic daemonology. Fortunately there has been an impressive and invaluable amount of recent work on the tensions and productive exchanges between literary modernism, Freudian and post-Freudian psychoanalysis, and other early-twentieth-century discourses of psychology.[14] And this, admittedly, is one of the reasons that I have not given psychoanalysis a more prominent place in the pages that follow. Instead, in my attempt to take a fresh look at four modernist writers and their commitments to emotion and passivity, I have chosen to rely upon the dichotomy between passion and action in hopes that this philosophical framework will prove spacious enough to accommodate the divergent modernist psychologies without imposing a single, dominant theory to which each artist either subscribes or does not.

PHILOSOPHIES OF PASSION AND ACTION

A brief and very selective glimpse at aspects of the classical philosophical discourse on the passions will help to clarify the terms with which I have framed this study. The specific meaning of "passion" as emotional upheaval is actually derivative of the broader distinction between "action" and "passion," a conceptual opposition that the Western philosophical tradition inherits from Aristotelian metaphysics and psychology via the medieval scholasticism of Aquinas. That the term remains in widespread use today testifies to the way it has become structurally embedded in our view of human psychology. In short, the terms "action" and "passion" designate the relationship between an entity that *acts* or *originates movement* and an entity that is *acted upon* or *moved*. As Susan James succinctly puts it, the difference between them amounts to "a difference between the power of an object to be moved (which is a passion) and the power of an object to move itself (which is an action)."[15] Or as the phenomenon is formulated with equal lucidity by the foremost contemporary thinker of passion, French philosopher Michel Meyer, "to have a passion, in the original sense of the word *pathos,* simply means that the soul has suffered a movement."[16] Whether they are humans or objects, all entities can be understood to share certain degrees of passivity and activity, based upon the perspective from which we observe them. Descartes adopts the Aristotelian terms to formulate his definitions in *The Passions of the Soul:* "I note that whatever takes place or occurs is generally called by philosophers a 'passion' with regard to the subject to which it happens and an 'action' with regard to that which it makes happen. Thus, although an agent and a patient are quite often different, an action and a passion must always be a single thing which has two names on account of the different subjects to which it may be related."[17] A baseball can be either an agent or a patient depending on whether it is breaking a window or being hit by a baseball bat; a person can be either an agent or patient depending on whether he or she strikes the baseball or is struck by it.

In the Cartesian paradigm, the umbrella of "passion" encompasses four subcategories of perceptivity, including external objects of sense perception, bodily perceptions (such as hunger and pain), perceptions of the soul or emotions, and what Descartes calls "imaginings."[18] In this broad sense, emotions such as anger or pity are clearly passions, but so are rancid smells and chicken pox, an aching back or a daydream. For Descartes and others, we "perceive" an emotion like joy or sorrow in much the same way that we perceive a thornbush or a tornado, that is, as something that acts upon us "from without," something that affects us and is caused by a force that is not our volition. Mental passions are all "perceptions" insofar as they are "thoughts which are not actions of the soul or volitions."[19] What unites these disparate phenomena—products of the passions of the body and those of the soul—is that we, however temporarily, become passive before them. It is important to note that Descartes makes a place for the imagination among these nonvolitional passions. As long as "our will is not used in forming them," imaginative visions and illusions can press upon our mind just as vividly as sense objects press upon our sensual organs.[20] Just as heat from a boiling kettle acts upon the hand, disturbing its natural equilibrium, so too do emotions and imaginings cause disturbances in the mind; and "until this disturbance ceases they remain present to the mind in the same way as the objects of the senses are present to it while they are acting upon our sense organs."[21]

There are two important implications of the philosophical discourse on the passions to which I would like to draw attention here. First, no matter how normal and necessary a place the passions assume in the various typologies of human experience, they are still construed as a temporary disturbance or departure from which we must recover. For Aristotle, passion "carries a man away"; for Descartes, it is always "accompanied by some disturbance which takes place in the heart."[22]

The gear in which the normal, balanced mind idles is almost always active, conscious, and deliberate. It would seem that nothing could be more human than passion. Yet if we define "the human" with an eye toward our capacity to think, judge, and will action, passion can prove "dehumanizing" insofar as it interferes with all of these. Even the humanistic, anti-stoical thinkers in the Western tradition for whom passion is both necessary and justified nonetheless maintain that it departs from the normative states of the human organism.[23] And if the human process of creative composition is fundamentally active, if the act of writing words on a page (as opposed to the imaginative passivity often characterized as inspiration) entails a self-possession and deliberate control, then passion is equally disruptive of literary craft. No matter how freely the balloon of the imagination may drift and sway (to use Yeats's metaphor), it must eventually be hauled down by the active mind in order for composition to occur.

The second implication that I would like to remark is that "passion" tends to blur the conceptual boundaries between psyche and soma. Most thinkers agree that heartburn is not a psychological event and that solving a mathematical equation does not involve the digestive tract. But just how far anger or depression, for instance, crosses into or originates from somatic territory is not nearly so commonly agreed upon. Suffering of most sorts, it seems, often has the effect of eliding the distinction between mind and matter, or between the human and the object. In this sense, both the physical and psychological passions hasten the disturbing realization of what Eliot calls "the reluctance of the body to become a *thing*," that is, our reluctance to admit our kinship to the world of objects (*CPP* 384). The philosophical and experiential proximity between the bodily and the psychological passions is what will allow Virginia Woolf to claim that we need a new "hierarchy of the passions" that gives equal weight to the throes of fever, the pitch of emotion, and the ecstasies of inspiration (*Essays* 4.194). And it is what underlies Thomas Mann's suggestion that the infectious spread of disease, the building momentum of lust, and the slow-growing energies of creativity are all variations on a single theme, which he calls "the devastating invasion of passion."[24] These apparently dissimilar phenomena are brought together insofar as the normally active, choosing, and self-determining human agent becomes, in relation to them, a patient with qualities not dissimilar from a mute object.

In its traditional senses, then, passion is always an aberrant intervention of psychosomatic conflict and discord; it is a threatening, unusual phenomenon that demands all of our conscious powers to control and discipline it into abeyance. The pedagogical hyperbole with which philosophy frequently treats its threatening potential only serves to bring the threat into better focus. Descartes argues unconvincingly in *The Passions of the Soul*, "Even those who have the weakest souls could acquire absolute mastery over all their passions if we employed sufficient ingenuity in training and guiding them."[25] A consistent theme for moralists from

Cicero to La Rochefoucauld, the desire to train, guide, and master the passions reflects our suspicion of their fundamental foreignness and of the ways in which that foreignness threatens to divide us, perhaps permanently, from ourselves.

SENTIMENTAL AND SUBLIME PASSIONS

The philosophical discourse on the passions veers most sharply toward literary concerns in the eighteenth and early nineteenth centuries, when it becomes a key component in discussions of the sentimental and the sublime. Because contemporary scholarship has recently discerned the formative influence of these two inter-related aesthetic modes on early modernism, it will prove worth our while to linger over them for a moment.[26] Although sentimentality properly refers to the conventions of a genre of eighteenth-century fiction, its emphasis on the various modes of passive perception—sensitive, affective, intellectual—makes it a useful way for us to address how early modern "passion" transformed from an abstract philosophical problem to an urgent point of contention among the immediate predecessors of the modernists in the late nineteenth century.

From Descartes' passions and the similar preoccupations of the seventeenth-century Cambridge Platonists, the broader discourse surrounding "sentimental-ism" makes its way through the eighteenth-century ethical philosophies of Hume and Locke, is transfigured in Edmund Burke's theories of the sublime, and reaches a turning point of sorts in the Romantic poets that were eventually so maligned in certain circles of modernism. In terms of this simplified chronology, the "sentimental" refers to the focus upon the primacy of affect in the economy of mental experience, its role in ethical and political judgment, and its centrality to the creative process. Surprising as it may seem given the term's contemporary cultural usage, scholars of eighteenth-century literature have long recognized that sentimentality provides the affective spectrum upon which we situate, at the farthest, white-hot end, the idea of the sublime. The sentimental hinges upon the mind's passive powers or its capacity to feel, and the sublime is (as Burke says) a product of "the strongest emotion which the mind is capable of feeling."[27]

At its uppermost extreme, the sentimental verges toward Burkean sublimity, the mental state that occurs when the passions are wrought to such a high pitch—that is, when they demonstrate their indisputable primacy by annulling all other mental faculties—that our response is limited to mute astonishment or reverence. The historical debate about whether the sublime is an external, objective characteristic or an internal, subjective response is a direct result of the ambiguity that allows the Cartesian passions to straddle both internal and external perceptions. Burke's sublimity is primarily an arbiter of passion in the sense of both emotion and passivity; part 2 of his *Philosophical Enquiry* (1757) begins explicitly with the subtitle, "the passion caused by the sublime." The sublime provokes astonishment, fear, a "delightful terror" not dissimilar from what Wordsworth would later call the "beauty, which . . . hath terror in it" or from Eliot's "awful daring."[28] But it also renders the mind's active faculties bewildered and ineffectual. The soul's conscious motions are helplessly suspended, Burke says, while the passion of the sublime "hurries us on by irresistible force."[29] For the purposes of my argument, Burke's most compelling insight into the sublime is its connection to self-preservation and thus its relationship to the classical model of catharsis. Whatever pleasure we derive from the sublime, he suggests, arises from what it reveals about our tenuous hold on life.[30] That is, Burke discerns in the sublime an escalated version of the same threatening, dehumanizing potential of passion in the philosophical sense, the power to disrupt and disturb those actions whereby we define human physical and mental activity.

Burke's emphasis on cathartic self-preservation helps to explain the facility with which the passion of the sublime could paradoxically become, in the hands of Romantic poets, not only a reification of the self but a mode of self-transcendence, of the self's dialectical approach to the infinite and withdrawal back into temporality. In book 1 of *The Prelude*, for instance, Wordsworth registers the spontaneous outburst of receptivity, feeling, and poetry as both a blessing and a temporary disturbance to be allayed; eager to "give / A respite to this passion," the speaker hastens toward more moderate, less overwhelming pleasures. In the second book he returns to the "extrinsic passion" of Nature and how it "peopled the mind with forms sublime." And before long he elevates passion to its rightful place in the Romantic hierarchy of feeling, referring to it as "passion, which itself / Is highest reason in a soul sublime."[31] The Wordsworthian speaker explicitly pairs sublimity and the passions, and he suffers the sublime passions as if they were part of an existential test, an initiatory trial that seems to endanger but ultimately exalts the unity and transcendence of the self.

With no small help from the classicist philosophies of Irving Babbitt and T. E. Hulme, many modern writers learned to distrust this possibility, which came to seem wishful and self-aggrandizing. Thus they could not subscribe to the sublime as a singular, aberrational state, one into which the mind perilously descends only to make its timely, triumphant recovery. But they were not willing to dismiss it from the necessarily capacious emotional spectrum of modern poetics, nor from the realm of intuitive possibilities toward which Henri Bergson's influential philosophy had gestured. So in effect modernism seeks to free sublimity from a mute, anomalous state of response—or from a state of "poetic" rapture and emotional excess—and instead to make it a fundamental aspect of creative activity in general, one whose threat to self-preservation and psychic autonomy does not impede but rather "hurries on" (in Burke's phrase) literary composition.

Insofar as the sentimental in all of its forms was often aligned with the Romantic and the "feminine" literary traditions, it earned the censure of modernists like T. E. Hulme and Ezra Pound. Their advocacy of technical craftsmanship and

Augustan classicism (especially in Eliot's and Pound's quatrain poems of 1918–20) was articulated in explicit opposition to the formal liberties that, they suspected, resulted from the overvaluing of emotion. The mainstream modernism of Lewis, Pound, Woolf, Eliot, and Joyce, it is often argued, constituted itself precisely by denying its sentimental heritage. Critics remind us of Pound's desire for a poetry that is "austere, direct, free from emotional slither," or Hulme's directive that emotion in art be subservient to clarity and precision.[32] In short, we have learned—at times from scholars, at times from the artists themselves—to view the sentimental as modernism's other, as a force operating from within modernism whose potential for subversion was realized solely by feminist and politically progressive artists in opposition to the conservative philosophy of more mainstream writers.[33] On the contrary, I hope to show that Eliot, Yeats, Woolf, Mann, and others, despite their frequent diatribes against the sentimental tradition and the Romantic sublime, were deeply invested in the kind of intense emotional self-awareness to which the commitments of these traditions gave rise.[34] It was, in fact, Eliot who brought the term "sensibility"—a standard term in the lexicon of sentimentalism—back into widespread use in literary criticism. The various discourses of passion allowed modernists like Eliot to recapture the emotional primacy of the sentimental tradition—including the role of the sublime not only in the reception of literary forms but in their creation as well—while distancing themselves from those elements of it that they considered dangerously "feminine" or passive, though as I demonstrate, these more dangerous elements were precisely those that fascinated them the most. Although I do not often refer to them explicitly, the discourses of the sentimental and the sublime will help us to grasp the historical and philosophical basis for the conflicts that I outline in the following chapters, and they are a crucial subtext for the later-nineteenth-century repudiation of passive suffering and the modernist tensions that it engendered.

MODERNISM AND THE NINETEENTH-CENTURY PASSIONS

Of the many influential pressures that later-nineteenth-century poets exerted on subsequent theories of poetics and emotion—the development of the new dramatic monologue and the objectification of Romantic expressivity are among the two most often remarked—few were so crucial to modernism's own self-definition as the tensions surrounding the role of passion and emotional expression, in terms of both psychology and artistic creation.[35] Adela Pinch has demonstrated, for instance, that nineteenth-century writers in England were deeply fascinated by both the power and the threat of what she calls "the vagrancy of emotions." Victorian passions, she argues, seem to possess an independent, "transpersonal" life of their own, an extravagant autonomy that threatens to invade and infiltrate certain segments of society like an infectious disease.[36] Another scholar reveals that even popular discourse in Victorian dictionaries and magazines connected the passions of the mind and those of the body—heartaches may cause heart attacks, for instance, and excessive joy may end in "instantaneous death"—in vivid admonitions against weakness and passivity. "The obsessive manner with which writers treat the relation between disease and emotion, body and feeling," she argues, "is itself an indication of the anxiety that the subject could provoke."[37] The Victorians passed this anxiety along to their modernist descendants, who sensed and suffered it even more keenly because of their growing certainty that such dangers were intrinsic to the artistic enterprise. Nowhere is the anxiety so immediately legible as in modernist critiques of Victorian artists, whom they invariably portray as succumbing to the wrong passions.

Though it is often accepted as the definitive modernist statement on passivity, Yeats's repudiation of World War I poetry in his introduction to the 1936 *Oxford Book of Modern Verse, 1892–1935,* offers a valuable example of modernism's tendency to adopt and renegotiate Victorian tensions about passion. His introduction is a withering condemnation of passivity that, for long afterward, cinched his reputation as the Nietzschean poet par excellence, champion of modern iconoclasm and the indomitable will: "Passive suffering," Yeats famously declares, "is not a theme for poetry." When it becomes one, he suggests, the poet no longer traverses the frontiers of sublime tragedy; instead, "some blunderer has driven his car on to the wrong side of the road—that is all" (*LE* 199). In light of such a stark and trivializing censure, my claims about the centrality of passion to modernist thought might seem to be swerving dangerously toward the blunderer's side of the road as well.

Of course, as with so many of his seemingly ex cathedra aphorisms, Yeats's admonition relies for its force both upon the tensions that it consciously elides in his own work and those that it unconsciously reproduces from the late-nineteenth-century literary tradition. His resistance to passivity and his recourse to its ethical implications as viable criteria for aesthetic judgment explicitly point us back to Matthew Arnold's similar warning in the preface to his *Poems: A New Edition* (1853). In the preface Arnold rejects the poetic value of passivity—in terms that rely similarly upon its ethical dimensions—by condemning his own "Empedocles on Etna," a narrative in which he himself had tipped the scales between passion and action too far. "What are the eternal objects of Poetry?" Arnold asks; "they are actions; human actions."[38] Certain literary themes, however, do not promise the kind of noble enjoyment necessary for a great work of art to persist, he continues: "What then are the situations, from the representation of which, though accurate, no poetical enjoyment can be derived? They are those in which the suffering finds no vent in action; in which a continuous state of mental distress is prolonged, unrelieved by incident, hope, or resistance; in which there is everything to be endured, nothing to be done. . . . When they occur in actual life, they are painful, not tragic; the representation of them in poetry is painful also."[39]

Arnold's well-known critique is directed not toward suffering or passivity it-self, which can attain the status of tragedy if the will defiantly rises to meet it, but toward the prolongation of suffering that finds no release valve in action. What most troubles him is the possibility that passion might prove to be an inescapable psychological condition and not a temporary state, that the will might encounter forces—especially internal forces or "mental distress"—that it simply cannot resist or overcome. One might say that Arnold glimpses the potential permanence and irrevocability of passion but cannot envision this state in terms other than debili-tating distress.

Perhaps we could take this declaration at face value if "Empedocles on Etna" were not the product of his own imagination, if he himself had not grotesquely envisioned the human soul as a mirror that the Gods have strung upon a vast cord, a "gusty toy" passively battered by the wind and capable only of offering partial reflections of the expanses over which it dangles and whirls. In this context, Empe-docles asks, "Can our souls not strive, / But with the winds must go, / And hurry where they drive?"[40] And in the same volume—this time without the safety net of the *dramatis persona*—Arnold's speaker declares, "We cannot kindle when we will / The fire which in the heart resides; / The spirit bloweth and is still, / In mystery our soul abides."[41] If the intention of Arnold's warning in the preface is to exalt the aesthetic and ethical virtue of action over passion, its ultimate effect is to register his own profound ambivalence about the roles of passion and passivity in art, their potentially painful and permanent consequences both in life and literature.

The tension carries over from Arnold's thinking about aesthetic judgment to his more speculative thinking about poetic composition as well. In fact, the very aspect of his own work that he so strenuously resists in the preface—the diminish-ment of the will, its "feminine" tendency to passively receive and perceive—later becomes the primary basis for a critique of his own foremost Romantic predeces-sor. Thus Arnold in the preface he contributed to the 1879 edition of Wordsworth's *Poems* writes, "To give aright what he wishes to give, to interpret and render suc-cessfully, is not always within Wordsworth's own command. . . . Here is the part of the Muse, the inspiration, the God, the 'not ourselves.' In Wordsworth's case, the accident, for so it may be called, of inspiration, is of peculiar importance. No poet, perhaps, is so evidently filled with a new and sacred energy when the inspiration is upon him; no poet, when it fails him, is so left 'weak as is a breaking wave.'"[42]

According to Arnold, Wordsworth's passive dependence upon the "not him-self" runs a risky gambit; it lifts him to great heights but also drops him from those heights into tedium and mediocrity. In Arnold's eyes, Wordsworth's passive atten-dance upon a force foreign to his own will brings him too close to Empedocles' prolonged suffering at the hands of the gods. "Nature herself seems to take the pen out of his hand," Arnold famously writes of Wordsworth, "and to write for him with her own bare, sheer, penetrating power."[43] Arnold's gendered metaphors essentially feminize his predecessor, whom he imagines to have been passively ravished and penetrated by nature itself. More important, he can effectively conflate Wordsworth—a sometime prophet possessed by the energies of Nature—with his own fictional Empedocles—a lifeless mirror blown about by the winds of fate or chance—because what compels his resistance to both is not the particular agent to whom poet and hero are patients but rather the disturbing effect of *becoming a patient at all.* Whatever inscrutable entity or force we choose as the agent of such a passion (perhaps Arnold puts it best by concluding his list of possibilities—Muse, inspiration, or divine—with simply the "not ourselves"), the aesthetic and psychological dangers to the recipient, the patient, remain the same.

If the Victorian ambivalence toward passion is, as I believe, a complex inheritance of the sentimental and sublime traditions as they intersected in Romanticism, then we can expect to find that Arnold is not alone in his anxieties about passivity and the "not ourselves"; we can expect to find his contemporaries engaged in a similar critique of their Romantic predecessors. And we will not be disappointed if we turn directly to Walter Pater and his thought about the passive and active aspects of composition. In his essay on Wordsworth in 1874, Pater invokes the dialectic to a similar purpose: "He who thought that in all creative work the larger part was given passively, to the recipient mind, who waited so dutifully upon the gift, to whom so large a measure was sometimes given, had his times also of desertion and relapse; and he has permitted the impress of these too to remain in his work. And this duality . . . gives the effect in his poetry of a power not altogether his own, or under his control, which comes and goes when it will, lifting or lowering a matter, poor in itself; so that the old fancy which made the poet's art an enthusiasm, a form of divine possession, seems almost literally true of him."[44]

Pater discerns the risks associated with this kind of passivity and distinguishes them from the benefits with perhaps even more urgency than does Arnold. If Wordsworth's poetry has a fault, it is precisely that it does not seem the product of the active, deliberating craftsman, whom he portrays unsurprisingly as "the gem engraver blowing away the last particle of invisible dust."[45] The mysteries of art, for Pater—its ambiguities and opacities—should occur in the realm of reception, not production; that is, how it affects us is mysterious, not how it is made. The artist, he suggests in "Style" (1888), should labor at his craft like the carpenter at his workbench, and the work, upon completion, should embody and make manifest the gestures of the triumphant will. It should dazzle us with "all the freshness of volition," not the mysteries of inspiration.[46] The strongest art, Pater implies, bears the indelible imprint of a strong, active will. Instead Wordsworth was often the victim of "periods of intense susceptibility," and during those times "he appeared to himself as but the passive recipient of external influences."[47] While Pater nowhere denies the potential of such passivity in terms so harshly derisive as Arnold's, he does resist the idea that the artist must suffer himself to be possessed for his work to come to fruition. He touches briefly upon this modernization of Plato's divine "mania" in his essay on Dante Gabriel Rossetti, pausing only long enough to remind us that poetry of this sort possesses "a mere insanity incidental to it . . . into which it may lapse in its moment of weakness."[48] Like Arnold, Pater implies that passion in art—whether in its role as creative force or thematic focus —ought to consistently demonstrate its own transience, its accidental, nonnormative character.

As with Arnold's admonitions, however, these warnings do not quite veil Pater's own ambivalence about the centrality of passion and receptivity to the creative act. It is, after all, his own Marius the Epicurean who—in a moment with tremendous implications for modernist theories of impersonality—desires to transform himself into a "complex medium of reception."[49] And Pater himself takes great pains to emphasize the centrality of "passion" in the closing passages of *Studies in the History of the Renaissance* (1873), invoking it with chant-like repetition. "High passions," "great passions," "poetic passion": how appropriate that so conflicted a term appears among the final notes struck by the famously conflicted and misunderstood "Conclusion."[50]

An identical tension animates John Ruskin's best-known appraisal of the imaginative faculties in the third volume of *Modern Painters* (1856), particularly in his discussion of the pathetic fallacy. Ruskin grants a degree of respectability to the artist who allows himself to be overwhelmed by emotion. Clearly, he argues, a dry rationality or a dull insensitivity to affective forces is less desirable than a keen albeit confused receptivity to "emotions which are strong enough to vanquish, partly, the intellect."[51] It would be difficult to overstate the importance of Ruskin's parenthetical qualification, "partly"; this sort of hesitance is paradigmatic of the ambivalence toward passion in Victorian poetics. States of aesthetic passion are, he continues, "more or less noble" in proportion to the strength of the emotions which motivate them. But these are also the sort of dangerous psychological conditions—when the mind is "borne away, or over-clouded, or over-dazzled by emotion"—that result in the errors in judgment and perception that the pathetic fallacy reveals in the artist. More desirable than the strong emotions themselves, he concludes, is the ability of the mind to subject them to its dominance, "to assert its rule against, or together with, the utmost efforts of the passions."[52] As before, the conscious mind preserves its sovereignty only by exercising its will against ("or with," in Ruskin's formulation, which means essentially the same, in that the intellect marshals the passions against themselves) that which threatens it. In distinguishing the levels of this hierarchy, Ruskin makes explicit the tensions that both Arnold and Pater intimate. The uncontrollable, he implies, is of crucial importance to art, but only insofar as it is ultimately controlled, insofar as the imagination asserts and reifies its essentially active condition, proving passion temporary and subordinate.

Yeats and Eliot not only inherit this ambivalence toward passion but eventually find themselves struggling to balance the tensions that I have remarked in their Victorian predecessors. Pater's formative influence on Yeats has been widely remarked. And I cannot help but imagine that the tensions in Pater's prose contributed to the peculiar "attitude of mind" that, Yeats suggests in *The Tragic Generation*, sent the poets of the 1890s tiptoeing precariously across a tightrope in the midst of a raging storm (*Au* 235). Was it Pater, Yeats wonders, who led his early contemporaries astray, who lured them toward the Hodos Chameliontos, that overpowering, uncontrollable realm of imaginative fantasy and nightmare that Yeats aligned with madness and loss of control?

Eliot's agonistic relationship with Arnold mirrors Yeats's with Pater. In the Charles Eliot Norton lectures that he delivered at Harvard in the winter of 1932–33, Eliot gives "Empedocles on Etna" a singular, ascendant place in Arnold's poetic corpus. The very stone that Arnold rejected, Eliot implies, should have been the foundation for his other work. This gesture alone should signal Eliot's desire to renew and reestablish the tensions between passion and agency that, in his mind, Victorian poetry had so insistently suppressed. As if in direct response to Arnold's original criteria for rejecting the poem and its theme, Eliot claims that Arnold lacked a "discipline of suffering," a capacity for confronting and engaging the kind of radical passion that prompted both the composition of "Empedocles" and its ultimate dismissal.[53] Decrying the rarity with which Arnold's prose addresses the actual experience of composition from the poet's point of view, Eliot suggests, "One feels that the writing of poetry brought him little of that excitement, that joyful loss of self in the workmanship of art, that intense and transitory relief which comes at the moment of completion and is the chief reward of creative work."[54]

Of course, because this speculation depends for its evidence wholly upon the absence of any evidence at all, it tells us little about Arnold's poetics. It is, however, an oblique and revealing commentary on Eliot's singular interpretation of Arnold and on how he allowed that interpretation to shape and influence his own experience of creative composition. Elsewhere Eliot returns to this passive, momentary "loss of self"—which he envisions occurring simultaneously with active workmanship—with even greater emphasis on the conflicting emotional upheavals that it entails and the sense of irrevocability that follows. Both intense and exciting, joyous and horrific, for the poet who is willing to confront it in all of its complexity, this experience is "something very near annihilation, which is in itself indescribable" (*TVP* 30).

Not only does this description significantly complicate his earlier, widely misunderstood claims in "Tradition and the Individual Talent" about the relationship between poetry and emotion, but it also situates his creative engagement with Arnold as one of the primary catalysts of the influential theory of impersonality. In confronting the radical passion of poetic composition and in accounting for the full range of affective experience that this passion provokes, Eliot is consciously responding to a shortcoming that he perceives in his foremost literary predecessor. He is attempting to reveal and reinstate the tensions that Arnold aimed to elide in the preface, tensions that—once back in play—challenge the poet's status as the self-transparent, conscious agent of his work. In short, Eliot discerns in Arnold's resistance to passion and passivity a willful refusal to surrender the "self" that, in his view, the composition of poetry puts at risk.

It is striking, then, to return to Yeats's introduction to the *Oxford Book of Modern Verse* and find the same critique rehearsed by a poet who, only pages before, had repudiated the poetic value of passive suffering altogether. In fact, when he begins to discuss Eliot explicitly, Yeats admits that it is precisely these themes—the relationship between passion and action, or between suffering and doing—that he finds most captivating in his younger contemporary's work. While he was preparing his introduction, Yeats began to meet with Eliot more regularly than ever before, arranging for new contributions to the *Criterion,* introducing him to the poetry of Dorothy Wellesley, and even discussing the possibility of staging the recently completed *Murder in the Cathedral* (1935) with the Group Theatre. He was present for director Martin Browne's lecture on Eliot's new play at the Abbey in September 1935, and he attended a performance of it two months later at the Mercury Theatre, where the reflections on passion and patience in *Murder in the Cathedral* seems to have struck a familiar chord with him. When it came time to offer his concluding remarks on Eliot for the *Oxford Book* introduction, Yeats intuitively turned to these troubled elements of the play. "'They know and do not know,'" he quotes at length from Eliot's opening act,

> that acting is suffering
> And suffering is action. Neither does the actor suffer
> Nor the patient act. But both are fixed
> In an eternal action, an eternal patience
> To which all must consent that it be willed
> And which all must suffer that they may will it.
> (*LE* 194)

I do not think it an accident that, in the midst of one of his rare written commentaries on Eliot, Yeats quotes precisely these lines. In Eliot's meditations on the paradoxical simultaneity between passion and action ("Can I neither act nor suffer / Without perdition?," the same protagonist demands elsewhere [*CPP* 193]), Yeats finds a mirror for his own ambivalence about passion and poetry, for the tensions that he had inherited from Pater and that he hoped to simplify by issuing his edict against passive suffering and excluding the World War I poets from the modern canon. Surprisingly, however, his one concern about Eliot's new work is not that it places too much emphasis on passion and surrender. In fact, Yeats claims quite the opposite: "There is little self-surrender," he concludes, "in [Eliot's] personal relation to God and the soul" (*LE* 192). How strange that Yeats—the self-proclaimed herald of the imaginative will-to-power—would find Eliot to be lacking in the capacity for self-surrender. Wasn't it Eliot, after all, who had claimed that art demands nothing less than continual self-sacrifice and surrender of the artist to the work? Isn't this the author of *The Waste Land*'s most urgent question and its unexpected answer: "what have we given? / . . . / the awful daring of a moment's surrender" (*CPP* 49)?

Poets are notoriously bad at reaching a proper estimation of their contemporaries. Though they are intuitively sensitive to the problems faced by other artists (primarily because those problems are theirs as well), they are too close to the fray, too occupied with struggling against the same rough beast, to give a reliable account of the battle. I'd like to conclude by turning to a poet whose generational distance from the early modernists enabled him to see more clearly the stakes and widespread ramifications of the debate that I've been tracing thus far. In *The Struggle of the Modern* (1963), Stephen Spender distinguishes between the two modes of ego or self-identification that he sees at work in early-twentieth-century literature: the "Voltairean I," which appears to stand outside of temporality, claims to adjudicate with reason and intellect, and belongs to those whose "sensibility was not the product of the times that they deplored," and the "modern I," a more fragile, contingent, historical self whose decisions and judgments are characterized by fallibility, incompleteness, and suffering. He continues: "What I call the 'Voltairean I' participates in, belongs to, the history of progress. When it criticizes, satirizes, attacks, it does so in order to influence, to direct, to oppose, to activate existing forces. The 'Voltairean I' of Shaw, Wells, and the others acts upon events. The 'modern' 'I' of Rimbaud, Joyce, Proust, Eliot's *Prufrock* is acted upon by them. The Voltairean 'I' has the characteristics—rationalism, progressive politics, etc.—of the world the writer attempts to influence, whereas the 'modern' 'I' through receptiveness, suffering, passivity, transforms the world to which it is exposed."[55]

I know of no other poet or scholar willing to claim so boldly that what is "modern" about modernism is its capacity for receptiveness, suffering, and passivity, and that these common attributes are not merely negative but instead possess a positive, substantive, transformative value. The distinction that Spender draws between the "I" that originates action and the "I" that is acted upon cuts to the heart of my argument here, even if it supports a dichotomy that the modernists whom I address will challenge and complicate. If, as Spender concludes, "the modern is the realized consciousness of suffering," then it is a suffering that creates and transforms, a passion that is simultaneously an action of the highest caliber.[56]

This is a tension, I believe, that will not be resolved by recourse to the conventional paradigm wherein passion is simply a momentary departure from action, a temporary aside on the path to self-possession and rational autonomy. The burden of this book will be to follow the ways that modern writers struggle to articulate this tension—so important to their thinking about both poetics and human experience—and to perform it in ways that do justice to the affective extremes to which the mind is given when its self-sovereignty is threatened, to the emotional and psychological turmoil that each passion scene attempts to recapture.

CHAPTER OVERVIEW

Eliot is at the center of my argument, and the two chapters in part 1 set the conceptual boundaries for the rest of the book. Yeats is a counterpoint of sorts; part 2 shows how his drastically different phantasmagoria of passion arises from a set of concerns very similar to Eliot's and central to broader modernist preoccupations. The four chapters on Eliot and Yeats follow a similar structure: The first chapter on each investigates how the poet envisions an ideal imaginative response to passion. The second then takes up an alternative model of passion and its theoretical implications: in Eliot's case, a realization of psychological limitation characterized by suddenness and surprise; in Yeats's, an aesthetic upheaval characterized by anxiety and emotional turmoil. The two shorter chapters in part 3 explore alternative modes of passion in the fiction of Woolf and Mann, both of whom emphasize the painful physicality and materiality of being moved, Woolf from without, Mann from within.

The first chapter discusses Eliot's changing ideas about how the mind responds to passion—affectively, intellectually, and imaginatively—and about how one might experience passion as a normative and creative mental state rather than an aberration or temporary suspension of activity. With the etherized patient as my guiding thread or passion scene, I address how Eliot learns to imagine and dramatize a state of permanent passion—one which is psychologically constitutive rather than transient. I gauge the pressure that this realization exerts on his aesthetic theories by demonstrating that he increasingly makes a place, late in his career, for intuitive and noncognitive elements of creativity that would have been antithetical to his early classicist ideals. I conclude by arguing that a more thorough estimation of Eliot's ideas about passion, in turn, offers us a corrective to long-standing critical perspectives based solely on his early, best-known essays.

In chapter 2 I focus on a complementary model of passion in Eliot, which he develops by experimenting with what he calls the "recognition scene." I trace the development of this scene to show how he learns to calibrate the relationship between intense emotions and the limitations of the human mind. I first address the philosophical and psychological theories that Eliot uses to formulate the recognition scene, a disturbing realization of mental incompleteness that he captures by imagining himself surprised by a ghostly presence standing just over his shoulder. Eliot uses the recognition trope to envision a sense of internal vulnerability or doubling and, ultimately, to confront the emotional implications of the mind's loss of self-sovereignty and self-transparency. His repeated and increasingly complex attempts to dramatize this ambivalence reveal the value that he places upon receptivity, emotional intensity, and the mind's capacity for dwelling within limitations.

Chapter 3 turns to Yeats with concerns parallel to those that the first chapter addressed with Eliot. I examine how he envisions the ideal imaginative response to passion, one that will do justice to its violent energies without relinquishing a degree of control and self-possession. I discuss how he enlarges the conceptual precincts of passion to accommodate what he calls the "abnormal restlessness" of the mind, that is, how he envisions the paradoxical simultaneity of action and passion in the mind's movement toward the visionary. I suggest that while Yeats contributes to the characteristically modernist discourse of the decentered subject, what he calls "the dissolution of the fixed personality" actually arises from an intensification of affective conflict and sensitivity rather than—as is usually supposed—a fascination with literary form or symbolic abstraction.[57] Drawing on a number of unpublished letters and manuscript materials, I conclude by offering a revisionary account of Yeats's daemonic theories of inspiration and by situating these theories as a dynamic fulcrum in his dialectical volume *Last Poems and Two Plays* (1939).

In chapter 4 I shift focus to examine Yeats's aesthetic passion, that is, to demonstrate how another Yeatsian passion scene—the Japanese fable of the "painted horses"—demands that we rethink conventional ways of conceptualizing modernist perspectives about the aims and "afterlife" of art. For Yeats, all art must assume an autonomous ("independent," "self-moving") life of its own, especially if it is to bring about personal and political change. I address the risks and emotional upheavals that result from Yeats's theory, and I show how his genuine concerns over these risks pervade even his later work, where the painted horses seem to have all but disappeared. The implications of this theory of art's autonomy pose a trenchant challenge to the still-prevalent critical perspectives on modernism's commitment to "aesthetic autonomy," which involves a text that somehow remains closed and insulated to external cultural and historical forces. With recourse to Frank Kermode's discussion of the "Romantic Image," I argue that this Yeatsian passion scene takes the symbolist aesthetic to its logical extreme, making it impossible for such an insulated autonomy to exist.

My starting point in chapter 5 is Virginia Woolf's well-known essay "On Being Ill" (1926), wherein she issues her call for "a new hierarchy of the passions," one that will account for the intense ambivalence and the rich yet dangerous vulnerability of artistic perception (*Essays* 4.139). I show that Woolf's myth of the origins of personality—in which the inchoate mind is shaped by an atomic storm—is predicated upon a violent passion that precedes human consciousness, and I argue that this violence remains an integral part of a passion scene that recurs throughout her career, that of the wounded or vulnerable human eye. The profoundly sensitive membrane of the artist's eye is, I propose, the site of Woolf's most complex and conflicted thinking about passion, and I conclude by discussing how she dramatizes this conflict in two complementary characters in *The Waves*.

If Woolf's passions emphasize a physical violence from without, Thomas Mann's passions relentlessly turn our attention toward a physical, even biological, violence within. The final chapter examines how Mann conceptualizes passion in terms of disease, specifically as a hidden, invisible infection devastating its victim slowly and imperceptibly before its presence becomes known. Drawing from each of the major novels and a number of political essays, I discuss how his protagonists all struggle with the suspicion of an intrinsic susceptibility to internal corruption and disease but also with the resemblance that this condition bears to the ecstasies of artistic inspiration. I examine the development of a narrative strategy that Mann uses to reproduce the infectious manifestation of passion on a structural level, and I demonstrate how his political commitments in the decade before World War II intensify his longtime ambivalence toward the dangerous, noncognitive aspects of passion. *Doctor Faustus* (1947), I conclude, dramatizes this ambivalence by coupling the protagonist's moral and emotional devastation with his ultimate success in bringing passion into enduring, artistic form.

PART 1

T. S. ELIOT

1

PASSION AND SURRENDER

The Sinking Blackness of Ether

> These things may seem to you delusions, or truisms; but for me they are dark truths, and the power to put them into even such words as these has been given me by an ether dream.
>
> William James, *The Varieties of Religious Experience* (1902; quoted from "a manuscript by a friend in England")

> [Eliot] is a cadaver, dissecting himself in our sight. . . . Of course it hurts him more than it does us, and yet it hurts some of us a great deal at that.
>
> Elinor Wylie, "Mr. Eliot's Slug-Horn" (1923)

Not long after his much anticipated second book, *Ara V[o]s Prec* (February 1920), appeared and while he was still busy preparing for *The Sacred Wood* (November 1920) to "emerge into obscurity," T. S. Eliot finally found a moment to write to his mother on 20 September about his heartening prospects for the coming months (*Letters* 209). He and Vivienne were in the midst of packing for their long-awaited move to 9 Clarence Gardens, a more spacious London flat where he hoped to escape the noise, nightly arrests, and "one-night cheap hotels" (as Prufrock calls them) that had made their residence on Crawford Street unbearable. And though he did not expect his new living quarters to bring immediate relief, he did sense his creativity stirring for the first time in months: "I want a period of tranquility," he writes in the famous first mention of *The Waste Land*, "to do a poem that I have in mind" (*Letters* 408). Tranquility, however, was not what the coming weeks held.

In late October, Vivienne Eliot's father, Charles Haigh-Wood, fell seriously ill. What at first seemed merely a case of food poisoning soon turned deadly when the specialists arrived to examine him. Within hours they operated on Haigh-Wood and discovered a stomach abscess that, as the surgeon told Eliot and his wife, would have killed him within minutes had it not been treated immediately. The sudden discovery of such a threatening and previously unsuspected condition disturbed Eliot greatly; he immediately began to obsess about his own health, and he took great pains to be sure that Vivienne would be secure if he should suffer a similar disaster.[1] He began, that is, to imagine *himself* as the unsuspecting patient. What if, he must have asked himself, some horrific disease were secretly thriving within his own body, slowly corrupting his internal organs without a hint of its malign, insidious growth? Once Eliot's father-in-law recovered enough strength, the surgeons operated again, this time with the hope of uncovering the cause of the abscess. What they found unsettled Eliot only further. He wrote to his mother again with the results in December: "We have of course been on pins and needles about Vivien's father the whole time. When we think that the surgeon, one of the most skilled in London, was so horrified when he opened him, at the second operation, at what he found inside that he wanted simply to sew him up and let him die in peace—we are absolutely terrified to believe that it is now possible, and even probable, that he will recover. I am really uneasy the whole time" (*Letters* 423).

If this morbid, hyperbolic account sounds more like something out of Edgar Allan Poe or Oscar Wilde than an accurate reporting of a medical surgeon's findings, there is good reason. Eliot had been reading them both extensively and, in fact, had been plagued by nightmarish fantasies of precisely this scenario for years by the time it tore through the thin veil of literary fiction and into his own life. Such dark visions are present from his earliest manuscripts in *Inventions of the March Hare* (1996), in which the anesthetized patient fears that his shameful secret will finally be revealed, to "The Death of Saint Narcissus," "The Love Song of J. Alfred Prufrock," and "Sweeney among the Nightingales," all of which dramatize, in one way or another, the protagonist's terror at just this sort of revelation. Laid out at the mercy of another, either literally or figuratively "etherised upon a table," Eliot's early speakers all struggle against the terrible fact of their own vulnerability, against their unknowing and helpless susceptibility to harm and danger, and with the shameful suspicion that inside of them there abides something so vile and repulsive that it must never be exposed (*CPP* 3).

Eliot's imagination returns insistently to similar scenes of passion—in the broad sense of the word that I shall be using throughout this book, as a sustained state of suffering or being moved. His father-in-law's operation only reawakened in him the difficult questions he had already been asking himself about the capacity of the mind to endure pain and suffering—its potential to be moved or harmed, to receive and suffer rather than give and act—and about his ambivalence toward what he eventually calls the "immense passive strength" that allows the artist to encounter the passions in all of their overwhelming, minute complexity (*SE* 423).

How should the mind best respond, emotionally and intellectually, to energies that overwhelm it? What is the most fruitful artistic response? Eliot would later seek answers by immersing himself in the mysticism of Richard of St. Victor and the negative theology of John of the Cross, but the questions themselves are prompted not by theological inquiries but by emotional turmoil, not from a desire to attain spiritual transcendence but from his attempts to grapple with fear, self-disgust, and powerlessness in his earliest poetry.[2] In the early poems included in *Inventions of the March Hare* and in "Prufrock," he begins to experiment with physical paralysis as a correlative to the traumatic affective states of helplessness and vulnerability. The tensions underlying these experiments come to a head when, in his early literary criticism, he addresses this kind of passion or radical passivity as an essential but dangerously ambivalent element of the poet's vocation.

In the pages of the *Criterion* and elsewhere, Eliot and his circle undertook a scathing critique of artistic "intuition" and the "inner voice," those Romantic and Emersonian concepts which, in his eyes, privilege passivity and reduce the creative process to bursts of "fitful lyric inspiration," thereby denying the active, rational mind of the craftsman its rightful place.[3] The poet must be, Eliot quotes from Paul Valéry, neither an automaton nor a madman but a "'cool scientist, almost an algebraist, in the service of a subtle dreamer.'"[4] But Eliot also suggests that poets must cultivate "a kind of sense, a receptive medium" and that in all great poetry "there is always a hint of something behind, something impersonal, something in relation to which the author has been no more than the passive (if not always pure) medium."[5] In his 1919 lecture for the Arts League of Service, he goes so far as to claim that the poet does his best work "not through a desire to express his personality, but by a complete surrender of himself to the work."[6] From his earliest critical writing, he is torn between the dangers that passion poses and the virtues it promises, both for the craft of poetry and the life of the emotions.

This chapter examines Eliot's lifelong attempt to find a way to respond to passion that neither ignores its threatening aspects nor elides its potential for creative and emotional transformation. Drawing from unpublished letters, manuscript drafts, and a wide range of uncollected essays and reviews, I chart the course of his experiments with a single, emotionally fraught scenario—the "patient etherised upon a table," a scene that bears what he calls an "exact nightmare correspondence to some spiritual terror"[7]—as it twists and turns throughout his career, accompanied at each stage by dramatizations of possible responses to passion and the intense emotional upheavals that accompany them. Eliot believed that how the poet relates to passion (and to the range of emotions that it provokes) directly influences the creative process; he believed, as well, that the creative act itself often takes the form of a passion. So a secondary aim of this chapter is to discuss the close ties that he envisioned between writing and passion, and to show how his maturation as an artist eventually helped him to reconcile his ambivalence about the imminent dangers and potential benefits of passivity and powerlessness. More than twenty years intervene between the etherized patient's earliest precursors in *Inventions of the March Hare* and its late, drastically transformed appearance in *East Coker* (1940); the pages that follow aim to tell the story of that transformation.

One of the most important elements of Eliot's ongoing, revisionary self-dialogue—and perhaps the most urgent challenge facing scholars who wish to think about him against or beyond the critical ethos of irony, skepticism, and rationalism still prevalent in many circles—is his attempt to reflect upon passion in terms that do not reduce it to psychological pathology, epistemological certainty, or philosophical transcendence; that is, in terms that reflect the ceaselessly uncomfortable and often threatening ways in which passion both shapes and disfigures our experiences of self-possession and creativity.

PASSIONS OF THE MARIONETTE

Although Eliot had begun to think about how the mind might respond to the realization of its own powerlessness long before his emotional and physical "breakdown" in the winter of 1921, his convalescence at Margate and afterward in Lausanne gave him the opportunity to reconsider it in a much more urgent and personal light. In the "London Letter" (1922) that he wrote upon his return to London, he applauds one of his literary mentors for recognizing the transformative potential of physical and emotional suffering: "Dostoevsky had the gift, a sign of genius in itself, for utilizing his weaknesses; so that [they] . . . cease to be the defects of an individual and become—as a fundamental weakness can, given the ability to face it and study it—the entrance to a genuine and personal universe."[8]

Not long after he had been forced to confront a disabling manifestation of his own fundamental weakness, Eliot rediscovered in Dostoevsky the possibility that this sort of passion might become a passage, a threshold of possibility that opens not outward onto self-transcendence, cognition, or universality but inward onto new ways of accounting for the highly individual, unpredictable life of the mind. In his eyes, Dostoevsky's novels diagnose not only the temporary afflictions of the individual but the ways in which those afflictions ground and inform all that we conventionally consider to be psychologically healthy and self-sufficient. Reflecting upon and dwelling with one's own weakness, Eliot learns, also demands that we rethink the conventional distinctions between those aspects of the psyche that originate action and those which are, whether by volition or by violence, acted upon. He did not need to wait until his "breakdown" in 1921, however, to reach these conclusions. Over a decade before his "London Letter," he had already begun to anticipate Dostoevsky's gift for "utilizing" weakness by experimenting with tropes for paralysis and horrific scenarios of forced, passive suffering.

The predecessor to the etherized patient in Eliot's phantasmagoria is the marionette, and both *Poems Written in Early Youth* (1967) and *Inventions of the March*

Hare include a variety of poems that adopt the uncanny puppet as a figure for various states of passivity and helplessness. Most of them are, however, different from the later trope in one significant respect: instead of confronting the emotional consequences of the experience directly, they attempt to elide or escape it through the Laforguean irony that pervades so much of Eliot's early writing. For instance, there is the marionette's sentimental exclamation in "Convictions (Curtain Raiser)"—"Where shall I ever find the man! / . . . / I'd give my life to his control" (*IMH* 11)—behind which one senses Eliot's youthful sneer at the absurdity of a puppet's desire to abandon the control that, of course, it does not actually possess. Questions of self-control—and the doubts and fears associated with relinquishing it—assume a singular urgency in Eliot's early poems. And it is clear that this urgency intensified during his philosophical studies at Harvard a few years later. In an unpublished paper that he likely gave to the Philosophical Society in 1913–14, for instance, he contends that our ordinary, mundane experiences are characterized by an exhausting struggle between mechanism and volition, both of which often incite the desire for mental escape.[9] His earlier experiments with the marionettes repeatedly work to ensure that escape, as in the following mock-visionary lyric wherein the puppets transform into the legions of the undead:

> The neuropathic winds renew
> Like marionettes who leave their graves
> Walking the waves
> Bringing the news from either Pole
> Or knowledge of the fourth dimension:
> "We beg to call to your attention
> "Some minor problems of the soul."
> (*IMH* 29)

The corpse, undead or otherwise, will later become an important part of the etherized patient scenario; here it is merely a sly analogy (marionettes, lifeless vehicles, risen corpses), contrived to undercut the poem's metaphysical pretensions with an air of absurdity. However, in a subtle twist with implications that will soon become apparent, Eliot portrays these early marionettes as propelled by the winds of a nervous disorder ("neuropathy") that allows them to convey messages from elsewhere, as might the Pentecostal prophet filled with the divine *afflatus,* or the Platonic poet maddened by the Muse. In fact, Eliot would later claim that Kipling, whom he admired as a visionary poet, possessed the gift "of transmitting messages from elsewhere" (*A Choice* 22).

As disappointing as these early experiments may be aesthetically, I want to linger for a moment over the conclusion of this last marionette poem, which employs another distinctive metaphor to which Eliot will later return. "Your seamanship is very neat," the speaker declares, "Your language nautical, complete; / There's nothing left for me to do. . . . [but] gladly leave the rest to fate" (*IMH* 29). Few have recognized this persona as a precursor to the speaker who fears relinquishing control of a similar vessel in the final stanzas of *The Waste Land.* When Eliot returns to the nautical metaphor in "What the Thunder Said," he changes the earlier "hand expert with sail and oar" to the caretaker of the human heart, which responds in turn by "beating obedient / To controlling hands" (*CPP* 50). The marionette reappears in "Humouresque," and then once again when the speaker of "Goldfish (Essence of Summer Magazines)" mocks the absurdity of a puppet that has surrendered its "will" to a human vice: "Like the cigarettes / Of our marionettes / Inconsequent, intolerable" (*PWEY* 24; *IMH* 26).

In *The Waste Land,* the Thunder's voice prescribes voluntary surrender as a mode of spiritual transcendence. But these early speakers are not sure whether to hold on or let go, whether relinquishing control is a dangerous threat or a welcome release. The only certainty is that each finds himself at the mercy of another's will, and that Eliot is not yet certain how to handle that experience artistically without the use of irony and obliquity. If the wooden figure of the marionette gives the young poet a way to begin thinking about the experience of helplessness, it also proves a useful tool (not least because it had become, thanks to the nineteenth-century French revival of the Commedia dell'Arte, a clichéd literary trope by this time) for keeping the disturbing emotional consequences of that experience at bay. Puppets, Eliot eventually concludes, are a dead-end. After "all the reminiscent tunes" of the marionettes' monotonous waltz have ended, "What answer?" he asks. The best conclusion is that which a "tired Sphinx" offers listlessly and with a characteristically Laforguean shoulder shrug: "We cannot discern" (*IMH* 26).

EARLY PATIENTS

When he began composing "The Love Song of J. Alfred Prufrock," Eliot's various figures for passivity crystallized into a conceit that not only characterizes Prufrock with one deft masterstroke but that would remain central to Eliot's poetic "universe" for the rest of his career. "Let us go then," he begins: "you and I, / When the evening is spread out against the sky / Like a patient etherised upon a table" (*CPP* 3). Of course Prufrock's "Love Song" is replete with figurations of the speaker's affective states ("the nerves in patterns on a screen," in Eliot's phrase), from the feline fog lingering in the street to the ragged claws on the ocean floor, but the first conceit is perhaps the most psychologically acute and surely the closest in kinship to the marionette (*CPP* 6). If the tragedy of this poem consists in Prufrock's fear of (and failure to risk) vulnerability, the first line configures that fear ironically with a correlative for a radically vulnerable, physical paralysis, a body whose dulled awareness remains but which cannot move to protect itself; it is a living marionette with its strings severed. Later in the poem Eliot experiments with other tropes for helplessness, as Prufrock envisions himself "formulated, sprawling on a pin," or "pinned and wriggling on the wall" (*CPP* 5). In "Portrait of a Lady" (1915) he temporarily replaces etherized paralysis with a less menacing "tobacco trance," a drowsed mental state with consequences as meaningless, circular, and nonhuman as those that befell the marionettes: "dance, dance / Like a dancing bear, / Cry like a parrot, chatter like an ape. / Let us take the air, in a tobacco trance—" (*CPP* 11). Eliot's training in classical philosophy had taught him that rational consciousness is the faculty of the human soul that distinguishes it from animals; his "intolerable" marionettes and chattering apes imply that when the will is overwhelmed and rendered helpless, the human is no less mechanical and automatic than the animal.

The etherized patient remains Eliot's most succinct embodiment of the sensation of helplessness; he puns on it again in "The Burnt Dancer" (1914) when the speaker imagines himself a "patient acolyte of pain, / . . . / Caught on those horns that toss and toss" (*IMH* 63). The significance of the pun—and, in fact, of his use of other "patients" in the early poems—rests upon his knowledge that the word "patient" pertains to "patience" in the modern sense but is also etymologically linked with passion and passivity. In his reading of scholastic theology, he would have found the noun "patient" (*patiens*) distinguished from the "agent" (*agens*), as the entity which is acted upon differs from the originator of the action.[10] It is the nature of the patient to suffer movement inflicted upon it by an agent, but it is essential to remember that this movement need not necessarily involve violence or fear. For instance, one may be *pulled* from the path of a moving train or *pushed* onto its tracks; in both cases, a patient has been acted upon by an agent. The emotional turbulence that Eliot's personae experience—their oscillation between relief and terror—is particularly striking because it arises not from *what* they are forced to suffer, but rather from the fact *that* they suffer.

He returns to this ambivalence in "The Death of Saint Narcissus" and "The Love Song of St. Sebastian," both of whose speakers confess a terror of, but compelling attraction to, passion and passive suffering. However, unlike Eliot's beloved Arnaut Daniel in Dante's *Purgatorio,* these early personae possess none of the purgatorial virtues that result from choosing passivity. They fear paralysis, and their fear produces a craving for relief, which results in an ambivalence that only paralyzes them further. In his penetrating essay on Eliot, Ted Hughes agrees that Saint Narcissus, alongside the other early personae whom we have examined, "shares that curious neurasthenic self-awareness of himself as a thing, a puppet on strings."[11] When Eliot allows himself to engage more "directly" with the passion of mental paralysis, he invariably fixes his attention again upon its closest physical correlative.[12] In this remarkably prescient, untitled lyric ("Do I know how I feel?") from *Inventions of the March Hare,* his speaker foresees a grotesque scene of his own dismemberment:

There will be a smell of creolin and the sound of something that drips
A black bag with a pointed beard and tobacco on his breath
With chemicals and a knife

Will investigate the cause of death that was also the cause of the life—
Would there be a little whisper in the brain
A new assertion of the ancient pain
Or would this other touch the secret which I cannot find?
. . . .
There will be a blinding light and a little laughter
And the sinking blackness of ether
I do not know what, after, and I do not care either.
(*IMH* 80)

This speaker imagines the Mephistophelean surgeon's approach with metonymic swiftness; in his panic, he notes only a few salient, threatening details—black bag, chemicals, knife—before hurrying on toward an overwhelming question: Would this figural operation only confirm his fears by bringing into the light the shameful evidence of his internal corruption and decay ("the ancient pain")? Or might the seemingly horrific experience have some other, self-revelatory effect? Might it somehow bypass the labyrinthine defenses of the conscious mind, those frivolous and not so frivolous "matters that with myself I too much discuss" that prevent Eliot's speakers, time and again, from confronting the reality of their own suffering (*CPP* 61)? Not unlike Prufrock, the speaker proves unable to follow the question through to an answer. The poem dramatizes his fear by dismissing the scenario at the moment of the malevolent surgeon's approach, refusing to entertain the outcome of the imagined operation.[13] This version of the etherized patient evokes the same fear of helplessness that was embodied less poignantly in the marionettes, a fear that remains central to Eliot's sensibility into *The Waste Land,* and not only in the Thunder's diagnosis of our need for the "awful daring of a moment's surrender" (*CPP* 49).

In *The Waste Land* this emotionally dense scenario assumes an airiness to shift with the winds and, like the ether itself, insinuate itself into the poem at precisely those moments when Eliot wants to address passion and powerlessness. Take, for instance, part 2, "A Game of Chess," which portrays a speaker whose senses are overwhelmed by the pungent perfumes of the woman whom he anxiously approaches:

In vials of ivory and coloured glass
Unstoppered, lurked her strange synthetic perfumes,
Unguent, powdered, or liquid—troubled, confused,
And drowned the sense in odours; stirred by the air
That freshened from the window, these ascended
In fattening the prolonged candle-flames,
Flung their smoke into the laquearia,

> Stirring the pattern on the coffered ceiling.
> (*CPP* 40)

The detached, baroque style of this passage too often diverts our attention from its crucial focus: not the aristocratic woman but the speaker himself, who undergoes something like a Prufrockian passion. Unless we allow for a doubtful degree of narrative obliquity, there is no paralyzed patient here, no supine victim awaiting the chemicals and knife. However, the sensual and emotional momentum of the passion scene with the etherized patient—which moves swiftly from the ether's sinking blackness to the fear of violence and helplessness—is distinctly echoed here. Dazed and disoriented by the strange, synthetic chemicals, the speaker allows his gaze (the compass for the psychological movements of the poem, its imaginative shifts and progressions) to follow the candle smoke as it drifts upward to the well-known "sylvan scene" waiting above:

> The change of Philomel, by the barbarous king
> So rudely forced; yet there the nightingale
> Filled all the desert with inviolable voice
> And still she cried
> (*CPP* 40)

The violent rape of Philomel—her forced transformation into a passive object—recaptures the radical passion that Eliot associates with the etherized patient. Her mournful song— "'Jug Jug' to dirty ears" —will sound its painful note again later in the poem, still carrying with it the primary emotional burden of the scene: "So rudely forc'd" (*CPP* 43). Like his earliest paralyzed patient, and like the "human engine" later in "The Fire Sermon" that "waits / Like a taxi throbbing waiting," Philomel's rape is a way for Eliot to entertain imaginatively the possibility of becoming a mute, defenseless object, of being "possessed" and violently acted upon in a way that affects an irrevocable change.

However, like the hint of possibility in "Do I know how I feel?" (recall the speaker's piercing but unanswered question, "would this other touch the secret which I cannot find?"), there is an ambivalence here that Eliot chooses to leave unexplored. Only after this disastrous rape does the nightingale begin the mournful song that is sustained throughout the poem and that is, as at least one scholar has suggested, an emblem of the poem itself, of the origins of the poetic voice.[14] Eliot will later recognize the visionary potential inherent in the passion scene, the creative possibilities that arise when the artist allows himself to be possessed, to experience "a moment's surrender" in all of its abandon. The tragedy (or properly speaking, the origin) of *The Waste Land* is, perhaps, that this possibility remains hidden and submerged beneath the speaker's emotional horror and spiritual writhing, a latent potential to which Eliot will need to return years later in order to discover fully. The speakers of *The Waste Land* and his other early lyric personae can only tremble at the thought of such daring; their attraction to passive suffering results not from a desire for self-awareness but from a yearning for their own dissolution.[15] They exemplify what Eliot would later call the "tendency to collapse, the recurring human desire to escape the burden of life and thought."[16]

ORIGINS OF THE PATIENT

In the decade that brackets the composition of *The Waste Land,* Eliot's ambivalence toward control and surrender repeatedly drew him to other thinkers who sought to reconsider the mind's response to passion and suffering in innovative and dramatic terms. Studying and annotating the writings of William James as a philosophy student at Harvard, for instance, he gravitated toward accounts of ether-induced states of altered consciousness or "anesthetic revelations" and especially what one of James's acquaintants (who had recently experienced an anesthetic revelation) calls "the passivity of genius, how it is essentially instrumental and defenseless, moved, not moving."[17] In the narrative that James relates at great length, the patient under ether suffers excruciating mental pain but is also afforded a visionary glimpse into the creative processes of the human mind. Eliot also turned to Edgar Allan Poe, whom he considered another master of suffering and vulnerability. His preparation for a 1927 review of Hervey Allen's biography of Poe, *Israfel,* likely led him to discover an account of one of Poe's more outlandish lovers, who was known to appear in public conspicuously clutching a handkerchief soaked in ether, its "faint, deathly sweet odor" trailing behind her everywhere.[18] Poe was no stranger to the sinking blackness of ether, and Eliot may have caught the scent of a similar anesthetic that makes its way into the short stories as well. In "Shadow—A Parable" (1835) Poe's narrator offers a hypochondriac's description of his degenerative nervous state, of its stifling "sense of suffocation—anxiety," which he likens to "that terrible state of existence which the nervous experience when the senses are keenly living and awake, and meanwhile the powers of thought lie dormant."[19]

Rereading Poe may also have led him back to "The Premature Burial" (1844), which features a narrator with whom Eliot would have sensed a disturbing affinity. Poe's narrator explains that he suffers from catalepsy—a nervous condition that leaves its victim in a paralyzed state bearing an uncanny resemblance to the scenes from Eliot's own early poetry—and that he is therefore haunted by the fear of premature interment. The unfortunate sufferer of a cataleptic episode, he describes meticulously, enters into a state of "semi-syncope, or half swoon . . . without pain, without ability to stir, or, strictly speaking, to think, but with a dull lethargic consciousness of life and of the presence of those who surrounded my bed."[20] Poe's narrator suggests that such horrific fantasies of paralytic helplessness give our world "the semblance of a Hell."[21] For Eliot, however, the "hell" that the etherized patient endures is neither a mere semblance nor a passing torment; it is, rather, a revelation of something fundamental about human consciousness, of something within its inscrutable depths that remains always "simple, terrible and unknown."[22]

When he wrote the introduction for Christopher Isherwood's translation of *Journaux intimes* in 1930, Eliot applauded another master of pain and affliction, Charles Baudelaire, for cultivating an "immense passive strength" to endure physical and emotional suffering. In the process of rereading *Journaux*, he would have rediscovered Baudelaire's description of love as "an application of torture or a surgical operation . . . in which one of the players must forfeit possession of himself."[23] Beneath the surface of Baudelaire's distinctive analogy and his undaunted inquiry into the passions of suffering, Eliot claims, lies "the possibility of a positive state of beatitude" (*SE* 423). The jarring trope of love-as-surgery would also have recalled to him Baudelaire's essay "Some Foreign Caricaturists" [*Quelques caricaturistes étrangers*], which Eliot read along with "On the Essence of Laughter" [*De L'essence du rire*] when he began to model himself in the image of the "savage comedian" in the 1920s.[24] Baudelaire's essay features a lengthy description of William Hogarth's woodcut *The Reward of Cruelty* (1751), and it applauds the moral significance underlying Hogarth's ghastly depiction of "a corpse stretched out stiff and flat on a dissection table" and "the surrounding figures of all those British doctors."[25] It was a scene with which Eliot had become too well aware, on many levels. In short, his sustained tutelage under James, Baudelaire, Poe, and their paralytic and tortured protagonists taught him to cultivate an imaginative and affective capacity for the most extreme modes of passion, for the kinds of weakness and suffering that can become both arbiters of shame and guilt and pathways to spiritual and artistic transformation.

But he did not need to rely solely on the paralyzed patients of recent literary history for firsthand accounts of ether, surgical operations, and the passions of physical paralysis. By now Vivienne Eliot's addiction to the substance has been well documented. Scholars have also determined that she had been prescribed "Hoffman's anodyne" and paraldehyde to treat her nervous condition, both anesthetics that exude a strong scent of ether.[26] In an account that bears an uncanny resemblance to that of Poe's notorious lover and her ether-soaked handkerchief, Lady Ottoline Morrell recalls visiting Vivienne in her room and finding her flustered and fatigued, her breath filling the air with the smell of ether.[27] According to Valerie Eliot, the receptionist at Faber frequently remarked that "the smell of ether on Vivienne was frightful—it nearly knocked her out."[28] And Aldous Huxley, who first met Vivienne in 1917, gives a similar account: "Vivienne was an ether addict. Her face was mottled like ecchymotic spots, and the house smelled like a hospital."[29]

Even if his wife's ether addiction actually began later than scholars suspect, Eliot himself experienced the effects of the substance firsthand as early as September

1925 when, as he tells his friend and publisher of the *Criterion* Richard Cobden-Sanderson in an unpublished letter, it was administered to him during an unexpected operation on his jaw.[30] After weeks of complaining about severe pain in his teeth and jaw, he agreed to undergo what he anticipated would be a "minor" operation to relieve the distress. Perhaps a few years before then, when Eliot and his wife dined with the Woolfs in April 1919, Virginia Woolf had chanced to tell him about her own visit to the dentist and the "queer little excursion into the dark world of gas" that accompanied it.[31] After a dental operation less than a month before, she had allowed herself to wonder what would happen if "one woke" from the anesthetic "to find the deity himself by one's side" instead of the attending physician.[32] But if Eliot had the benefit of her warning, it did him little good. As he tells Cobden-Sanderson in the letter—a wrinkled half sheet of paper scrawled in pencil and with an uncharacteristically shaky hand—he went unsuspectingly into the surgeon's office expecting to be out in ten minutes. Instead he spent more than an hour under the anesthetic, all the while (he claims) with a vague awareness of the surgeons chipping and scraping at his jaw. A mere two years before he would be baptized into the Anglican church, Eliot wrote to Cobden-Sanderson that he could do nothing but utter curses at God upon reviving from his drugged state and staggering into midafternoon London. Even aside from its physical effects and the minor blasphemy they induced, the disorienting experience had a much more permanent and jarring impression on Eliot's sensibility than the strangely lighthearted tone of his letter suggests. He tells Cobden-Sanderson that perhaps it would have been a blessing had he simply not revived from the ether at all, but his implicit self-deprecation does not quite distract us from the vivid possibility that he had allowed himself to entertain: What if he had remained paralyzed upon a table like Poe's narrator or his own early personae? What if the passivity to which he willingly succumbed did not dissipate along with the ether?

As if Eliot were desperate to find an answer to this question in the work of his masters, the essays and reviews written after his operation repeatedly turned to poets who seem to have shared his own fears about the passions of paralysis and tortured helplessness.[33] He returned to Shakespeare, for instance, whom he now claims was intensely "occupied with the struggle . . . to transmute his personal and private agonies into something rich and strange" (*SE* 137). And he turned to his friends as well. In an unpublished letter to John Hayward in 1931, Eliot admits to finding it immensely difficult to learn from intense suffering, to use it consciously as an instrument of self-reflection or enlightenment.[34] He proposes, however, that a pattern often emerges long after the agony has passed, one which surprises the sufferer with its sudden illumination and that helps him to make the experience meaningful. Though he does not name it as such, the "sinking blackness" of ether was, I believe, just such a pattern. By his later work, it had assumed both an acute personal resonance and an allusive literary one associated with vulnerability and the surrender of the will. Whatever its provenance, though, in Eliot's mind, the trope of the "etherized patient" expands to encompass the wide range of conflict-ing emotions involved in his attempt to reconcile the virtues of passion to its more hidden and threatening dangers, dangers which became increasingly vivid for him on two related fronts: the psychological theory of the renowned doctor who treated him in 1921, Roger Vittoz, and the Thomistic theory of a contemporary theologian and trusted friend, Jacques Maritain.

NOISES IN THE CELLAR

In 1921, on the advice of Ottoline Morrell and Julian Huxley, Eliot agreed to leave the "nerve" doctors of London behind and travel to Lausanne, Switzerland, to undergo psychological treatment at the clinic of Dr. Roger Vittoz (*Letters* 480). At stake was not only his marriage or his career, but apparently also the possibility of spiraling downward toward that etherized blackness he had envisioned so fearfully in the years before. The emotional and psychological strain of the months leading up to his decision, he wrote to Sydney Schiff, "has been paralyzing" (466). If Eliot was searching for reassurance that this new doctor could help him to escape the sinking blackness—the psychological powerlessness and anesthesis he had begun to sense—he found it even before he left London when he consulted the treatise that Vittoz had written explicitly for the benefit of his patients, *The Treatment of Neurasthenia by Means of Brain Control* (1911).

The strict dichotomies that structure Vittoz's theory of neurasthenia and men-tal control—between action and passion, control and powerlessness—likely reso-nated with Eliot's desperate need for clarity and reassurance. The mind is divided into two "centres," Vittoz claims: the subjective, comprised of a seething cauldron of ideas, sensations, and emotions, and the objective, the seat of reason, judgment, and all those faculties with which the mind ostensibly bridles and controls its impressions. For Vittoz, all mental pathology—but especially the nervous affliction termed "neurasthenia"—results from an imbalance between the two, specifically from an insufficient ability control the unruly subjective center. Under the heading "lack of brain control," he observes: "It is easy to imagine the state of one lacking this regulating faculty; his uncurbed brain would, without a controlling power, be indeed in a state of anarchy. A prey to every impulse, subject to all fears, unable to reason or weigh an idea, forced to receive all the impressions of his subjective brain, he is nothing but a wreck, doomed to a life of suffering."[35] The rhetoric of Vittoz's diagnosis portrays the pathological neurasthenic as the victim par excel-lence. He is remarkable not only for *what* he suffers—the particular violence or force which his own mind threatens to inflict upon him—but for the very fact *that* he suffers, for his enduring and helpless vulnerability to suffering itself. In the syn-tax of experience, the neurasthenic is always the direct object.

The symptomatology that Vittoz offers is unsurprising in most respects: con-fusion, worry, anxiety, depression, all neurological evils to which both Eliot and his wife had already been prey in the years preceding. But remarkable for my

purposes is the one symptom with which Vittoz begins the list, the one that is perhaps most common to his patients and most indicative of the onset of neurasthenia. Even if the insufficiency of brain control is very mild, he claims, the patient
can become "troubled and even distressed by being only half awake and in a sort
of half-dreamy state from which he cannot escape"(Vittoz 7). Over and again Vittoz cites this "dreamy state, a semi-conscious condition" as the most indicative and
most dangerous symptom demonstrated by his patients, not least because of the
profound ambivalence it provokes in the mind of the sufferer. It is not always
either troubling or distressing; on the contrary, the patient may sometimes find it
"by no means disagreeable to himself," or even worse, may simply remain unaware
of its pervasiveness and therefore ignorant of its danger (19). The risk that this
condition of mental paralysis might go unnoticed seems most apposite here. Vittoz's warning situates this unconscious passivity in chilling proximity to everyday,
"normal" consciousness. In effect, he makes it less a temporary state and more an
enduring condition that may be, at any moment, affecting the patient without his
awareness. Eliot will later contemplate the implications of precisely this unsettling
possibility.

Vittoz's programmatic method for regaining control of the brain by means of
repetitive behavioral exercises in concentration, however, demands that the doctor ignore this disruptive implication of his theory and insist, instead, upon a clear
and observable demarcation between the passive and active conditions of the
mind. *Treatment of Neurasthenia* is, after all, a guide for the perplexed and must
reassure his patients of their ultimate curability. To this end, Vittoz reintroduces
the dichotomy with which he began—between the subjective and objective
"centres" of the mind—now under the rubric of the two psychological conditions
between which the neurasthenic oscillates: the active or "normal" condition and
the passive one. Of the latter, he claims: "Every variety of want of brain control
is to be found in this condition. Such brain may be conscious but is never voluntary, that is to say, governed by the will. Psychically speaking, it is characterized by a peculiar receptiveness and is like a door open to all weaknesses,
obsessions, and fears. All these psychical symptoms only exist in the passive condition, which is, therefore, eminently an unhealthy one" (Vittoz 56).

"Every passive thought," Vittoz concludes, "does harm and causes moral and
physical discomfort" and acts, in his words, "as a real toxine on the human organism" (106). Perhaps because Vittoz's treatise seems so rudimentary, scholars
have tended merely to reduce it to one of the many source texts for *The Waste
Land,* pointing to the most vivid evidence of its influence in the final section of
"What the Thunder Said." Eliot's biographers have likewise treated it as little more
than a confirmation of his earliest thinking about the modern weakness of the
human will, citing it as a source for Eliot's own self-diagnosis (which he mentions
briefly in a letter to Richard Aldington shortly after he had read Vittoz's text) of

"aboulie," a weakening of the volitional faculty (*Letters* 486).[36] Strangely enough, these accounts underestimate Eliot's own claim that his nervous condition arises from an enduring emotional complex—"*aboulie* and emotional derangement which has been a lifelong affliction," in his words—and they do not address the ways that Vittoz's text fits into his "lifelong" reflections on passivity and on the vulnerability of the mind to its own violent energies (486). With its striking similarity to the lexicon of Eliot's own early literary essays, Vittoz's description of vulnerability as a helpless, unsafe openness— "a door open to all weaknesses"— becomes permanently associated in his mind with the risks of passivity. It is a trope that would haunt his imagination in the years following, especially when he encountered it again—almost verbatim—in the work of the prominent philosopher and theologian whose name and work figured frequently in the debates of the *Criterion*.

In 1927 Eliot pseudonymously translated "Poetry and Religion" by the French philosopher Jacques Maritain, a neo-Thomist whom he celebrates as "the leader of the Catholic rationalists," "the most conspicuous figure, and probably the most powerful force, in contemporary French philosophy."[37] In this essay and elsewhere, Maritain proposes a rationalist philosophy of art that allows for the role of "creative intuition"—which he admits is not strictly rational—but severely limits the value of passivity in matters both spiritual and artistic. He applauds modern poets like Baudelaire and Rimbaud for allowing the passive mind to wander beyond its conventional frontiers, but his misgivings about the results assume an ominous tone that likely intensified Eliot's own uncertainties. Poets like Baudelaire and Rimbaud "made modern art pass the frontiers of the mind," Eliot translates, "but those regions are the regions of supreme dangers; . . . it is there that the good and evil angels war with one another, and the latter disguise themselves as messengers of light."[38]

Eliot now found himself cornered on two fronts: Maritain's prognosis shifts the emphasis from the psychological dangers of passivity (upon which Vittoz had focused) to the moral dangers of relaxing the vigilance of reason. Maritain inveighs against any sort of mystical surrender to the impulse of the unconscious *psyche*, claiming that "disguised as an angel of counsel, it will lead the human soul astray on false mystical paths."[39] A similar suspicion and ambivalence apparently manifested itself not only in Eliot's work but in his private life as well: Ezra and Dorothy Pound remember feeling that he was always "'wrestling with a devil or an angel.'"[40] In his writings on art and creativity, Eliot shows signs of gradually becoming convinced of the need for surrender, but the danger that passivity might lead the mind into madness or into moral depravity posed a significant challenge to the development of his aesthetic ideals. His translation of "Poetry and Religion" concludes with a stern warning, and its strikingly apposite challenge to his own ideas about passion and passivity could not have gone unnoticed: "The demonologists know that every *passive state* in which man puts himself," Eliot translates, "is a door open to the devil."[41]

The personae of Eliot's early poems all seem to have heeded a similar warning. Each one harbors the secret fear that, in Maritain's phrase, he has left "a door open to the devil" and by surrendering the defenses of the active mind, has made himself susceptible to the nightmares and impulses that originate in its hidden regions. Later, the chorus in *The Family Reunion* (1939) articulates this fear again, anxiously pleading: "to be reassured / About the noises in the cellar / And the window that should not have been open" (*CPP* 243). Vittoz's "door open to all weaknesses," Maritain's "door open to the devil," and Eliot's inadvertently opened window all aim to convey the fearful sense that the house of the psyche is not safe, not entirely its own; a menacing, foreign entity has entered and claimed the cellar for its own. And this unnamed force is influencing, moving, and even directing the mind without its conscious intention or awareness.

Once again, however, Eliot encounters the familiar tension between his psychological discoveries and his artistic convictions: whatever crept in through the open window or the devil's door also bears a threatening resemblance to that mysterious entity which guides the artist when he experiences the sensation of "being a vehicle" in moments of heightened poetic inspiration (*SE* 405). Vittoz's dangerous subjective "centre" also houses all of those aspects of psychological experience that Eliot most valued in poetry, including sensation, emotion, and receptivity (Vittoz 2). Eliot intimates elsewhere that both Dante and Kipling experienced the sensation of being spoken through in a kind of literary "possession," but he is nowhere so explicit as when he suggests in "The *Pensées* of Pascal" (1931) that the mystical inspiration that transformed Pascal into "a vehicle rather than a maker" may well have resulted from "communion with the Divine" (*SE* 405).[42] For Eliot, artistic surrender to the creative spirit, psychic surrender to the "subjective" center, and spiritual surrender to "the devil of the stairs" are all dangerously similar (*CPP* 63). Stripped of their defenses either by choice or by force, body and mind are vulnerable to both physical and psychological possession, be it possession by an angelic muse or what he explicitly calls "the *diabolic*."[43]

Students of Eliot's rationalism might be reluctant to concede his genuine belief in spiritual possession, his certainty that the human will can act as an instrument for the forces of both good and evil. Admittedly he was averse to Yeats's brand of séance and table rapping, and he considered attempts to "describe the horoscope" and "riddle the inevitable / With playing cards" examples of the "usual / Pastimes and drugs, and features of the press" (*CPP* 135–36). But Eliot did believe in the spiritual reality behind the demonic and angelic allegories, and in "Personality and Demonic Possession" (1934) he explicitly assents to the possibility of "a positive power for evil working through human agency" as well as to the danger that evil "might operate through men of genius of the most excellent character." While he may not have subscribed to homunculi and exorcists in the literal sense, he was intensely concerned, as he claimed of Baudelaire, "not with demons, black masses, and romantic blasphemy, but with the real problem of good and evil" (*SE* 427). A year after "Personality and Demonic Possession," and in the same year that he first brought to the stage *Murder in the Cathedral* and its demonic tempters, Eliot offered a more concrete example of the perilous proximity between passivity and evil. In "Religion and Literature" (1935), he warns against the dangers brought about by "excessive possession by any one literary personality," and he suggests that the literature which we read "'purely for pleasure'" or with the attitude of "pure passivity" may have "the easiest and most insidious influence upon us" (*SE* 394–96). In matters of literary passion and possession, even the seemingly innocuous activity of reading becomes morally significant; the overly passive reader is just as "helplessly exposed" as the saint or martyr to the influences of a veritable and imminent spiritual danger (*SE* 398).

PASSIONS AT EAST COKER

In *East Coker,* Eliot attempts once again to find a satisfactory way of relating to passion—as well as making sense of his own experiences of paralysis and helplessness—by returning once again to the figure of the etherized patient and the emotional upheavals that it provokes. As does each poem in *Four Quartets, East Coker* sketches the movements of the narrator's mind as it reflects upon a single sensory experience with "personal poignancy" and then expands outward from this "acute personal reminiscence (never to be explicated, of course, but to give power from well below the surface)."[44] The sense of joy and personal discovery in the rose garden provides the starting point for *Burnt Norton* (1936), just as Eliot's visit to the chapel at Little Gidding in May 1936 sets in motion the meditations of the last of the *Quartets*. The reflections in the second movement begin in the hazy shade of "the deep lane" that leads into the village of East Coker, which Eliot visited in August 1937 during his stay at West Coker with Sir Matthew Nathan.[45] But more important, they begin with the sunken lane's persistent effects (the road itself "insists on the direction") upon the drowsed speaker who is "in the electric heat / Hypnotised" (*CPP* 123). In the "warm haze" and "sultry light" of the afternoon, the speaker moves almost without volition, his mind slumbering with the flowers, which "sleep in empty silence" (*CPP* 123). It is this muddled state of mental and physical lethargy—so remarkably similar to Vittoz's semiconscious "dreamy state," induced even in the absence of the paralytic catalyst—that prompts the meditations of *East Coker,* not the village itself or the spectral apparitions of Eliot's ancestry.

As the narrator nears the village—and as the poet's imagination allows its characteristic associations with this drowsy, "dreamy" state to take form, just as they did in *The Waste Land*—we witness what initially seems a joyous marriage celebration:

> In that open field
> If you do not come too close, if you do not come too close
> On a Summer midnight, you can hear music
> Of the weak pipe and the little drum
> And see them dancing around the bonfire
> The association of man and woman
> In dausinge, signifying matrimonie—
>
> . . . .
>
>   Feet rising and falling.
> Eating and drinking. Dung and death.
> (*CPP* 124)

With a disorienting mental haze obstructing his vision, the speaker refuses to see the virtue in this ancient ceremony. His mind flits past the pipes and drums to the mechanical, repetitive movements of the dancers, which he immediately aligns with the visceral automatic processes of the body: eating, drinking, excreting waste, and dying. For him, these are the instinctive movements to which the human animal, at its worst, is reducible, but they also resemble those habitual patterns into which it falls when it foregoes the faculties of reason and volition. Only one year before, Eliot had incorporated an early version of this scene into *The Family Reunion*, where he allowed himself to make its association with paralysis and automatism painfully explicit:

> The sudden solitude in a crowded desert
> In thick smoke, many creatures moving
> Without direction, for no direction
> Leads anywhere but round and round in that vapour—
> Without purpose, and without principle of conduct
> In flickering intervals of light and darkness;
> The partial anaesthesia of suffering without feeling
> And the partial observation of one's own automatism
> While the slow stain sinks deeper through the skin
> Tainting the flesh and discolouring the bone—
> (*CPP* 235)

Like the unguent perfumes in "A Game of Chess," this strange, gaslike substance ("thick smoke," "that vapour") substitutes for Eliot's earlier anesthetic agent, the more familiar ether. And as the "partial anaesthesia" in this scene begins to take effect, the speaker's mind moves immediately to the unthinking automatism of the earlier marionettes, until finally settling to dwell upon the internal decay and corruption that he fears to be slowly overtaking him without his knowledge or consent (the "slow stain" sinking "deeper through the skin"). The emotional trajectory here recalls the terror that Eliot experienced upon hearing the surgeon pronounce his father-in-law's horrible affliction; it retraces the fear of physical violence and shameful exposure that his earlier speakers suffered when they imagined their helplessness before the surgeon's knife; but more important, it sets the stakes for the emotional turmoil that *East Coker*'s meditations on surrender and passion will attempt to resolve. The psychological upheaval at the beginning compels the speaker through the following sections, which dramatize his halting attempts to find a way to respond to this experience that can account for its emotional and imaginative complexity.

Parts 2 and 3 of *East Coker* sketch two contrasting versions of this response, each of which involves a different form of surrender. First, the speaker looks to his literal and literary ancestors, the "quiet-voiced elders," whose example initially seems to offer the "autumnal serenity" that ought to result from the mind's surrender of its anxious watchfulness (*CPP* 124). Will surrender bring, as the "wisdom of age" promises, the "long looked forward to / Long hoped for calm" (*CPP* 125)? For a brief moment, the narrator finds that such calm offers him a satisfactory analogue to his own dulled mental state, and his fear of infection and automatism dissipates. But he soon suspects this serenity to be merely the product of a surrender to routine and habit, what he calls a "deliberate hebetude" that is ultimately useless in the darkness "into which they peered" or (as he reconsiders) "from which they turned their eyes" (*CPP* 125), the darkness, that is, of the ether. The serenity of the elders only offers the semblance of surrender; its true source is instead a surrender to fear, "fear of possession, / Of belonging to another, or to others, or to God" (*CPP* 125–6). In part 2 the narrator concludes that this surrender produces merely the illusion of self-control and self-possession, one that will dissolve the moment that an emotional upheaval proves the mind not the sole master of its own precincts. Refusing to dismiss the threatening, dangerous aspects of passion in favor of an easier path, a more "secure foothold," he circles around to begin again in the "etherized" shade of the sunken lane: "O dark dark dark. They all go into the dark" (*CPP* 125–6).

The narrator of part 3 revisits the state of the hypnotized traveler from the opening stanzas, following his dulled, darkened mind into the parallel darkness of the landscape, "the vacant into the vacant," and searching for analogies that will make the disorienting, trancelike experience meaningful (*CPP* 126):

I said to my soul, be still, and let the dark come upon you
Which shall be the darkness of God. As, in a theatre,
The lights are extinguished, for the scene to be changed
With a hollow rumble of wings, with a movement of darkness on darkness,
And we know that the hills and the trees, the distant panorama

And the bold imposing façade are all being rolled away—
Or as, when an underground train, in the tube, stops too long between stations
And the conversation rises and slowly fades into silence
And you see behind every face the mental emptiness deepen
Leaving only the growing terror of nothing to think about;
Or when, under ether, the mind is conscious but conscious of nothing—
I said to my soul, be still, and wait without hope
(*CPP* 126)

Eliot's personae have attempted in vain to follow this path into silence before: "Prufrock's Pervigilium" ends abruptly when the Madness opens his mouth and the world falls apart; Prufrock himself ends his "Love Song" as the chambers of the sea close over him; the narrator of "Do I know how I feel?" averts his imagination from an identical impending darkness ("I do not know what, after, and I do not care either" [*IMH* 80]). They have all, like the fearful elders of part 2, "turned their eyes" from the darkness and have become prime examples of what Eliot calls "the human soul in the process of forgetting itself" (*CPP* 125).[46] This time, however, the results are very different. If *East Coker* takes the etherized patient scenario further than any of Eliot's previous attempts, then we must ask what Eliot did differently when he returned to the scene in 1940 that allowed him to achieve this new level of imaginative depth and complexity. In other words: What allows the speaker of *East Coker* to go where the others could not? To see past the sinking blackness of ether and into a clearing of sorts, one that promises to balance the extreme emotions that the passion scene evokes?

The first difference is perhaps the most striking: this time, the etherized patient does not occupy center stage; instead he appears only in the last of three similes that the speaker invokes in the attempt to make the paralysis—what he calls "the silent funeral" or "the darkness of God"—meaningful in a way that does not elide its dangers (*CPP* 126). By connecting them with the coordinating conjunction "or" (instead of "and" or simply no conjunction at all, as is often the case), Eliot implies that all of these tropes are tentative, explorative possibilities; in effect, the stanza declares itself to be uncertain, still reaching after an adequate correlative. The order of the progression, then, is paramount. It traces a mental learning curve in reverse, beginning with an advanced cognitive "knowledge" ("we *know* that the hills and the trees") and moving to a sensory vision ("you *see* behind every face") before settling on the vacant, object-less awareness of our familiar patient ("*conscious but conscious of nothing*" [*CPP* 126]). With the degenerative mental arc traced by these verbs, Eliot brings the sinking effects of the ether to an excruciating, slow-motion pace; never before have his speakers been capable of sustaining the kind of emotional pressure necessary to follow the scenario through to its end, much less to stretch the fearful anticipation beforehand to nearly twenty lines. On their own, the similes are not especially compelling, but in the emotionally fraught context that Eliot has built up around the etherized patient, they represent an impressive feat of imaginative suffering that approaches the "immense passive strength" that he so admired in Baudelaire's work (*SE* 423).

The second significant difference between this scene and its predecessors involves Eliot's use of what I call an "intertextual reprise," a strategy that is examined in greater detail in the next chapter. In the reprise, he recalls salient tropes from his own earlier poems to both evoke and revise the emotional resonance they have acquired. It is a gesture that performs, we might suggest, what Yeats calls the "quarrel with ourselves" that alone produces great poetry. The first—"as, in a theatre, when / The lights are extinguished"—is the most striking. It recalls Prufrock's inner theater of the mind, where a "magic lantern threw the nerves in patterns on a screen" (*CPP* 6). Now, however, the magic lantern of the unruly fantasia is darkened; no "monsters," "fancy lights," or "enchantments" (as the speaker here recalls them) intervene between the mind and its internal darkness: the anesthetic has done its work (*CPP* 125). Likewise for the next simile, which focuses on the vacuous faces on a stopped subway car ("you see behind every face the mental emptiness deepen" [*CPP* 126]). When Eliot's earlier speakers thought of a lifeless, paralyzed face, they were tormented by grotesque visions of "pearls that were his eyes," or "daffodil bulbs" staring "from the sockets of the eyes" (in *The Waste Land* and "Whispers of Immortality" [1919]) (*CPP* 41, 32). As in the previous trope, this speaker will not allow his own fearful imagination to divert his attention by projecting its monstrous, horrific visions upon the darkness; instead, when "mental activity fail[s]" (as Eliot had more accurately phrased it in an earlier draft), it simply fails, and we are left only to await the imminent revelation.[47] In short, this narrator has blinded the "blind eye" that "creates / The empty forms between the ivory gates," the tremulous mental activity that (as he had discovered in *Ash-Wednesday*) deceives with its seductive illusions (*CPP* 66). This self-imposed blindness may not seem the more demanding imaginative path, until we consider that even the fantastic, grotesque shapes of nightmare can seem, to the dreamer, preferable to absolute nothingness. When he finally arrives at the familiar etherized patient, he is willing to follow the scenario through to its conclusion. Only now, after he has grappled with the deeply ambivalent emotions associated with paralysis and surrender, does Eliot turn to his paraphrase of the famous lines from the *Ascent of Mount Carmel* ("wait without hope / For hope would be hope for the wrong thing" [*CPP* 126]) to buttress his personal and emotional conclusions with the weight of the mystical tradition.

In the earlier poem, Eliot's paralyzed patient refused to entertain the possibility that the menacing surgeon might discover his shameful secret, hidden even from the patient himself, while the speaker of another poem could only imagine with fear his own exposure and vulnerability: "We are helpless. . . . Some day, if

God— / But then, what opening out of dusty souls!" (*IMH* 49). But by the last stanzas in part 3 of *East Coker*, finally prepared to face the revelation in its stark, unem-
bellished reality, the narrator presses past the intellectual and emotional collapse
that had stunted his predecessors. The result is not the evidence of innate moral
corruption, nor is it the kind of hidden internal disease and infection that had so
utterly shocked the surgeons when they operated on his father-in-law in 1920. It is,
rather, one of the most striking and compelling moments of emotional release in
Eliot's verse, perhaps second only to the "lost lilac" and the "bent golden rod" that
temporarily alleviated *Ash-Wednesday*'s purgatorial anguish in the final stanzas
over a decade earlier (*CPP* 66). It holds out the promise, if only briefly, of an exhilarating breath of air in the midst of the sinking suffocation of the ether:

> Whisper of running streams, and winter lightning.
> The wild thyme unseen and the wild strawberry,
> The laughter in the garden, echoed ecstasy
> Not lost, but requiring, pointing to the agony
> Of death and birth.
> (*CPP* 127)

Each of these images of sensual pleasure and emotional anticipation is muf-
fled or half hidden by the forest terrain ("running streams"), the color of the sky
("winter lightning"), or the foliage ("the wild thyme" and the "laughter in the garden," both of which point us back to the children's voices in *Burnt Norton*). Each
is in the slow process of emerging from its hiding place, of revealing itself; as
such, each re-creates the gesture of revelation toward which the earlier speakers
were so ambivalent. It is as if Eliot recaptures the affective and spiritual lightness
of the *Landscapes* poems (1934–35) and submerges them just beneath the surface
of the fear-filled scene.[48] These tokens of hopefulness do not elide the "agony" of
the passion scene nor its painful proximity to "death and birth." They do, however,
portray the possibility that the formerly malevolent surgeon might uncover—or
rather, that he might allow to emerge on its own—an emotional richness that the
speaker himself cannot. They imply, in short, a more measured response to the
passion scene, one which is not ultimately governed by shame and self-hatred.

In part 4 Eliot picks up where he had left off more than twenty years before by
reintroducing the familiar surgeon, this time without the malicious attributes that
so frightened the speaker of "Do I know how I feel?" in *Inventions of the March
Hare*:

> The wounded surgeon plies the steel
> That questions the distempered part;
> Beneath the bleeding hands we feel

The sharp compassion of the healer's art
Resolving the enigma of the fever chart.
(*CPP* 127)

Although it is helpful to discern the parallels between the stanzas in section 4 and André Gide's *Le Prométhée mal enchaîné,* and although we cannot ignore the Christian connotations of this redemptive healer, we should not allow a zeal for allusions or spiritual transcendence to divert our attention from one important fact: the emotional contours of this scenario have drastically changed since Eliot last sketched it. These terse, controlled stanzas (indicative of the speaker's calmer, more measured state of mind this time) follow the imagined scenario of the etherized patient beyond any of Eliot's previous forays into what he calls "the dark cold and the empty desolation" (*CPP* 129). They return to add a more ambivalent, complex dimension to Baudelaire's ironic description of love as a "terrible pastime, in which one of the players must forfeit possession of himself."[49] The forfeiture of self-possession is a condition for the narrator's rediscovery of hope (whether we call it secular hope, religious faith, or Christian *caritas* matters less than its broader emotional import, which is identical for all three), although the surrender is no less terrible than Eliot has previously imagined it. Under this surgeon's "constant care," the speaker discovers that surrender does not promise serenity, that it is not an escape from the turbulent emotions attending human vulnerability; it is a way of accounting for those emotions as the quiet-voiced elders could not. Its joy is not the illusory condition that results from habit or willful ignorance, but rather that which abides only on the far side of passion, only once the mind has undergone the passivity and paralysis that destroy its pretensions to self-possession and control. In contrast to the seeming self-possession that the narrator disclaimed in part 2, this is the way of dispossession, wherein the illusion of self-sufficiency and perfectibility (our "sound, substantial flesh and blood") is supplanted by an acute awareness of limitation, by what Eliot calls the liberating spirit that "will not leave us, but prevents us everywhere" (*CPP* 128). Within the strict boundaries of these limitations and preventions, Eliot discovers the possibility of an emergent, recaptured joy unknown to his previous speakers. *East Coker* transforms the valence of the passion scene from a horrific, shameful obstacle to a necessary and ambivalent condition of the speaker's artistic and emotional development.

This transformation, we must note, is not accomplished by logical means. Eliot does not "prove" that hope and joy may accompany the passion scene alongside fear and anguish; nor does he borrow his conclusions from a systematic theological or philosophical tradition. Instead, by performing the transformation, by dramatizing its imaginative and affective changes step by step, *East Coker* sketches the *possibility* of a more varied and complex set of emotional responses. In short, he has modulated the emotional and dramatic paradigm of the scene, not its logic, by experimenting with what he claims are the poet's primary materials, "feelings, sensations, emotions, and their possible chemical combinations."[50] I believe that this is precisely what Eliot has in mind when he suggests that the function of poetry "is not intellectual but emotional" and thus "it cannot be defined in intellectual terms" (SE 138).

Ten years later, Eliot returns to the etherized patient once more in The Cocktail Party (1950), where he is finally able to allow himself to think more philosophically about the trope that had compelled so many of his early speakers into nightmare. Edward, the play's protagonist, encounters a literal doctor this time in Sir Henry Harcourt-Reilly, whose whimsical but profound advice promises his patient freedom from a prison of spiritual apathy and isolation (a condition that Eliot portrays in recognizably Prufrockian terms). Humility is the only escape, Harcourt-Reilly suggests, and the path to humility begins when "you're suddenly reduced to the status of an object— / A living object, but no longer a person" (CPP 307). Such awareness reminds one of the acute vulnerability and passivity that constitute an abiding condition of the mind, and although this condition may not always be readily apparent, it is nonetheless (as Eliot contends in a draft) "often happening; / Only, we contrive to forget about it quickly."[51] One becomes aware of its presence—and of what Harcourt-Reilly calls the "reluctance of the body to become a *thing*"—when, for instance, one misses the last step of a staircase and comes to startling "jolt" at the bottom (CPP 384, 307). Harcourt-Reilly proposes this singular, jarring experience as the physical correlative to a spiritual reality, but his next example more directly addresses the attendant state of the mind:

> Or, take a surgical operation.
> In consultation with the doctor and the surgeon,
>   . . . you are still the subject,
> The centre of reality. But, stretched on the table,
> You are a piece of furniture in a repair shop
> For those who surround you, the masked actors;
> All there is of you is your body
> And the "you" is withdrawn.
> (CPP 307)

After the conclusion that his narrator had reached in East Coker, Eliot can now return to reexamine the etherized-patient trope with the detached, analytic tone proper to Harcourt-Reilly's psychoanalytic vocation. Harcourt-Reilly's advice prescribes the voluntary withdrawal of the same "you" that Prufrock so infamously addresses ("Let us go then, you and I"), the conscious mind fearful of relinquishing its illusory control or what Eliot calls in Ash-Wednesday the "power of the usual reign" (CPP 3, 60).

Eliot's drafts repeatedly reveal his tendency to delete passages that too explicitly address the philosophical precepts behind the poetry, and a deleted passage from *Little Gidding* (1942) hints at the philosophical problems underlying Harcourt-Reilly's monologue. As the draft demonstrates, Eliot had originally planned for his Virgilian guide, the "composite ghost," to propose a disabused state of awareness identical to that which Harcourt-Reilly advocates in *The Cocktail Party:* "the awareness of the / fact that one was moved while / believing oneself to be the mover."[52] In addition to recalling the account of "anesthetic revelation" that Eliot had encountered in William James's footnote ("the passivity of genius, how it is essentially instrumental . . . moved, not moving"), this passage overtly employs the Aristotelian categories of causality to address the human psyche's status as both an active form and a passive instrument, as both agent and patient.[53] In the theological terms with which Eliot had begun to apprehend the problem, the awareness that Harcourt-Reilly conveys in the draft of *The Cocktail Party* involves a recognition of the divine influences that operate within the soul, moving it either without its conscious knowledge or in tandem with its own inclinations. The temporary loss of control over the will (such as occurs during etherized paralysis), he implies, only reveals the extent to which the conscious mind is never the "centre" of its own will nor entirely in control of its own movements. Now, Eliot never underestimates the primacy and ultimate value of the human will; he even claims that "a strong and positive misdirection of the will" is at the root of the decay of modern spirituality.[54] The conclusion he reaches in *Four Quartets* and *The Cocktail Party* neither abdicates the will's freedom nor downplays the significance of the conscious mind in making decisions; rather, it demands that we attend to the unknown influences that make that freedom possible and that lend our decisions a wider, more far-reaching significance than mere isolated moments of evaluation and judgment. It demands, he claims, the sort of "hypersensitive awareness" that alone grants the individual some degree of "helpless power among the helpless."[55]

Eliot's conclusion is ultimately that the mind may feign surrender by relying on falsifying routines or the illusion of human perfectibility; it may simulate passivity while actually preserving its defenses under the guise of idealism or despair (we recall the devil in *Ash-Wednesday,* who "wears / The deceitful face of hope and of despair" [*CPP* 63]). But only the harrowing experience of realizing itself a passive object rather than a motivating agent, the thing-moved rather than the entity-moving, will finally afford it a glimpse of what Thomas Becket means by losing one's "will in the will of God" (*CPP* 199). Only when the mind refuses any secure foothold—even the ominous certainty that the "diabolic" often offers—can it become, as Thomas continues in *Murder in the Cathedral,* "the instrument of God" (*CPP* 125, 199). It is precisely this belated discovery of passivity before the divine movement within the soul that motivates the long monologues on martyrdom and the human will in *Murder in the Cathedral,* that stands behind Harry's escape from the psychological phantoms in *The Family Reunion,* and that even precipitates Lord Claverton's spiritual resignation in *The Elder Statesman* (1959). Each protagonist must learn, in his own way, to confront those passions which are inscrutable and beyond his conscious control; each must endure the risks inherent to spiritual surrender and passivity; and each must find a way to face those risks that accounts for the broad, varied range of emotions that accompanies the passion scene.

PASSION AND CREATIVITY

In his later essays, Eliot returns to address the persistent tension between his mature understanding of passion and surrender and his misgivings about passivity and inspiration in literary matters. Before concluding this chapter, I would like to linger over several of these unduly neglected essays to demonstrate how his affective resolutions to the questions of passion and passivity in *East Coker* and *The Cocktail Party* make their way into his critical theories of composition and inspiration. I have chosen not to address such well-known essays as "Tradition and the Individual Talent" or "Hamlet" at any length, because, despite their intriguing articulations of passion and instrumentality, I believe that the excessive critical reliance upon them—and the way in which they are often misleadingly presented as indicative of a stable and unchanging theory that Eliot held—has blinded us to more compelling and complicated readings of Eliot's career as a whole.

Despite his early, well-known statements about, for instance, the artist as a "medium" or a "vehicle," Eliot sets no store by surrealist experiments or the trend of automatic writing; he refuses to substitute submission to the unconscious "dark embryo" for the labor and craftsmanship of technique.[56] In his 1916 Harvard dissertation on Bradley's philosophy, he denies even the need for the term "unconscious."[57] Elsewhere, he asserts that he has "no good word to say for the cultivation of automatic writing as the model of literary composition" (*SE* 405). But toward the later half of his career, he proves increasingly willing to reserve a privileged, unmistakable place for the inscrutable psychological movements that compel the poem and dictate its form. It is not a negligible coincidence that it was in 1941— one year after he had found a form to balance the affective intensities of passion and surrender in *East Coker*—that he contributed a provocative and seemingly uncharacteristic introduction to his selection of Kipling's poetry in *A Choice of Kipling's Verse.* At first glance Kipling would seem to be the perfect test case for Eliot's classicist argument in favor of the conscious, deliberate craftsmanship of Augustan verse against the ecstatic, Pindaric rhapsodies of Romantic poetics. The occasional nature of much of Kipling's verse, his intense awareness of social strata and cultural proprieties, his strict metrical regularity—according to our conventional view of the younger Eliot, all of these factors should have combined to make Kipling a paradigm of classical constraint and intellectual sensibility.[58] Instead of applauding his craftsmanship, however, Eliot takes the opportunity to discuss the essential difference between "the poem which forces its way into the consciousness of the poet" and "the poem which the writer himself forces" (14). In the latter, he proposes, the artist attempts to exert intellectual control over all of the various elements and signifying mechanisms of the poem. He conceives his meaning, chooses appropriate figures of speech to convey it, and manipulates the sound and rhythm of the language accordingly. He is the example par excellence of the "'cool scientist, almost an algebraist, in the service of a subtle dreamer.'"[59]

But for the later Eliot, the cool, calculating instruments of the scientist are no longer enough to account for the passions of creativity and inspiration. The poem that "forces" itself upon the poet results only from an "awful daring" of surrender and abandon to the same mystical or psychological energy to which Eliot refers when he suggests that Dante composed "by surrender and assent" rather than by means of "a strong will."[60] At times, he suggests, Kipling seems to be "possessed" by this clairvoyant energy, a powerful affective force "over the development of which he has, as a poet, no control" (*A Choice* 19; 17). It is no accident that now— a year after he had upbraided the "quiet voiced elders" for mistaking hebetude for self-control and for using that illusory control to turn their eyes away from the darkness—he calls artistic control an obstacle to the vital energies of a visionary poetry. For a poet like Eliot—who once so vehemently refuted the optimistic, Arnoldian idea of the "inner voice," and who once, armed with Maritain's severe warnings against artistic passivity, led the classicist charge against intuition's capricious whims—these are aesthetic propositions of bold and striking significance.

In the lecture he delivered to the National Book League in November 1953, *The Three Voices of Poetry* (1954), Eliot turns to the German poet and critic Gottfried Benn for help in further calibrating the uneasy relationship between passion and the creative process. The poet, Eliot writes, begins a poem with "nothing so definite as an emotion, in any ordinary sense"; instead he is prompted by what Benn calls "an inert embryo or 'creative germ'" (*TVP* 28). Eliot translates Benn's metaphor for the source of inspiration into what he calls an "unknown, dark *psychic material*"; he suggests that the poet makes himself into a vehicle for this obscure energy and that his artistic submission is accompanied by an emotional upheaval not dissimilar to that which his own etherized patients repeatedly underwent. "He is oppressed by a burden," Eliot writes, "which he must bring to birth in order to obtain relief": "Or, to change the figure of speech, he is haunted by a demon, a demon against which he feels powerless, because in its first manifestation it has no face, no name, nothing; and the words, the poem he makes, are a kind of form of exorcism of this demon" (*TVP* 29). Most notable about this demon of artistic creativity is its utter unnotableness: it is a formless, featureless force, a nightmare without images, a mirror in the dark. Eliot's entirely negative characterization reveals this demon to be merely the anonymous arbiter of passion, a dim placeholder for the agentless energy that transforms the poet into a patient. Most important, it shifts our attention from the origins of the artistic haunting to its emotional effects, that is (to recall Eliot's early tropes), from the nimble gesticulations of the puppeteer to the powerless gestures of the marionettes.

Powerlessness, it seems, of the sort that we have been referring to as passion, is the condition upon which the creative act is predicated. Without submitting himself to the now-familiar state of the "patient etherised upon a table," the artist cannot access the urgent and pressurized emotional energy that will compel him into speech. Like the poems that forced their way into Kipling's consciousness, this demonic creative material "dominates" the poet's sensibility. "The psychic material," Eliot continues, "tends to create its own form," a form which the poet's conscious mind can neither predict nor control (*TVP* 36). Even in the case of the poetic drama, in which the dramatist perhaps more consciously conjures an emotional situation and then allows the "particular story" to emerge accordingly, Eliot admits that the writer possesses far less control than he normally supposes. He may exert a degree of control over the dramatic unfolding of the story. But "it is likely, of course, that it is in the beginning the pressure of some rude unknown psychic material that directs the poet to tell that particular story" (37).

A look at one more of his late, largely neglected lectures should make the developments in Eliot's post-*Quartets* thinking about passion and creativity unmistakably clear. A year before *The Three Voices of Poetry,* he delivered a little-known lecture titled "Scylla and Charybdis" (1952) at a literary conference in Nice. Here he offers a more complex (albeit also more brief) account of the simultaneity of action and passion involved in the composition of poetry, that is, of how the poet is both an active maker and a passive vehicle at once. To register the full impact of his claims in that essay, however, we must turn for a moment to Paul Valéry's comments in *The Art of Poetry* (1958), the volume of translations for which Eliot wrote a laudatory if somewhat ambivalent introduction. In "Poetry and Abstract Thought," Valéry distinguishes between the necessary caprice of inspiration (which he reverently calls "irregular, inconstant, involuntary, and fragile") and the subsequent mental action required to compose a poem.[61] The passive poetic state, he affirms, "is not enough to make a poet, any more than it is enough to see a treasure in a dream to find it, on waking, sparkling at the foot of one's bed."[62] Despite his impressively nuanced and complicated theory of creative composition, Valéry clings to the traditional Aristotelian distinction between the passion of inspiration and the action of creative composition. There is a "profound difference," he argues, "existing between spontaneous production by the mind . . . and the fabrication of works." And again he asserts, "poetic feeling and the artificial synthesis of this state in some work are two distinct things, as different as sensation and action."[63] In Valéry's essays, passion (as either reception, sensation, or passivity) is always only a precursor to composition, that is, a temporary departure from the normative state of mental action, the state of control and volition to which the mind must subsequently return if the work is to come into being. In the phrase of Valéry's foremost theoretical descendent, Maurice Blanchot, it is always the "impatience" of the poet—that is, the mental actions that distinguish him from the passive thinker, the patient—that accompanies the origination of the work.[64] If the dreamed-of treasure is to be found at the foot of the bed, it is up to the impatient artist to forge and craft it during his waking hours.

However, as we have seen in matters not directly related to poetic composition, Eliot does not abide by the conventional psychological paradigm that distinguishes between action and passion, between the mind operating under its own control (or the agent) and the mind operating at the whim of another (the patient). His realizations in *East Coker* and afterward have convinced him that passivity is more than an aberrant mental or physical condition from which we must recover and reassert the mind's sovereignty; it is, rather, an abiding and ambivalent element of the emotional life, one which the mind can choose to ignore but which it cannot master. It is notable that Eliot turns repeatedly to Valéry in his 1952 lecture, calling him "the great explorer of thought, feeling, and language" and applauding the ways that his *Le Jeune Parque* and *La Cimetière Marin* both possess meaning beyond their ostensible subject matter.[65] Eliot brings Valéry to his side because he knows that Valéry's poetry itself challenges the facetious distinctions between inspiration and creation that essays such as "Poetry and Abstract Thought" pursue. In the lecture, he compares the poet's struggles with diction to the Homeric navigator, perpetually struggling to avoid the wrong path. This active, conscious deliberation with language and rhythm, Eliot proposes, is more than enough to occupy the poet's mind; poets should limit their attention to "a better choice of words, a neater turn of phrase, and a more orderly arrangement," that is, to problems of craft rather than content.[66] While the mind's will-to-action is satiated in this respect, while it is fully engaged with resolving the technical difficulties of composition, another, less apprehensible energy exerts itself upon the poem: "In avoiding the several dangers of navigation, the poet cannot be too much concerned with the choice of port he eventually hopes to reach. It is necessary, certainly, in a poem of any length, to have a plan, to lay a course. But the final work will be another work than that which the author set out to write; and will, as I have already suggested, be something of a surprise to the author himself."[67]

The poet writes; the poem is written. Even though they occur simultaneously, Eliot implies, these two clauses do not describe an identical phenomenon. It would be more in keeping with Eliot's lecture to say that *while* the poet writes, the poem is written. Elsewhere he had formulated this paradoxical simultaneity another way, with characteristic obliquity: "such poets find it expedient to occupy their conscious mind with the craftsman's problems, leaving the deeper meaning to emerge, if there, from a lower level" (*A Choice* 18). The "emergence" of a deeper

meaning, the surprising way it "forces" itself upon the poet, returns us immediately to the signals of affective emergence in *East Coker,* the "wild thyme," "running
streams," and "laughter in the garden" that Eliot had captured in the process of
becoming visible and audible. There these tokens of emotional lightness allowed
the speaker to entertain the possibility of rebirth in the midst of a seemingly debilitating passion and paralysis; here they similarly gesture toward the possibility of
poetic meaning emerging, still half hidden, in the midst of the passion of composition. And as before, when the speaker recognized in these emblems an "echoed
ecstasy / Not lost, but requiring, pointing to the agony," so now the poet does not
escape the demonic, agonizing burden of the creative passion. As I suggested earlier, Eliot's ability to recalibrate the affective scales of passion and surrender in *East
Coker* and afterward has an unmistakable effect on his aesthetic theory. It allows
him to see that the poet is always, despite his conscious labors, a patient; that the
passive nature of inspiration coincides with—rather than opposing or obstructing
—the active processes of the conscious mind.

It should not be surprising that here, in the attempt to define passion and surrender in an aesthetic sense, Eliot adopts nautical metaphors—navigational dangers, choice of port—similar to those he had used in an affective context many
years earlier: in "Goldfish" ("Your seamanship is very neat"), *The Waste Land* ("The
boat responded / Gaily, to the hand expert with sail and oar"), *Ash-Wednesday*
("The white sails still fly seaward"), and "Marina" ("the hope, the new ships")
(*IMH* 29; *CPP* 49, 66, 73). The subtle integration of these formerly distinct metaphors for passion and surrender into a single artistic paradigm is indicative of his
expanded, mature understanding of passion and the role that it plays not only in
the range of affective experience but in the dark, uncertain processes of creative
composition. If in his early essays such as "Tradition and the Individual Talent"
and "Modern Tendencies in Poetry" Eliot begins to articulate the radically passive
character of creativity but seems unwilling to grant it its full weight, his persistent
experimentation with the figure of the etherized patient and its affective paradigms eventually allows him to bring his literary ideals into accord with his spiritual and emotional understanding of surrender. As I have tried to show, Eliot's late
emphasis on a poetics of possession and surrender is not a product of his old age
nor a blatant reversal of his earlier position. Instead, as he himself recognizes in
Kipling's later writing, "this later work is the continuation and consummation of
the earlier" (*A Choice* 32).

CONCLUSIONS: JOHN DAVIDSON

Late in his life, Eliot revisited the haunting work of poet whom he had long admired when he delivered a radio tribute to John Davidson in the summer of 1957
and, four years later, composed the preface for Maurice Lindsay's edition of *John
Davidson: A Selection of His Poems* (1961).[68] Davidson's ability to gaze unflinchingly

upon the ruins and terrors of modernity, Eliot claims, "impressed me deeply in my formative years between the ages of sixteen and twenty."[69] Scholars have long discerned the influence of Davidson's attention to what he calls "agony unutterable" on Eliot's earliest work, and Eliot himself reveals that the speaker of Davidson's "Thirty Bob a Week" "has haunted me all my life."[70] Another of Davidson's speakers that the young Eliot could not have overlooked, and that seems to have had a similarly haunting effect on him, relates with philosophical detachment the details of a ghastly vivisection that he performed on a dying man whom he had taken into his care. "I study pain," the narrator of Davidson's "The Testament of a Vivisector" explains before dismembering the paralyzed man, "measure it and invent it."[71]

If the young Eliot sensed a "fellow feeling" and a dark kinship with a poet who could envision the details of dissecting a living, paralyzed body, his own mature conclusions about passion and paralysis likely strengthened this sense when he returned to reread Davidson with renewed interest in 1957.[72] By that time, Eliot's persistent attention to the etherized-patient trope had taught him that vulnerability and spiritual surrender might be accompanied by not only terror but joy as well, and he would have discovered a striking portrayal of this conviction when he chanced to reread Davidson's "Insomnia." Davidson's protagonist awakens to find himself not quite on a dissection table like the patient in "Prufrock" but instead "stretched upon his living bier"—"a golden rack / Inlaid with gems"—while all around him a conspicuously familiar "ether hovered black."[73] Rather than a sadistic "vivisector" or Eliot's early Mephistophelean surgeon, two angelic Seraphim attend this paralyzed patient, intent on what initially seems to be torture but what Davidson eventually reveals as a form of divine purgation: "The Seraph at his head was Agony; / Delight, more terrible, stood at his feet."[74] Eliot must have looked upon the scene knowingly: a paralyzed patient, the embodiment of spiritual surrender, caught midway between agony and ecstasy but nonetheless in the constant care of the divine Seraphim, whose "implacabl[e] intent" he undoubtedly realized to be at one with that liberating spirit he addresses in The Family Reunion as the "love and terror / Of what waits and wants me, and will not let me fall" (CPP 281).[75] Eliot's belated encounter with Davidson's helpless patient in "Insomnia," so reminiscent of his own Prufrock but transfigured in the light of the divine, must have helped him to draw his long-standing struggle to engage and relate to passion toward a completion of sorts. Looking back on his cigarette-smoking marionettes, or on the malicious approach of the bearded surgeon with his chemicals and knife, perhaps Eliot eventually came to affirm, alongside Harry in The Family Reunion, that "in the end / That is the completion which at the beginning / Would have seemed the ruin" (CPP 275).

2

WHO STOOD OVER ELIOT'S SHOULDER?

Passions of Recognition in His Later Work

I begin by calling to mind the following stanza from *The Waste Land,* if only to postpone returning to it until the closing pages of this chapter:

> Who is the third who walks always beside you?
> When I count, there are only you and I together
> But when I look ahead up the white road
> There is always another one walking beside you
> Gliding wrapt in a brown mantle, hooded
> I do not know whether a man or a woman
> —But who is that on the other side of you?
> (*CPP* 48)

Surely the young T. S. Eliot had not yet envisioned this mysterious, hooded "third" or the ominous Fourth Tempter from *Murder in the Cathedral* when he suggested, in one of his first published poems, that "ghosts are fellows whom you *can't* keep out; . . . For often they drop in at awkward moments."[1] Nor could he have foreseen the amount of creative energy that he would eventually expend investigating these "awkward moments"—spectral or otherwise—and the pressure that they exert on the creative imagination. Although we must abandon the hope of glancing over Eliot's shoulder to find an answer, the question posed by my title nonetheless addresses precisely such a moment, and the reverberation of that moment throughout his work presents us with a challenge that will not be so easily abandoned. Its origins in experience may remain hidden, perhaps even from Eliot himself. Or perhaps they are hidden in full view, too familiar to be distinguished, since being caught off guard by someone (or something) is a consequence not of character, culture, or the supernatural but of the simple fact that our organs of sight both face in the same direction. Our ability to focus at all, we might say, is predicated upon the possibility of being surprised from behind. In matters of sight—both physical and psychological—blind spots are neither an unfortunate accident nor an avoidable obstacle; they are a structural, organic necessity.

We can begin to register the importance that the "awkward moment" assumes as a poetic figure for Eliot by recalling its early appearances in "Portrait of a Lady" (1915)—when the narrator claims to "feel like one who smiles, and turning shall remark / Suddenly, his expression in a glass"—and in the last section of *The Waste Land,* when "the third" appears suddenly behind the shoulder of the narrator's companion (*CPP* 11). As different as they may initially seem, both scenes are instances of what Eliot eventually calls spiritual "recognition," a phenomenon that occurs when the mind's eye is caught off guard by a presence that appears suddenly in its peripheral vision, as familiar as a reflection but as foreign as a stranger, as opaque as the mirror's quicksilver, and as terrifying as a roaming phantom.

How does the recognition trope relate to what I have been calling the passion scene? First, like the etherized patient that we explored in chapter 1, it is a compressed node of feeling, thought, and image that Eliot seems compelled to revisit over a lifetime of creative work, one that seems to exercise as much power over his imagination as his imagination does over it. Second, the recognition trope also engages passion thematically, that is, it confronts the emotional and intellectual upheavals provoked by the mind's vulnerability to being "moved" by forces not subject to conscious control. Moreso even than the etherized patient, however, the recognition scene aims at calibrating the relationship between passion and psychological limitation, between emotion and suffering, on the one hand, and the range and blind spots of consciousness on the other. The scene is part of Eliot's ongoing inquiry into the ways in which the limitations of the human mind—rather than merely obstructing our normal activity or impeding our otherwise fluid self-awareness—actually shape and structure our experience of the world and of ourselves in productive and imaginatively substantive ways.

Rather than starting with "Portrait of a Lady" or *The Waste Land,* where the recognition scene is only beginning to gather a conceptual resonance, to vibrate with the distinctive hum of Eliot's creative and intellectual urgency, this chapter examines the later stages of Eliot's artistic and conceptual experimentation with the scene, from the essays that lead toward its first full articulation in "Marina"(1930) to its complex development in the work that follows.[2] Calling on a number of his unpublished letters and uncollected essays, it determines how the various instantiations of the scene reveal Eliot's changing understanding of psychological vulnerability, how this conceptual trajectory informs his development as a poet, and how it demands that criticism rethink certain entrenched assumptions about his classicist allegiances, his relationship to romanticism, and his theories of human emotion. In "Marina," Eliot achieves an ideal vision, a telos of sorts, which seems—

however vague and distant—to offer an adequate way of engaging limitations and vulnerability without reducing them to temporary, accidental disturbances of the psychological status quo. But only after nine years of experimentation with the scene does Eliot finally achieve this vision and use it to make sense of the volatile, strangely autonomous world of emotion through which the conscious mind haltingly stumbles.

My claim, in short, is twofold. First, the recognition scene is Eliot's way both to explore and to enact the mind's sudden and disturbing realization of its own radical incompleteness and vulnerability, of the fact there are inscrutable realms within its own precincts which it can neither illuminate nor elide. It is a gauge to register what he calls elsewhere the "ultimate spiritual pressure."[3] And second, Eliot's attempt to calibrate the emotional responses to this realization leads him, over the course of the career, to rethink the psychological value of affective intensity, to ask what this intensity might reveal about the mind's ability to know itself, and to integrate the answers to these questions into a theoretical paradigm capable of accounting for the mind's limitations in both transcendent and immanent terms. In the process of offering a corrective to widespread misconceptions about Eliot's commitment to emotion in poetry, my conclusions about the recognition scene promise to give us new ways of conceptualizing two commonplaces of modernist criticism—the decentered subject and the critique of Enlightenment rationality. In that vein, and insofar as it identifies a jarring self-difference and discontinuity at the heart of Eliot's ideas about psychological limitation, this chapter is in productive dialogue with scholars such as Jean-Michel Rabaté (*The Ghosts of Modernity*), William Melaney (*After Ontology: Literary Theory and Modernist Poetics*), and Walter Kalaidjian (*The Edge of Modernism*), each of whom discerns an aporetic, noncognitive element operating at the center of modernist literary discourse and haunting its margins and peripheries.[4]

I find it expedient to use the admittedly overdetermined terms "soul" and "unconscious" in the pages that follow—the first word because Eliot uses it frequently and not without great care, and the second because it is an accepted contemporary term to designate those psychological processes that occur beyond or beneath our conscious awareness. In *Fantasia of the Unconscious* (1922), a book that Eliot regarded with uncharacteristic admiration, D. H. Lawrence goes so far as to align the two terms unambiguously: "As a matter of fact, *soul* would be a better word. By the unconscious we do mean the soul."[5] I am not willing to go that far, but as we discuss Eliot's metaphors for the dark, inscrutable regions of the psyche, it is essential to remember that "soul" need not always carry its conventional religious associations. In ancient thought, it encompassed not only the unconscious but the conscious mind and the organic processes of the body as well. As it was for F. H. Bradley, the philosopher whose work he studied in graduate school, so for Eliot in his early philosophical writing, the "soul" remains an umbrella term for all of

the movements of the psyche, conscious or otherwise. It is, to borrow Eliot's metaphor, the garden in which the flowers of intellect, volition, and emotion all take
root, thrive, and wither according to the unpredictable seasons of the inner life.

EARLY RECOGNITIONS

In the *Times Literary Supplement* on 31 March 1921, Eliot published an essay on
Andrew Marvell that reveals some of the conceptual problems that he was enter-
taining not long before "the third" made its awkward appearance in *The Waste
Land.* There he characteristically praises precision and clarity as paramount virtues of versification; he applauds Marvell for the same lucid self-control and crys-
talline hardness that T. E. Hulme predicted would dominate poetry in the coming
age of classicism. To distinguish Marvell's precision from the lamentable vague-
ness of his contemporaries, Eliot quotes a passage from William Morris's "The
Nymph's Song to Hylas," in which the narrator wanders through "a little garden
close" and wishes he might remain there "from dewy dawn to dewy night, / And
have one with me wandering" (*SE* 299). If only briefly, Eliot trains his attention on
the seemingly innocuous ambiguity of the "one" in Morris's last line, claiming to
sense in it "some indefinite person, form, or phantom," a vague and eerie presence
that Marvell would have revised into clarity (*SE* 299). As usual, his censure is even
more revealing than his praise. However inferior Eliot considered it in terms of
clarity and precision, Morris's relatively inauspicious lyric must have struck a mystical chord with the young poet. Later in the essay, he reveals the rationale behind
his seemingly unwarranted discovery of this mysterious presence. Poems like this
one startle us, he claims (emphasizing the element of surprise), because they
involve "a recognition, implicit in the expression of every experience, of other
kinds of experience which are possible" (*SE* 303). Something in this concise articulation apparently pleased him; on 16 December 1935, Eliot wrote to F. R. Leavis that
the Marvell essay had retained for him a permanent value that others had not.[6] Perhaps he sensed a significant intellectual breakthrough here, sensed himself beginning to set the intellectual and affective stakes of what he would eventually call the
"recognition scene." Although still conceptually vague, Eliot's early understanding
of recognition entails a startling realization of the multiple levels upon which the
psyche registers a single experience. These include the conscious levels as well as
unconscious and spiritual ones, "forms" and "phantoms" that slip nimbly past the
mind's doorways and corridors and which consciousness must gradually, sometimes painfully, learn to discern. "Most people are only very little alive," he later
reminds us, and "need to be aroused to the perception of the simple distinction
between the spiritual and the material."[7]

Perhaps the difference is neither so simple nor so binary; in fact, Eliot had
been thinking about how the soul negotiates these multiple levels of experience
since his time as a graduate student in philosophy at Harvard. In his dissertation

on F. H. Bradley, he imagines the soul as a kind of reservoir for the various perceptual data of experience, which flood the mind and the senses simultaneously (in the rush of what Bradley calls "immediate experience," a phenomenon so immediate that we do not experience it at all) but are immediately channeled into multiple psychological foci, what he calls "points of view" or "units of soul life" (KE 147–49).[8] From Eliot's perspective, the soul both perceives and preserves the many simultaneous levels of experience, yet because so many of these levels remain unconscious—only potentially conscious "points of view"—it is neither self-transparent nor explicable as the sum of its experiences.[9] In a vast house with many windows, the soul looks out from all of them at once, and it preserves not only each view but its own response to the view, and its response to that response, et cetera; in fact, we would more properly say that the soul is *itself* the house, throbbing with receptive life, humming with a keen and vibrant self-awareness. Consciousness, however, can only peer out from one window at a time; however frantically it races from one window to the next, it will never see a visitor coming up the walk from every angle. Any single conscious state, Eliot contends, is only "an inconsistent aspect" of the many that comprise the soul's totality, and as a result the conscious mind can never encompass the myriad aspects of experience that constantly beset it (KE 28). At best it can address an experience under only one of its multiple aspects at a time, hoping to correct each partial view by discerning as many of these dimensions as possible (KE 19). Drawing on the philosophy of Gottfried Wilhelm Leibniz, Eliot concludes that "the life of a soul does not consist in the contemplation of one consistent world but in the painful task of unifying (to a greater or less extent) jarring and incompatible ones" (KE 147–48).[10]

Eliot's early theory of "soul life" and the multiplicity of experience implies an inexorable condition of partiality and incompleteness, or of loss and desire, one in which the conscious mind longs to revisit and recuperate the affective and spiritual dimensions of experience that it has "missed" but that remain hidden elements, potential points of view, as it were, of the soul. This early formulation of the psychological necessity of incompleteness and loss is extremely important, I believe, for several reasons. First, it prefigures Eliot's later, better known theories of the structural incompleteness of the psyche itself and of its vulnerability to foreign influence. Second, insofar as the sense of loss is motivated by "missed" experience, it implies a desire that scholars are rarely willing to associate with Eliot: the desire to intensify sensory and emotional receptivity rather than escape or deflect it. Expanding and intensifying the mind's receptivity would mean that it ultimately "misses" less. But perhaps most important, Eliot's paradigm implies (although he would have been loathe to admit it in 1916) the attempt of the rational mind to delve into those dark coffers of the psyche that were well known by that time as the unconscious.[11] If the mind cannot expand its receptive capacity to consciously register the multiple dimensions of experience, then at least it can hope to recover those dimensions later if they remain somehow preserved in the unconscious. In effect, the mind longs either to absorb or to recover the multiple dimensions of reality that Eliot discerns in Morris's poem, those embodied in the vague companion who may be person, form, and phantom simultaneously. It longs for the eradication of the mental blind spots that seem to prevent a richer, more complex experience of the world through which it moves. To adapt a trope from one of Eliot's unlikely bedfellows, the mind *would like to be* a vast transparent eyeball, a house constructed entirely of windows.

These multiple levels and "worlds" of experience are not merely products of Eliot's early thinking, nor are they limited to his poetic theory. As late as 1946, he applauds the Christian novelist and poet Charles Williams for demonstrating the unique "mystic faculty" to "live in the material and spiritual world at once." And perhaps deliberately using the recognition trope, he laments the atrophied state of our "capacity for recognising the realities to which Williams was trying to draw our attention" in his mystical writing.[12] And again Eliot reveals the enduring personal value of his theory in a letter written to the Reverend William Turner Levy on 21 August 1954, when he consoles Levy for the loss of a close friend by suggesting that even a single experience, such as one shared with a beloved yet seldom-seen friend, may penetrate into and remain submerged within multiple and unexpected levels of consciousness.[13] What changes over the course of Eliot's career, as we shall see, is not his theory of the irreducibly multiple planes of experience but his belief in our ability to reconcile, unify, or recapture them.

Eliot contends that such multiplicity pertains primarily to the psychological processes over which the mind has little awareness and even less control. If a single experience affects the conscious mind singly, it also provokes myriad nonapprehensible movements in the soul, and these unconscious movements (which he strongly aligns with sensitivity and feeling, "unconscious" passions as it were) in turn affect conscious thought and emotion. What is a feeling if we do not feel it consciously, Eliot seems to ask? What are these multifarious movements that seem so much like conscious feeling but will not come forth to be counted, gauged, and reconciled? In their furtiveness, temerity, and epistemological recalcitrance, Eliot concludes, they constitute "the substratum of our being, to which we rarely penetrate."[14]

If this gnomic pronouncement sounds more like an excerpt from his 1916 dissertation than a passage in a literary lecture from 1933, there is good reason: Bradley's philosophy of feeling and immediate experience was its starting point. In an essay that Eliot read when he was completing his work at Havard, "In What Sense Are Psychical States Extended?" (1895), Bradley pursues the possibility that spatiality or extension might apply not only to physical objects but to psychological states as well. He implies, albeit cautiously, that the spatial metaphors that we use for psychological processes (like realm, region, area, or backdrop) might be more accurate than we think. In a state of psychological receptivity, he suggests, our mental perception assumes a distinctively spatial character, becoming "not spatial merely, but spatial even visually."[15] What he calls "the psychical field of struggle" (and for Bradley, there is no psychological state that does not entail struggle) may not itself be a space, but nonetheless "when I dwell on it, becomes localized somehow in a visual field."[16] Although he finally decides against it, Bradley even wonders if these localized psychological states might not collide with one another, a possibility that Eliot implicitly embraces in his formulation of the "jarring and incompatible" levels of experience (KE 148).

It is in this context that Bradley envisions the existence of a "background of feeling, before which every object must come," a sort of internal affective stage upon which the objects of the mind act and gesture, or a vast emotional canvas upon which they cast their shadows.[17] The canvas itself is not an object of consciousness, but rather it is the condition for our consciousness of the psychological actors upon it; in this way it is, as Eliot puts it, the "substratum" of our mental life. When he confronts the existence of this unconscious, affective background in his dissertation, Eliot distinguishes between it and the objects of our conscious attention with a spatial metaphor that, under Bradley's enduring intellectual tutelage, he would soon indelibly associate with the actual internal landscape of the soul: "There is no clear line to be drawn between that of which we are conscious and that which as 'feeling' melts imperceptibly into a physiological background. But so far as this fringe is contrasted with that which is actually conscious, it is merely an object" (KE 29). However close they may be figurally, Eliot's fringe is different from Bradley's background in one very important way. It implies at least a limited, restricted visibility or intelligibility not merely of our conscious, active states but also of that unconscious substratum against which they appear. Like the solar corona, that fringe of lighted atmosphere around the sun that is always present but visible only during an eclipse, the substratum manifests itself at the edges of conscious mental objects. Eliot's fringe implies, in short, a confidence in the mind's capacity to detect the multiple, unconscious levels of experience and the hidden psychological and physiological movements that attend them.

As Eliot's inquiry diverges from Bradleian metaphysics toward an immanent psychology—from the sources of mental movement to its effects—he becomes less interested in whence these obscure psychological currents originate than in what they imply about the occluded nature of the human psyche, how it is moved and influenced without its conscious awareness. Long afterward, he returns to the spatial trope from his dissertation to recuperate what had since become one of his most penetrating and persistent metaphors for these unconscious movements, one that implies—contrary to the conventional "depth" model—that they are not lodged within an impenetrable, vertical abyss but, on the contrary, are immanent and close by, a sphere encircling the pinpoint of consciousness at their center, or a shadow cast on all sides at once.[18] They partake of a "penumbral consciousness," he suggests, of which the waking mind is dimly if ever aware: "It seems to me that beyond the nameable, classifiable emotions and motives of our conscious life . . . there is a fringe of indefinite extent, of feeling which we can only detect, so to speak, out of the corner of the eye and can never completely focus."[19]

This circular, surrounding "fringe" is not inscrutable per se; we detect it, sense it, become aware of its hazy, circumferential existence. In 1916 the unconscious mental periphery was "merely an object" like other objects, one which could be (at least partially) examined, contextualized, and mastered; in 1957 it is still both unconscious and peripheral, but it no longer promises to become an object. In fact, it strenuously resists the focused gaze that would allow it to assume object-hood. It has become a permanent and irremediable blind spot, a retinal floater on the mind's eye, forever flitting at the corners of mundane vision, intruding when ignored, retreating when discovered.

The mind's sudden, incomplete awareness of this unconscious, affective periphery may bring intense emotional upheaval, but it also promises artistic intensity for the poet capable of registering its disquieting effects. Despite (or perhaps because of) its disturbing psychological implications, that is, Eliot the poet discerns its poetic value. In an essay written two years after his dissertation, he describes the disconcerting sense of "doubleness" provoked by an awakening awareness of this multiplicity: "There is something terrible, as disconcerting as a quicksand, in this discovery," he suggests. "And it makes the reader, as well as the personae [of the play], uneasily the victim of a merciless clairvoyance."[20] Eliot might more accurately have included the poet himself among those "victimized" by this severe clairvoyance, since it is he who must undergo its tumultuous upheavals before the work even begins. He senses a similar clairvoyance in the work of Chapman and Dostoevsky as a sort of disquieting double vision, and he contends elsewhere that "the greatest poetry, like the greatest prose, has a doubleness" about it.[21] Later, he applauds the doubleness that allows Shakespeare to "somehow disclose . . . a deeper reality than that of the plane of most of our conscious living" and to "remove the surface of things."[22]

By the time he writes The Dry Salvages (1941), he has learned to call the moment of clairvoyance a "sudden illumination" that erupts from behind even the most seemingly inconsequential experiences, and he is even more convinced of the spiritual ordeal that recognition involves and that turns the mind—of the artist especially—into a "victim," the patient of a violent, unwilled, and uncontrollable action (CPP 133). In such moments the conscious mind glimpses, he claims, "Something that is probably quite ineffable: / The backward look behind the assurance / Of recorded history, the backward half-look / Over the shoulder, towards the primitive terror" (CPP 133).

If the causal, linear narrative of history assures us that we are the intentional and knowing agents of our actions and experiences, the backward glimpse "over the shoulder" toward the mind's periphery robs us of such assurances by revealing some foreign, enduring presence, not merely contingent upon a set of remembered or suppressed experiences but partaking of the very structure of the psyche itself, a constituent element of primal, unknowing blindness in the organ of mental and physical sight itself. At times the intimate though inscrutable nature of this other presence prompts Eliot to align it with the Absolute, as in an early lyric such as "Afternoon," when the narrator sketches the psychic trajectory of a mundane experience through the conscious mind and onward "toward the unconscious, the ineffable, the absolute," and again later when he agrees that Lancelot Andrewes, at such moments, is "alone with the Alone" (*IMH* 53).[23] Perhaps, he implies, the conscious mind is not always as alone as it seems.

"MARINA"

Eliot begins to complicate his ideas about the poet's conscious emotional response to these radical realizations of incompleteness and vulnerability when he revisits the recognition scene in "Marina." First published on 25 September 1930 as a slim volume in Faber's *Ariel Poems* series, "Marina" combines Shakespearean imagery, biblical rhetoric, and the features of a New England coastline to dramatize the spiritual awakening of the narrator, whose state of mind undergoes a gradual transition from initial puzzlement (dramatized by the continuous syntax of the opening line: "What seas what shores what grey rocks and what islands") through severe meditation (declarations couched in patristic rhetoric: "Those who suffer the ecstasy of the animals, / . . . Are become unsubstantial") and finally to personal discovery and reclamation ("I made this, I have forgotten / And remember"; *CPP* 72). It seems to end on an expectant high note—"The awakened, lips parted, the hope, the new ships"—full of promise for the advent of the speaker's long-lost daughter, whose return is signaled by the "woodthrush calling through the fog" (the bird that later reappears as the deceptive thrush of *Burnt Norton*). But a strong undercurrent of dread troubles its optimistic surface from the outset. Just a few months before, the narrator of *Ash-Wednesday* had glimpsed from the corner of his eye "the devil of the stairs" but had hurried past the demonic vision in his purgatorial ascent (*CPP* 63). Though few have recognized it as such, "Marina" is Eliot's belated attempt to re-descend that very step to probe its complex, ambivalent significance.

Not long before he began writing "Marina," Eliot encountered and proclaimed his admiration for G. Wilson Knight's commentary on the Shakespearean recognition scene or motif in "Myth and Miracle: On the Mystic Symbolism of Shakespeare" (1929). A variation on the Aristotelian convention of recognition in tragedy, Knight's recognition scene involves a formerly disguised or apparently lost personage who is revealed to an overjoyed beloved. In a letter to E. McKnight Kauffer in 1930, Eliot revealed the centrality of Knight's Shakespearean "Recognition Motive" to his intentions in "Marina."[24] Eliot personally inscribed a copy of "Marina" for Knight, wrote the introduction to his subsequent book, and adapted tropes from Knight's "Myth and Miracle" into his verse as well.[25] No doubt "Myth and Miracle" influenced him, providing him with a classical literary hook upon which to hang his own philosophical reflections about recognition and the multiplicity of experience. But Eliot's certainty of the treacherousness, the psychological dangers, and the fear-driven emotions involved in his own version of "recognition" prompted him to resituate the scene into a darker, more uncertain landscape.

Despite Knight's confidence that "Marina" was "a perfect poetical commentary" on his own scholarly insights into Shakespearean recognition,[26] it is clear that Eliot sensed something missing from Knight's optimistic assessment of the scene as a parable or symbolic representation of Christian rebirth, a moment in which death (or a father's grief at the loss of his daughter, for instance) is ultimately defeated in a sudden, unexpected, and grace-filled moment of rebirth and recovery (the unexpected return of the daughter to her father). The emotional momentum of Eliot's "Marina," however, comes not so much from its "perfect poetical" recovery of what was lost as from its structural attempt to "crisscross" (in Eliot's own phrase) "two extremes of the recognition scene," one from Shakespeare's *Pericles,* when Pericles finds his long-lost daughter alive, the other from Seneca's *Hercules Furens;* the epigraph to the poem reads, in translation, "What is this place, what country, what region of the world?" which are the questions that the disoriented Hercules asks when he wakes to find that he has murdered his family.[27] Our grasp of the first, Shakespearean motif is certainly well framed by Knight's theological paradigm: it entails grace, light-filled happiness, and near-celestial revelation. But to predict the allusive pressures of the second—the opposing emotional energies it exerts, by way of allusion, upon Knight's optimistic recognition—we only need recall Eliot's own early description of doubleness and recognition; this discovery will also be "terrible," "merciless," and "disconcerting as a quicksand."[28]

In this poem of ambivalent discovery, the narrator catches glimpses of a new world appearing in the corner of his eye: "What images return / O my daughter," he asks, as the returning image of a face appears "less clear and clearer," "less strong and stronger," coming in and out of focus (*CPP* 72).[29] With a familiar visual trope, the speaker discerns images that are "more distant than stars and nearer than the eye" (*CPP* 72). That is, they resemble the earlier "fringe" of indefinite extent, which was also both too far and too near for the eye to bring into focus. The result of this recognition, as Eliot had hinted, is the speaker's realization that the strangely familiar images in his peripheral vision are indeed previously hidden aspects of his own soul, an "unknowing, half conscious, unknown" that is nonetheless unmistakably "my own" (*CPP* 72). But lurking always behind the narrator's apparent joy—

a joy which Eliot embodies in "whispers and small laughter between leaves," nostalgic but hopeful elements of a nascent, rediscovered world of experience—is the emotional tension that he intends by appending the Senecan epigraph to the poem (*CPP* 64).

No ghosts leap out from the curtains in "Marina," nor does any demon sneak up to linger behind the shoulder, but the speaker's response to his sudden and difficult realization here constitutes Eliot's first clear articulation of this particular passion scene and of the emotional ambivalence between horror and ecstasy that accompanies spiritual recognition. Is the speaker, like Pericles, elated by the discovery of a new life in which his lost experience has been restored to him? Or does the shade of Hercules speak through his lips? Is he horrified by the new, monstrous world into which he has awakened, where he will live with the knowledge of having killed, in Wilde's phrase, the very thing he loved? Or perhaps, Eliot asks, could he somehow be both, simultaneously healed and horrified by a doubling, shifting, Protean form not unlike the ominous "person, form, or phantom" in Morris's poem? Even if the Senecan epigraph fails to achieve artistically the sustained complexity that Eliot initially envisions for "Marina"—and I do not disagree with those who have found this to be the case—it nonetheless clearly indicates an intentional *telos* that he will strive to attain for nearly a decade afterward.[30]

For years scholars have consistently misconstrued Eliot's explicit program for "a more severe and serene control of the emotions by Reason."[31] We have imagined him at times as Joyce's aloof, mythy artist, paring his fingernails far above the fray of the work's emotional drama, or else as an cool mathematician of the mind, clacking the beads on the abacus of his unruly emotional life to calculate its order, weight, and value. It is long past time to recognize that, on the contrary, Eliot's pronouncements do not entail an extirpation of the emotions but an increased capacity to experience them without simplification or reduction. In "Personality and Demonic Possession" (1934), he cites D. H. Lawrence and Thomas Hardy as examples of "extreme emotionalism," critiquing their "heretical" tendency to identify extreme emotion with what is most fundamentally human.[32] But as is clear from our discussion of the Bradleian "fringe" and of the contending emotional extremes in "Marina," Eliot does not object to the significance of extreme emotion, only to the belief that "there is something admirable in violent emotion for its own sake."[33] Violent emotions are not valuable in themselves, he claims, but only insofar as they lead toward something else, something other than themselves. (Perhaps certain early indications of this belief were what led Lady Ottoline Morrell to suggest, after dining with him in March 1916, that Eliot "has lost all spontaneity and can only break through his conventionality by stimulants or violent emotions."[34] As he would later indicate, the extremity of conventionally "unsuitable" emotions is a necessary part of the mind's awakening to its own multiple planes of experience: "It's only when they see nothing / That people can always show the suitable emotions—" Harry contends in *The Family Reunion.* "They don't understand what it is to be awake, / To be living on several planes at once" (*CPP* 266). In a letter to John Gould Fletcher written in September 1920, Eliot suggests that experience of any sort is always accompanied by an irreducible flurry of correspondent emotions, and what he discovers in the "Marina" recognition, what makes the scene so valuable for him, is that the extreme emotions that it provokes offer insight into the nature of the psyche—its tantalizing, unpredictable blind spots, its strangeness to itself, and the range and limitations of its self-awareness (*Letters* 409–10).

LATER RECOGNITIONS

If we are to understand how Eliot eventually reconciles the extremes of the recognition scene intertwined in "Marina," we must begin by paying close attention to the chronology of his work in the following years. In each of the subsequent poems and plays—*Murder in the Cathedral* (1935), *Burnt Norton* (1936), *The Family Reunion* (1939), and the three remaining parts of *Four Quartets* (1940–42)—he is compelled to return to the scene and to reconsider it. The key to Eliot's mature understanding of how recognition irrevocably affects the life of the mind rests in the subtle stylistic, thematic, and philosophic differences between these scenes.

In *Murder in the Cathedral,* the joy-filled grace of the Periclean recognition vanishes completely, and the half-hidden world that reveals itself is a harrowing one of sin and temptation. Thomas Becket's exchanges with the Tempters externally dramatize the inner dialogue that Eliot had represented obliquely in "Marina," and it is the Fourth Tempter who now induces Thomas's surprise and recognition. "Do not be surprised," he tells the alarmed archbishop, "I always precede expectation" (*CPP* 190). If the first three Tempters represent alluring but merely ephemeral temptations, the fourth stands for some intimate, abiding aspect of Thomas himself. He is out of place, unexpected; his appearance compels the archbishop's formerly hidden, half-conscious desires and motivations into the light of consciousness, and the revelation is not a pleasant one. The Fourth Tempter's furtive, unsettling, and menacing appearance calls to mind, in fact, the passage in *The Waste Land* that Eliot adapts from Marvell: "But at my back in a cold blast I hear / The rattle of the bones, and chuckle spread from ear to ear" (43). This ribald chuckler seems to know something the speaker does not, and, like a demonic Cheshire Cat, he seems poised to reveal the sordid, decaying reality lurking just beneath our illusions of solidity and permanence.

In *Murder in the Cathedral,* Eliot imagines that the startling figure whom he has sensed lurking behind his shoulder for so long is purely malevolent, and this fear leads him to equate his earlier metaphysical recognitions with the realization of sin and depravity. In the moment of surprise and fearfulness, that is, all of the trope's former semantic richness and multivalent possibility collapses into a single, threatening figure. In Eliot's later description from *The Cocktail Party*, Thomas represents "the Saint in the desert / With spiritual evil always at his shoulder" (*CPP* 385). Pride, impure motivation, or ambition "comes when early force is spent," catching the mind off guard and vulnerable; it "comes behind and unobservable" (*CPP* 196). In short, the recognition scene in *Murder in the Cathedral* represents the awkward revelation of what Eliot later calls "the shame / Of motives late revealed," the universal proclivity for moral corruption that lingers unseen behind seemingly virtuous actions (*CPP* 142). Despite the extraordinary success of the play as a whole—both artistic and popular—I believe that Eliot must have remained dissatisfied in part with its treatment of the recognition scene, which elides the emotional ambivalence that he had earlier desired to sustain. *Murder in the Cathedral* temporarily disentangles the crisscrossed emotional knot of "Marina," whose tension and uncertainty seemed to demand a more complex resolution than this. When Eliot returns to the figure a year later, it is in the hopes of recapturing and elaborating its former complexity.

Four years after the publication of "Marina," he visited the manor house at Burnt Norton in Gloucestershire, reuniting with Emily Hale in what must have seemed (at least in part) a private, joyous recognition scene of his own. So it should come as little surprise that when he composed the first poem of *Four Quartets* two years later, he returned to the joyful elements of "Marina" that had been left conspicuously absent from *Murder in the Cathedral*. In the meanwhile, though, he had encountered an equally ambivalent version of the recognition scene in Djuna Barnes's *Nightwood* (1936), one which incorporates both a seemingly sacred "disc of light" (not unlike his own "penumbral consciousness") and an unsettling sense of apprehension. In a dream, the protagonist has a startling, disconcerting vision of her lover, Robin Vote: "A disc of light, which seemed to come from someone or thing standing behind her and which was yet a shadow, shed a faintly luminous glow upon the upturned still face of Robin, who had the smile of an 'only survivor,' a smile which fear had married to the bone."[35] The luminous glow is not dissimilar from the grace-filled recognitions in "Marina," and this fearful smile seems less akin to a demonic Cheshire Cat's chuckle or the Fourth Tempter's arrogance and closer to the whispers and pastoral laughter that are Eliot's enduring figures for joy and liberation. *Nightwood* had come into his hands at Faber and Faber months before it first appeared in England in October 1936, early enough for it to have been on his mind (and certainly it was, given that he contributed the laudatory introduction to its first edition) when he began to reconstruct his visit to the rose garden at Burnt Norton and the half-fearful, half-hopeful illuminations it shed upon his own would-be lover.

In *Burnt Norton*, the symbols of Periclean joy from "Marina"—the "whispers and small laughter between leaves"—reappear as "hidden laughter / Of children in the foliage," figures for the mysterious, grace-filled discovery of another world, half hidden but discernible beneath the autumnal landscape of sense (*CPP* 122). The children's whispers and laughter alert us to Eliot's desire to restore the element of joy and possibility to the complex of emotions involved in the recognition scene, to recapture the ecstasy that was lost in the Fourth Tempter's negative revelations. But more important, *Burnt Norton* begins with a recasting of the recognition scene itself, in which Eliot subtly returns to his earlier figure, the glimpse from "the corner of the eye" or the "backward half-look / Over the shoulder" (*CPP* 133):

> There they were as our guests, accepted and accepting.
> So we moved, and they, in a formal pattern,
> . . . .
> And the pool was filled with water out of sunlight,
> And the lotos rose, quietly, quietly,
> The surface glittered out of heart of light,
> And they were behind us, reflected in the pool.
> Then a cloud passed, and the pool was empty.
> (*CPP* 118)

The mysterious "guests" stand just behind the narrator's back and appear only as reflections cast by the light of clairvoyance. Should he turn to face them, one presumes, they would vanish like "the third" in *The Waste Land* or, as will the "familiar compound ghost" several years later in *Little Gidding,* fade upon "the blowing of the horn" (*CPP* 140–42). In one sense, they are likely echoes or reflections of Eliot and Hale as they might have been; they are spectral manifestations of alternate selves like the revenant that Eliot seems to have admired in Henry James's "The Jolly Corner." But as Eliot had argued in his dissertation, they also partake of a more expansive psychological reality not wholly absorbed in conscious desire and nostalgia, a jarring reality that includes those half-hidden levels of experience which are "so mad and strange that they will be boiled away before you boil them down to one homogenous mass" (*KE* 168).

In terms of the goals Eliot has set for himself, I believe that the recognition scene in *Burnt Norton* constitutes both a success and a failure. By including both anxiety ("Go, go, go, said the bird") and serenity ("accepted and accepting") in the scene's emotional spectrum, he initially restores the ambivalence that he had intimated in "Marina" (*CPP* 118). This time, however, he more clearly suggests that the emotional upheaval of recognition results from the mind's startling realization of its own incompleteness, its inability to see itself clearly without the intervening presence of some foreign other. Gazing into the visionary pool, the speaker of *Burnt Norton* unmistakably resembles Narcissus, that mythical figure for self-reflection who infamously lingers over the pool in a similar rose garden in ancient and medieval narratives.[36] From Dante and other medieval thinkers, Eliot had learned that the Narcissus myth allegorizes the soul's reflexive confrontation with itself. He had studied the Christian exegetes of the tale, who discerned the didactic value of Narcissus's death as a lesson in *humilitas,* that virtue whereby the self realizes its fundamental limitations by measuring itself against the divine, "passing through" its own image and toward the *Imago Dei* after which it is fashioned.[37] Unlike Narcissus, whose allegorical introspection yields only his own image, the narrator of *Burnt Norton* senses behind him reflections both familiar and foreign, figures for those inscrutable regions of the soul that Eliot aligns with the "Alone" or the Absolute. The foreignness of the reflections reconfigures the presence of what he calls, quoting theologian Friedrich von Hügel, "the otherness of God."[38] Even without the theological substructure, the thematic implications of this moment are clear. Wondering about the "perpetual possibility" of what might have been, in other words, contemplating the various experiences he might have enjoyed but did not, the speaker looks at himself and sees not the experiences themselves nor an entirely different self, transformed in the light of a different necessity. What he sees, rather, are strangely foreign, strangely familiar presences hovering just at the "fringe" of his field of vision, in the blind spots of his internal, self-reflective sight. However, despite the achievement in the first part of *Burnt Norton*—a symbolic rendering of the mind's recognition of its fundamental foreignness to itself and its dependence upon an other—the meditations that follow the opening vision significantly undermine its effects.

The thrush dramatizes the speaker's surprise by hurrying him onward—"Go, go, go, said the bird: human kind / Cannot bear very much reality"—but this particular reality reminds us more of Pericles' joy than Hercules' horror, and the recognition scene's more troubling elements disappear entirely in the following stanzas, just as the scene's affective complexity collapsed in the opposite direction in *Murder in the Cathedral* (*CPP* 118). As in "Marina," a "grace of sense" settles upon the speaker, and he awakens to find both "a new world" and even "the old world made explicit, understood / In the completion of its partial ecstasy, / The resolution of its partial horror" (*CPP* 119). But Eliot's characteristically relentless self-scrutiny does not allow for easy endings, and he decides that his holistic reconciliation has gone too far. The "completion" and "resolution" of multiple worlds implies the possibility of a metaphysical wholeness by which the conscious mind could grasp itself under all of its aspects or units of soul life at once and fuse those aspects into a unity. It implies the holistic psychological reconciliation that Eliot seemed to desire in his dissertation, what he would later call "a degree of self-consciousness of which mankind has never been capable, and of which, if attained, it might perish."[39] The premature resolution describes a state of mind that he elsewhere joins John Middleton Murry in critiquing as a delusory vision of wholeness and self-understanding that would make the human soul god-like, self-sustained and self-transparent.[40]

Eliot dramatizes his displeasure with this optimistic conclusion in the third section of *Burnt Norton,* when the narrator invites us to forego the earlier resolution and to "descend lower, descend only / Into the world of perpetual solitude" (*CPP* 120). Foregoing the ambivalence of both worlds for the solitude of a single one, the narrator can only regard joy as a momentary liberation which actually intensifies the suffering it is meant to alleviate: "Quick now, here, now, always— / Ridiculous the waste sad time / Stretching before and after" (*CPP* 122). Though it promises a timeless "always," the Periclean joy is restricted to the moment of recognition. By Eliot's own standards, the insight of the recognition scene retains an enduring significance only if it is not restrained to isolated moments of illumination; rather, it must extend its influence to the self's daily experience in the world, whether "now and in England," in his words, or "never and always" (*CPP* 139). Despite the achievements of its first part, *Burnt Norton* ends on a note of frustration, a failure to address the "larger whole of experience," and it becomes clear that the speaker has much to learn before the culmination of his reflections in *Little Gidding* (1942; *SE* 251).

THE FAMILY REUNION

After the premature resolution in *Burnt Norton,* Eliot returns to verse drama to experiment with yet another version of the recognition scene in *The Family Reunion.* In light of its intense personal significance and reflections on the soul's most intimate secrets, *The Family Reunion* constitutes a turning point for Eliot just as important as (if not more so than) the spiritual conversion represented in *Ash-Wednesday.* Eliot would later reveal that his method of composing verse drama was to begin with "a particular emotional situation" and then to allow "characters and a plot" to emerge from it, and his modern versions of the Greek Eumenides are the figures that emerge from the emotional upheaval that compelled *The Family Reunion* in the first place (*TVP* 36–7). They assume the role of the vague reflections in *Burnt Norton* and the Fourth Tempter in *Murder in the Cathedral.* Harry, the protagonist, describes them in terms strikingly similar to those Eliot had used in the previous recognition scenes. "Can't you see them?" he asks frantically:

> I knew they were coming.
> In Italy, from behind the nightingale's thicket,
> The eyes stared at me, and corrupted that song.
> Behind the palm trees in the Grand Hotel
> They were always there. But I did not *see* them.
> (*CPP* 232)

Like Thomas's Fourth Tempter, who always approaches furtively from behind and brings with him the gravity of an ancient curse, the Eumenides possess a

significance more far-reaching than Harry's imagined sense of guilt for the death
of his wife. They are not merely, as one reviewer disparagingly suggests, the symbolic outpouring of "trivial 20th-century guilt . . . and misplaced anguish"; their
significance is not historically contingent, either upon the play's imagined history
or the author's personal life.[41] Like the similarly unidentified "they" in *Burnt Norton* (but different here of course in their corruptive rather than restorative potential), they are figures for hidden aspects of the soul, psychological blind spots
which Eliot can only describe as "the shadow of something" that lurks, appropriately, "behind our meagre childhood" (*CPP* 273). Mary, the play's heroine, accurately discerns that the Eumenides might be a part of the protagonist's inner
world, and in response Harry reverts to a familiar trope to describe their haunting, peripheral existence:

> Something inside me, you think, that can be altered!
> And here, indeed! where I have felt them near me,
> Here and here and here—wherever I am not looking,
> Always flickering at the corner of my eye,
> Almost whispering just out of earshot—
> (*CPP* 250)

The Eumenides, it seems, are also figures for the region of the soul that Eliot calls
the "fringe of indefinite extent." They are, as Harry relates, a "ring of ghosts with
joined hands" (*CPP* 278).

With help from Agatha (the aged *Sophia* figure of the play), the protagonist
learns about "the loop in time," when the soul frees itself from its solipsistic
wars by returning to an image of its past state and discovering, in the seemingly
unconnected actions of the conscious mind, a deeper design orchestrated by
the inscrutable workings of the divine (*CPP* 229). Following this realization, he
comes to understand his recognition of the startling Eumenides as neither wholly
terrifying (like Hercules') nor wholly joyful (like Pericles'). Instead the recognition reveals for him both the "love and terror / Of what waits and wants me, and
will not let me fall" (*CPP* 281). Here, Eliot is able to sustain the tension between
both emotional components of the recognition: he will not blur love and terror
into one, but neither will he eclipse one with the other. When Cleanth Brooks
claims in a 1939 review of *The Family Reunion* that it "may be said to be a restate-
ment of *Burnt Norton* in terms of drama," he overlooks the play's significant
advances over the earlier poem's abortive resolution.[42] In fact, while Eliot was
reworking the recognition scene for *The Family Reunion* in 1938, he wrote urgently to his protégé George Barker about the artist's continual challenge to never
repeat himself, to avoid ever doing the same thing twice.[43] If, as he suggests in
the letter, the daily changes in the artist's emotional landscape make reinvention
less a challenge than a necessity, we can be sure that the recognition scene in

The Family Reunion embodies a significantly different set of assumptions than it did previously.

Unlike *Burnt Norton,* in which the speaker experiences recognition as a serene but momentary resolution of worlds, *The Family Reunion* now represents it as an ongoing realization, an intense emotional insight that continues to influence the conscious life of the mind long afterward. The experience of recognition will remain present to attend "the pilgrimage / Of expiation," the "long journey" that Agatha foresees for Harry (*CPP* 293, 278). Instead of the purely negative realization of sin and depravity in *Murder in the Cathedral,* this new recognition scene perhaps allows us, as Eliot speculates elsewhere in the same year as *The Family Reunion* appeared, "to return, with greater spiritual knowledge, to our own situation," to reevaluate the appearances of quotidian experience in its light.[44] One might be tempted to inquire into the causes and motivations for Harry's dramatic realization, into the thematic details that lead to his newfound understanding. And in fact, the absence of such details sparked much contemporary debate about the play.[45] But the focus of this chapter is neither the particulars of the play nor the transformation of the protagonist's character; rather, what matters is that Eliot has learned to represent dramatically and symbolically the mind's emotional response to the upheaval that attends spiritual recognition. He has attained the *telos* that he had earlier articulated by including the Senecan epigraph to "Marina" in order to "crisscross" the two scenes of extreme emotional volatility.

A more pertinent question for our purposes would address not the plot of the play but the artistic mechanisms that allow this recognition scene to succeed where the earlier versions did not. How does Eliot's representation of the scene in *The Family Reunion* differ from his earlier attempts to articulate its implications directly, either in prose or in dramatic declaration? One reviewer of the play in 1958 glibly claims that its characters seem to be "engaged in a struggle that they are not eager to explain"; however, as the protagonist himself suggests, "explaining would only make a worse misunderstanding; . . . There is only one way for you to understand / And that is by seeing" (*CPP* 250).[46] To measure Eliot's success at sustaining the emotional ambivalence of the recognition scene, one must address how he avoids the propositional logic of "explaining" and instead allows the audience to "see" by employing the tools at the poet's disposal. One of his most effective techniques for enacting rather than explaining is what I have called in the previous chapter, for the sake of convenience, the intertextual reprise, the use of a trope that (not unlike a palinode) depends on chronology insofar as it invokes and revises another trope from his own earlier work. As opposed to the passion scenes we have been tracing—which are characterized by the peculiar force they seem to exert over the author's imagination—this strategy often seems conscious and deliberate, the self-reflexive equivalent of Eliot's more well-known mythical or literary allusions and pastiche. Two such reprises coincide with Harry's first dramatic recognition of the Eumenides in act 1 of *The Family Reunion,* and their precise ordering is designed to elicit a familiar range of emotions. The first evokes the terror-filled landscape of *The Waste Land,* where a speaker inquires of Stetson: "That corpse you planted . . . / Has it begun to sprout? Will it bloom this year?" (*CPP* 39). Echoing this anxiety about the possibility of life amid decay and corruption, Harry asks anxiously, "Do not the ghosts of the drowned / Return to land in the spring? / Do the dead want to return?" (*CPP* 251). Harry's ghosts are submerged alongside Eliot's personal memories of Jean Verdenal and the drowned body of Phlebas the Phoenician in *The Waste Land,* and the protagonist's description of spring as a "season of sacrifice" recalls the terrifying Herculean recognition in "Marina" as well (*CPP* 251). If this first passage relies for its pathos on the agony of the cruelest month, the allusion which almost immediately follows it calls to mind the joy-filled recognition of *Burnt Norton,* which was accompanied by the singing thrush and the heart of light. Several lines later, Harry exclaims, "You bring me news / Of a door that opens at the end of a corridor, / Sunlight and singing" (*CPP* 252). The two allusions encompass the emotional arc between horror and joy that we have seen Eliot traverse in his previous configurations of the recognition scene, from the purely negative realization in *Murder in the Cathedral* to the joyous resolution in the first part of *Burnt Norton.*

But the movement is not continuous and unbroken; rather, inserted directly between the two allusions and interrupting their emotional arc, an utterance by another character offers the possibility of a kind of balance between the two extremes. "Pain is the opposite of joy," Mary suggests simply, "but joy is a kind of pain" (*CPP* 251). Mary's pronouncement may initially seem too simple, too mundanely epigrammatic to address the problem's complexity adequately, but Eliot does not intend to communicate a platitude with it. In fact, the statement serves more of a structural purpose than a discursive one. Because of its position between the two allusions, Mary's utterance functions as a dramatic fulcrum between the horror of *The Waste Land* and the joy of *Burnt Norton,* both of which have been precipitated by Harry's recognition. Her suggestion takes the form of a chiasmus, a trope that implies the reversibility of two terms by inverting them in the second clause of a series (pain is joy; joy, pain). Instead of subsuming one into the other, as metaphor would, the balance of the chiasmus implies that both emotions might be present simultaneously; it is a trope that rhetorically performs the "crisscross" Eliot had attempted less effectively in "Marina." But even more important, the rhetorical mechanism that balances the scene's emotional ambivalence is articulated by someone outside of the speaker's psychological "war of phantoms," as if Eliot were attempting to recapture the realization of incompleteness that he had intimated at the pool in *Burnt Norton* (*CPP* 276). In the midst of his extreme emotional upheaval, Harry needs someone else to discern the balance that he cannot, someone to break through the "the spectres and the 'bad dreams'" of isolation, what Eliot calls elsewhere "the ceaseless question and answer of the tortured mind."[47]

Later the play repeats the identical movement, from a terror evoked by figures from *The Waste Land* to a joy recaptured with tokens from *Burnt Norton,* when the Eumenides appear again and Harry moves from imagining "shrieking forms in a circular desert" toward the quiet, intimate moment when "I ran to meet you in the rose-garden" (*CPP* 277). This time, it is Agatha instead of Mary through whom Eliot articulates the balance, as she symbolically steps into the Eumenides' place (Harry's blind spot, the emblem of his vulnerability) and relates that the curse of awakening exists always alongside the joy of rebirth, and that the joy of love may resemble the pain of cruelty (*CPP* 279). In the tripartite movement of this structure, Eliot achieves a symbolic enactment of both conceptual components of the recognition scene with which he has struggled: the philosophical and psychological content, in the mind's realization of its limitations, and the emotional upheaval, in its ambivalent oscillation between terror and ecstasy. *The Family Reunion* constitutes, in terms of the artistic struggle discussed here, a conceptual and aesthetic watershed.

We need only glance at *East Coker,* which appeared in the Easter number of the *New English Weekly* shortly after the publication of *The Family Reunion,* to register the striking changes that occur in Eliot's representations of the recognition scene following his conceptual achievement in *The Family Reunion.* The second poem of *Four Quartets* does not attempt to recast the recognition scene itself. Eliot has learned, in Harry's words from *The Family Reunion,* that success does "not consist in getting what one wanted / . . . / But in a different vision," and he returns with a different vision, not directly to the rose garden and its reflections, but to the emotions that their jarring appearance originally evoked (*CPP* 275). Looking back on the earlier experience, he can now claim that "the laughter in the garden" performs two functions: it echoes an "ecstasy / Not lost," but it also points the way toward "the agony" of finitude and incompleteness (*CPP* 127). Eliot can now admit the necessity of both emotions without diffusing the intensity of either by unifying them. The speaker realizes that the value of the conscious mind's startling recognition of incompleteness lies not only in a single experience, but in the integration of that experience into the stretches of time before and after:

> Not in the intense moment
> Isolated, with no before and after,
> But a lifetime burning in every moment
> . . . .
> There is a time for the evening under starlight,

A time for the evening under lamplight
(The evening with the photograph album).
(*CPP* 129)

The awakened mind now does not yearn to grasp entirely all of the soul's unconscious, potential states at once, nor to resolve the multiplicity of experience, but
to more fully engage each in its own time and place. Neither does it fuse the old
world and the new, as in *Burnt Norton;* rather, it can experience both metaphysical ecstasy and terror at the vastness of the infinite ("under starlight"), and their
mundane counterparts, joy and regret, under the intimate light of its own memory ("under lamplight . . . with the photograph album"). Eliot implies that the
emotional lessons of the recognition scene need not remain isolated in a single
moment of heightened consciousness, but instead may remain to inform the tri-
als of both spiritual and mundane experience. In the later parts of *Four Quartets,*
the backward glance over the shoulder "towards the primitive terror" exists alongside the "moments of happiness" and the "sudden illumination" (*CPP* 132–33). As
Eliot realizes, both are fundamental elements of the mind's experience of its own
incompleteness, and both characterize the soul's recognition of its proper place in
what he calls "the middle way," its painful task of negotiating the many material
and spiritual worlds of experience (*CPP* 128).

RECOGNITION AND EXPERIENCE

After the conceptual achievement of *Four Quartets,* Eliot finds that he can use this
highly charged passion scene—the "backward half-look / Over the shoulder" and
similar figures—to envision the implications of recognition not only in the spiritual life, "the evening under starlight," but in the "lamplight" as well, the temporal
life of everyday human experience (*CPP* 133, 129). The two variations of the recognition trope that appear in *The Elder Statesman* (1959) pertain not to the heights
of divine love and the depths of spiritual depravity, but to the mundane experiences of nascent romantic love and lingering regret for what Eliot calls merely
"shabby behavior" (*Plays* 323). There is "the reflection in the mirror of the face
behind you" that haunts Lord Claverton's shame-filled memories, but there is also
Monica's description of her newfound love for Charles, which "crept so softly /
. . . and stood behind my back" long before "I felt its presence" (*Plays* 314, 298). The
mind's fundamental limitations, its inability to grasp itself entirely, may lead (as
it does with Lord Claverton) to guilt and shame when we find our motivations to
have been tainted or impure. But the same weakness may also be what propels
us to feel a need for others (as with Monica and Charles), offering the unique possibility for an intimacy unavailable to a spiritual celibate like Narcissus. As Eliot
has learned by his prolonged scrutiny of the recognition scene, this ineluctable

vulnerability is both a blessing and a curse, and thus may always be accompanied by both fear and joy.

His most incisive later treatment of the recognition scene, however, occurs five years earlier in *The Confidential Clerk* (1954), in the portrayal of Colby Simpkins's attempt to negotiate the multiple professional and spiritual worlds at the intersection of which he abides. Not unlike the young Eliot once did, Colby acutely feels a jarring incompatibility between the worlds, both of which become "a kind of make-believe," illusions symptomatic of the madness of the isolated mind (*Plays* 238). Colby uses the familiar rose garden from *Burnt Norton* as a metaphor for what he calls the soul's "inner world" but reveals that his isolation makes it impossible for him to experience either the soul or the material world as real (*Plays* 244).[48] If he were a religious man, he thinks, God would walk in his "garden" and render both worlds real and acceptable, assuring an absolute reference point by which to gauge their reality. But when Lucasta, the play's heroine, asks him if no one else could enter the garden in order to free him from isolation, Colby replies:

> I should not see them coming.
> I should not hear the opening of the gate.
> They would simply . . . be there suddenly,
> Unexpectedly. Walking down an alley
> I should become aware of someone walking with me.
> That's the only way I can think of putting it.
> *Lucasta:* How afraid one is of . . . being hurt! (*Plays* 246)

Colby's imagined encounter—now so remarkably free of the sudden terror and clairvoyance that characterized the earlier recognitions— deliberately blurs the distinction between the mundane and the spiritual, the division that Eliot himself has so long attempted to negotiate. Like the "one with me wandering" through the garden that caught Eliot's eye in Morris's poem, the "someone" who would surprise Colby in the garden might be either "a person, form, or phantom," the spirit of either a god or a lover (*SE* 299). Eliot sees no need to elide this ambiguity in order to specify which; as he has learned, the recognition scene can address both experiences, the metaphysical and the mundane.

But most important, he suggests that only the startling presence of this mysterious "someone walking with me" will offer the soul an escape from its isolation. By unveiling the presence of some mysterious Other within its own circumference, the soul's recognition offers some assurance that it is not alone with its "awful privacy," that it will not be "crushed by the terrible awareness of [its] isolation" (*CPP* 276).[49] The agony that the mind experiences upon realizing its incompleteness and vulnerability—a vulnerability emphasized by Lucasta's fearful (if sentimental) response—is also the ecstasy of its release from the isolating delusion of self-sufficiency, the illusion that it can encompass and reconcile the inner worlds of the soul into a single, unassailable reality. Eliot had once envisioned the sudden recognition of this startling presence as an event that renders the world unreal, that tears experience apart into jarring and incompatible layers. Now, after nearly forty years of reflection, he comes to apprehend that recognition plays an essential role in the soul's experience of the "otherness of God." In addition to enduring the intense emotional upheaval that attends recognition, "what's so difficult," Eliot admits in the guise of his protagonist, "is to recognise the limits of one's understanding" (*Plays* 274). His use of the word "recognise" here is far from accidental. The recognition scene has become his shorthand for the mind's response to discovering its limitations and for its ability to apprehend the consequences of those limitations in its interactions with others.

BACK TO "THE THIRD"

It is with a certain degree of hesitation that I return to the question in *The Waste Land* that prompted this chapter and that appears on its first page: "Who is the third who walks always beside you?" (*CPP* 48). Retrospective interpretation—in this case, reading back into Eliot's earlier work the eventual conclusions and confirmations of his later work—is always a tricky venture. But I am confident that we will benefit from the new light that it sheds upon a blind spot in the poem for which scholars have not yet fully accounted.

If we can agree that, on one level, *The Waste Land* is a narrative of psychological descent, or at least that it undergoes progressively intensifying affective modulations, then I suggest that the descent reaches its nadir in sections 3 and 4, with the Augustinian invocation of Carthage, the bitter, burning fragments of the speaker's lament, and the drowned body of Phlebas the Phoenician. And if there is any moment in the poem that promises an upward turn or shift in momentum (anticipating the revelations of the final stanzas), it is here, at the outset of "What the Thunder Said." This earliest of the recognition scenes appears, therefore, at a very propitious moment. If there were a time for the speakers of the poem to benefit from the affective revelations that Eliot's later speakers enjoy, it is now. Only a few stanzas later, the "damp gust / Bringing rain" arrives, and the prophetic voice of the Thunder rumbles its declarations (*CPP* 49). The thundering deity diagnoses three sicknesses of the psyche, each of which results from the isolation implicit in the failures of the poem's various personae: from the fumbling clerk and indifferent typist, to the hysterical wife and brooding husband, and finally to Phlebas himself, the embodiment of utter isolation; to be drowned in the "chambers of the sea" is a fate that the equally isolated Prufrock rightfully feared would be his own (*CPP* 7).

In addition to introducing a religious presence amid the barrenness of the ruined landscape, the startling and unexpected appearance of the Emmaus scene offers the speaker an opportunity for the recognition that so transforms Eliot's later protagonists. If *The Waste Land* is an allegory of the psychological tortures of isolation, the appearance of "the third" represents a moment of potential liberation from the mind's solipsistic privacy, from what Eliot calls "the spectres and the bad dreams which live inside the skull."[50] But unlike Harry in *The Family Reunion*, Colby in *The Confidential Clerk*, or the narrator of *Four Quartets*, the speaker is unable to benefit from the moment's awe-filled potential. As we have seen, the recognition scene propels the imagination between emotional extremes, which must be calibrated and balanced lest the mind delude itself into believing in its own invulnerability or, alternately, its own nothingness. In this instance, the speaker's horror at the startling presence of "the third" eclipses the possibility of any other emotion; in Eliot's terms from "Marina," the Senecan recognition completely overwhelms the Shakespearean one. While the scene itself seems almost void of emotion, the images that immediately follow it betray its frightening impact on the speaker. *The Waste Land* plunges back into nightmare, and the "hooded," half-hidden "third" transforms and multiplies into "hooded hordes swarming over endless plains," peering toward the narrator like "bats with baby faces in the violet light" (*CPP* 48). In the terms that Eliot eventually settles on for *The Family Reunion*, this downward spiral is the path that Harry might have followed were it not for Agatha and the emotional equilibrium that her paradoxes bring. W. B. Yeats had once claimed that "when one looks into the darkness, there is always something there," and Eliot will eventually realize as well that the darkness of the mind is never empty or exhausted.[51] But in this land of waste and decay, which arose in part from so torturous a period of Eliot's personal life, the mind remains alone with itself and its delusions; it can only cry out from the bottoms of "empty cisterns and exhausted wells" (*CPP* 48), seemingly severed from the foreignness of the Other, whether sacred or secular.

To Carthage then we come. I believe that Eliot uses the allusive momentum of Augustine's narrative as a counterpoint to his own, invoking it at precisely the moment when the contrast between the two is most crucial: just before the appearance of "the third." In the *Confessions*, Augustine arrives in Carthage with his mind still under the sway of the Manichees, whose metaphysical dualism perhaps recalled to Eliot his own early philosophical frustrations at reconciling the "mad and strange" worlds of experience. The author of "Prufrock" would have also been likely to identify with Augustine's estimation of his own frightful condition upon arrival, when bodily and spiritual sickness convince him that "I was on the verge of going down to hell, carrying with me all the sins that I had committed."[52] In alluding to Augustine's arrival at Carthage, Eliot invokes the trajectory of the first half of the *Confessions*, a movement that parallels the increasingly self-isolated, downward spiral of *The Waste Land*. The timely appearance of the third offers the possibility of following Augustine's path out of what he calls the "region of unlikeness" [*regione dissimilitudinis*] and into the clarity and sight of transcendence.[53] In book 10 of the *Confessions,* Eliot would have found a passage that possesses a striking significance for his own theories of the mind's vulnerability and incompleteness, its inability to comprehend its own circumference. "Great is the power of memory," Augustine declares, reflecting on the inscrutable depths of the psyche: "Exceeding great is it, O God, an inner chamber, vast and unbounded! Who has penetrated to its very bottom? Yet it is a power of my mind and it belongs to my nature, and thus I do not comprehend all that I am. Is the mind, therefore, too limited to possess itself?"[54]

Augustine's answer, as Eliot's will eventually be, is yes: "Within me are those lamentable dark areas wherein my own capacities lie hidden from me."[55] Under the searing eye of the divine, Augustine finds that he has become a riddle to himself, and that this riddle is both an infirmity and a blessing. While it presents an insurmountable obstacle to his self-knowledge—one that actually halts the progress of the narrative, in the case of the *Confessions*—it also allows him to entertain the presence of the Other within the inscrutable, individual psyche and the possibility for Grace to free the soul from its blindness and suffering. As we have seen, Eliot's recognition scene offers the possibility for a similar realization, in which the terror and joy of human incompleteness and vulnerability are held in mutual suspension under the light of the Absolute. The divergence of *The Waste Land* from Augustine's trajectory at precisely this moment, as the poem veers toward nightmare instead of the balanced intensities of ambivalence, serves to emphasize the tragic, missed opportunity that "the third" represents in the poem. After *The Waste Land,* it would be years before Eliot would successfully endow the recognition scene with a rich, philosophical significance distinctly reminiscent of Augustine's own aporetic declaration: "I truly labor at this task, and I labor upon myself. I have become for myself a soil hard to work, and demanding much sweat. . . . It is no matter for wonder that what I am not is far distant from me; but what is closer to me than myself?"[56]

By the conclusion of *The Waste Land,* Eliot can articulate the necessity for surrender, he can imagine the possibility of escape from the mind's prison, but the dramatic potential implicit in the recognition scene has been lost. Or perhaps it is more accurate to say that he exploits its negative dramatic potential by contrasting the conversion of the Augustinian narrative with the halting yet downward movement of *The Waste Land,* and the result is the opposite of the transfiguring recognitions that his later protagonists will undergo. Instead of the performative, symbolic transformation that he achieves in *The Family Reunion,* he can only declaim the existence or the possibility of such a transformation. The Thunder's dogmatic prescriptions conclude *The Waste Land* with the same propositional directness that prompted Eliot to excise the Thomistic passage on the unmoved mover from *Little Gidding.* They advocate a surrender to the foreign Other within the soul, an obedience to "controlling hands," whether these be human or otherwise (*CPP* 50). However, as prescriptions and propositions, they fail where Eliot's later dramatizations succeed: at capturing the emotional ambivalence and intensity of such a surrender, at performing and enacting the imaginative turmoil with which the mind confronts its own limitations. If the appearance of "the third" represents the fleeting possibility of liberation in *The Waste Land,* it also reveals the failure at the poem's center (and in turn, one of the reasons for its over-whelming success), the mind's "tendency to collapse" before the burden of its own inscrutable mysteries.[57]

CONCLUSION

In the fall of 1950, an eager and awkward undergraduate named Donald Hall bor-rowed his roommate's convertible and drove to a Harvard University guesthouse to accompany Eliot, who was visiting at his alma mater, to a party hosted by the *Harvard Advocate* where he was to be the guest of honor. Eliot was sixty-two, and as Hall recounts, professors and students alike revered the literary magus with dis-tance and awe, flocking to the party to "observe the lion" out of his natural habi-tat.[58] But what remained in Hall's memory was not the party itself, where his friends scrambled and scuttled for a glimpse at the literary lion, but the awkward and embarrassing moment when he first picked Eliot up at the guesthouse: "Two young women sat inconspicuous in the back seat of the convertible—one of them my date, the other a literary person from Bennington engaged to the roommate from whom I borrowed the car. As Mr. Eliot bent to enter the seat beside the driver, I realized that he had not observed the occupants of the back seat. I hastened toward protocol, waving urgently in the direction of the back seat and shouting, 'Mr. Eliot, I'd like you to meet. . . . ' He twisted and jumped, seeing them, reaching for his hat, and rising all at the same moment, so that with an abrupt jerk upward he hit his head on the doorframe of the car and knocked his hat off."[59]

We can only speculate what must have gone through Eliot's mind as he picked up his hat, swallowed his pride, and settled back into the car for a proper intro-duction. Perhaps, once he had recovered his composure, he sensed the consum-mate fittingness of this moment. After a lifetime of reflection on precisely such awkward moments of recognition, and nearly thirty years after the protagonist of *The Waste Land* suffered a similar unease at the presence of "the third" just behind his companion's shoulder, he found himself still entirely susceptible to the hum-bling surprise and embarrassment of the experience, whether it be at the hands of the Fourth Tempter, the spectral Eumenides, or simply two nervous undergradu-ates, lurking innocuously just out of view in the backseat.

Who stood behind Eliot's back, lingered over the shoulder of the narrator's companion in *The Waste Land,* and appeared in the reflecting pool of *Burnt Nor-ton*? By now, we can see that it matters little whether it was "the silent observer" or "the primitive terror," the face "behind the smiling mirror" or the reflections in the rose garden; whether Morris's "one with me wandering" or Colby's "someone walking with me," a person, form, or phantom.[60] As Eliot himself realizes while producing *Murder in the Cathedral*, we cannot even say whether it is the figure of an angel or a devil.[61] Eliot's investment in the recognition scene depends wholly upon the emotion that the figure evokes and the passion, in the broad sense, toward which it leads. What matters is the mind's response, the terror and ecstasy of discovering the presence of an Other within itself, in that inscrutable circumference where the many jarring and incompatible spiritual worlds ordain consciousness with its most painful, impossible of tasks. In response to its startling recognition of incompleteness, Eliot asks urgently, does the mind turn away, as Prufrock and the "quiet-voiced elders" of *East Coker* do, distracted from distraction by distraction (*CPP* 125)? Or does it learn to submit to and endure the intense emotions that arise from the limitations of human experience, with all of its doubt and mystery? In reply to the question he poses in *The Waste Land* ("Who is the third who walks always beside you?"), or in "Marina" ("What is this face, less clear and clearer / The pulse in the arm, less strong and stronger [?]" [*CPP* 48, 72]), Eliot learns to weigh the consequences of a fearful silence against the vulnerability of a response, to risk an invocation not unlike the one which the narrator of *Little Gidding* addresses to his own familiar ghost, and to find that, in the end, "the words sufficed / To compel the recognition they preceded" (*CPP* 141).

PART 2

W. B. YEATS

3

YEATS'S ABNORMAL RESTLESSNESS

> As I look backward, I seem to discover that my passions, my loves and
> my despairs, became so beautiful that I had to be constantly alone to
> give them my whole attention. I notice now, for the first time, that what
> I saw when alone is more vivid in my memory than what I did or saw in
> company.
>
> *Reveries over Childhood and Youth* (1916)

> I cannot discover truth by logic unless that logic serve passion, and only
> then if the logic be ready to cut its own throat, tear out its own eyes.
>
> *Pages from a Diary Written in*
> *Nineteen Hundred and Thirty* (1944)

Although he was admittedly given to fits of romantic melodrama, W. B. Yeats
wrote to his friend and confidante Lady Gregory in September 1917 from (this time
he was certain) the brink of emotional collapse. In this as yet unpublished letter,
he foresaw an onslaught of work and a threatening "crisis of my affairs": "I am getting ready for a mass of work to start on in Dublin and London if I can make some
settlement in my life. I am just now too restless."[1] Iseult Gonne's disappointing
rejection of his marriage proposal two months before had reawakened the anxious
restlessness and frustration that he had suffered repeatedly after equally unsuc-
cessful propositions to her mother, Maud, over the past thirty years. "I thought
I loved Iseult," he writes confusedly to Gregory, "and would love [her] to my life's
end."[2] Redoubling the anxieties and frustrations he was already facing from a bevy
of practical matters—urgent monetary pressures, plans for renovating the tower
at Ballylee, a collapsed lecturing arrangement at the University of Edinburgh—
these crushing rejections had taken their toll on his emotional energy. "My sheer
bodily strength was worn out," he confessed.

His sudden proposal and engagement to George Hyde-Lees in the midst of this emotional and physical exhaustion did not offer the succor for which he had hoped. His family was stunned; Lady Gregory reproved him for what seemed to her a reckless, rash decision; even Yeats himself soon feared that his proposal had been "a kind of suicide," a way to end the "emotional strain that had become unendurable." In the days before the wedding, he suffered a feverish nervous attack and "fell into wild misery."[3] He was dogged by nightmares of abandonment and by fears that the revelation of some shameful secret in his past might forestall the marriage. Less than a week after the two were married, a revelation did indeed occur, but not of the sort that he dreaded. On 27 October 1917, while the two anxious honeymooners were staying at the Ashdown Forest Hotel, his newfound wife sensed the spirits tapping at her shoulder, and thus began the visionary automatic writings that would energize and inspire Yeats's imagination for years to come. After years of frustration and rejection, and in a state of extreme "restlessness" and emotional collapse, Yeats received the revelation for which he had long hoped.

Three months later, his creative philosophical treatise *Per Amica Silentia Lunae* (1918) was published, bearing an introduction and conclusion dedicated to Iseult under her honorary nom de plume, "Maurice." In one brief sentence undoubtedly composed with her in mind, Yeats manages not only to sketch his troubled courtship with Iseult but to foresee the unexpected visionary revelations that would ensue in the following months. "The passions, when we know that they cannot find fulfillment," he had written only a short while before his marriage, "become vision" (*LE* 15). With uncanny foresight, Yeats had apparently predicted that his own unfulfilled desires would transfigure themselves into precisely those turbulent imaginative energies that would culminate in the elaborate phantasmagoria of *A Vision* (1925; 1937). Or perhaps it was not so uncanny. Years before, he had declared with utmost certainty that "the subject of all art is passion" (*Ex* 155). But just how art should approach that unruly and unpredictable subject, just how the artist should encounter and relate to his own passions was, perhaps, only now becoming clear to him.

However, as Yeats believed, one never really owns a passion; when I say "my" passion, I refer not to something that I possess but rather to something that possesses me. So foreign and beyond the intellect's control are the passions that they often seem to possess an external reality of their own, a vivid, detached foreignness that the afflicted mind observes as if it belonged to another person. And in fact this is precisely how Yeats often imagines such an encounter: as a meeting with a god, a woman, a troop of ravenous demons, his own doppelgänger, or the shape-changing Daemon, which embodies all of these at once. Passions are neither bodily nor mental in origin, he suggests in 1900; rather, they are invisible beings "whose footsteps over our hearts" make us tremble and quake with emotion.[4] My preliminary aim in this chapter is to examine several salient instances of this dramatic encounter that recur with startling regularity throughout Yeats's career—reiterations of a passion scene, as I've been calling it—and to see what they can tell us about his early theories of passion and frustration.

Of course, Yeats's aphoristic claim—"The passions, when we know that they cannot find fulfillment, become vision"—cannot hold true for everyone. We can all relate to unfulfilled passion, but precious few of us have witnessed the visions of the poet. The missing element of Yeats's claim is an explanation of how the artist calibrates his response to the unfulfilled passions. He was no believer in wish fulfillment, so we cannot assume that art merely substitutes for the fulfillment denied by experience, that passion becomes vision because it cannot find its own consummation *qua* passion. Instead, I believe, his approach to the passions implies two distinct ways in which the poet might relate to the passions, two apparently contradictory possibilities embodied most vividly in Yeats's antithetical figures of the saint and the hero.

The first possibility that I examine is the way of renunciation, which Yeats associates with the saint: it implies that an unfulfilled passion teaches the mind the futility of all passion, and thus the need to surrender that which it cannot control. According to the saint's logic, the will is inherently an obstacle; vision comes to those who renounce affective and intellectual activity in favor of a trancelike state of meditation, a receptivity akin to the *via negativa* of the medieval and Neoplatonic mystics whom Yeats so admired.[5] The second possibility that I outline, and the one that I believe to be Yeats's most significant contribution to the long-standing philosophical and literary discourse on the passions, is that vision depends upon the mind's capacity to continually confront its disappointment and renew its resolve in the face of an unfulfilled passion. This is the hero's way, and it depends on the poet's ability to sustain the energies of passion even in the face of their own certain and repeated disappointment. The Yeatsian model of the heroic has been the subject of much critical speculation. Yeats owned and studiously annotated a selection of Nietzsche's works, so we can assume that the *Übermensch* always stands not far behind his defiant heroes, as do the various models of Victorian hero worship that he encountered as a young man.[6] What interests me here, however, is not the literary or cultural origins of the Yeatsian heroic but the psychological function that it plays for Yeats, its role as a paradigm of response to emotional intensity.

Whether they label him the last Romantic or the first Modernist, critics and scholars have generally adhered to Yeats's compelling self-portrait as a Faustian artist of will and domination, a living symbol approaching its own fulfillment and completion by coaxing the mind's dark, exotic mysteries into reason's light and marshaling them into discipline and order. In Yeats's own lifetime Edmund Dulac agreed unequivocally that "his imagination was under perfect control."[7] Scholar Larry Brunner writes of Yeats's all-consuming drive to be "self-possessed,

self-made, and self-determining," to attain a "lofty self-mastery"; Richard Ellmann, of his desire to complete "the process of what he himself described as 'self-
conquest'"; and Phillip Marcus, of his bardic dedication to an "artistic power"
capable of deliberately reshaping both self and nation.[8] So far as I can tell, Daniel
Albright comes the closest to seeing through Yeats's mask of self-possession when
he wonders "if Yeats did not secretly rejoice in [the] destructive tidal-wave of imagination," in the overwhelming energies that render the mind vulnerable and powerless.[9] Contrary to the prevailing scholarly consensus, I hope to demonstrate that
Yeats was fascinated by powerlessness, by the prospect of losing control entirely.
Most important, I intend to show that the Yeatsian heroic is not an arbiter of
power, self-possession, and transcendence, but rather an alternate mode of achiev-
ing the intense passivity and receptivity that Yeats believed to be paramount to the
artist's vocation. Yeats's efforts at control and artistic domination, in fact, all aim
at their own dissolution, at that paradoxical point where the poet succumbs to the
transfiguring force of his passions, where he becomes the sufferer, the victim, the
patient. The Yeatsian model of passion that I am proposing, ultimately, draws both
saint and hero out of their isolated opposition and into creative simultaneity.

In the following pages, I look first at the simultaneous development and unrav-
eling of these binary principles—the saintly and the heroic—in his youthful work.
I show that even during the time when Yeats was most energetically invested in
modeling himself after the saint's passive acceptance, he was allowing the principles of the hero's active resistance to formulate themselves, so to speak, between
the lines. I then address how he transforms these principles of emotional response
from abstract psychological propositions into the affective dramatizations proper
to literary art in the two versions of his symbolic play *The Hour-Glass* (1903; 1914)
and in the dialectical lyrics of his final volume, *Last Poems and Two Plays* (1939).

THE WAY OF THE SAINT

Yeats frequently asserts that the active mind must surrender its anxious strivings
in order to attain the frenetic imaginative state of poetic vision. The vocation of
the poet, he suggests—or the task of conjuring symbolic images—demands a
continual and rigorous mental surrender: "One must allow the images to form
with all their associations. . . . If you suspend the critical faculty, I have discovered, either as the result of training, or, if you have the gift, by passing into a slight
trance, images pass rapidly before you. If you can also suspend desire, and let them
form at their own will, your absorption becomes more complete and they are
more clear in colour, more precise in articulation, and you and they begin to move
in what seems a powerful light" (*LE* 17).

The more complete the surrender, Yeats implies, the more acute this visionary
procession becomes, and the more complete becomes the union between the mind
and its imaginative objects ("you and they begin to move"). Thus Yeats filters the

familiar light of medieval mysticism through the prism of his modern literary and occult praxis. In a similar vein, he envisions the poet as a kind of neglectful gardener whose sole task is to plant the seeds of vision—"parasitic vegetables," as he calls them—and then allow their coiling tendrils and vines to grow uncontrollably, to envelope the artist in a thicket of twisting, spiraling images until poet and poem become one indistinguishable bramble (*LE* 23). Gazing back toward the mystical origins of this poetic theory, he claims that those poets and conjurers who adhere to "the old rule"—meaning both ancient occult practitioners and his own mystical contemporaries—seek to quiet both body and mind into the absolute stillness of trance. They aim to become "polished mirrors" in which their extraordinary visions are reflected but not altered (*LE* 23). The mystical gardener of the "old order," in other words, is more mental guardian than mental gardener; he keeps watch over the wild growth but is forbidden to prune a single shoot.[10]

Yeats's occult experiments with trance and mediumship in the 1890s certainly helped to propel him along this path—the passive, meditative way that his occult predecessors followed—as did his studies in Irish folklore and mythology, in which he often read of faeries that enter and subtly manipulate the bodies of their chosen while they are asleep or ill.[11] He had the dubious good fortune to experience this radical occult possession for himself in 1888 at a private séance, the memory of which reverberates throughout his poetry and plays for years afterward. In *Reveries over Childhood and Youth,* Yeats recalls that as he took his place at the séance table and quieted his mind, he felt at once a violent electric current course through him. And then, by his own fantastic account, "my whole body moved like a suddenly unrolled watch-spring, and I was thrown backward on the wall" (*Au* 106). His friends assured him that if he did not resist, he would become a medium for a visiting spirit. Yeats was less than persuaded. He struggled; he resisted; he even tried to pray, though he could remember only the first few lines of *Paradise Lost* and so shouted those instead.[12] "I was now struggling vainly with this force," he remembers, "which compelled me to movements I had not willed" (*Au* 106). Reflecting on the séance in 1916, he admits that both the terror and the exhilaration of this involuntary passivity remained with him long after the séance had ended: "For years afterward I would not go to a séance or turn a table and would often ask myself what was that violent impulse that had run through my nerves. Was it a part of myself—something always to be a danger perhaps; or had it come from without, as it seemed?" (*Au* 107).

Even if we approach this account with suspicion, we should remember that, in terms of the way he imagined himself and his own mind, it forms a part of Yeats's imaginative biography. In fact, at stake in his urgent question are precisely the two categories—the subjective and the objective, or what he called the antithetical and the primary—that would occupy his philosophical imagination for decades. The Great Wheel and the interlocking gyres in *A Vision* are plotted according to precisely this dichotomy, the distinction that he draws here between "a part of my-self" and "from without." The primary or objective mind is moved by a force from outside of itself; in the landscape of the mind, it is increasingly an object that merely receives action, that exists to gauge the impressions of that which "comes from without." The antithetical or subjective mind, on the other hand, is forceful and originating, a cause rather than an effect; it is the actor and maker of its mental universe. Yeats's question after the séance strikes at the heart of his philosophical system because it challenges the distinction between the two categories, causes him to sense himself both actor and acted upon, both the vessel and its occupant.

The unsettling exteriority of the violent impulse—the possibility that it "came from without"—foreshadows the strange foreignness that Yeats will eventually attribute to elements of his own mind. His firsthand experience of spiritual passivity and possession may have made him wary of séances for a while, but it also compelled him toward a lifelong investigation of similar experiences in his creative work. He revisits it with an almost obsessive intensity in the years that follow, asking each time, in effect: What might have happened had he remained passive? Had he renounced both the desire to resist and the fear of being overpowered, and instead allowed the spirit to speak through him as it seemed poised to do?

In one of Yeats's first attempts to integrate the disorienting experience of possession and his other occult experiences, the narrator of his early, unpublished novel, *The Speckled Bird,* awakes from a deep sleep "to hear a voice speaking through his own lips, but as if it were of another voice . . . . It seemed to him as the strange voice spoke that his body had become impersonal and magical."[13] It matters little whether his account of this strange enunciation actually originates from the séance or from an earlier experience akin to it; what matters is the force with which the sense of passive possession struck Yeats's imagination, leaving an impression vivid enough that he was compelled to recount it several more times, in the early drafts of his "Autobiography," in *The Stirring of the Bones,* and in *Per Amica Silentia Lunae.*[14] In each instance, the spirit speaks through him as if through "lips of stone" or through what Michael Robartes (one of Yeats's many artist-surrogates) calls his "wire-jointed jaws" (*VP* 382). In the metamorphosis of inspiration, Yeats's poet transforms into a puppet, dangling from the nimble fingers of the Muse, like Leda from the rude clutches of Zeus: "Constrained, arraigned, baffled, bent and unbent / By these wire-jointed jaws and limbs of wood, / Themselves obedient, / Knowing not evil and good" ("The Double Vision of Michael Robartes," *VP* 382). He recasts the scene again in *At the Hawk's Well* (1917), this time shifting emphasis from the externality of the puppeteer to the uncanny internality of the voice: "It was her mouth, and yet not she, that cried. / It was the shadow that cried behind her mouth" (*VPl* 408). The shadow that cries from within and behind the mouth recaptures his own uncertainty after his séance experience: Does the violent power of the spirit come from within or from without? Is it one with the other psychological processes over which the disciplined mind might gain control? Or is it invulnerable to the will's jealous energies, an imperturbable foreign presence lurking in the mind's otherwise familiar precincts?

The tropes of this poetic theory effectively reduce the creative psyche to the passivity of an object, to the state that T. S. Eliot later compares to an anesthetized patient on an operating table, when "all there is of you is your body / And the 'you' is withdrawn" (Eliot, *CPP* 307). Yeats revisits the scene in his 1903 narrative poem *The Old Age of Queen Maeve* as well, casting the prophetic speaker in a state of immobilized slumber: "Suddenly Ailell spoke out of his sleep, / And not with his own voice or a man's voice, / But with the burning, live, unshaken voice / Of those that, it may be, can never age" (*VP* 183).

Sleep and trance, for Yeats, are close cousins. The slumbering body appears to neither think nor feel; from the outside, it seems to have renounced not only the voluntary activities of thought and motion, but also the often involuntary affects—anxiety, fear, desire—that characterize the waking mind. Yeats recognized this resemblance and took advantage of it repeatedly; his verse itself, he insists, is composed "Of things discovered in the deep, / Where only body's laid asleep" ("To Ireland in the Coming Times," *VP* 138). Three years after he and his wife began their automatic writings, they agreed to a daring new tactic for coaxing the spirits to speak through her, which he duly recorded in a notebook: "New Method: George speaks while asleep."[15] Years later, in a lecture that he presented to the United Arts Club titled "A New Theory of Apparitions," he expounds on the "semifreedom" that the sleeper enjoys, during which he can be most easily visited by the visionary dreams of the spirit world. He connects the passivity of sleep with that of hypnotism, suggesting that both transform the normally active mind into a mute, objectlike vehicle: "People under the influence of hypnotism are in a receptive state of dream, and so become *media* for the incarnation of wandering ghosts."[16] According to the *Irish Times* reporter who attended the lecture, however, Yeats concluded with a characteristic warning about the dangers of entering into such a state: "Dreams are irresponsible things and the medium is, therefore, an irresponsible person."[17] Foster suggests that the moralistic tone sounds dubiously un-Yeatsian, but I believe that Yeats's apparent hesitation to commit entirely to the virtues of hypnotic passivity rings true. He consistently senses danger in relinquishing the mind's active, protective control over itself, and even his most credulous and enthusiastic writings about the subject never fail to register a note of apprehension about that risk.[18]

Intertwined from early in his career with his occult beliefs and mystical experiments, this model of passion-as-possession becomes one of Yeats's most reliable ways of thinking about poetic inspiration. In his early essays he repeatedly suggests that Blake, Shelley, and Dante Gabriel Rossetti all experienced a similar artistic possession in their creative pursuits. Each one welcomed the great creative spirits to speak through him by cultivating a mental "idleness," and in turn, each was granted an ability that Yeats desired and idealized, "the power to create beautiful things without labor" (*E&I* 78; 55). It is the curse of Adam, he says, that forces upon the poet the necessity of mental labor, the immense work of evoking and shaping the visions that will become the poem. And he was always attracted to the possibility of an art where (as he puts it in "Among School Children") "labor is blossoming or dancing," rather than toiling to wring "blear-eyed wisdom out of midnight oil" (*VP* 446). "Passion" in this radical sense not only allows the poet to compose without effort but also runs counter to the expressivist theories of art that he so vehemently repudiated throughout his career. As Albright rightly suggests, the Yeatsian poem is precipitated by an "imaginative convulsion" instead of a deliberate intent to express.[19] Like Eliot's, Yeats's theory of impersonality derives not only from his studies in aesthetics but also from his prolonged examination of the ways that passion transforms the poet into a imaginative vehicle, a passive instrument, or what he calls "a vessel of the creative power of God" (*E&I* 202). As for Eliot, impersonality for Yeats is never simply one mode of lyric among many; rather, it is a structural element of poetic composition itself.

In the mystical terms that Yeats preferred, this is the *via negativa,* the way of negation and renunciation. But in terms of poetic praxis, in terms of an artist seeking to find a fruitful way of relating to the passions and how they affect his own creative experience, there is a less exotic explanation. Yeats's renunciation of agency means that the poet's emotions bear an inverse relation to the intensity of his vision. The greater the emotional turbulence, the less likely the mind will be to attain a meditative state conducive to composition. The more empty the mind becomes, on the other hand—that is, the more successful the poet is at renouncing affective and intellectual strife—the more powerful and moving will be the vision. There is a marked distrust of human consciousness underlying the Yeatsian saint's meditative poise, one which (as I believe he suspected) is at odds with his Blakean affirmations of the Tree of Life and its fruits. Nevertheless, his experiments in artistic and dramatic symbolism, his lifelong emphasis on the trance-inducing effects of musical and rhythmic patterns in verse, and his belief in minimal dramatic action are all symptoms of his early conviction that the poet must surrender both emotion and intellect to become a vehicle for the inhuman, impersonal energies of a symbolic art.[20]

This, however, is only half of the story. Like that of his master Blake, Yeats's imagination operates most dynamically in the dialectic mode, when it is forced to weigh and sustain two positions with equal yet opposing energy. Although it remained alluring to him, he sensed that this model of passivity and surrender did not quite fit his own artistic experience, which often seemed more at home on the heroic battlefield than in the monastic cloister. At times, his mystical theory seemed to him too full of what he insensitively calls "feminine sensitiveness" and a weakened will, both attributes that he believed were the ruin of his Victorian predecessors.[21] As early as 1888, he wrote to his close friend Katharine Tynan of the frustration that he had experienced after following the advice of a certain clairvoyant, who admonished him for his restlessness and recommended that he become passive "for a long time" in order to center himself (*CL1* 92). This sort of passivity, he replied immediately, destroys the will and blunts creativity.[22] He echoes this denunciation years later in a handwritten inscription in Mabel Dickinson's copy of *Stories of Red Hanrahan* (1904): "All our follys are from drowsiness of the will."[23] Yeats often liked to use and reuse the same dedicatory inscription for years at a time, so it is altogether likely that this austere self-criticism had become a kind of mantra for him during this time.

A brief glance at the archives will demonstrate just how deliberately Yeats went about revising his own early theories of passivity and creative mediumship. In a rarely cited essay he wrote for the April 1900 issue of the *Spectator* titled "The Way of Wisdom," he recalls nostalgically his first encounter with Mohini Chatterjee, the Indian Brahmin whom he first met and greatly admired in Dublin in 1886. Chatterjee's teachings on surrender and selflessness were a formative spiritual and philosophical influence on Yeats, who later admitted that the Brahmin's lectures in Dublin "did much for my intellect, gave me indeed my first philosophical exposition of life."[24] Chatterjee taught him to distinguish between egotism and acquiescence, the two affective modes between which the human soul sways, and to value acquiescence above all else. Egotism is the way of will and power; acquiescence, the only way to wisdom. Even prayer, Yeats affirms, is too full of egotism— too motivated by desire and self-will—to partake of "that acquiescence that was his beginning of wisdom" (*EE* 290). "All action and all words that lead to action," Yeats concludes his admiring summary, "were a little vulgar, a little trivial" (*EE* 290). Chatterjee esteemed the way of the saint, and the young Yeats approved unequivocally.

However, when he revised "The Way of Wisdom" less than a decade later for inclusion in his 1908 *Collected Works*—now under the more neutral title, "The Pathway"—his admiration had remarkably dimmed. He softened his praise for his early master, and he deleted an epigraph linking him to another of Yeats's creative touchstones, Villiers de L'Isle-Adam. Most important, he scratched his pencil through the original essay's concluding line, which ambiguously reads: "nor am I certain that any among us has quite awoke out of the dreams [Chatterjee] brought among us." If the essay's new version was to reflect his current state of mind, he knew that such saintly dreams must be repudiated; he must rouse himself from the dangerous slumber of the will. "Ah, how many years it has taken me," he asserts vigorously in the new version, "to wake out of that dream!"[25] It is a subtle, seemingly insubstantial revision, but it marks a definitive change of mind: the sleeper has now awakened and cast off his saintly dreams of mystical passivity and possession. By 1908, Yeats had become disillusioned with his early theories of passive creativity and trancelike states of receptivity; he had begun to embark on the hero's path.

Or had he, in actuality, already been on it by that time? It is essential to grasp the full extent of Yeats's early commitment to passivity and surrender, if only because scholarship has sorely underestimated it. But the orderly narrative of Yeats's growing dismay that I have assembled thus far leaves out, admittedly, a dialectical counternarrative, one that was simultaneously committing itself to the virtues of heroic action and resistance. Discussing the serene quietude of passive meditation in 1917, he confesses, "I had no natural gift for this clear quiet, as I soon discovered, for my mind is abnormally restless" (*LE* 17). By the time Yeats explicitly admitted that his own mind did not easily follow the traditional *via contemplativa,* he had already begun to forge an alternative model. It was his predilection for intellectual and imaginative activity, I believe, that compelled him to find another way to attain the passive, trancelike creative states that he so idealized, to invite those "turbulent" images that, as he says, "hurry from unmeasured mind / To rant and rage in flood and wind" (*VP* 139). But what would this alternate model look like? How could relentless action lead the poet toward the passivity and "unmeasured mind" of trance meditation?

Yeats's alternate model, he knew, must sustain rather than surrender the unfulfilled passions. That is, it must continue stoking the timbers of emotional intensity despite his knowledge that the fire will not catch. It must attain a visionary passivity but, simultaneously, find a place for the action of the restless mind—the grasping, searching intellect that longs to bring the vision into the regions of volition and control. The poet must become, in terms of Yeats's own iconography, both saint and hero; the impossible task that Yeats sets for himself, in essence, is to make passion and action simultaneous. And I propose to begin examining how he accomplishes that task by reexamining one of his earliest volumes, where the precursors to the Yeatsian emblems of action and passion first confront one another and stake out their opposing territories in the darkness of what he calls "the inmost cave of man's mind" (*E&I* 88).

THE WAY OF THE HERO

Long before he assigns them their fixed positions on the great lunar wheel of personality in *A Vision,* Yeats sets a much more lyrical, dynamic version of saint and hero at loggerheads in *The Wanderings of Oisin* (1889).[26] As are all of his antithetical personae—wise man and fool, or Conchubar and Cuchulain—the saint and the hero are, at least on one level, archetypal principles of mental activity.[27] In this case, they embody the passive and the active faculties of mind, two halves of the Wordsworthian distinction between perception and creation ("both what he half

perceive and / what create") with which he was quite familiar. At the center of the
narrative, on the second of the three islands to which his quest takes him, Oisin
encounters the earliest precursor of the shadowy Daemon that will eventually help
Yeats to bring the two psychological principles into equilibrium.

Oisin's adventures lead him to The Isle of Victories, a darkened plateau where
he soon discovers a cave in which "a dusky demon dry as a withered sedge / Swayed,
crooning to himself an unknown tongue" (*VP* 39). The hero's confrontation here
represents one of Yeats's first attempts to give figural form to the parts of the
psyche that he cannot control, to those unruly forces that he both champions as
poetic catalysts and fears as arbiters of madness and powerlessness (*E&I* 88). But
what shape does one give to that which resists and eludes the shape-making powers of the mind? What image could give definitive form to those forces whose very
power rests in the agility with which they refuse a single image, form, or definition?
Oisin's lover Niamh hints at the mythical answer to this question when she warns
that the demon is "strong and crafty as the seas" (*VP* 35). Yeats's headstrong hero
only grasps her meaning once it is too late:

> Amid the shades of night, he changed and ran
> Through many shapes; I lunged at the smooth throat
> Of a great eel; it changed, and I but smote
> A fir-tree roaring in its leafless top;
> And thereupon I drew the livid chop
> Of a drowned dripping body to my breast;
> Horror from horror grew
> (*VP* 40–41)

The demon parries the hero's every lunge by splitting and multiplying, shifting
and morphing, as if his stable form were only a thin meniscus, waiting to be agi-
tated and swirled so as to free the many monstrous shapes swelling just beneath
the surface. It is as if, in fact, Oisin's frenzied struggle actually brings forth these
phantasmagorical transformations, which Yeats will eventually transplant from
the demon's lair to the gong-tormented waters of Byzantium.

Oisin defeats the shape-changer after three days of constant struggle, only to
find the same "dull and unsubduable" monster reemerge in a newly healed form
(*VP* 43). A century of futile battle ensues, until finally the hero abandons the Isle
of Victories in search of his next challenge. Yeats himself, however, was not willing
to leave this scene behind quite so easily. Something about Oisin's never-ending
struggle to subdue the demon—and more specifically, about the perpetual renewal
and frustration of that struggle—must have struck him as representative of the
poet's heroic yet ever-frustrated vocation, that "quarrel with ourselves" that alone
gives rise to all strong poetry (*LE* 8). Though Oisin's demon vanishes, Yeats returns
to the emotional contours of this scene time and again in the coming years. Like

the fantastic scenario of mediumistic possession, it becomes what I have called a "passion scene," an imaginative shorthand for a particular node of feeling and thought, a kind of lightning rod for his imaginative energies.

He includes a similar confrontation in his novella *Dhoya* (1891), in which the protagonist battles with a devilish, scarlet-capped stranger whose cunning proves just as frustrating (if not quite as mythical) as the crooning demon's. "For a long while they fought," the narrator relates: "Underneath them the feet of Dhoya beat up the ground, but the feet of the other as he rushed hither and thither, matching his agility with the mortal's mighty strength, made neither shadow nor footstep on the sands. . . . [Dhoya] closed with his enemy and threw him, and put his knee on his chest and his hands on his throat, and would have crushed all life out of him, when lo!, he held beneath his knee no more than a bundle of weeds."[28] Though it is much abbreviated from his other hero's century-long battle, this scene recaptures in miniature the salient emotional features of Oisin's confrontation: the surging energy and force of the active will and the crushing sense of disappointment and frustration as that activity proves futile, as the nearly defeated enemy metamorphoses to elude the hero's grasp. It is the same endless energy and force for which the protagonist of *Where There Is Nothing* (1902) cries out, "I want the happiness of men who fight, who are hit and hit back, . . . the endless battle, the endless battle" (*VPl* 1097). In keeping with their fairy tale aura, Yeats relates these early narratives of endless battle with simplicity and detachment, with a brisk factuality that allows for no elaboration of the scene's emotional import. If we want to gauge the full affective weight of the battle scene, we must look instead to the fears and doubts to which he gives voice in a journal entry written several years afterward.

As we have seen, Yeats later claims to possess an "abnormally restless" mind that impedes the lucid dreams of trance. But in 1909 this minor "abnormality" seemed to him to border on the pathological: "I begin to wonder," he writes, "whether I have and always have had some nervous weakness inherited from my mother": "The feeling is always the same: a consciousness of energy, of certainty, and of transforming power stopped by a wall, by something one must either submit to or rage against helplessly. It often alarms me; is it the root of madness?" (*Mem* 157). This passage is particularly illuminating because it reveals—in a way that his early Spenserian allegories rarely do—the emotional turmoil, the fear, rage, and helplessness that underlie each of his scenes of battle, confrontation, and disappointment. The intransigent psychic wall recalls the vivid foreignness and exteriority—something "within" that seems to be "without"—that he wondered about after his séance misadventure. Even the "transforming power" to which he refers here insinuates itself figurally into the heroic battles, transferred from the gathering force of his own mind to the powerful, shape-shifting capacities by which his enemy eludes him. In one of his last publications, a transcript of a radio broadcast that appeared in the *Listener* in 1938, he speculates again about the fear that he actually suffered from "some psychological weakness" as a young man, a temperamental irritability that prevented him from concentrating.[29] Tempting as it may be to read Yeats's career-long obsession with scenes of frustrated struggle as a symptom of his inherited psychological "weakness," I think it more fruitful to suggest that this recurrent scenario—surging energy, battle, frustration—is rather the powerful, transfiguring lens through which he came to view his most urgent concerns, creative and personal alike.

It is unsurprising, then, that this lens helps him to appreciate a similar scene in an 1899 *Bookman* review of Fiona Macleod's collection of folktales, *Dominion of Dreams*. In one pastoral tale upon which Yeats dwells at length, a shepherd desperately gives hunt to a shadowy piper whose malleable form repeatedly eludes his pursuer just as the chase seems close to an end. In his paraphrase of the ordeal, however, Yeats allows himself to interpolate the emotional contours of the scene even more fully than in his own work: "Being terrified, and angry because he was terrified, he tried to seize the piper with his hands, and fell against a rock, striking his head, and as he fell he saw the shadows change to a flock of curlews and fly away."[30] The Irish legends and fairy tales that he so earnestly gathered with Lady Gregory were filled with similarly strange, metamorphic figures, and Yeats did not fail to integrate these shape-changers, body snatchers, men-becoming-shadows, and shadows-becoming-birds into his own personal mythologies of failure and frustration. They reappear in *The Two Kings* (1914), when the heroic King Eochaid draws his sword against a mystical stag who then "vanish[es] like a shadow" in the midst of the struggle, "crumbling away, / Till all had seemed a shadow or a vision" (*VP* 278). And later in the same narrative, a stranger of unnatural majesty accosts King Eochaid's queen, only to slip away again midbattle in a perfect reenactment of the conclusion to Dhoya's much earlier struggle: "And now the shape // My hands were pressed to vanished suddenly. / I staggered, but a beech tree stayed my fall" (*VP* 285–86). With its repeated, insistent appearances throughout his early career, this scene captures a complex emotional energy that Yeats finds particularly compelling, one that veers toward disappointment, frustration, and exhaustion and yet seems magically self-renewed and self-renewing, that thrives upon the continuous exertion of its own forces.

The phantasmagorical shape-changers of the Yeatsian passion scene are undoubtedly connected to the deluge of symbolic images that beset the visionary poet at the height of inspiration, and nowhere is this relationship more explicit than in the early poem from *The Countess Kathleen and Various Legends and Lyrics* (1892) "Fergus and the Druid," in which Yeats performs the relationship between the hero's futile struggles and the transformative abundance of the poet's vision. "This whole day I have followed in the rocks," the exhausted Fergus exclaims to the mythical druid whom he has finally cornered:

And you have changed and flowed from shape to shape,
First as a raven on whose ancient wings,
Scarcely a feather lingered, then you seemed
A weasel moving on from stone to stone,
And now at last you wear a human shape,
A thin grey man half lost in gathering night.
(*VP* 102)

Unlike Yeats's other antagonists, however, the druid does not vanish. Instead, in a gesture reminiscent of the Spenserian allegory that Yeats so admired (and one to which he will return many years later), the druid offers his pursuer a token for his troubles, a reward for his frustrations in the form of a "little bag of dreams": "Unloose the cord," he instructs, "and they wrap you round" (*VP* 104). Endowed with this emblem of the poetic visionary gift, Fergus finds himself suddenly transformed from shape to shape just as the druid was, awed and overwhelmed by the whirlwind of images that enwraps him. By "knowing all," he laments at last with sorrow, "I have grown nothing" (*VP* 104). It is as if, after much effort, Fergus finally brings the spinning toy top to a sudden halt when he himself, fantastically absorbing its momentum, begins to reel and whirl. Once this gyre of imaginative transformation begins, Yeats must have asked himself, who can tell the dancer from the dance?

There is a subtle but distinct change in the Yeatsian paradigm here, though, one which could pass almost unnoticed were it not so integral a part of his later theories of poetry and imagination. This hero, strained to the very extremes of his active, conscious will in pursuit of the shape-changing druid, is granted the sort of mystical vision that is typically reserved for those who have entered into trance, those who surrender their minds for polished mirrors, who were the mystic gardeners of the old order. Just as a trance seems to rob the subject of his sense of self-possession and allow another to speak through his lips, so Fergus finds that he is no longer a single, solid individual but rather like a clear, crystal vase that assumes the color and character of whatever is poured into it. Instead of the locus of a unique, expressive identity, the hero's body becomes a vehicle for the self-multiplying, self-renewing images that haunt the visionary imagination.[31]

This instantaneous self-dispersion—so similar to that which Oisin's morphing demon underwent, yet now on the hero's side—is still foremost in Yeats's mind in *The Wind among the Reeds* (1899). In a review written not long before, he had sternly criticized the strange dissolution of personality that turns Henrik Ibsen's *Peer Gynt* (1867) into a theater of loose, shifting forms: "Peer Gynt lets sheer phantasy take possession of his life, and fill him with the delusion that he is this or that personage, now a hunter, now a troll, now a merchant, now a prophet, until the true Peer Gynt is well-nigh dissolved."[32] In *The Wind among the Reeds*, Yeats sets out to find the counterweight to this passive dissolution, a way to experience its mad fluctuations without surrendering "possession of his life." In "He Thinks of His Past Greatness," he collapses the shape-changing druid and the poet's metamorphic imagination into a single entity; that is, he finally allows us to see that Fergus and the druid are both but elements of a single mind. He has been a hazel tree, the speaker declares, a rush trampled by horses, a man battling the wind, a beast of the wilderness, and a bird of the air. He is both the seeker and the sought after, caught up in the instantaneous "pulsation" of the Blakean artery. He is both the active hero and also the embodiment of Mohini Chatterjee's teachings on surrender and acquiescence.[33] And as Fergus does, he exclaims, "I weep because I know all things now" (*VP* 177). Like Fergus's despair, the speaker's weeping registers the emotional implications of what Yeats calls elsewhere "the dissolution of the fixed personality."[34]

This confrontation—whether between Fergus and the druid, Oisin and the demon, or King Eochaid and his shadowy opponent, for they are all one in Yeats's phantasmagoria—is a paradigmatic moment in the Yeatsian model of poetic imagination. It reveals the intricate conceptual linkage between passion in the strictly affective sense (the frustrated emotional struggles of the hero) and passion in the broader sense (the state of radical passivity, of being overtaken and violently overcome). In Yeats's formulation with which we began, this is the missing transition between the unfulfilled passions and the vision into which they transform. The poet must find a way to sustain his affective energies until they reach exhaustion, until every conscious faculty is strained in struggle and effort, and only then—when the will is completely consumed by its efforts—is the mind emptied enough to become a vehicle for the creative energies that Yeats seeks. Only then can the poet fall headlong into that dangerous world of visionary clairvoyance that he later calls the Path of the Chameleon. At the height of his conscious, willed activity, at the moment when he seems most fully in control of himself and his intellectual powers, Yeats asserts, then the hero paradoxically possesses himself the least. This is when he enters into the most dangerous states of helplessness and passivity, the states which also hold the most explosive artistic potential.[35]

DAEMONOLOGY

In an essay published in the 1904 issue of *Samhain*, Yeats takes a step back in order to think about this frustrated battle scenario from a more abstract, theoretical perspective. Modern art has declined, he suggests, because the artist no longer relates to his "dominant passion" correctly; he no longer envisions the emotions "moving before him, living with a life he [does] not endeavor to control" (*IDM* 68). Passion is not merely an accidental attribute of a self-possessed being; we must encounter it as if it were another living thing, a foreign deity, foe, or lover. The ancient dramatists, Yeats continues, knew that the most powerful tragedy arises not from attempting to control passion by eliciting it from a sequence of external events but from allowing it to emerge during those unpredictable moments when "will br[eaks] itself upon will and passion upon passion" (*IDM* 68). This is the ineluctable deadlock, the end point toward which, in Yeats's mind, all art must move: the heroic exhaustion of a will struggling with that which it can never conquer.[36] "The desire that is satisfied is not a great desire," Yeats affirms with Blakean grandiosity, "nor has the shoulder used all its might that an unbreakable gate has never strained."[37]

He returns to the artistic significance of this impasse in phase 22 of *A Vision*, one of the many lunar cycles in which we can discern more than a hint of self-diagnosis on Yeats's part. An artist in this phase of his creative life (as several scholars have pointed out, the dizzying cosmology of *A Vision* becomes infinitely more understandable if we consider it in terms of artistic maturation rather than metaphysics)[38] not only pushes his imaginative efforts to the point of utter frustration and exhaustion but also "discover[s] this exhaustion of will in all that he studies" (*Vision* 159). Of course Yeats had been rediscovering moments of exhaustion in every aspect of his own creative work and in that of his most admired predecessors. But lest we confuse this exhausted passion with the meditative silence of the saint's prayer, he takes pains to make the distinction clear: "The man himself [of phase 22] is never weak, never vague or fluctuating in his thought, for if he brings all to silence, it is a silence that results from tension, and till the moment of balance, nothing interests him that is not wrought up to the greatest effort of which it is capable. . . . The mind exhausts all knowledge within its reach and sinks exhausted into a conscious futility" (*Vision* 159). This "silence that results from tension" is Yeats's answer to the mystical silence that results from renunciation. Although both saint and hero move toward silence, although both mental principles ultimately lead the artist into a state of passive receptivity and meditation, only one mode demands all of the artist's conscious faculties that Yeats found it so difficult to abandon. Only the heroic principle accounts for both the "conscious futility" of unfulfilled passion and the role of the abnormally restless mind in a creative process that must ultimately surpass the reaches of both consciousness and volition.

Yeats's desire to discern an ancient pattern at work in this exhausting struggle leads him to develop the theory of the protean Daemon, the Platonic personification of that shape-shifting phantasm that Fergus pursued in the form of the druid. In "Swedenborg, Mediums, and the Desolate Places" (w. 1914; 1920), he suggests that his mental restlessness—which once prevented him from entering a trance like his fellow occultists—is not an aberration at all but the product of a *psychomachia* essential to creativity itself. In the profound depths of the psyche, he claims, we find neither peace nor solitude; rather, we perpetually confront and do battle against "the other will that wrestles with our thought, shaping it to our despite" (*Ex* 56). "We meet always," he reiterates elsewhere, "in the deep of the mind, whatever our work, wherever our reverie carries us, that other Will" (*LE* 12). This internally opposing will is a later version of both his early morphing enemies and the immovable wall against which Yeats felt his transforming psychological energies break, that force which he realized he must either submit to or rage against helplessly. The Daemon is internal, autonomous, and implacable; it submits neither to reason's subtle inquiries nor the will's brute force. It is the source, for Yeats, of the mind's self-difference, a blind spot for which one cannot compensate.

For a poet such as Yeats who dreams of an absolute Unity of Being—a grand realization in which the human soul grasps itself fully, transparently, and without obstruction—the Daemon is both the only guide and the ultimate obstacle.[39] Because it knows all that the self does not, possesses all that the self lacks, and refuses to yield its secrets without interminable struggle, the Daemon is the sole object of the most intense and insatiable desire. In fact, Yeats invokes the paramount shape-changer of classical mythology to describe the Daemon more fully. When we speak of the Daemon, he suggests, "we speak, it may be, of the Proteus of antiquity which has to be held or it will refuse its prophecy, and there are many warnings in our ears. 'Stoop not down,' says the Chaldean Oracle, 'to the darkly splendid world wherein continually lieth a faithless depth and Hades wrapped in a cloud, delighting in unintelligible images'" (*Ex* 57). In Yeats's narrative of inspiration, the effort to conquer the protean Daemon grants the poet access into the hidden sources of his powers: the druid's bag of tumultuous dreams, the swarming images of the Hodos Chameliontos, the symbols of the *anima mundi*, or as he later puts it so memorably in "Byzantium," the torrent of "images that yet / Fresh images beget" (*VP* 498). Oliver Hennessey rightly maintains that, for the later Yeats, "revelation is closely associated with active pursuit" as opposed to passive waiting, but he insists that this fact "does not negate the opportunity for revelation through passivity or mediumship."[40] In fact, I think Hennessey understates the strangeness of Yeats's paradox: passive revelation does not merely occur *in spite of* or *along with* the artist's conscious activity; it actually demands and requires that activity.

It seems important, however, to avoid getting caught up in cataloging these daemons and deities, to avoid mistaking them for the principles of mind which they represent; they are still metaphors for the poet's struggle to engage and sustain his own passions. They are still Yeats's way of understanding how unfulfilled passion translates itself into imaginative intensity for those who are willing to confront and sustain it. Simply put, the mythical confrontation with the Daemon is also the mind's vain struggle to encounter and suspend those unruly passions that threaten to overwhelm and overpower it. The Daemon, he clarifies elsewhere, is simply the dramatic incarnation of "my own buried self," a way to envision his own half-conscious passions moving before him with a life he cannot control (*Au* 279). The confrontation with this buried self is dangerous because the struggle to engage such forces, to bring them under the light of consciousness, involves the mind in energies beyond its ken. Not only, Yeats says, does the Daemon "demand a painful daily service, but it calls for the denial or dissolution of the self" (*Au* 275). The Daemon is the psychological equivalent to the shape-shifting enemies of Yeats's early literary personae; it allows him the opportunity to explicitly systematize what he had formerly intuited in lyric glimpses and flashes, namely, that passion comes only at the apex of psychic activity, only when the mind has fully engaged all of its turbulent, frustrated powers in a single, impossible struggle.

PASSION IN *THE HOUR-GLASS*

I'd like now to discuss two pairs of texts in which this shift in Yeats's response to passion—from the ascetic mode to the heroic—makes itself most keenly felt: first, the two versions of *The Hour-Glass,* and second, a pair of lyrics from *Last Poems and Two Plays.* A deepened awareness of the paradigmatic changes that underlie these works promises to offer new purchase on their otherwise familiar achievements; and the dramatic richness and polyvalence of the texts themselves promise, in turn, to complicate and refine the question of passion as I have explored it thus far.

I begin with *The Hour-Glass,* the play that Yeats published first in 1903 (in prose) and again, after much revision, in 1913–14 (in verse). It is an exemplary instance insofar as the two drastically different versions are separated by the decade of Yeats's life during which the daemonic psychology of the battlefield was becoming increasingly important to him. He borrows the play's plot from an Irish tale called "The Priest's Soul," which tells of a proud, intellectual clergyman who finds salvation only by adopting a child's faith. Yeats's dialectical imagination immediately splits the protagonist in two, and in his letters to Lady Gregory in the summer of 1902, he alters the title to "The Fool and the Wise Man" to reflect this new internal division. Initially, however, the plot seemed unchanged: the scornful, intellectually aloof Wise Man is visited by an angel, who promises him salvation if only he can find one believer unsullied by his anti-Christian teachings. The ostensible crux of the play, according to most readers, is the dialectical debate between simple faith and learned wisdom.[41]

As Yeats set about making the play his own, however, he all but erased the Wise Man's priestly origins and granted him the hero's mantle, allowing the Fool, in turn, to assume the saint's role. By the time he finished the second version, what began as merely a "morality play" (Wade 397)—he also called it "a little religious play" (*VPl* 644)—had transformed into a powerful statement of his new theories of creativity: "I took the plot of 'The Hour Glass' from an Irish Folk Tale," Yeats relates, "but tried to put my own philosophy into the words."[42] The drastic revisions that he undertook between the first version in 1903 and the second in 1913–14 reveal Yeats's growing confidence that renunciation is not the sole path toward vision, that there may exist a way that demands all of the poet's conscious energies and emotional intensity.

Like the other narratives we have examined, *The Hour-Glass* works by means of a dialectic between two Yeatsian antinomies, two principles of the mind embodied in the Wise Man and the Fool.[43] The Wise Man of Yeats's play is analogous not to the saint (as the play's source material would suggest) but to the Yeatsian hero: he follows the straight, forceful ways of the active mind rather than the meandering, unpredictable path of the passive imagination. In his abnormal restlessness, in his searching for material evidence and proof of spiritual events, he distinctly resembles the younger Yeats, who often upbraided himself for his abiding incredulity and his desire to verify spiritual discoveries with scholarly, historical proof.[44] In contrast to the Wise Man's fervent intellectual zeal, Teigue the Fool remains quiet and receptive; when the angel of retribution arrives to reprove the Wise Man, the Fool keeps his silence. And in the 1903 version, Yeats explicitly associates the Fool's quietude not with "simple faith" but with the saintly scenes of possession and spiritual mediumship that I discussed earlier in this chapter. He alone has witnessed the celestial visions, and when the Wise Man questions him about them—"When do you see them?"—Teigue replies, "When one gets quiet, then something wakes up inside one, something happy and quiet like the stars . . . like the fixed stars" (*VPl* 590).

In the early drafts of this exchange, the Fool had simply claimed to see angels everywhere; but just before its publication Yeats inserted this passage, with its subtle nod to the "old rules" of occult meditation: the cosmological patterns and the still, shimmering (starlike, or as he said before, mirrorlike) reflectivity of the meditative mind.[45] This internal "something" and the fixed stars also recall the unshaken voices of eternity that speak through Yeats's early protagonists while they slumber or enter states of meditative trance. And Teigue's strange awakening is precisely what Yeats had in mind when he wrote years before that "it sometimes happens to a man that when this outer world has grown utterly blank there exists within him a spiritual illumination."[46] It is a familiar theme for Yeats: the Fool's vacancy is the glassy blank of the mirror's face, an immobile surface polished by abandoning emotional extremity and intellectual striving, by casting off, as Albright suggests, "every inflection of personality, every impurity of the medium."[47]

When he returned to revise *The Hour-Glass* over the following ten years—the decade in which his energies were beginning to move toward the violence of the heroic mode—he shifted his emphasis from the play's explicit pedagogical import to its implicit aesthetic commentary on the path to artistic vision. In the first version of the play, the Wise Man poses no opposition to the Fool's quiet. He questions Teigue desperately about the afterlife and about his visions of angels. But as his death approaches, he finally admits the truth behind the Fool's proclamations. In the quiet of renunciation and passivity, he declares, the self abandons its restless emotions and dissolves into the mystical nothingness of its maker: "My last hope is gone and now that it is too late I can see it all. . . . We sink in on God, we find him in becoming nothing . . . strange that I never saw it until now" (*VPl* 634–36). Something about the Wise Man's utter submission, however, remained displeasing to Yeats. When he was preparing the first version for the stage in 1902, he told Lady Gregory that the actor playing the Wise Man should not look too old or haggard; from the beginning, Yeats envisioned him as "a man in the full vigour of life" (Wade 378). Perhaps this disparity—between the protagonist's physical stature and his psychological dissolution—helps to explain why he sensed an element of platitude in the Wise Man's final gesture, something which (as he admits) rang false on the stage.[48] It seemed false to the dramatic demands of the play, false to the dialectical principles that the two figures represent, and in fact, as he writes in a note to the second version, "false to my own thoughts of the world" (*VPl* 646). If the Wise Man does not struggle, if he does not achieve a futile rage and battle in vain against an immovable force, then in essence Yeats has admitted that his new way to enlightenment is false. He has admitted that passion leads to vision only through its own self-immolation.

In the later version, the Wise Man (or as Yeats now calls him sympathetically, "my philosopher" [*VPl* 646]) comes into his own. Early in the play Yeats gives him a portentous dream in which "Reason" grows dim and useless, yielding not to the Fool's quiet but to a drum-beating, Dionysian "Frenzy" that laughs and screams in the face of his philosophies. By granting the Wise Man his own nightmarish dream visions to match the Fool's serenely angelic ones, Yeats begins to balance the dialectic that had languished in the earlier version. Yeats's early revisions also prepare us for the Wise Man's new realization, one that is drastically different from his humbled submission at the conclusion of the first version. In the 1903 production, he had found it "strange" to think that the Fool had been right all along, that vision entails the death of the passions. But now, he discovers an altogether different strangeness:

> Yet it is strange, the strangest thing I have known,
> That I should still be haunted by the notion
> That there's a crisis of spirit wherein
> We get new sight, and that they know some trick
> To turn our thoughts for their own needs to frenzy.
> (*VPl* 599)

Yeats's Wise Man is haunted by an idea that, in fact, had haunted Yeats himself for years; his description of the "crisis of spirit" draws overtly from the terminology that Yeats uses elsewhere to describe the frenzy provoked by the Daemon, the struggle that brings the mind's emotional and imaginative energies to the frenetic levels necessary to begin the poet's vision, the "new sight" for which he becomes a radically dispossessed vehicle. Yeats is still certain of the Wise Man's ultimate end—the nothingness of God, the utter dissolution and dispersal of the self into the chain of images that overpower it—for he barely changes these lines at all from the first version.[49] But the path toward this nothingness has, to borrow a phrase, changed utterly. Now he imagines that it leads only through a "spiritual terror" of consummate effort, an ordeal in which "our hold on life is troubled" (*VPl* 625). Only at the point of utter frenzy (as he had written in an earlier draft) are "all the faculties whereby our minds / Are masters of their state" scattered and swept away, "as though in Autumn's wind."[50]

Midway between the two versions, in February 1906, Yeats wrote to Florence Farr asking that she help him to learn the meditative techniques of the old masters. He admitted that he was hopelessly divided; without her help, he could not reconcile his own vain attempts at passive trance meditation with what he knew to be the "fiery understanding" of poetic vision (Wade 472). By 1914, he comes to understand that perhaps such a reconciliation does not exist. Instead the way of quiet and trance must abide alongside the "fiery cloud" of passion and heroic struggle; the Fool and the Wise Man must coexist in what Yeats calls elsewhere the paradox of a truth and countertruth (*Mem* 170). As if to make absolutely certain that the Wise Man joins the ranks of his past heroes, such as Oisin and Dhoya, Cuchulain and Fergus—all those who arrived at their own "fiery cloud" in the bitter frustration of a struggle that cannot be won—Yeats allows his rejuvenated philosopher to invoke the battlegrounds of these heroic ancestors in his final plea. "Go call my pupils—I can explain all now":

Say to them

> That Nature would lack all in her most need,
> Could not the soul find truth as in a flash,
> Upon the battle-field, or in the midst
> Of overwhelming waves
> (*VPl* 625)

If draft manuscripts can imply certainty, Yeats was quite certain about the necessity of this new passage; it is untouched throughout the otherwise heavily revised manuscripts, a clearing of clean script amid a forest of revisions and cancellations.[51] And for good reason. This battlefield is one and the same with the Isle of Victories whereon Oisin first fights his interminable war with the crooning demon; it is the same ground where the heroic King Eochaid battles his metamorphic enemy. The familiar waves evoke not only Cuchulain's wild, futile battle against the sea (another passion scene that Yeats revisited throughout his career),

but also the poet's ceaseless struggle with the shape-changing Proteus, the gate-
keeper of the dangerous path of the chameleon who doubles as the Daemon of the
mind, which must be held lest it refuse its prophesies.

Yeats's drastic revisions make it clear that the poet, in his eyes, must depart
from the path of the mystic. In a later diary entry, he proudly recalls his father
denying that either the painter or the poet lives the contemplative life; the poet's
weapon, he asserts, is closer to the sword than to the cross.[52] And in the same
pages, he reiterates that his familiar daemonic spirits have repeatedly turned him
away from the Fool's quietude and toward a region of battle and swordplay, that
they have insistently repudiated "all that is not conflict, that is not from sword in
hand" (*Ex* 301). As I have argued, however, the frenzy of the hero's swordplay exists
only to lead him toward an intensified version of the same stillness enjoyed by
his saintly counterpart. It is a stillness that results from a dizzying, ceaseless whirl
of activity, like that of a wheel when the blurring spokes spin faster than the eye
can follow.

LAST WORDS, *LAST POEMS*

Given the dogged persistence with which Yeats struggled to renew and sustain
these tensions throughout his career, it is entirely fitting that he should offer his
last words on the subject of passion in a pair of dialectical lyrics in his final, posthumously published volume. At least two other poems in this volume, "Man and
the Echo" and "The Circus Animals' Desertion," function in the dialectic mode
as well, the latter challenging the resolutions of the former (the speaker of the
first poem concludes with the relief of distraction from his theme, while the
speaker of the second begins in search of reestablishing a theme). If there is any
doubt that the exhaustive struggles and passionate frenzies still hold sway over
Yeats's imagination, one need only glance at a lyric like "Long-legged Fly," whose
enigmatic refrain—"*Like a long-legged fly upon the stream / His mind moves upon
silence*"—vividly recaptures the "silence that results from tension" that he had
foreseen in phase 22 of *A Vision* (*VP* 617; *Vision* 159). Or we can turn to "Under Ben
Bulben," wherein Yeats addresses once again the frustration of unfulfilled passion
by contrasting it sharply with satiety of the superhuman sages and horsemen of
mythology, those eternals who have won "completeness of their passions" (*VP*
637). Into the midst of these oblique reflections on passion and fulfillment, Yeats
reintroduces his tragic hero Cuchulain, whose mute submission in "Cuchulain
Comforted" finds a surprising counterbalance in the exhausted, frustrated, but
unrelenting resistance of the guardsmen in "The Black Tower." Many scholars have
pointed out the daring and unforeseeable irony with which Yeats gives his embattled hero, Cuchulain, the role of the surrendering saint.[53] But to my knowledge,
none has recognized the antithesis to this gesture in "The Black Tower," which
quite literally contains Yeats's last words on the subject; he dictated it from his

deathbed on 21 January 1939, a week after the Cuchulain lyric and only a week before his death. As a consequence, we have missed entirely Yeats's final attempt to sustain the frustration of the hero until it becomes a passion resembling the saint's. We have missed, as it were, the rich ambivalence of his last words on the paradoxical unity of his two lifelong psychological emblems.

Much has been written about "Cuchulain Comforted" and its place at the end of the hero's dramatic sequence, so I mention it only briefly here to indicate its function vis-à-vis its underestimated companion poem, "The Black Tower." The action of "Cuchulain Comforted" is fairly straightforward: the newly murdered, Dantescan hero enters the wood of the underworld and encounters his antithetical doubles, cloaked in shrouds, who identify themselves as "convicted cowards" (*VP* 634). In Yeats's phantasmagoria, they are the hero's daemonic opposites, those entities to whom he must reconcile himself in the purgatorial period of the afterlife that he calls "The Shiftings."[54] As is also the case with its companion poem, "Cuchulain Comforted" works by way of two interwoven, contending movements or trajectories, discernible most vividly in the progression of verbs and verbals. The primary movement is traced by the hero: he progresses gradually from the bellicose stride of the warrior, to the posture of an exhausted soldier, and finally to the utter passivity and awe-filled gaze of a victim (the verbal progression moves from the active "strode," to the resting "leant," to a passively obedient "taking up" of the shroud, and finally to his mute gaze at the poem's conclusion [*VP* 634]). In short, the hero's momentum is slowing, subsiding, and withdrawing. Against Cuchulain's progressive diminishment, Yeats sets in motion the contending movement: the forward momentum of the Shrouds, who first "stare" passively, then "creep" with caution toward the hero, and finally proclaim the nature of their characters before launching into their transformative song ("Now we must sing," "They had changed") at the poem's end (*VP* 634–35). Theirs is a momentum of building: it escalates, it steps forth, and it reveals.

These dual movements, in short, structurally perform the saintly, ascetic aspect of the Yeatsian visionary model. Like Cuchulain, the poet slows his intellectual and emotional activity, submits to the demands of the "old rule," and approaches a state of meditative trance. His renunciation, in turn, allows the Daemon, the spirit of inspiration and imaginative frenzy, to slowly emerge from the darkness and speak through him. The transformation of the Shrouds into songbirds at the conclusion dramatizes, in brief, the protean transformations of imaginative vision, which overtake this speaker just as they had overwhelmed Fergus or Ailell in the earlier works. The cycle is complete, with Cuchulain's ultimate submission revealing (in Yeats's phrase from "The Phases of the Moon") what it means "to triumph / At the perfection of one's own obedience" (*VP* 376).

Many have viewed this magisterial Dantean lyric as the capstone to Yeats's thinking about tragic vision and the fate of the modern artist-hero. It makes a

final, definitive case, Vendler contends, on behalf of "the claims of the contemplative life" and against "the heroic claims of martial action."[55] Admittedly, it accords
with his late preoccupations with the meditative practices of Zen Buddhism and
Eastern spirituality.[56] "Cuchulain Comforted" does not, however, account for the
marked emotional ambivalence of his earlier thinking about passion and passivity, nor does it make a place for the "abnormal restlessness" of mind that Yeats had
insistently attempted to incorporate into his model of imagination and artistic
inspiration. In an unpublished letter to Dorothy Wellesley written only two years
before his death, Yeats reminded his confidante of their longtime, shared conviction: "Some few of us," he writes vehemently, "have in the very core of our being
the certainty that man's soul is active."[57] As we have seen, Yeats's certainty was not
always so steadfast. But such a vigorous statement should, at least, warn us away
from placing too much credence in Cuchulain's ultimate submission. To gauge its
place in Yeats's mature work, we must weigh the lyric momentum of "Cuchulain
Comforted" against the only poem in the volume that musters an equal but opposite force, "The Black Tower."

The poem is divided into six stanzas, which alternate between narrative and
refrain. Three focus upon the beleaguered "men of the old black tower" as they
defend their stronghold against an unnamed foreign invasion; the other three
interrupt the narrative (and conclude the poem) with an ominous refrain that
ends, "*They shake when the winds roar / Old bones upon the mountain shake*" (*VP*
635–36). The anonymity of the poem's contending forces—both the besieged and
the invaders—suggests that Yeats is once again experimenting with dialectical
principles of mind rather than, as some scholars would have it, a political allegory. As Hazard Adams justly claims, the lyrics of his final volume not infrequently
deploy "a kind of shorthand that requires knowledge of what has come before" in
the Yeatsian oeuvre.[58] Before pointing out the intersecting movements of "The
Black Tower," I would like to spend a moment elucidating this shorthand, beginning with the tower that was, for Yeats, a lifelong symbol, a lyric talisman, and a
sometime home. In his early essay ("The Philosophy of Shelley's Poetry," 1903), he
suggests that the tower in Shelley's poetry is always a Platonic symbol of "thought's
crown'd powers"; it is, in other words, the locus of imaginative effort and awareness (*E&I* 86). When he bought his private tower at Ballylee in 1916, he stepped
squarely into the realm of his Romantic master's symbolism and set about making it his own (or as Pound memorably put it, taking possession of his very own
"phallic symbol on the bogs—Ballyphallus or whatever he calls it").[59]

Years later in the masterful sequence "Meditations in Time of Civil War" from
the 1928 volume *The Tower*, he envisions a solitary, Miltonic poet toiling by candle-
light high atop the same tower. From his vantage point below, the speaker of "Meditations" imagines this isolated habitant suddenly possessed by what he calls "the

daemonic rage" of creativity (*VP* 419). And by the last part of the 1928 sequence, Yeats's speaker himself climbs high atop the same tower, supplants the *penseroso,* and is suddenly overwhelmed by a similar imaginative rage and tumult from below: a torrent of "monstrous familiar images," a "rage-driven, rage-tormented, and rage-hungry troop" of men waving foreign banners and shouting political slogans (*VP* 426). Among these raging images there are also unicorns, hawks, and beautiful women, all of which are familiar, protean inhabitants of the path of the chameleon. In fact Yeats had begun thinking about the violent uproar of this scene at the tower when he was composing *The Stirring of the Bones* (1922), in which he describes a time when his mind seemed to have grown helpless before its own powers. As a writer, he had lost his way on the Hodos Chameliontos; everything that he wrote seemed to assume a powerful, autonomous life of its own and escape his imaginative control. He admits to feeling helpless before his own imagination, much like the protagonist of the novel he was planning, who was forced to "see all the modern visionary sects pass before his bewildered eyes" but remain unable to stop or make sense of them (*Au* 283). Here Yeats aligns the invading foreign forces and visionary sects that beset his tower—whether they be "modern visionary sects" or the "rage-hungry troop" in "Meditations"—with the threatening imaginative upheaval of the Hodos Chameliontos, and even the brief invocation of them brings with it an admission of helplessness and bewilderment. In short, the speaker in the last section of "Meditations" has approached, just as Fergus and Oisin before him did, the visionary threshold and the world of the shape-changers. He has begun to lose control over the images that he has conjured, and in the process, the Yeatsian tower has assumed yet another symbolic valence, this time as the site of the poet's exhausting climb (rather than the more conventional descent) toward the path of the chameleon.

How intriguing, though, that in "Meditations in Time of Civil War," Yeats's speaker recoils in fear and exhaustion from the phantasmagorical frenzy that his imagination conjures: "I turn away and shut the door," he says at the poem's conclusion, "and on the stair / Wonder how many times I could have proved my worth" (*VP* 427). It is as if he reaches the pinnacle of conscious effort, that threshold of utter exhaustion and failure toward which the Daemon always leads, but suddenly turns aside at the last moment, not unlike Yeats himself claims to have done when threatened by the invading spirit at his disastrous early séance. When he returns to the tower for a final time in *Last Poems,* he does so with these earlier moments of imaginative frenzy, invading armies, and disappointment foremost in his mind.

He had entertained nightmarish fantasies of a similar psychic invasion in "The Tower" as well, wherein a squadron of fantastic, armored knights arrive on his doorstep and demand entrance:

And certain men-at-arms there were,
Whose images, in the Great Memory stored,
Come with loud cry and panting breast
To break upon a sleeper's rest
While their great wooden dice beat upon the board.
(*VP 412*)

As in "Meditations," the ghostly soldiers pounding at the tower's door are not real. Although they have their origins in the dissident violence and rebel uprisings to which Yeats was witness when he lived at Thor Ballylee in 1922, they have now become a part of the Great Memory, the collective imaginative storehouse of history.[60] They are emanations of the *anima mundi,* figments of the dreamer's imagination grown unruly and hostile because he has not properly confronted them, because he has (as "Meditations" reveals) turned away in terror. They are bad dreams, in a sense, that return impetuously night after night, threatening to force their way into the dreamer's embattled psyche. In contrast to these previous poems, whose speakers gaze primarily upon the swarm of monstrous images gathering below the ramparts, "The Black Tower" remains doggedly within the tower's walls. In effect, it is a deliberately revisionary poem: Yeats sets himself the demanding task of delving backward into the mind of his earlier speaker to explain why, in the previous poem, he had proven unable to sustain the exhausting effort, unable to successfully engage with what he calls elsewhere the "invasions of the soul" (*Mem* 155).

To plumb fully the complex moment of siege and invasion in "The Black Tower," however, we must go even farther back than 1928, to an eager letter that Yeats wrote in 1901 to the members of one of his early hermetic orders. Arguing vehemently against the inclusion of certain rogue groups in the ranks of the exclusive Order, he reaches into his druid-bag of tropes for a striking simile, one that will resonate with the shared vocabulary of his fellow occultists. "Sometimes," he warns, "the sphere of an individual man is broken . . . and a form comes into the broken place and offers him knowledge and power if he will but give it of his life. If he give it of his life it will form a swirl there and draw other forms about it, and his sphere will be broken more and more, and his will subdued by alien wills" (*CL3* 44).[61] Here Yeats uses individual psychology to describe the actions of the group: just as the mind is vulnerable to foreign invasion, so too is his exclusive hermetic order. In "The Black Tower" (as well as in "Meditations" and "The Tower"), he reverses the trope: the actions of the group now allegorize the individual psyche. This early scenario forecasts the fear and anxiety that causes the speaker in "Meditations" to turn away from his rapturous visions, the same fear that underlies the oath of fealty professed by the black tower's embattled watchmen. It is the fear not of military invasion but of mental invasion, of psychological possession by an alien, other force stronger than the individual will and capable, if permitted, of redoubling its protean forms to threaten the mind's autonomy.[62] In the physical, materialist terms that Thomas Mann uses for the same scenario, it is the fear of mental infection. In Yeats's paradigm of creativity, as we have seen, visionary "possession" must result not from submission to an "alien" will but from a consummate conscious effort that sustains passion in the face of its certain disappointment. The black tower's watchmen, with their stubborn refusal to yield to the alien banners threatening to overtake them, bring this distinction into salient focus.

As with its dialectical counterpart, "The Black Tower" works by means of two contending movements. The watchmen's repudiation of the threatening armies enacts the primary movement, which begins in the first stanza:

> Say that the men of the old black tower
> Though they but feed as the goatherd feeds
> Their money spent, their wine gone sour,
> Lack nothing that a soldier needs,
> That all are oath-bound men
> Those banners come not in.

And continues in the third and the fifth:

> Those banners come to bribe or threaten
> Or whisper that a man's a fool
> Who when his own right king's forgotten
> Cares what king sets up his rule.
> If he died long ago
> Why do you dread us so?
> . . . .
> The tower's old cook that must climb and clamber
> Catching small birds in the dew of the morn
> When we hale men lie stretched in slumber
> Swears that he hears the king's great horn.
> But he's a lying hound;
> Stand we on guard oath-bound.

Not including the antiphonal refrain, each narrative stanza but the second begins by recounting the overwhelming odds against their victory (their "money spent," their "wine gone sour," the "small birds" that they must catch for food). Each narrative stanza begins, in other words, to build the case for the watchmen's eventual submission by making its seem inevitable, a product of sheer physical necessity. Each one concludes, however, with a reaffirmation of their resolve, with the resolute decision to prolong their defense of the tower despite the certainty of defeat. So the primary momentum of this poem is thematically iambic, if you will, surging upward from certain failure toward unqualified resolve, from despair to determination. If the second narrative stanza pauses to consider the opposing arguments, the tempting reasons according to which the watchmen should surrender their autonomy, it is only in order to buttress the hopelessness, and thus the heroism, of their refusals. The watchmen's resolve is not simply sustained from beginning to end; rather, it is tested—from within and from without—and must prove itself capable of enduring the emotional struggle of self-renewal again and again, of pursuing a passion that will not be fulfilled. In short, it must assume the character of visionary resolve: "We who are poets and artists," Yeats asserts elsewhere, "must go from desire to weariness and to desire again, and live but for the moment when vision comes to our weariness like terrible lightning" (*LE* 15). If the watchmen exemplify the first clause of this statement—the alternation between desire and weariness—the refrain aims at evoking the possibility of the second clause, the terrible lightning for which poets and artists all must wait.

The secondary movement of the poem occurs in the italicized stanzas of the refrain, each of which reasserts—with slight variations—the enigmatic invocation of the shaking bones: "*They shake when the winds roar / Old bones upon the mountain shake.*" So much depends upon how we understand these lines, on whether or not they can muster an affective force compelling enough to justify the watchmen's tenacious resistance. If they can—if the rumbling bones are omens of the dead king's imminent return—then "The Black Tower" becomes the lyric capstone to Yeats's psychology of frustrated passion. If they cannot—if the king's lifeless bones merely tremble with the earth's tremors—then we must grant "Cuchulain Comforted" the last say. That is, if the latter is true, then the implication of the refrain would ironize the resolve of the watchmen's stanzas; it would undercut Yeats's conviction that unfulfilled passion, passing through exhaustion and disappointment, finally becomes vision.

I think an appropriate valence for these shaking bones might be derived from a scene in the appositely titled volume of memoirs, *The Stirring of the Bones*. It is there that Yeats relates the startling experience, familiar to us by now, when "lying upon my back with all my limbs rigid," in the supine position of the dead, "I woke ... to hear a ceremonial measured voice, which did not seem to be mine, speaking through my own lips" (*Au* 284). As we have seen, the stirring of this alien voice from his own lips haunted Yeats throughout his career, as did the "rigid," deathlike sensation that he experienced in his limbs upon waking. It was as if he were already dead, he imagines, and the spirits trembled into speech through his body. In Yeats's penultimate volume, the speaker of "An Acre of Grass" had entertained a similar fantasy, pleading for the Muse to bring his aged body a creative uprising that would invigorate his failing imagination. At the end of that poem, Yeats once more imagines himself posthumously, wrapped in the winding-sheet, and he envisions the infusion of an imaginative power forceful and invasive enough to bring him back from the dead, one that "inspired by frenzy" could "shake the dead in their shrouds" (*VP* 576). And in "A Prayer for Old Age," written only a few years before, the desolate speaker begs that he be spared from the desiccated, impotent ideas of the crippled intellectual, from "those thoughts men think / In the mind alone" because their bodies have all but decayed. Instead, as he had foretold in "Sailing to Byzantium," where the visionary soul of the poet claps and sings despite the body's decrepitude, he now reaffirms that the poet's music originates not in the mind or the flesh but in the stirring, trembling bones themselves: "He that sings a lasting song / Thinks in a marrow bone" (*VP* 553).

The "stirring" bones of the *Autobiographies,* the "marrow bone" of "A Prayer for Old Age," and the "shaking" of the dead in *New Poems* are all one and the same with the trembling mountainside bones of "The Black Tower." They are not about death and resurrection at all; they are not about the bones of the buried body but about the "rag-and-bone shop of the heart," that psychic region wherein the poet's imagination stirs and trembles with life and renewal. Each dramatizes the internal imaginative agent of inspiration, what Yeats had called the "implacable will, not his, though within his," to which "man must surrender" or against which he must rage (*Ex* 279). What could be so ours, so essential, and yet so utterly foreign and strange to our experience of ourselves as our own bones? If the watchmen are emblems for the part of the poet that resists and struggles with the unconquerable, invading Daemon, then the shaking bones stand in for that part of him that will soon be overtaken by an exhilarating, overpowering force from within his own psyche.[63] This is surely what Yeats had in mind, only a few years before in *A Vision,* when he described the radically dispossessed state of one who has reached this ultimate state of passion: "He is nothing . . . he no longer even possesses his own body" (*Vision* 181). The constant, relentless thrust of the antiphonic refrain, then, provides the counterpoint to the drastic fluctuations of emotional despair and renewal in the watchmen's stanzas.

If the watchmen's momentum is like a gathering wave breaking itself upon a reef, then the momentum of the refrain is the shower of spume cast up, suspended motionless in the air, when the wave breaks; or else it is the array of fantastic, luminous prisms that glimmer in the spray. We might say, in fact, that each time the old guard renews its resolve in the face of certain failure, the refrain holds out the promise of what is to come, of the bone-stirring visionary upheaval that awaits the poet on the far side of his disappointed passions, his failed and unfulfilled desires and fears: the passion, in the most radical sense, on the far side of the passions. Unlike "Cuchulain Comforted," Yeats's last poem concludes with no visionary climax, no otherworldly transfiguration. The refrain offers no promise of transcendence; the surging energy of the preceding stanzas, it implies, will simply continue as heretofore, with neither submission nor transcendence intervening to bring the struggle to an end.

Twice before Yeats had attempted to capture this heroic passion by rewriting Cuchulain's death scene: first in the 1892 narrative poem later titled "Cuchulain's Fight with the Sea," and fifty years later in his last play, *The Death of Cuchulain* (1939). Only now, in his final attempt, does he discover that his hero must stand down, that he must cede his place in the drama of daemonic visitation to the impersonal, anonymous soldiers of "The Black Tower" and their relentless emotional struggle.

CONCLUSIONS

I would like to conclude by invoking a singularly revealing moment that will return us to where this chapter began, with Yeats's own frustrations over the discouraging, unfulfilled passions of his unimaginably persistent love affair with Maud Gonne. In the spring of 1938, he admitted to Gonne (who was still a regular correspondent) that his days as a public intellectual and touring lecturer were finally over. His doctors had ordered him to avoid all strain and excitement, and as a result, he writes, he dare not venture out of the house even to see friends. Even the doctor's most severe restrictions, however, could not deter his creative activity, which had only gained in momentum since his forced seclusion began: "I am writing poetry & thinking of nothing else," he tells her conspiratorially. "I have written more in the last few months than in any similar period of my life. Think of me as [a] monk of some strict order."[64] However, if the elder Yeats had begun to abandon the hero's armor for the monk's habit, it was—as he predicted six years before, in his well-known letter to Olivia Shakespear from June 1932— "not without vacillation" (Wade 798). He knew that Gonne was in the midst of finishing her autobiography, *A Servant of the Queen* (1938), and that his name would feature prominently in its pages. Perhaps he feared that his saintly self-identification would give her the wrong impression, that she would record only one aspect of the dialectic between hero and saint that he found so integral to both his personality and his poetry. Or perhaps, as we have seen repeatedly, he simply refused to dissolve the tension between the two by choosing one over the other. In either case, his next letter to Gonne on 16 June 1938 contains a gentle but unflinching directive, carefully formulated to preserve the balance he had struggled for so long to achieve: "Yes of course you may say what you like about me. I do not however think that I would have said 'hopeless struggle.' I never felt the Irish struggle 'hopeless.' Let it be 'exhausting struggle' or 'tragic struggle' or some such phrase. I wanted the struggle to go on but in a different way."[65]

Composed around the time when he was writing "The Black Tower"—while he was bolstering the confidence of its embattled soldiers to continue their struggle against the invading psychic army—this letter gives voice yet again to Yeats's longtime desire to sustain and renew the unfulfilled, unfulfillable passions to the point of exhaustion and collapse. And though he addresses the struggles of Irish nationalism and independence, we cannot help but detect here a double meaning, a knowing wink directed toward the woman who had been for so long the ever-changing, ever-withdrawing object of his exhausting personal struggle, who had been the sweetheart conspiring in whispers with the Daemon in order to set ablaze, with the "sudden lightning," "the passive and active properties" of the imagination (*LE* 29).

4

THE TURBULENT LIVES
OF PAINTED HORSES

Had things gone the way he hoped, Yeats would have been in Japan by 1921, comb-
ing the museums and mountains for ancient paintings and statuary, or perhaps
wandering through "some forgotten city, where the streets are full of grass" and
"where there is no sound but that of some temple bell."[1] Instead, on 27 June he was
still in Oxford writing wistfully to his friend Yone Noguchi, the poet who had
visited him and Ezra Pound at Stone Cottage in 1913, spent time with him in New
York in 1919, and then returned to Keio University in Japan to arrange an invitation for him to lecture there for two years. "I wish I had found my way to your
country a year or so ago," Yeats admits regretfully, "and were still there."[2] He had
received the invitation two years before, on 9 July 1919, had written about it with
growing excitement in the following months, but in November his eminently
frugal "Instructors" (with no little assistance from his wife) firmly directed him to
decline the offer.[3] By the time he wrote to Noguchi in 1921, he had reluctantly
resigned himself to poring over books of paintings by Japanese artists, to settling
for an ancient Japan of the imagination, composed mainly of "the lives . . . of these
painters." "Their talks, their loves, their religion, their friends," he implores Noguchi, "I would like to know these things minutely."[4] Perhaps it was this sense of disappointment (since we now know how keenly the poet valued disappointment
and frustration) and the subsequent renewal of interest in Japanese painting that
provoked a boyhood memory only a few months before, when he was preparing
his autobiographical essay, *Four Years: 1887–1891,* for its upcoming serial publication in the *London Mercury* and the *Dial.*[5] Without warning and in the midst of
a discussion of psychic symbols, Yeats turns his imagination once again toward
those Japanese painters whose lives and legends he longed to discover for himself: "I had found when a boy in Dublin on a table in the Royal Irish Academy a

pamphlet on Japanese art and read there of an animal painter so remarkable that horses he had painted upon a temple wall had slipped down after dark and trampled the neighbours' fields of rice. Somebody had come into the temple in the early morning, had been startled by a shower of water-drops, had looked up and seen painted horses still wet from the dew-covered fields, but now 'trembling into stillness'" (*Au* 186).

Something about the seemingly digressive account of the painted horses obviously remained important to him; despite the hundreds of revisions that he inflicted upon the two manuscripts and various published versions of *Four Years,* this passage remained almost entirely untouched from the first.[6] Yeats mentions the Japanese fable again in the same section, in connection with one of his fanciful psychic testimonies, but he only arrives at its deeper significance several pages later, when he returns briefly to the painted horses to reveal the privileged place he has allotted to them in his thought about aesthetics and its incursions into the political realm (*Au* 187). Hoping to inspire and unite Ireland under the ancient, mythic images of poetry and drama, he wonders if "perhaps even these images, once created and associated with river and mountain, might move of themselves and with some powerful, even turbulent life, like those painted horses that trampled the rice-fields of Japan" (*Au* 194).

In the years between his youthful discovery of the pamphlet in the Royal Irish Academy and December 1920 (when he finished *Four Years*), the tale of the painted horses had assumed significance for Yeats as an allegory of art itself, as a symbol for the function of symbols in general;[7] or rather, for the ways in which symbols—if they are to have either artistic or political effect—must act autonomously, independently of the author's purpose and aim. It had become, in short, what I have been calling a passion scene, a scenario fraught with the emotional turmoil that arises when the mind registers its own loss of control and sovereignty, its vulnerability to the forces that move and threaten it. Theoretically the implications of the trope seem clear: instead of a mere artifact, imprinted and inflected by history and culture, poetry might possess the power to influence and affect history and culture, that is, to trample religious, political, and artistic rice fields of all sorts.

The crucial role that Yeats envisioned for drama and poetry in the shaping of the cultural and political spheres has been the focus of a number of recent studies.[8] But none has addressed in any detail the potential dangers that he foresaw in relying upon so volatile and unpredictable an entity as art to accomplish specific social or political goals. He knew all too well that the meaning of any work of art is inevitably transformed with each generation, "modified in the guts of the living" as Auden said, and put to purposes the author could not have imagined.[9] He also knew that in order to figuratively trample the neighbors' rice fields, poetry must do more than merely communicate an idea. It must assume "some powerful, even turbulent life" of its own, an affective and semantic momentum that surpasses the poet's limited control and intentions. But if, in Yeats's aesthetic theory, poetry assumes an autonomous life of its own—if the Yeatsian artistic apprentice proves himself to be a successful Pygmalion—how can the poet be certain that it will act as he intends? When the poem is meant to woo a beloved or encourage a rebellious uprising, how can he be sure that it will not do just the opposite, that it will not enrage the lover or appease the Crown?

In this chapter I shift my attention from the role of passion in Yeats's theories of psychology and creativity to the paramount place that it holds in his aesthetic thought, that is, to the way that it informs his convictions about the effects and "afterlife" of art. I begin by consulting a hitherto unrecognized source that illuminates how Yeats imagines art to assume an independent, autonomous life of its own, to achieve an agency before which the poet takes on the role of the patient. The escape of the painted horses from their temple wall is my passion scene in this chapter, and I trace the horses' persistence through Yeats's work as emotionally ambivalent figures for the unpredictable and often disastrous effects of poetry once it is out of the poet's hands. I then discuss how they draw upon both early-twentieth-century accounts of Japanese art and Victorian and fin de siècle aesthetics, and I conclude by demonstrating how they dramatize both the origins and inevitable exhaustion of what Frank Kermode called, in his classic 1957 study of the same name, the "Romantic Image."

Because I believe that Yeats's conclusions will help us to complicate conventional perspectives about modernism and its commitment to "aesthetic autonomy," I want to clarify my terms up front. I use "autonomy" frequently throughout this chapter to mean "independent" or possessing the power to move and direct one's own actions. When later I discuss "aesthetic autonomy," on the other hand, I intend the cluster of theoretical perspectives (associated with some strands of modernism and, later, with certain proponents of the New Criticism) that posit the text as detached and insulated from ostensibly extrinsic forces like culture or history. In the concluding pages of this chapter, I argue that Yeats's ideas about passion lead him to a theory of autonomy (in the first sense) that forcefully reveals the illusions and impossibility of aesthetic autonomy (in the latter sense).

DISCOVERING KANAOKA'S HORSES

The painted horses had apparently been on Yeats's mind for some time before *Four Years;* versions of them appear repeatedly throughout his *Two Plays for Dancers* (1919). The "Stranger" in *The Dreaming of the Bones* spots one of them straying far from the temple wall—"An old horse gone astray. / He has been wandering on the road all night"—and they return with threatening urgency in *The Only Jealousy of Emer,* transfused with the mythical steeds of the sea god, Manannan mac Lir: "Hear how the horses trample on the shore," Cuchulain's double exclaims, "hear how they trample!" (*VPl* 765, 561). Even when Yeats revisited the much earlier–composed "Easter 1916" to include it in *Michael Robartes and the Dancer* (1921), he would have found yet another menacing "horse that comes from the road": "A horse-hoof slides on the brim, / And a horse plashes within it" (*VP* 393). Around the same time, he prophesies about the danger of the increasing prevalence of logic and science in intellectual quarters. For Yeats, logic is anathema to all imaginative endeavors; it is a brute that must be tamed, that must blind and restrain itself if it is to properly serve passion. "Logic is loose again, as once in Calvin and Knox," he urgently warns readers of "If I Were Four-and-Twenty" (1919), and "the wild beast cannot but destroy mysterious life" (*Ex* 277). In the painted horses, Yeats finds and celebrates an opponent worthy of challenging this wild beast of logic, one that will always battle (he believes) under the banner of the "mysterious life" of art and imagination.

It seems doubtful that he could have intuited the symbolic significance that the painted horses would eventually accumulate for him when, sometime between 1887 and 1891, he stumbled upon the pamphlet containing Ernest Hart's lectures to the "Society for the Encouragement of Arts, Manufactures, and Commerce" entitled *Lectures on Japanese Art Work* (1887) in the Royal Irish Academy. Dean of St. Mary's hospital in London and a prominent ophthalmic surgeon, Ernest Abraham Hart was also one of the foremost collectors of Japanese art in Europe, and in the printed version of a lecture delivered to the Society on 18 May 1886, he recounts an apocryphal story of the ninth-century Japanese painter Kanaoka and his masterfully painted horse:

> Among the stories of Kanaoka's skill, which are most popular, is one which relates that the peasants of the province of Omis, much disturbed at night by the nocturnal ravages of some creature which trod down their gardens, destroyed their flowers, and ate the herbs, laid wait for him one night, and gave chase to the intruder who proved to be a wild horse. They chased him till he disappeared into the temple. Entering the temple he was not to be found, but as they stood wondering in the hall, drops of moisture fell upon their heads, and looking up they found that they were falling from one of the horses in a picture by Kanaoka; so lifelike was he that he had escaped from the canvas and had only just resumed his place, and was still sweating.[10]

The Pre-Raphaelite in Yeats may have preferred to remember a troupe of dew-drenched steeds instead of a single, sweating horse, and rice fields instead of flowers or herbs, but his account of the tale more than twenty years later in *Four Years* is otherwise impressively accurate. We search the *Lectures* in vain for a horse "trembling into stillness"; the phrase is Yeats's own subtle addition, a quotation not from Hart but from his own earlier essay "The Tragic Theatre" (1910).[11] Hart suggests that similar fables appear frequently in Asian traditions, and the versions of the legend of Kanaoka that appear in Siegfried Bing's monthly journal *Artistic Japan*

(June 1889) and Henri L. Joly's *Legend in Japanese Art* (1908) offer even greater detail, including the whereabouts of the temple itself and one monk's valiant and quick-witted attempt to anchor the roving horse by adding a tether and peg in the corner of the painting.[12] Yeats no doubt found similar accounts in Laurence Binyon's *Painting in the Far East* (1908) and *The Flight of the Dragon* (1911), and throughout the works of Lafcadio Hearn, as both writers played prominent roles in the early-twentieth-century dissemination of popularized accounts of Eastern art, architecture, and legend.[13]

THE LIVING IMAGE

Through the similar fables by Binyon and Hearn, Yeats would have eventually learned of the Eastern belief that the truly inspired artist endows the figures in his paintings with souls of their own, so that (like the woman painted on a screen in one of Hearn's tales) "they [become] by their own will, really alive."[14] As early as 1902, he intuitively adapts the Eastern belief to the ancient narratives of Irish mythology, claiming that no teller of such enduring tales, "even when he had added some new trait, or some new incident, thought of claiming for himself what so obviously lived its own merry or mournful life" (*Ex* 6). Yeats's first reference to Kanaoka's painted horses bears the same mythical trappings. Although he had only recently encountered Hart's *Lectures* when he began work on *Dhoya* sometime late in 1887, the painted horses had already become a part of his supernatural landscape.[15] The tale of the heroic Dhoya takes place in an age of myth and mystery, the narrator relates, "long ago, before the earliest stone of the Pyramids was laid, before the Bo tree of Buddha unrolled its first leaf, before a Japanese had painted on a temple wall the horse that every evening descended and trampled the rice-fields."[16] By elevating the horses beyond legend and toward the realm of primordial myth, Yeats implies that they articulate some fundamental, originary phenomenon, even if he remains as of yet unsure of exactly what the phenomenon could be. Although these early painted horses are still a vague narrative frame, it is nonetheless clear that they struck his imagination with a singular and memorable force. It was not long before the tale of Kanaoka's horses submerged to a deeper, more permanent place in his phantasmagoria, before they began to appear and reappear—like the other passion scenes that we have examined—with a nearly compulsive regularity, as figures for the wild unpredictability of art and imagination.

In his early short story "The Crucifixion of the Outcast," from *The Secret Rose* (1897), the protagonist Cumhal embodies the connection between the horses and an unpredictable visionary frenzy exclaiming, "My soul is indeed like the wind, and it blows me to and fro, and up and down, and puts many things into my mind and out of my mind, and therefore am I called the Swift Wild Horse."[17] Unsurprisingly, Cumhal is a poet figure, a wandering bard who curses in rhyme and sings the mythic songs of ancient Ireland, the very mythology which Yeats would later claim "so obviously lived its own merry or mournful life." However, unlike the nimble, clever escape of the painted horse back onto the temple wall, Cumhal suffers a gruesome death: he is crucified, with wolves gnawing at his feet and vultures circling overhead, while his fellow outcasts abandon him. The protagonist's anguished, tragic end hints at Yeats's growing awareness of the fable's more ominous implications. Even though Cumhal cannot control the unpredictable movements of the visionary imagination—"They are," as Yeats says of his own waking dreams, "ever beyond the power of my will to alter in any way"—he is nonetheless held firmly accountable for the havoc and upheaval that results from them.[18] Thus the conceptual quandary posed by this passion scene begins to emerge more explicitly: If art must always transcend the conscious intentions of its maker, what assurances can the artist have that it will not function contrary to his desires? What if, Yeats asks implicitly, the painted horses trample the wrong rice fields?

The possibility that his own poetry may not follow his intentions presents Yeats with a genuine risk, one that registers on the personal, political, and spiritual levels of his imagination all with equal urgency. Though it might seem fanciful to claim that it haunted his sleep, he later relates a dream in which he himself enacts this very possibility: "I dreamed very lately that I was writing a story, and at the same time I dreamed that I was one of the characters in that story and seeking to touch the heart of some girl in defiance of the author's intention" (*LE* 26). As he acutely discerns, both the unruly movements of the imagination and the unpredictable meanings of poetry are forces that extend beyond the author's control, forces that may always rise up, like his dreamer, in defiance of his intentions. "Art, in its highest moments," he asserts, "is not a deliberate creation," and thus it is not subject to the deliberate control of its maker (*IDM* 60).

For Yeats, this possibility poses not merely an abstract theoretical dilemma but a concrete moral and ethical one as well. One need only recall his guilty self-questioning in the late poem "Man and the Echo": "Did that play of mine send out / Certain men the English shot?" (*VP* 632). It may have eventually earned him Paul Muldoon's parodic censure in "7, Middagh Street" ("If Yeats had saved his pencil-lead," Muldoon asks in reply to "Man and the Echo," "would certain men have stayed in bed?"), but his acute sense of the artist's accountability for the consequences of his work was no joking matter amid contemporary Ireland's political violence and turmoil.[19] Later in his career, looking back upon the unforeseen and unintended consequences of his work, Yeats would attempt to clear his conscience, to "measure the lot; forgive myself the lot" (*VP* 479). But in *The Stirring of the Bones,* he seems far from this ideal of acceptance: "I count the links in the chain of responsibility, run them across my fingers, and wonder if any link there is from my workshop" (*Au* 368). Despite Muldoon's suspicions to the contrary, I do not believe that this is merely feigned concern or veiled megalomania.

Yeats's anxiety about the afterlife of his art was real enough that he brought it before the Senate floor in a related context. Returning to the "chain of responsibility" again in a Senate speech in June 1923 he publicly discusses the tragic suicides that were said to be "inspired" by Goethe's *Sorrows of Young Werther* (1774) and Synge's *Riders to the Sea* (1904).[20] Yeats's explicit preoccupations with the risks and consequences of art are one and the same with the keen sense of personal and artistic accountability that lends the painted horses their profound emotional valence. They may be figures for poetry's turbulent afterlife, but they also carry the weight of his own deep-seated ambivalence about the poet's vocation, that precarious tightrope walk between the idealism of art's social and political efficacy and the awareness of its potential dangers and destructiveness.

Of course, as symbols or figures themselves, the emotionally charged painted horses must function according to the same artistic principle that they embody. Instead of associating them with the natural forces of river and mountain, as he foresees in *Four Years,* Yeats connects them with the unwieldy, phantasmagoric terrain of his imagination, and they soon assume the power and unpredictability characteristic of his other symbols (*Au* 194). They begin to reappear incessantly in various forms, to multiply themselves and roam the landscape of his poems as horses of the sea god, mythological unicorns, and Platonic steeds of the soul. But the painted horses nonetheless always retain the emotional connotations of turbulence, upheaval, fear, and anxiety with which Yeats first encountered them. No matter their guise, they always appear treading the brink of disaster, as instruments of an overwhelming force not to be tamed or tethered. Almost ten years after he came upon Hart's pamphlet, he introduces this more ambivalent version of them to the pages of the *Savoy* (January 1896) in "The Shadowy Horses":

> I hear the Shadowy Horses, their long manes a-shake,
> Their hoofs heavy with tumult, their eyes glimmering white;
> . . . .
> The Horses of Disaster plunge in the heavy clay:
> Beloved, let your eyes half close, and your heart beat
> Over my heart, and your hair fall over my breast,
> Drowning love's lonely hour in deep twilight of rest,
> And hiding their tossing manes and their tumultuous feet. (*VP* 154)

The later note that Yeats added to this short poem—a formal lyric in which the poet seeks relief from the creatures of his imagination by turning to the Muse herself, the source of their creation—attempts to divert our attention to certain horse-shaped "Fomorian divinities" and "the horses of Mannannan," both symbols of "the drifting indefinite bitterness of life" (*VP* 808). But the painted horses are there alongside them, plunging into the same symbolic clay, as figures for the unpredictable "drifting" of the symbols themselves and the "indefinite bitterness" of the poet's own troubled conscience.

Several months after "The Shadowy Horses," Yeats confronts the burden of the poet's vocation more explicitly, without the painted horses this time, though with an optimism more suitable for the iconoclast who once declared himself the herald of "the revolt of the soul against the intellect" (*CL1* 303). In "William Blake and His Illustrations to the *Divine Comedy*" (1896), he suggests that the artist always aspires to become, not unlike the masterful animal painter of Japan, "an enchanter calling, with a persuasive or compelling ritual," beautiful and horrendous creatures "that he never imagined, out of the bottomless deeps of imaginations he never foresaw" (*E&I* 141). It is clear from this subtle Dantesque allusion that Yeats had submerged himself in the imaginary of the *Commedia* in preparation for his essay on Blake's illustrations. Without explicitly invoking the text, he likens his prototypical artist-enchanter to Dante's pilgrim in *Inferno* XVI, who waits anxiously upon the precipice of Malebolge in the seventh circle of hell. With his copy of the *Commedia* (likely in Cary's translation) close at hand, Yeats would have encountered Dante's description of the pilgrim hurling his knotted waist-cord over the cliff's edge to summon a creature whom he cannot foresee but upon whom he must depend to ferry him and Virgil down the rock-face. "Quickly shall come," Virgil warns him, "that whereof thy thought is dreaming."[21] The grotesque creature whom Dante summons from hell's "bottomless deeps" is Geryon, that monstrous embodiment of fraud who is (as Yeats says) "ignoble" and "demonic" and who represents the dangerous, perverse means to which the fables of the imagination may be put. Although this rough Dantean beast has certainly descended from no temple wall, its striking two-sidedness (Geryon is both a monstrous terror of the deeps and an obedient instrument of Dante's descent) nonetheless recaptures for Yeats the emotional and mythical complexity of the painted horses, as well as the aesthetic problem that they allegorize.

By the time of the Blake essay, the phenomenon represented by the painted horses no longer pertains merely to the exceptional case of an ancient fable but to a fundamental criterion for the success of any art unwilling to submit to narrow mimetic constraints or to what Yeats calls elsewhere "the barrenness and shallowness of a too conscious arrangement" (*E&I* 87). If the poet is willing to risk the burden and uncertainty of daemonic struggle, Yeats believes, his work cannot help but assume a life of its own. "Every artist who has any imagination," he suggests in a 1900 issue of *Beltaine*, "builds better than he knows" (*IDM* 160). And a year later, in February 1901, he claims with confidence that "whatever we build in the imagination will accomplish itself in the circumstance of our lives" (*CL3* 40). Almost two decades before *Four Years*, he discerns the connection between Kanaoka's horses and his own artistic ideal well enough to employ the legend's unmistakable details as shorthand for the success of the 1902 production of George Russell's

Deirdre. After the production, he had written to Lady Gregory of his admiration for the play: "It is thin & faint but it has the effect of wall decoration. The absence of character is like the absence of individual expression in wall decoration" (*CL3* 167). This is a bit oblique, but shortly thereafter he clarifies exactly what kind of wall decoration he has in mind: "The actors moved about very little," Yeats writes in a letter to the *United Irishman* on 12 April 1902, "and there were moments when it seemed as if some painting upon a wall, some rhythmic procession along the walls of a temple had begun to move before me with a dim, magical life" (*CL3* 171).[22] There is even evidence that, as early as 1904, Yeats had begun to connect the magical life of Kanaoka's paintings with the majestic Byzantine mosaics that would figure so prominently in "Sailing to Byzantium"—"O Sages standing in God's holy fire / As in the gold mosaic of a wall." Certainly the painted horses would be fitting if unlikely models for Byzantium's mosaic sages, especially when we recall that Yeats's speaker summons them to come alive, descend from the wall, and ravish him with their living fire: "Come from the holy fire . . . / And be the singing-masters of my soul" (*VP* 408).[23]

As we have seen, he senses the "dim, magical" life of the painted horses in Dante as well, and he eventually appraises a contemporary's verse in terms of the same criterion: "It had, as it were, organized itself, and grown as nervous and living as if it had, as Dante said of his own work, paled his cheek" (*Au* 241). It would seem that the artistic principles embodied in the legend of Kanaoka's horses even cross the threshold of the spirit world: "So too when you write a play," Yeats's mystical alter ego, Leo Africanus, reminds him, "the characters seem to move & live of themselves."[24] He articulates a similar phenomenon *in propria persona* in a letter to Frank Fay in January 1904, written while he was feverishly revising Cuchulain's dialogue in *On Baile's Strand:* "I write of [Cuchulain] with difficulty for when one creates a character one does it out of instinct & may be wrong when one analyses the instinct afterwards. It is as though the character embodied itself. The less one reasons the more living the character" (*CL3* 527). What better way to be certain that Cuchulain becomes an embodiment of "wandering passion" than to envision the fictional character effectively creating himself, imposing his own autonomous force on the poet's passive imagination (*CL3* 527)? How else could he become, in Yeats's shorthand, the product not of an action originated by the poet but of a passion suffered by him? If it is fanciful to imagine Cuchulain impressing himself upon Yeats's imagination, then one must admit that it was Yeats's fancy, and he took it quite seriously: we need only recall his account of the composition of "Leda and the Swan," over which he admits losing imaginative control.[25]

So confident does Yeats become in the effectual, autonomous power of art and the imagination that, by the time of his American lecture tour, he detaches the painted horses from their literary and legendary origins and incorporates a nuanced version of them into the nationalistic context in which they would eventually appear in *Four Years*. "It may be that it depends upon us," Yeats tells his audience in 1904, "to call up into life the phantom armies of the future. If we keep that thought always before us, if we never allow ourselves to forget those armies, we need have no fear for the future of Ireland."[26] The "phantom armies" of Ireland are none other than the painted horses writ large, and the poet who will call them "up into life" is one and the same with the "enchanter calling" to his aid the powerful, monstrous, and utterly unpredictable creatures of the imagination.

THE ROMANTIC IMAGE AFTER ROMANTICISM

Yeats may have stumbled into the rice fields of the painted horses by way of Orientalists such as Hart, Binyon, and Hearn, but the path there had been paved for him not only by Eastern spiritualism but also by the aesthetics of several of his most influential Western predecessors and contemporaries. The idea of the work of art as living thing, an organism infused with the vital life of the imagination and not merely a mechanism of moving parts and cogs, assumed a singular prominence during the latter half of the nineteenth century. Intellectuals from Carlyle and Pater to Wilde and Symons became increasingly concerned about art's potential autonomy from the dictates of its maker, so that by the time Yeats encountered *The Symbolist Movement in Literature*, he could not have failed to notice some of his own fears and anxieties beginning to play out on much a broader scale. If I am temporarily obliged to leave behind the painted horses to explore the tradition into which Yeats integrates them, it is only to gauge both their debt to and definitive departure from that tradition and from the aesthetic assurances of what Frank Kermode labeled "the Romantic Image."[27]

Despite his sometimes ill-reasoned antipathy toward Thomas Carlyle—"No, I have not read him," he once snarled at Cruise O'Brien, but "my wife, George, has read him and she tells me he's a dolt"—Yeats would have undoubtedly found a kindred spirit in such a stalwart proponent of the power of symbols, the freedom of the imagination, and the prophetic nature of the poet's vocation.[28] Carlyle professed a lofty admiration for the heroic works of the intellect, for the architectural structure and proportion that the poet's rational mind imposes on the vast spectrum of experience that constitutes his raw material. Nowhere is this consummate artistic control and organization so apparent as in the *Commedia,* he suggests in *On Heroes, Hero-Worship, and the Heroic in History* (1841). Yet, he admits, something in Dante's masterpiece never fails to reach beyond what we consider the natural limits of conscious craftsmanship.[29] He recognizes a similar excess in Shakespeare, a force that gives the plays meaning and life that were seemingly beyond the playwright's power to give. In Shakespeare's case, Carlyle proves more willing to speculate about the origins of this vitality: "If I say, therefore, that

Shakspeare is the greatest of Intellects, I have said all concerning him. But there is more in Shakspeare's intellect than we have yet seen. It is what I call an unconscious intellect; there is more virtue in it than he himself is aware of. Novalis beautifully remarks of him, that those Dramas of his are Products of Nature too, deep as Nature herself. I find a great truth in this saying. Shakspeare's Art is not Artifice; the noblest worth of it is not there by plan or precontrivance. It grows-up from the deeps of Nature, through this noble sincere soul, who is a voice of Nature."[30]

In Carlyle's eyes, the works of a great poet are not merely analogous to natural creatures; they partake of the thriving, self-sustaining world of nature itself. The poet is ultimately the vehicle or voice of "Nature," or of what the Neoplatonists before him would have called the *anima mundi,* the living form that (as Yeats also believed) animates the things of the world just as the human soul animates the body. Carlyle maintains the necessity of the artist's intention in the process of "utmost conscious exertion and forethought" necessary to bring the work into being.[31] But he nonetheless insists that the art of a great master must "grow up withal unconsciously, from the unknown deeps in him;—as the oak-tree grows from the Earth's bosom, as the mountains and waters shape themselves; with a symmetry grounded on Nature's own laws, conformable to all Truth whatsoever . . . like roots, like sap and forces working underground!"[32]

Here I cannot help but recall the great rooted blossomer at the end of "Among School Children," but, more important, those "rivers and mountains" whose enormous power Yeats hopes to transfer to Kanaoka's painted horses when he reflects on them in *Four Years* (*Au* 194). The great poet, for Carlyle, gives bodily form to these vast living forces in his work, whether through dramatic characters such as Lear and Othello or by way of evocative symbols, whose mysterious revelations (he argues at length in *Sartor Resartus*) offer us the momentary embodiment of the infinite.

Surprisingly enough, when Yeats turned to the consummate fin de siècle theorist of such revelatory moments, Walter Pater, he would have found a tonic for Carlyle's ecstatic proclamation of art's organic autonomy. In his 1889 volume *Appreciations,* Pater traces the theory back to Coleridge, quoting passages in the *Biographia Literaria* that claim for Shakespearean drama an internal principle of life and development: "'a vitality which grows and evolves itself from within.'"[33] In the thought of both Wordsworth and Coleridge, he observes, "the work of art is likened to a living organism."[34] Pater admits that this paradigm does justice to the phenomenology of art—to the way we experience and appreciate its wholeness and unity—but not to the painstaking intellectual processes of selection and association that create it. He senses a similar devaluation of the artist's "supreme intellectual dexterity" in Wordsworth as well, whose passive, receptive theories of inspiration he associates with "that old dream of the anima mundi."[35] Pater's solution to the problem, however, is not to deny art its autonomous, independent life, but instead to transfer the life-giving force from the immanent divinity of "Nature" or the *anima mundi* to the artist himself. As the artist approaches the completion of his immense intellectual exertion, he realizes that "his work now structurally complete, with all the accumulating effect of secondary shades of meaning, he finishes the whole up to the just proportion of that ante-penultimate conclusion, and all becomes expressive. The house he has built is rather a body he has informed."[36]

What begins as an organized, architectural structure becomes, at the conclusion of the artist's endeavors, a living body, an organism with a soul that is as mysteriously present as the soul of a human being.[37] Instead of a Prometheus, who merely borrows the vital spark from elsewhere, the artist assumes the guise of a Pygmalion or a Dr. Frankenstein, creating it entirely by his own devices, a fully independent, self-sustaining creature. Pater does not address them, but obviously there are tremendous moral implications to this seemingly slight modification, which shifts the responsibility for the unpredictable afterlife of the work of art from an immanent, impersonal, and all-seeing Spirit of Nature to the finite, imperfect, and socially invested artist. They are moral implications that Yeats would come to feel acutely.

Though *Dorian Gray* (1891) addresses with excruciating detail the moral implications of art's unpredictable autonomy, it is actually to Oscar Wilde's "The Critic as Artist" that Yeats would have eventually turned for an unequivocal assertion of what Carlyle and Pater intimate more or less obliquely. "Those great figures of Greek or English drama," Wilde declares in the 1890 essay, "possess an actual existence of their own, apart from the poets who shaped and fashioned them."[38] These literary figures are by no means inferior for having received their life from an artist instead of a god; in fact, he insists, their sheer breadth and depth of personality guarantee them a life more varied and meaningful than most things we normally consider "living." It may be characteristically overstated, but Wilde's reversal means that it is not the artist who deceivingly dangles his marionettes but Life itself, which "cheats us with shadows, like a puppet master." The work of art no longer channels nature's energies, walks through nature's world, or strives to be a natural being; it is now more natural, more alive, than Nature itself. In Wilde's perverse museum, we ourselves are the lifeless paintings upon which the Mona Lisa gazes and in whom she quickly loses interest. The true critic must therefore "always be reminding us that great works of art are living things—are, in fact, the only things that live."[39]

Wilde also possesses an eminently more practical (and in retrospect, more Yeatsian) understanding of precisely what constitutes the autonomous afterlife of a work of art. A poem does not suddenly develop complex motor systems or opposable thumbs; instead it "lives" because of its capacity to convey a multitude of different meanings to generations of readers after its inception. It is the work of art's excess of signification—or as Pater says, its many "shades of meaning"—that

makes it unpredictable and uncontrollable once out of the author's hands. Wilde
cautions the apprentice critic to wholeheartedly reject "those obvious modes of art
that have but one message to deliver" and to embrace instead those in which,
through symbol and association, one can discern "whispers of a thousand different
things which were not present in the mind of him" who created them.[40] Equally
important to Wilde as these myriad meanings is the fact that the artist could not
have intended them: "[Criticism] does not confine itself . . . to discovering the
real intention of the artist." In fact, he claims that a fine work of art "may be
marred, and indeed often is so, by any excess of intellectual intention on the part
of the artist. For when the work is finished it has, as it were, an independent life
of its own, and may deliver a message far other than that which was put into its
lips to say."[41] Wilde's suggestion—that the partial absence of intention is a requi-
site condition for poetry and not just a felicitous accident—situates the problem
squarely within the parameters according to which Yeats's early theories of symbolism operate as well. Similar sentiments animate Yeats's denigration of that
gloomy bird of prey (Yeats's metaphor for the intellect), the significant role he
affords to the Daemon (the dark spirit of the unconscious), and his lifelong interest in states of trance and spiritual possession.

In his impressive and influential *Romantic Image*, Frank Kermode examines
this and similar passages, suggesting that "in words like these Wilde concentrates
the nineteenth century [understanding of the image] for the benefit of the twentieth."[42] Kermode contends that the nineteenth-century theories of the autonomous, living work of art crystallize in the Romantic image, a product of Romantic
aesthetics in Germany and England that he also believes to be the origin of French
symbolism and modernist imagism or vorticism as well. For Kermode the image
represents the supreme reconciliation of all the difficulties that plague the art of
poetry as a result of its linguistic medium, the necessity that it attempt to signify
truth rather than merely embody it. He turns to music as a revealing counterpoint.
In both forms of art, "there must be an intense prior meditation by the artist—
indeed the quality of the work may be directly dependent upon this—but all the
planning and all the intellectual effort must be completely assimilated and dis-
tributed in the work, which must not *mean* but *be*. The art that most perfectly
achieves this state is music; in poetry there are difficulties of the sort that start
barren arguments about the status of the poet's thought extracted and discursively
considered."[43]

In music, he argues, there is no single paraphraseable meaning; it signifies
everything and nothing at once. Insofar as its form is coterminate with its substance, and insofar as its stillness is at one with its movement, music is the condition toward which poetry strives; it is the paradigm of an art which "must not
mean but *be*." Poetry achieves this independent existence only when it becomes
image, when it subsumes all that the artist consciously and unconsciously intends

in a single, all-reconciling form of the sort that music most perfectly embodies. The Romantic image brings about, in short, an Edenic state of unity and coherence, one that satisfies the artist's desire for wholeness by becoming, itself, a whole and living thing. And despite its apparent differences from the familiar "well wrought urn," Kermode admits, this ideal condition of unity is not far from the organic, self-sustaining principle that the New Criticism claimed for poetry in general, that aesthetic wholeness that contains "within itself all that is relevant to itself."[44] In short, the two senses of aesthetic "autonomy" converge in Kermode's paradigm: by becoming like a living thing, the poem also severs its links with the culture and society in which its author abides.

In light of Yeats's experiments with the phantom armies and painted horses, however, I have the suspicion that Kermode's prognosis too neatly assimilates the modern poet into the tradition of the Romantic image that he otherwise authoritatively traces. It seems certain that Yeats's aesthetic theory belongs to this tradition —that it develops, so to speak, under the auspices of romanticism via the late-nineteenth-century critics whom I have explored. But something in the disturbing emotional valence that Yeats attributes to the painted horses betrays an anxiety about the very Edenic unity and wholeness—and about the insulation of "aesthetic autonomy"—that they ought to represent. The most powerful fin de siècle precursor to this anxiety is to be found in Symons's *The Symbolist Movement in Literature,* which begins by quoting a passage from Carlyle's own chapter on symbols in *Sartor Resartus.* If, as Kermode suggests, Symons is heir to the tradition of the Romantic image, he is also its most cautious psychoanalyst. And his warnings about the unpredictable afterlife of such strangely "living" symbols capture Yeats's emotional ambivalence more precisely than Carlyle's ecstatic idealism or Wilde's iconoclastic nonchalance. Only the supreme artist will dare to conjure the autonomous creatures of the imagination, he warns: "The vague dreamer, the insecure artist and the uncertain mystic at once, sees only shadows. . . . He is mastered by the images which have come at his call; he has not the power which chains them for slaves. 'The kingdom of Heaven suffers violence,' and the dreamer who has gone tremblingly into the darkness is in peril at the hands of those very real phantoms who are the reflection of his fear."[45]

In Symons's apocalyptic vision, the Edenic ideal (its religious proportions enlarged by the biblical quotation from Matthew 11:12) is threatened by the creatures that were meant to create it; its condition of possibility becomes precisely that which it cannot sustain. And the "kingdom of Heaven," that ideal state of unity and wholeness wherein art lives (as Yeats says) its own merry or mournful life descends into a nightmare of violence and transgression. The aesthetic Eden begins to look more like Dante's infernal wood of the suicides, moaning with the voices of its own inhabitants as outlandish creatures rip and tear at the trees. Although he attempts to defuse its intensity by making it a risk to only the "lesser" artist,

Symons's bleak prognosis unveils a tension at the heart of the Romantic image as Kermode describes its development. The ravaged Eden is, so to speak, a possibility —perhaps even a necessity—implicit in the aesthetic ideals embodied by the reconciling image. If Yeats is, as Kermode claims "the great modern representative" of the cult of the image, it falls to him alone to confront this disastrous potential as he pursues his painted horses into the visionary garden at the center of *The Unicorn from the Stars* (1908).[46]

UNICORNS AND PAINTED HORSES

Despite the idealism of his political rhetoric and a growing confidence in his own artistic mastery—one of his speakers boldly declares, "I have come into my strength, / And words obey my call" (*VP* 256)—the older Yeats remains painfully aware of the painted horses' more dangerous implications, those which trouble his dreams and prompt Michael Robartes' desperate plea to his beloved in "The Shadowy Horses" to hide him from the "Horses of Disaster . . . their tossing manes and their tumultuous feet" (*VP* 154). In light of the developments in late-nineteenth-century aesthetics that we have explored, it is not difficult to understand why the horses eventually come to symbolize both the supreme fulfillment and the inevitable frustration of Yeats's early aesthetic ideal, that organic, reconciling image that promises the fulfillment of the artist's creative desires. Yeats's horses will inhabit, instead, both the unfallen Eden in which art lives a "merry or mournful life" of its own, a living testament to its author's skill and noble intent, as well as the ruinous, postlapsarian garden where the creatures of the imagination have displaced and inculpated their makers with havoc and destruction (*Ex* 6).

Nowhere does their simultaneous beauty and terror achieve a more compelling embodiment than in *The Unicorn from the Stars,* which begins with the protagonist Martin Hearne deep in the inner world of trance, where the phantoms of the imagination hold sway over the powerless intellect. Despite the relatively early composition of *The Unicorn* (nearly six years before the first drafts of *Four Years*), Yeats had been thinking about the painted horses since 1887 and, as I have shown, had long since begun to confront their emotional and aesthetic tensions. According to Thomas, Martin Hearne's uncle, the protagonist of *The Unicorn* has been long acquainted with them as well: "He used to be queer as a child, going asleep in the fields, and coming back with talk of white horses he saw" (*VPl* 649). To his great dismay, Hearne is finally awakened from the trance ("It was no dream, it was real," he argues [*VPl* 658]), and it is now that he relates the familiar phantasmagoria of his vision: "There were horses—white horses rushing by . . . —there was a horse without a rider, and some one caught me up and put me upon him and we rode away, with the wind, like the wind—" (*VPl* 659). At first, the vision seems to embrace the best of both worlds: Hearne bridles the rushing horses and, like his predecessor Cumhal had hoped, seems destined to ride the wild imagination "where it listeth" into the freedom of the visionary wind (*E&I* 197). It was ecstasy, he declares; he has seen "Paradise, in that happy townland" where the horses took him (*VPl* 688). Here, it seems, is the paradisal embodiment of the Romantic image —the great return to aesthetic unity that Carlyle and Pater seemed to intimate, where the creatures of the imagination do not merely signify but lead an independent existence.

But the painted horse is never a univocal figure for Yeats; it will not be easily tethered to a single semantic peg. With a prophetic warning ringing in his ears (not unlike Symons's in *The Symbolist Movement*), Martin Hearne soon finds his idyllic Eden no less vulnerable to its violence than those ancient "rice fields of Japan." He arrives at a sweet-smelling garden, which he thinks to be "one of the townlands of heaven": "Then I saw the horses we were on had changed to unicorns, and they began trampling the grapes and breaking them. I tried to stop them, but I could not. . . . They tore down the wheat and trampled it on stones, and then they tore down what were left of the grapes and crushed and bruised and trampled them. I smelt the wine, it was flowing on every side—" (*VPl* 659–60). Here the horses finally assume their full mythological stature. As an entirely imaginative creature, the unicorn attempts to reach beyond mimetic representation toward a reality of its own. In a way, they have become (in Wilde's phrase) more alive than that which really lives. More important, though, Hearne's apocalyptic vision of the horses-turned-unicorns encapsulates the tension between hope and frustration that abides at the heart of this increasingly complex trope. No longer do the escaped horses play a merely destructive role, trampling the neighbors' rice fields or, in Hart's version, treading their gardens and destroying the flowers. Now their wildness partakes in the transformation that presses, from the fallen vineyards of Eden, the consolatory draught of wine, the process that changes a raw material into something that we not only consume but in which we take pleasure. In other words, the aesthetic "product" does not merely benefit, accidentally, from the wild turbulence of a symbolic art; it positively depends upon that wildness. By the time he writes *The Unicorn from the Stars,* Yeats has learned—with the help of his early master Keats, who knew well the paradox that only a "strenuous tongue / Can burst Joy's grape"—that Eden and The Fall are one, that art cannot yield its vintage without risk and sacrifice.[47] Or, as he himself would later put it: "The poet finds and makes his mask in disappointment" (*LE* 12). The conclusion of Hearne's vision is also chillingly familiar. Alone in the ruined garden, he finds that "everything seemed to tremble around me," just as years later, in Yeats's reconstruction of the Japanese fable, the pursuer of the errant horse enters the temple to find the dew-soaked painting "trembling into stillness" (*Au* 186).

If there remain any doubts about the persistent hold that the painted horses exercised over Yeats's imagination, one need only glance briefly at the later volumes, in which they continue to reappear as Janus-faced figures for both artistic mastery and violence. In "Nineteen Hundred and Nineteen," the sound of "violence upon the roads: violence of horses" triggers the release of a Byzantium-like flood of poetic vision, and the symbol slides across a strong caesura into that which it symbolizes: "thunder of feet, tumult of images" (*VP* 432–33). Transfused once more with the steeds of the sea god, the painted horses menace the narrator of "High Talk"—"Those great sea-horses bare their teeth and laugh at the dawn"—and perhaps even trample invisibly through the mountain pass in the refrain to "Three Marching Songs": "*That is an airy spot, / And no man knows what treads the grass*" (*VP* 623, 614). Even when they do not appear explicitly, the painted horses are conceptually present each time Yeats envisions a work of art that seethes with an unruly and imaginative life of its own, that seems to transcend itself and its creator while simultaneously risking its own annihilation as a creation. They stir unmentioned behind the artistry of the stone carving in "Lapis Lazuli," intruding into the peaceful scene with "a water-course or an avalanche" awakened by the restless imagination (*VP* 567). And they rush equally unobserved alongside the whirling "Gyres" in "Under Ben Bulben," threatening the serenity of the quattrocento paintings in which elaborately detailed backgrounds initially tempt the speaker to return to Michael Hearne's as-yet-undisturbed Eden, with its transient and unattainable "Gardens where a soul's at ease" (*VP* 639). For Yeats, the aesthetic ideal is never simply one of Edenic fulfillment and reconciliation, such as the Romantic image would seem to promise. Instead poetry must be always on the verge of a catastrophe, a tragic consummation in which unity of meaning and semantic completion approaches and withdraws, materializes and disintegrates as the artist looks on in hope and terror. These later moments of threatened tranquility stand in contrast to Yeats's idealized visions of Byzantium, which set in such stark opposition the serene, static perfection of art and the turmoil of human experience and change figured by the "dolphin-torn" sea (*VP* 498). What he realizes in these final poems—what the painted horses have finally taught him—is that his art is neither a golden bird nor sacred mosaic, that it offers neither an escape nor an asylum "where a soul's at ease." Rather, it plunges the imagination into yet another cauldron of change and conflict, one with risks and consequences that will not be contained or elided by attempting to insulate art from culture, politics, history.

I believe that the painted horses allow Yeats to bring the assumptions of symbolist tradition to their inevitable conclusion and exhaustion. And I also believe that they offer an illuminating corrective to the critical discussions—which continue to be influenced by Peter Bürger's characterization of the avant-garde and its critique of institution and autonomy in *Theory of the Avant-Garde* (trans. Michael Shaw, 1984) and Andreas Huyssen's extension of its claims in *After the Great Divide* (1986)—that posit aesthetic autonomy as a central and ultimately lamentable feature of "high" modernism. Recent scholarship has persuasively contested this assumption by addressing the ways in which modernist poets were deeply influenced by and committed to politics and popular culture.[48] My conclusions here, however, imply that modernism's ambivalence toward aesthetic autonomy has its basis not only in the text's reception, the literary marketplace, and the poet's life but also in the tensions implicit in nineteenth-century aesthetic principles and in the tropes that poets such as Yeats deploy to test the limits of those principles.

In the final tally, perhaps it is best that Yeats chose not to accept the professorship that he was offered in 1919, that a young daughter and a reliably practical wife (along with the ever-persuasive "Instructors") dissuaded him from sailing to Japan in search of the painted horses. His confidence about the trip seems secure even up until the publication of "If I Were Four-and-Twenty," when he excuses himself from the mammoth task of instating a new epoch, "that of unity of being," by suggesting that he is "about to the move to the Far East" (*Ex* 280). Even if the temple of the painted horses never existed outside of legend (in any case, Kanaoka's temple painting was no longer extant when Hart delivered his lectures in 1886), they were surely not far from Yeats's mind when he wrote to Laurence Binyon in September 1919 of his desire to go to Japan "largely to see pictures which I have learned of through your books."[49] Nor had he forgotten them by 1924 when he recalled nostalgically "the descendants of Kanoka [*sic*]" and the "artistic genius of old Japan" (*Au* 547).[50] Years later, he received another invitation to visit Japan, and writing to Olivia Shakespear on 31 July 1929 about the tempting prospect, he allowed his mind to turn once again to painting and legend, envisioning himself a restless European "wandering about Japanese temples among the hills—all the best Chinese art is in Japan" (*Wade* 765–66).[51] Despite another disappointment— he suspected that his wife would "make up my mind for me in five minutes," and apparently George did just that—Yeats continued to pursue the imaginary painted horses in both his life and his art with an impressive persistence (Wade 766). Or, rather, they pursued him. He eventually came to realize that they offered him no more sanctuary from turmoil and tumult than did the daily struggles and frustrations of his own life in Ireland. Unable to free his mind from those "shadowy horses" and their alluring ideal, he must have concluded that the only way to abandon his lifelong pursuit of them was to contrive a scenario in which the painted horses would desert *him*. It should come as no surprise that his farewell poem to the horses and the other creatures of his phantasmagoria invokes a fabulous procession of "circus animals" rather than his well-worn motley coat or the emperor's drunken soldiery (*VP* 629). It was, after all, the tale of a remarkable animal painter that first set him on their trail.

PART 3

WOOLF AND MANN

5

VIRGINIA WOOLF
The Passions of the Eye

How could it be that T. S. Eliot—a longtime friend who had already devoted so much of his own energy to thinking about the transformative potential of illness and passivity—did not greet with unparalleled enthusiasm Virginia Woolf's "On Being Ill" (1926), the essay that she sent to him in December 1925 and for which he had been entreating her for months? Since September he had been desperately petitioning her—"What can I have of yours? . . . Please do not fail me"—to contribute something, anything, for publication in the *Criterion*.[1] Apparently, however, when her provocative meditation on illness and the human passions arrived, he greeted it with disappointingly lukewarm enthusiasm.[2] Could it be that the essay struck too close to home? That like his early reading of a chapter from Joyce's *Ulysses,* he feared that Woolf's ideas would exert too great an influence on his own thinking? (He had admitted to her just months before, in fact, that he found *The Common Reader* [1925] particularly important for his own future work.[3]) Or could it be that the seasoned ironist simply failed to discern the gravity behind the essay's playful tone, the urgent questions about perceptivity and passive experience that make "On Being Ill" an ideal starting point for my discussion of Woolf's ideas about passion and creativity?

Woolf fires the first salvo of her mischievously earnest essay by declaring the need for a new language for sickness, one that will more adequately describe physical pain and discomfort, that will be as well suited to the raging storms of desire as to the lightning bolts of a migraine. "Yet it is not only a new language that we need, more primitive, more sensual, more obscene," she presses on, "but a new hierarchy of the passions" (*Essays* 4.319). In Woolf's mind, sickness is a passion just as powerful as vehement emotion. Both are violent energies that cause us to suffer, that "move" us against our consent, and both compel us to recognize the vulnerability of the body, the same nakedness of that remarkably foreign, material aspect of ourselves that Eliot attempts to convey by means of the etherized patient. The passions, Woolf suggests, are far from secondary phenomena that we can safely relegate to the status of accident or annoyance; they are primitive, sensual, our primary point of contact with the world. They determine how the registers and instruments of perception will absorb everything from a sunrise to a mathematical theorem. In fact, she will eventually experiment with the idea that they actually precede and condition any "I" or "world" at all. For now, she concludes her modest proposal for a new hierarchy of the passions with an equally earnest jest: "Love must be deposed in favour of a temperature of 104; jealousy give place to the pangs of sciatica; sleeplessness play the part of villain, and the hero become a white liquid with a sweet taste" (*Essays* 4.319).

The fictive dramatization of the passions that Woolf proposes—with each passion playing the leading role, villain or hero, evil stepmother or Prince Charming —is not as outrageous as it may seem, especially when we consider the deliberate combination of allegory and psychological realism, of Homeric gravity and lyric agility, that she achieved only a few years later in *The Waves* (1931). Although many of the characters in Woolf's earlier fiction embody the fragile vulnerability and intense suffering that she associates with the passions, *The Waves* is her most ambitious and most complicated attempt to dramatize passion in its most radical, frightening (and thus most promising) forms. With Woolf's aesthetic and conceptual achievement in *The Waves* as both a point of departure and the port of arrival, I would like to touch briefly upon her ideas about passion's crucial role in the formation of human personality and upon the psychological primacy that she grants it as both a mundane necessity and a creative catalyst.

Most scholars who have examined Woolf's ideas about illness, passivity, and suffering focus their attention on the value that she assigns to the recovery and recuperation of the self rather than on the upheaval or sundering that necessitates such recovery. Gesturing to her well-known claims about the artist's "shock absorbing capacity" in the late volume *A Sketch of the Past* (1939–40; 1976), they suggest that Woolf thinks about writing as a mode of psychological recovery, a way for the wounded mind to heal itself either by asserting its control or dramatizing its own fragmentation.[4] Louise Poresky, for instance, emphasizes the psychic maturation whereby the fragmented "composite self" of Woolf's early novels "consistently moves toward Selfhood, until it reaches it and understands it."[5] Those scholars who discern the gravity of passion for Woolf—the centrality of suffering to her formation as an artist and her reluctance to ignore its most threatening aspects— tend to follow one of two paths: either they reduce it to a purely linguistic phenomenon or they pathologize it by discussing it under the rubric of masochism, as a self-inflicted violence that privileges suffering only insofar as it grants the sufferer moments of clarity and creative insight.[6] Focusing primarily upon writing as a healing process risks underestimating the psychological perils that Woolf

believes to be intrinsic to the creative process. And though the concept of masochism helps us to avoid this error, it risks relegating passivity and violence to the
realm of aberrance and accident. I propose the concept of passion, in the broad
sense that I have been using in the previous chapters, as a way of avoiding these
two mistakes and of grasping the complexity of Woolf's ideas about emotion, suffering, and creativity. For her, as for Yeats and Eliot in their different ways, passion
cannot be confined to a single psychic sphere; it is neither temporary nor aberrant.
Although it only becomes fully conscious during (in Woolf's well-known for-
mula) "moments of being," it is fundamental to the way that we experience ourselves and the world around us (*Moments* 70). Woolf's passions, even more so than
Yeats's or Eliot's, are bound up with sensation and perceptivity as well as with the
simple yet threatening fact that the objects of our perception—whether visual or
imaginative—are often not under our control. I will examine how Woolf first articulates and then revises her myth of the origins of human personality in order to
situate passion at the foundation of consciousness. And I will conclude by explor-
ing how she dramatizes several possible modes of engaging passion and the aesthetic consequences of each.

ORIGINS OF PERSONALITY

The Waves is peculiar in part because we are privy to the earliest childhood emotions of its protagonists from an impossible perspective: their own. Their inchoate
minds are bombarded by the storm of experience, both threatening and thrilling,
whose violent forces shape their inner lives throughout the novel and whose
impressions Woolf reveals in a series of distinct symbolic talismans: Rhoda's white
petals floating in a basin of water, Neville's deathly apple trees, the warm water
that rushes down Bernard's back in the bath, the flickering leaves that terrify Jinny.
Over the course of the novel, each of these early psychic talismans becomes like a
wound around which each character's skin of personality grows but does not quite
heal, an open scar to which each narrator repeatedly returns in order to make sense
of his or her emotional world. They are strikingly like Yeats's painted horses or
Eliot's "glimpse over the shoulder" in this way, as structural principles of creativity and personality, or the unique frames through which the maturing mind
learns to see and imagine the world. To use a metaphor closer to Woolf's own: they
are permanent scratches on the mind's eye, indelible grooves through which light
refracts into the unique pattern and color of each character's personality. In effect,
Woolf has brought the obsessive repetitions and reiterations of the passion scene
into the novel's own field of self-consciousness, as if each of her characters were
the novel's author, struggling to discern the significance of these urgent, compelling
scenes.

Of course, these permanent scratches and grooves are precisely the sorts
of tropes that Woolf had used, over a decade before *The Waves*, when she was

beginning to sketch out her ideas about the formation of human personality and the operations of consciousness in the well-known *TLS* essay "Modern Novels" (1919): "The mind receives a myriad impressions—trivial, fantastic, evanescent, or engraved with the sharpness of steel. From all sides they come, an incessant shower of innumerable atoms, composing in their sum what we might venture to call life itself; . . . Let us record the atoms as they fall upon the mind in the order in which they fall, let us trace the pattern, however disconnected and incoherent in appearance, which each sight or incident scores upon the consciousness" (*Essays* 3.33).

Although this brief passage has provoked an incessant storm of interpretations, its metaphors of scoring and marking are still useful for my purposes, not least because they will return with even greater effect when Woolf writes more explicitly about the origins of human personality.[7] For now, it is important to remark that she conceptualizes experience primarily as passive perception; she implies that the marks of passion—the "scores" left by the violent descent of the atomic shower—become personality's most enduring attributes, despite the fact that they are the least deliberate ones. Most important, she connects these scars of passion with seeing, with those "sights" that strike within our line of vision. That is, what most defines our intellectual and emotional lives is that which happens to us, particularly that which strikes our gaze without our intention or consent. One wonders, however, whether Woolf sensed something amiss here when she returned to revise "Modern Novels" in 1925 for its inclusion in *The Common Reader.* By that time, the "hierarchy of the passions" was doubtless already on her mind, and she must have sensed that her old atomic storm does not actually upset or revolutionize that hierarchy, especially if she aims to privilege passion over all other mental faculties. Although it is diminished to the role of passive receptor, consciousness still retains its primary, normative status as the beginning and end, as essence and *arche.* If it is present to be scored, it must exist before passion, which is thus reduced again to its conventional secondary role as accident or afterthought, an epiphenomenon rather than an origin. The ancient hierarchy remains firmly in place.

In the concluding monologue of *The Waves,* Woolf again revises the earlier analogy to give it the weight of an originary myth and to bring it closer to the radical ideas about passion and personality that she had begun to develop in 1926. "But we were all different," Bernard explains: "The wax—the virginal wax that coats the spine melted in different patches for each of us. The growl of the boot-boy making love to the tweeny among the gooseberry bushes; the clothes blown out hard on the line; the dead man in the gutter; the apple tree, stark in the moonlight; the rat swarming with maggots; the luster dripping blue—our white wax was streaked and stained by each of these differently. Louis was disgusted by the nature of human flesh; Rhoda by our cruelty; Susan we could not share; Neville wanted order; Jinny love; and so on. We suffered terribly as we became separate bodies" (*Waves* 241).

In this passage Woolf still imagines experience as a violent energy that acts upon or scores us, but she also implies that consciousness and personality (our "separateness") do not precede this violence but rather are the result of it. Neither the waxy sheath nor the inner nerve that it protects can actually be said to be "conscious" until they have been irrevocably acted upon, indelibly marked.[8] The ways of thinking and feeling that make us conscious individuals emerge only from those white-hot wounds through which the world begins to filter into distinctive symbolic shapes and patterns. We recall that she hints at this implication in "On Being Ill" when she figures passion (whether it be pneumonia or love) as the primary, determining factor in how we register and perceive the world. In effect, Bernard's monologue takes up the gauntlet that Woolf's earlier essay had thrown down so definitively: the necessity for positing a new hierarchy of the passions. Passion, in this radical sense that we have seen Yeats and Eliot use ("We suffered terribly," Bernard says), is not the result of some foreign, accidental energy that afflicts an already formed organism; it is not a temporary and aberrant departure from the norm; rather, it is a constitutive element of consciousness, one that not merely affects but actually conditions how we think, feel, and perceive.

Even more important, for my purposes, is that the children themselves do not invite these energies. They do not act in a way that causes certain experiences to wound them irrevocably, others to graze the surface, and still others to leave them entirely unscathed. Instead, according to the vividly physical correlatives that Woolf uses, their minds are utterly open and vulnerable to such foundational and random violence. Though ostensibly a protective covering, the permeable wax itself possesses no defense or protection; it is suddenly and forcefully singed away, after which the exposed interior becomes the most distinguishing but also the most agonizingly sensitive of registers. Woolf explicitly connects such primal, formative moments with the persistent emotional attributes of each character, like Louis's disgust, Neville's desires, or Rhoda's fear. In this more grave hierarchy—in which passion precedes and gives birth to consciousness—the same radical passions that bring us self-awareness also influence the rest of our lives as enduring and individuating emotional traits or patterns.

AN ENORMOUS EYE

If myths are often but the back-formations of how we understand and value present experience, then Woolf's emphasis on the passion and vulnerability at the origin of human consciousness only reflects the crucial place that she accords both of these in the daily operations of the mind. In "Street Haunting: A London Adventure" (1927), a *Yale Review* essay she finished not long after "On Being Ill," she returns to fine-tune the myth once again, this time to offer an account of the passions of the mature mind as it perceives and receives the same bombardment of atomic impressions by which it was formed and scarred at its inception. When we remain in the safety of our homes, she suggests before relating her evening venture through the London streets, we are securely ensconced in habit and familiarity: "But when the door shuts on us, all that vanishes. The shell-like covering which our souls have excreted to house themselves, to make for themselves a shape distinct from others, is broken, and there is left of all these wrinkles and roughnesses a center oyster of perception, an enormous eye. . . . But after all, we are only gliding smoothly on the surface. The eye is not a miner, not a diver, not a seeker after buried treasure. It floats us smoothly down a stream; resting, pausing, the brain sleeps perhaps as it looks" (*Essays* 4.481).

The opening and closing of the door—a figure that we shall encounter again in *The Waves*—is one of the ways that Woolf allegorizes those sudden moments when we are exposed to the harshness and violence of the "not ourselves"; it is a correlative for the breaking away of the shell-like covering and the singeing of our primordial waxen skin. Just as before, the safe coating is breached, but now the exposed interior is not a receptive nerve but a perceptive eye. As before, it is not active—it neither seeks nor discovers; it suffers and receives. And the effortless gliding that Woolf describes here, though seemingly so different from the harsh violence that her earlier metaphors evoked, is only another one of the ways in which she envisions the mind encountering and engaging passion. The current of perception catches us up; it overwhelms us, and we yield to its movements, as she will say four years later in *The Waves,* like a ribbon of weed in the water.

I certainly am not alone in discerning the intriguing parallels between Woolf's oysterlike "enormous eye" and Emerson's vast, transparent eyeball from "Nature" (1836). Woolf was a devoted, if somewhat guarded, student of Emerson, and both were believers—with admittedly quite different motives—in the crucial role that perceptivity plays in the formation of human consciousness.[9] Perhaps less anticipated, though, is the connection that I would like to draw between Woolf's metaphor and T. S. Eliot's own darker version of the Emersonian transparent eye from part II of *The Waste Land:*

> The hot water at ten.
> And if it rains, a closed car at four.
> And we shall play a game of chess,
> Pressing lidless eyes and waiting for a knock upon the door.
> (*CPP* 41)

Why are these eyes "lidless" if not to emphasize the fact that they cannot close to protect themselves, that they are forced to witness whatever monstrous vision will soon knock on the door and enter? Though he likely did not intend it as such, Eliot's "lidless eye" nonetheless captures in a single, piercing phrase his longtime antipathy toward Emerson and toward the Eliot family's own roots in American Unitarianism. For Eliot, Emerson's transparent eye sees all but is not seen, roams everywhere without obstruction, danger, or limitation; it is an emblem of the transcendent, invulnerable mind, comprehending itself and its surroundings in a single, instantaneous gaze.[10] Eliot's trope, on other hand (and Woolf's as well, as we shall see) presents a vision of the body's most sensitive, fragile organ, stripped of its instinctively protective membrane. It is not transparent but opaque, material, tangible; it "touches," and more important, it can be touched.

As I have demonstrated in earlier chapters, Eliot was deeply skeptical of claims to human invulnerability, and Woolf was perhaps even more skeptical. In the concluding paragraph of her review of Emerson's *Journals* in 1910, for instance, she critiques Emerson's lack of particularity, his way of writing "as if the disembodied mind were staring at the truth" (*Essays* 1.339). For Woolf, he is a prime example of the conventional error to which she returns in "On Being Ill," the classic mistake of believing "that the body is a sheet of plain glass through which the soul looks straight and clear" (*Essays* 4.317). Both Eliot's "lidless eye" and Woolf's drifting eyeball implicitly transform Emerson's metaphor for the transcendent, perceiving mind into tropes that convey the anxious, fragile vulnerability that both modern writers associate with perception, sensation, and imagination. Like the etherized patient, these post-Emersonian eyeballs return a visceral, physical dimension to the knowing subject, an opacity that intervenes between the knower and the known, and a horrific sense of anxiety that attends that obstruction. For Eliot, as we have seen, the primary burden of the metaphor is psychological; the mind, he implies, can be frightfully vulnerable to all sorts of violent influences. Woolf shares this sense of acute psychological vulnerability—the passions of the creative "eye" are the passions of the imagination—but she departs from Eliot in keeping her metaphors closely connected to the act of visual perception, that is, in extending this susceptibility to the organ of perception itself.

Given Woolf's close relationship with Eliot, I would not be surprised to learn that the two shared a conversation about this disturbing metaphor, or that they paused knowingly at this line when he read *The Waste Land* aloud to her in 1922, before it was published.[11] But this need not have been the case for us to recognize the striking way that it captures the similarities and differences between the two writers' notions of passion and helplessness. "We cannot stiffen peaceably into glassy mounds," Woolf says later in "On Being Ill," extending the metaphor of the naked, enormous eye into uncomfortably sensitive territory: "But with the hook of life in us still we must wriggle" (*Essays* 4.322). Glassy mounds pierced by the hook of life: Are these not, as unlikely as it may seem, naked eyeballs threatened by a fisherman's hook? Organs of perception menaced, snagged, caught by that which they perceive? If this is indeed one of Woolf's particularly nightmarish passion scenes, we can expect to find it elsewhere—doggedly asserting its urgency and emotional valence over and again, perhaps even when the context strays seemingly far away from passive perception and its dangers.

One particularly striking example occurs when she pauses in the midst of the vehement political essay "The Plumage Bill" (1920) to conjure a disturbing, violent scene of mutilation and blinding. "But since we are looking at pictures," she begins, drawing attention to the simple acts of observing and perceiving, as well as to the imaginative speculations she has entertained throughout the essay: "Let us look at another which has the advantage of filling in certain blank spaces in our rough sketch of Regent Street in the morning. Let us imagine a blazing South American landscape. In the foreground a bird with a beautiful plume circles round and round as if lost or giddy. There are red holes in its head where there should be eyes" (*Diary* 2.338). Woolf is pursuing a rhetorical strategy here with clear and urgent political motivations—her aim is to shift our attention from women's desire to wear feathers to the male brutality behind the fashion—but the visceral detail and violence of the imagined scene seems to reach deeper than pathos, to tap into an emotional reservoir concerned with more than persuasion or invective. And as if the first image of the mutilated, blind bird were not enough to achieve her purpose, as if the image forced itself back to the forefront of her mind when she strayed to describe other tortured birds in its fictive proximity, Woolf returns to the scene yet again moments later: "So, if we wish to go on making pictures . . . perhaps the most unpleasant sight that we must make ourselves imagine is the sight of the bird tightly held in one hand while another hand pierces the eyeballs with a feather" (*Diary* 2.338). There are two parallel kinds of violent compulsion dramatized here. First, there are the birds themselves, who are violently acted upon and blinded. But there is also the author, whose imagination seems compelled to revisit the scene. In other words, Woolf's essay implicitly couples the compulsion to watch with another "compulsion" that makes watching impossible, that blinds the perceptive organs through which any watching might occur. The interpenetration of these two passions—one substantively creative the other negating and destructive—is an integral and enduring part of Woolf's thinking about creativity and passivity.

She returns to this unforgiving trope again in *The Waves* when, as a child, Bernard finds his imagination foisting upon him horrible scenes of vicarious danger, violence, and disgust. And as before, the content of the scenes that are forced upon his mind's eye often includes other, more literal, eyes being acted upon: "We are in a swamp now; in a malarial jungle. There is an elephant white with maggots, killed by an arrow shot dead in its eye. The bright eyes of hopping-birds—eagles, vultures —are apparent" (*Waves* 23). When Bernard is older, the vivid figure of the pierced eye from his nightmare vision returns to him when he thinks about the emotional upheaval of falling in love—the slow effect of this amorous transformation on his confident self-possession and the sticky, remarkably waxlike membrane with which he is enveloped: "Moving oneself in this radiant yet gummy atmosphere, how conscious one is of every movement—something adheres, something sticks to one's hands, taking up a newspaper even. Then there is the being eviscerated—drawn out, spun like a spider's web and twisted in agony around a thorn" (*Waves* 250).

As uncomfortable as it may seem at first, Woolf imagines these sharpened hooks and jagged thorns coming within threatening proximity of the open eye—and even piercing it, in some cases—in order to stress the awful vulnerability of the passive, perceptive faculties of both mind and body, those which are especially susceptible to injury and violence. It is as if the only way for Woolf to gauge the centrality of perception is to investigate its limits, its vulnerabilities, in a lexicon that is, as she prescribes, both primitive (Bernard's dreams) and obscene (the slaughtered birds). Her imagination is unsatisfied with stopping at the thin membrane of the cornea; it wants instead to penetrate deep into the eyeball itself, to delve mercilessly into the reflecting chamber of rod and cone cells at the physical source of our vision.

THE ARTIST'S EYE

Particularly telling are those instances in which she associates the trope not only with everyday perception but with the receptivity of the artist. When she discusses, for instance, the wild and turbulent scenes of creative frenzy that English artist B. R. Haydon describes in his memoirs, Woolf retrieves the same unmistakable metaphor to suggest that such vast pictures of agony and uproar "begin, even as he sketches them in words, to scar and wound our eyes" (*Essays* 4.410). And she calls upon it again in a similar context in *To the Lighthouse* (1927), when Lily Briscoe prepares to transfigure the landscape onto her canvas: "the mass loomed before her; it protruded; she felt it pressing on her eyeballs" (*Lighthouse* 159). Woolf could have written that Haydon's pictures "strike" or "dazzle" our eyes, and that the scene pressed upon Lily's "mind" or even upon her "eyes" rather than the brutally physical "eyeballs." Instead the vulnerable eyeball has become for her a talisman, an artistic shorthand of sorts; its wounding is another modernist passion scene, a scenario that thematizes passive suffering while itself seeming to be the product of an analogous imaginative passivity or compulsion. In both of these instances—addressing the fictional Lily and the historical Haydon—it is a way for her to connect the creative potential of the artist's perceptions with the potentially debilitating pain and violence that those perceptions may bring, both to the artist and to ourselves.

If we step back from these visceral metaphors for a moment, we'll see that what Woolf wants to emphasize here is the double-edged sword of passive perception, whether it be sensory, emotional, or imaginative. Perceptivity demands a degree of openness, she implies; it obligates us to open and direct the receptive organs toward their objects, always a risky gambit when those objects are beyond

our control, even outside of our awareness. One gazes into the extraordinary spec-
tacle of a solar eclipse, for instance, only at the peril of permanently damaging the
eye and thus risking the physical capacity of ever witnessing the scene again. In the
same way, when an artist invites a spirit of memory or a phantasm of the imagination, or when she simply opens wide her eyes toward what Woolf calls in 1920
"the flux and fury of [her] impressions," she does so knowing that they may become, without warning, the ghostly nightmares of the waking mind, or the sharpened, ruthlessly indifferent objects of her gaze (*Essays* 3.205). And who is to say,
Woolf implies, that they will vanish as quickly as they appeared? They could turn
out to be more than motes to trouble the mind's eye. In short, the conclusion that
Woolf reaches with these metaphors of openness, nakedness, and violence is this:
The same vivid spectacles that enthrall the perceiving mind and compel its creative energies may also become the sources of its most vicious pain and injury. The
objects of perception, that is, may assume a frighteningly forceful agency, one to
which the modern artist must passively attune herself despite the dangers. Or to
choose terms perhaps closer to her own, the act of seeing demands that the artist
risk the mutilation and debilitation of her own eyes.

A willingness to confront this demand is something that Woolf found lacking
in Henry James, an insistent objection to her master's preternatural ability to gather
and sift his impressions. Reviewing a volume of James's letters for the *TLS* on 8
April 1920, Woolf calls him with admiration "a spectator, alert, aloof, endlessly
interested, endlessly observant" (*Essays* 3.201). Only an artist such as he, she imagines, could leave the insulated quiet and dark interior of a European cathedral and,
upon plunging into the midafternoon streets of a crowded, frantic city, maintain
an alertness and receptivity strong and particular enough to record the onslaught
of his perceptions with such cunning and accuracy (this tableaux, with which
she opens the review, bears a remarkable resemblance to the street scene in the
later essay "Street Haunting"). And yet this aloofness, this capacity to remain
"inscrutable, silent, and assured," has the effect of cloistering the novelist from
the violent swarm of impressions that he so faithfully transcribes (*Essays* 3.201).
We miss in James, she implies, the same thing that is lacking in Emerson: "What
we miss, perhaps, is any body of resistance to the impression—any warrant for
thinking that the perceiving mind is other than a stretched white sheet" (*Essays*
3.199). Instead of registering the anxious apprehension with which the material
eye both invites and defends itself against the myriad objects of perception vying
for its attention, James's style seems the product of an "alien in our midst," of a
"'solid and fixed and dense'" organ of reception as opposed to the quivering, exposed, intimately vulnerable eye with which her own artist-characters struggle
(*Essays* 3.205).

I cannot agree with Albright's contention that Woolf's exposed eyeball, in contrast to her raw nerve, "is not at all passive or reticent; it changes form, shuts its

lids, clouds itself with tears, hallucinates and storms."[12] All of these activities except the second are passive, largely involuntary, phenomena, and for Woolf, the artist must *not* shut her eyelids; the passive vulnerability of the naked eye is what makes the creative act so particular, so contingent, and so faithful to the objects of its vision. As Lily Briscoe asks urgently in *To the Lighthouse*, "Could things thrust their hands up and grip one; could the blade cut? The fist grasp? Was there no safety?" (*Lighthouse* 180). For Woolf, James never exposed himself to the blade to see if, in fact, it could cut; he kept himself always at a safe distance. She implies that even in moments of the highest imaginative intensity and apparent self-possession—when the creative "fist" seems most tightly clenched, as in James—the artist must recognize the presence of those energies that threaten to dissolve her creativity altogether, to ruin the perceptive faculties by which she defines herself.[13] When Woolf returns to James less than a year later, she admits that his penchant for ghost stories "removes the shocks and buffetings of experience" (*Essays* 3.320). Under the constant onslaught of these buffetings, she says, "the door must open; the hour must strike"; but in the dreamworld of James's fiction, "the door need not open; the clock need not strike" (*Essays* 3.321). In short, the Jamesian artist's mind need not open itself to suffering; it can keep its keen observations above the violent tussle and fray that Woolf found so full of both psychological danger and creative potential.

THE PASSIONS AND *THE WAVES*

In the essay with which I began this chapter, Woolf suggests that passion is not unlike a magician; whether in the form of physical illness or emotional turmoil, it "plays the same old tricks" (*Essays* 4.318). Her list of these peculiar tricks, appropriately enough, reads like a primer on the multiple faculties of the literary imagination: investing mundane creatures with divinity; working the mind into a frenzy of creative anticipation and anxiety; and wreathing around one's absent friends "thousands of legends and romances" in which the healthy mind simply would not indulge (*Essays* 4.318). She implies, that is, that passion's tricks are the wellsprings of fiction. For Woolf, passion is always intimately connected with the creative origins of art, with those elaborate tales and legends that the "healthy" mind might otherwise shun. Woolf knows, however, that art is not a one-person show with passion in the lead role as the magician extraordinaire. The artist must have a hand in the production; she must, Woolf implies, be like the volunteer from the audience who submits to being marvelously beheaded or sawed into sections on stage, to being acted upon by the magician. In short, the artist must find a response to passion that brings its tumultuous energies to creative fruition without ignoring its more dangerous, threatening potential.

Woolf's most vivid performance of the possible artistic modes of engaging passion—and the two corresponding states of literary creativity that result—occurs in *The Waves* with the characters Rhoda and Jinny. To an even greater degree than the rest, these two women feel and perceive their experiences as a raging storm akin to the shower of innumerable atoms that Woolf had borrowed from Pater in her earlier fables of personality. They are, in this way, the novel's most sensitive and reliable registers of passion. And recalling Woolf's own admission in response to a 1931 *Times* review of the novel—"Odd, that they (*The Times*) shd. praise my characters when I meant to have none"—I think that we can safely read them as both fictional personae and principles of mental states or aspects of mind (*Diary* 4.47).[14] In a single, crucial scene of *The Waves*—while all of the friends are at a restaurant awaiting the arrival of Percival—Woolf allows us to witness both women's very different responses to the same experiential storm. Or in terms of the ocular tropes that I have traced so far, one woman glides effortlessly like the enormous eyeball from "Street Haunting" (the creative mind in the ecstasy of surrender and submission) while the other is horribly pinned and pierced as if by thorns, arrows, or the sharpened end of a plume (the same creative mind registering passivity's more dangerous, threatening potential). When Jinny enters the restaurant, she becomes immediately and sensuously aware of this groundswell of movement and of her passive, receptive place in it:

> I slide easily on smooth-polished floors. I now begin to unfurl, in this scent, in this radiance, as a fern when its leaves unfurl. . . . I feel a thousand capacities spring up in me. I am arch, gay, languid, melancholy by turns. I am rooted, but I flow. All gold, flowing that way, I say to this one, "Come." Rippling black, I say to that one, "No." One breaks off from his station under the glass cabinet. He approaches. He makes towards me. This is the most exciting moment I have ever known. I flutter. I ripple. I stream like a plant in the river, flowing this way, flowing that way, but rooted, so that he may come to me. "Come," I say, "come." . . . Now with a little jerk, like a limpet broken from a rock, I am broken off: I fall with him; I am carried off. We yield to this slow flood. (*Waves* 105)

This is Woolf's most compelling vision of surrender and of the riches that passion can offer the imaginative artist. Like the enormous eye that floated passively along the stream of the London streets, Jinny's lithe, rippling body—which becomes surreal in Woolf's depiction of its liquidity and dissolution—yields to the affective and erotic energies that sweep past and consume her. She embodies, with her lightly rooted sweeps and flutters, the perceiving imagination—primitive and sensual—as it gives in to the tidal sway of its objects of vision. Woolf emphasizes the ambivalent eroticism and intensity of this moment—what she calls "the terror, the exaltation"—several years later in "The Moment: Summer's Night," in which she returns to the metaphors she had used to evoke Jinny's passivity and to the ocular tropes she has developed in the context of vision and vulnerability, now lending them a fiery sensation of burning to match their earlier connotations of pain and sensitivity: "to be consumed; to be swept away; to become a rider on the random wind; the tossing wind; the trampling and neighing wind; . . . to be part of the eyeless dark, to be rippling and streaming, to feel the glory of molten run up the spine, down the limbs, making the eyes glow, burning, bright, and penetrating the buffeting waves of the wind" (*The Moment* 8).

The molten lava that coats the spine (an offshoot of the earlier trope, the fiery atomic storm) makes its way directly to the eye, emphasizing the connection between seeing and being "swept away," rippling and streaming in the paradoxically eyeless dark. When the artist submits herself passively to such energies, Woolf observes, the eye is no longer pierced but glowing, no longer twisted in agony around a thorn but now bright and burning with vision. She recounts an identical experience in a 1928 diary entry, when she admits to allowing herself to be overpowered by the objects of her vision: "The look of things has a great power over me now," she writes, "so vivid to my eyes, & not only to my eyes: also to some nervous fibre or fanlike membrane in my spine" (*Diary* 3.191).

Elsewhere, Woolf wonders whether this kind of sensuous, conscious passivity might be the only authentic mode of experiencing the self. She asks whether its ambivalent sense of release and fear might not bring to realization something fundamental about artistic creativity and about the chameleon self, which "is neither this nor that, neither here nor there, but something so varied and wandering that it is only when we give rein to its wishes and let it take its way unimpeded that we are indeed ourselves" (*Essays* 4.486). We find her answer, at least one half of it, in Jinny's intense awareness of the passivity of her own rippling, streaming body. She is most herself, Woolf implies, when her "self" is swept away.

On an aesthetic level, Jinny is not unlike the figure of Fergus in Yeats's "Fergus and the Druid": Her passivity allows her to be transformed by the transforming shapes of the creative mind. Just as Fergus does, she runs the gamut of physical and emotional transformations; she is by turns "arch, gay, languid, melancholy"; she ripples in one direction, resists, and streams in another; she is not the locus of a single identity but rather the font of "a thousand capacities," each of which might find realization in the endless permutations of her movements. And in the passage that directly follows the one above, Woolf makes the artistic value of this creative passivity daringly clear: "Just behind my shoulder-blades some dry thing, wide-eyed, gently closes, gradually lulls itself to sleep. This is rapture; this is relief. The bar at the back of my throat lowers itself. Words crowd and cluster and push forth one on top of another. It does not matter which. They jostle and mount on each other's shoulders. The single and solitary mate, tumble and become many. It does not matter what I say. Crowding, like a fluttering bird, one sentence crosses the empty space between us" (*Waves* 105). In this passage, Woolf brings Jinny's significance as a double for the writer into the foreground; her experience dramatizes

with apposite urgency and excitement the effortless, un-meditated flood of words
that the writer enjoys in moments of creative inspiration. Perhaps as a result of
Woolf's tremendous sense of craftsmanship and artifice, we tend to forget that she
was as much a disciple of the Muse as she was an apprentice of the Masters. Jinny's
"rapture and relief" is the writer's rapture as well, when the anxious coaxing and
conniving of the technician give way to the free, unimpeded proclamations of the
oracle.

Not long after *The Waves* was first published, Woolf repeatedly chose the same
terms while composing the essays on Elizabethan literature and culture that would
eventually preface *The Common Reader: Second Series* (1932). There she uses Jinny's
crowding, fluttering birds to liken certain inspired portions of Sidney's *Countess
of Pembroke's Arcadia* to an "unformed babble of sound," "a chorus of intoxicated
voices singing madly like birds round the house before anyone is up" (*CR2* 44).
Similarly in Donne she points to the hurried, crowded "clipping and curtailing,
this abrupt heaping of thought on thought" that seems to imply that his "words
had urged him on too fast for grace or clarity" (*CR2* 25). She concludes that in the
midst of rapturous ecstasies of this sort, in which the spine is bathed in molten
lava, "lines of pure poetry suddenly flow as if liquefied by a great heat" (*CR2* 32).

In fact, it is precisely these terms that Woolf uses in "Letter to a Young Poet"
(1932), published in the *Yale Review* only one year after *The Waves,* to describe the
condition of the inspired poet. When inspiration reaches its highest, most rhythmic, pitch, she suggests, "the self offers no impediment; self joins in the dance; self
lends itself to the rhythm" (*Moth* 217). She concludes: "All you need now is to stand
at the window and let your rhythmical sense open and shut, open and shut, boldly
and freely, until one thing melts in another, until the taxis are dancing with the
daffodils, until a whole has been made from all of these separate fragments" (*Moth*
221). It is altogether fitting, in this letter about the art of poetry in particular, that
a taxi rather than the sublime Wordsworthian Self should be the one dancing with
the daffodils. In such a state, Woolf's post-Romantic aesthetic theory implies, the
self enjoys no spiritual enlargement from its creative sympathies; it is, in its most
intensely imaginative moments, barely even there to register them.

With this passage in mind, perhaps it will now be clear why the opening and
closing door holds so much figural weight for her—why it recurs at such crucial
moments in her essays on Henry James, in "Street Haunting," and in the restaurant scene of *The Waves*. Why, in fact, the gesture of opening and closing occurs
no less than ten times in *The Waves* as a whole: "The door is opening and shutting" (101); "a summer door will open and shut, will keep opening and shutting"
(156); "I move from dawn to dusk opening and shutting" (173); "Opening, shutting;
shutting, opening" (261). The insistent opening-closing movement aims to capture
both the fearful mind as it opens toward the atomic storm of experience and the
exhilarated imagination as it yields itself to the pulsing rhythm of creativity, as it

disperses and dissolves into the objects of its attention. Woolf invokes the same rhythmic surrender in *To the Lighthouse*, when Lily Briscoe experiences the rapture of inspiration before her canvas, her paintbrush suddenly beginning to move "as if it had fallen in with some rhythm which was dictated to her . . . by what she saw, so that while her hand quivered with life, this rhythm was strong enough to bear her along with it on its current" (*Lighthouse* 159). Like those of Lily's brush, the movements of Jinny's fluttering, rippling body are "dictated" by the forces that move her from without, by the rhythmic waves of the slow flood to which she willingly yields.[15]

"The door opens. The door goes on opening," Jinny excitedly proclaims, emboldened by the rhythmic, creative power she discovers in the act of surrender. "Here is my risk, here is my adventure" (*Waves* 105). However, as Woolf takes great pains to remind us—often through visceral scenes of mutilation and blinding—the swinging door through which we enter into the atomic storm of experience always holds another, less ecstatic, valence. The oracle always runs the risk of becoming the vulnerable, passive victim of madness. And in the passage immediately following Jinny's rapturous transformations, one is reminded once again of the ambivalence that Woolf so terribly conveys elsewhere with tropes of physical wounding and vulnerability. "The door opens," Rhoda repeats fearfully, altering the syntax of Jinny's rhythmic incantations to a fearful stutter, "the tiger leaps . . . terror rushes in; terror upon terror, pursuing me":

> I am thrust back to stand burning in this clumsy, this ill fitting body, to receive the shafts of his indifference, and his scorn, I who long for marble columns and pools on the other side of the world where the swallow dips her wings. . . . But I am fixed here to listen. An immense pressure is on me. I cannot move without dislodging the weight of centuries. A million arrows pierce me. Scorn and ridicule pierce me. I, who could beat my breast against the storm and let the hail choke me joyfully, am pinned down here; am exposed. The tiger leaps. Tongues with their whips are upon me. Mobile, incessant, they flicker over me. I must prevaricate and fence them off with lies. What amulet is there against this disaster? (*Waves* 105)

Rhoda's excruciating monologue dramatizes the other side of passion, the side that Woolf repeatedly attempted to articulate through her myth of the waxen shell and the raw, aching nerve left exposed by the slings and arrows of early experiences, by the very atomic storm that she now recaptures more solidly in Rhoda's references to storm and hail. The piercing arrows of scorn and indifference that she suffers hearken forward to Woolf's characterization of Samuel Taylor Coleridge (in a review that appeared in the *New Statesman* in 1940), whose extreme affective sensitivity, she writes, made him "a passive target for innumerable arrows, all of them sharp, many of them poisoned" (*Moth* 105). And they recall as well the

heightened sense of pain and vulnerability that she invokes in "The Moment,"
when she imagines plunging into the unbearable darkness (through yet another of
her familiar doorways): "The dark has stripped the fledge from the arrow—the
vibrations that rise red shiver as it passes through us" (*The Moment* 8). In Rhoda's
nightmare of passivity, the enormous perceiving eye is opened wide to the arrows,
thorns, and needles of experience; it writhes and winces, but the lid does not close.

If Jinny emblematizes the exciting sense of creative possibility with which mind
yields and bends to the imagination's autonomous energies, the abandon with
which it surrenders itself even to the point of dissolution, Rhoda embodies all of
the awful daring (in Eliot's phrase) of that passivity. Like Eliot's Prufrock or his
Saint Narcissus, she is "fixed," "pinned," "pierced," and perhaps worst of all—like
the agonizingly vulnerable eye of Woolf's earlier essays—she is "naked" and "exposed." While Woolf gives Jinny the freedom, force, and vitality of the first-person
singular ("I flutter," "I ripple," "I stream"), she saves for Rhoda the language of the
sufferer. Rhoda's way, then, is an alternative response to passion; or perhaps we
might better say the synchronic response—one half of the simultaneous attraction
and repulsion, Woolf implies, that characterizes our psychological experience when
faced with an overwhelming energy that we can neither control nor contain.

Rhoda's anxious response, however, is no less a mode of creativity than Jinny's
rapturous one. In fact, the product of Rhoda's response involves what Woolf often
admits to be the most challenging, daunting task of the artist: the slow, hesitating,
deliberate search for the right words. "I am not composed enough to make even
one sentence," Rhoda admits. "What I say is perpetually contradicted":

> Jinny rides like a gull on the wave, dealing her looks adroitly here and there,
> saying this, saying that, with truth. But I lie; I prevaricate.
>
> Alone, I rock my basins; I am mistress of my fleet of ships. But here, twist-
> ing the tassels of this brocaded curtain in my hostess's window, I am broken
> into separate pieces; I am no longer one . . . I doubt; I tremble; I see the wild
> thorn tree shake its shadow in the desert. (*Waves* 106–7)

Rhoda's direct reference to Jinny explicitly frames the contrast between them, and
her allusion to the wild thorn tree marks the return of that fearful vulnerability
that Woolf so compellingly captured in her essays the year before (and which Bernard echoes with his mention of the "spider's web . . . twisted in agony around a
thorn" [*Waves* 250]). But accompanying this fear, perhaps even propelled by it, are
the careful, calculated, and "deceitful" fabrications of the novelist. As Woolf knew
painfully well, novels rarely spring fully formed from the writer's head; however
much the artist must yield herself to her visions, surrender alone will not suffice
to amass and assemble that most cunning prevarication of all, the sustained and
finished work of fiction. Rhoda's ordeal, like Jinny's, is also the passion of the

artist. In Rhoda's hesitant, calculated response, Woolf dramatizes the necessarily intentional and deliberate choices of the active imagination as it attempts to confront, manage, and structure its overwhelming visions into a legible form.

SHOCKS AND CONCLUSIONS

Isn't Rhoda's response, in fact, but one half of the same dichotomy that Woolf had discovered years before, in her own creative process when she was writing *To the Lighthouse?* That book, she remarks, seemed to come together with "dashing fluency"—"Why am I so flown with words," she asks herself in a diary entry, "& apparently free to do exactly what I like?"—in comparison to the "excruciating hard wrung battles" she experienced when composing *Mrs. Dalloway (Diary* 3.76)?[16] It is Jinny's rapturous state that she foresees when she admires, two years later, the seeming effortlessness of Shakespeare's language in *Othello,* what she calls "the volley & volume & tumble of his words," the creative passion wherein the mind "tumbles and splashes" in a language of sound and delight (*Diary* 3.182). But it is the spirit of Rhoda's intricate lies and elaborate prevarications that animates her severe self-admonition, written around the same time, that "the perfect artist would revoke & rewrite & polish—infinitely" (*Diary* 3.181). Woolf's firsthand experience of the disconcerting shifts between states of effortless inspiration and periods of intense artistic struggle helped her to discover what she would later formulate with such dramatic elegance and subtlety in *The Waves:* not only the fact that the artistic mind must learn to operate on both levels, but that its modes of creativity are utterly beyond the artist's power to control. In short, that writing, like insomnia or fever, is a passion to be suffered.

Perhaps Woolf's most shrewd observation, though—in this new hierarchy of the passions, this vibrant and strikingly physical allegory of the creative process—is that both Jinny and Rhoda arrive at the same end. "I am to be broken," Rhoda recognizes with a Sophoclean clarity. "I am to be cast up and down among these men and women, with their twitching faces, with their lying tongues, like a cork on the rough sea. Like a ribbon of weed I am flung far every time the door opens. The wave breaks. I am the foam that sweeps and fills the uttermost rims of the rocks with whiteness. I am also a girl, here in this room" (*Waves* 107).

As with Jinny, who so boldly and ecstatically suffered the imagination's self-dispersal, its dissolution into the variegated objects of its attention, so too Rhoda undergoes a figurative dissipation; she breaks into a spray of foam upon the shore, is dispersed among the same atomic shower that accosts her. To label Rhoda's fate, as one scholar does, "a dispersal of the self of pathological proportions" is to miss the complementary place that it holds in Woolf's allegory of creativity; Rhoda is not unique.[17] Despite their widely differing responses, the ultimate similarity of the two women is unmistakable: Jinny becomes "a plant in the river," finally broken off and floating; Rhoda "a ribbon of weed," tossed and flung amid the crashing waves. We might say that both have succumbed to what one critic calls Woolf's desire "to dissolve all individuality and sink into a deathlike trance," but this is accurate only if we immediately add that the trance is also paradoxically productive, positive, and substantive, with unexpected and illuminating aesthetic consequences.[18] This is precisely the moment for which the artist, in Woolf's eyes, always strives.

It should be clear now that the insights into suffering and passivity that Woolf articulates so lucidly in *A Sketch of the Past* are but late reverberations, aftershocks, of the concerns with passion and powerlessness with which she had struggled for years. We can now understand, for instance, why she suggests that during those "moments of being" that constitute her earliest memories, she claims to have been "hardly aware of myself, but only of the sensation. I [was] only the container of the feeling of ecstasy" (*Moments* 67). It is because, according to Woolf's late theories of passion and conscious personality, there was as yet no "myself" to remember; in her eyes, the self emerged only with the "violent gusts of passion" that seemed to her, upon reflection, at once so threatening and so exhilarating (*Moments* 58). The phrasing in *A Sketch of the Past* may be new, but the idea certainly is not; it is implicit, as we have seen, in her early myths of personality and the atomic storm of experience. Whether they are positive or negative—her recollection of the flowers at St. Ives or her memory of being hit by her brother—each of these early impressions gave her a sense not of identity or self-sufficiency but of her own powerlessness, of emotional horror or physical collapse: "they seemed dominant," she recalls, "myself passive" (*Moments* 72). Even her well-known theory of the artist's passivity—as she puts it, "the shock-receiving capacity is what makes me a writer"—assumes a seemingly autonomous agency. The idea itself, she says, asserts a dominance before which she senses herself not the thinker but the vessel of thought: "This intuition of mine—it is so instinctive that it seems given to me, not made by me" (*Moments* 72).

With the highly conscious, self-reflexive account of passion and creativity in *A Sketch of the Past,* Woolf brings her new hierarchy of the passions to completion. What began as a myth of the origins of human consciousness becomes, by the time of *The Waves,* a statement of artistic creation, an appraisal of passion's crucial role in not only the ways that we experience the world and each other but also the ways that art transforms those experiences into meaningful patterns without eliding the fear, exhilaration, and intense vulnerability that accompany them. Woolf's vision of the artist's voluntary dissolution, embodied most poignantly in Jinny and Rhoda, is a version of modernist impersonality rooted not in detachment or aloofness, but in the intimate and personal experiences of weakness and powerlessness. Her enormous eyeball—now floating effortlessly along the current of experience, now veering toward the thorns of passive perception—is one of the most compelling modernist figures for the emotional and psychological stakes of what was once called negative capability, as well as for the fragile tension that the modern artist must sustain between the self-possession of action and the awful daring of allowing oneself to be acted upon.

6

THOMAS MANN

The Infectious Passions

In a well-known retrospective lecture given late in his life, Thomas Mann offers a succinct formulation of a motif that appears prominently in *Death in Venice* (1912) and that became, over the course of his sixty-year career, a constant point of return and a reliable source of creative energy and innovation: "Again my theme was the devastating invasion of passion, the destruction of a formed, apparently conclusively mastered life, which is degraded by the strange god."[1] Germany's disastrous political trajectory had been foremost in Mann's mind for over a decade by the time he composed the autobiographical lecture "On Myself" in 1940. With the results of what he viewed as the anti-intellectual frenzies of National Socialism becoming quite apparent, it is no surprise that Mann should retrospectively describe how passion operates in his earliest work in terms fraught with military connotations. Nor should it surprise us that, despite his long-held and complex ambivalence toward passivity and the daemonic, Mann should refuse to entertain the possibility that passion might produce other than devastating, destructive, or degrading effects.

For those familiar with any of Mann's major works, however, the language of invasion, infiltration, and internal destruction holds another, even more familiar valence: the bodily, the pathological, that which pertains to the invasion of a living organism by a foreign agent of infection (the "strange god"). In contrast to Yeats's psychological phantasms, Eliot's ether, or even Woolf's subatomic storm—all of which hinge on the occult, the spiritual, or a particularity so magnified that it becomes abstract—Mann's metaphors for the agents of passion always pertain to the human body: the infectious and the microscopic, the hidden organisms that secretively decay and corrupt the inner organs until the body finally succumbs to their overpowering forces. But like the other modernist writers whom I have examined, he also discerns the infectious passions' awful, daring potential as imaginative catalysts. The artist, he claims in "Goethe and Tolstoy" (1921), is never "normal, healthy, and according to rule." He is instead prone to disease and irritability; just as with his early protagonist who suffers the invasion of a "strange" or "foreign god," there is in the artist's physical constitution "always something foreign to the average man, affecting him uncannily" (*Essays* 152).

Under the unforgiving lens of Mann's artistic microscope, the passions become radically materialistic; they are transposed from the neuroses of mind to the neurons of the brain, from the breath of the spirit to the oxygen in the bloodstream. We sense them in the Blakean pulsation of an artery, or as Mann puts it in the early story "A Weary Hour" (1905), in the pulse of the blood and the corresponding pulse of the mind: "the rhythm of the blood, where thought [is] engendered" and "rhythmical urge of the creative force towards matter" (*Stories* 355, 361). For Mann, physical illness is not merely a metaphor for psychological suffering, whether emotional or creative; rather, the bodily and the psychological are intimately connected under the broader philosophical category of passion, which is expansive enough to include both the onset of an infectious disease and a fit of artistic inspiration. Perhaps because of what one scholar calls Mann's "personal mistrust of passion as such," or perhaps because he believed the body's organic processes to be so much more intimate, more inescapable, than the mind's impersonal movements, this transposition brings with it intensified dramatizations of shame, repulsion, and self-disgust.[2] It is accompanied by the horrid conviction (buttressed by Aristotelian philosophy, his protagonists hasten to add) that passion-as-disease only afflicts those who invite it, those whose bodies are already predisposed to corruption and infection.

My aim here is to remark the implications that Mann's materialization of passion possesses for the scheme that I have outlined thus far by charting the striking changes in his view of the relationship between passion and creativity from *Death in Venice* to *The Magic Mountain* (1924) and *Doctor Faustus* (1947). I can approach Mann's works only in translation, and I am undoubtedly slighting the later novels by devoting as much attention to them as I do to his brief essays and stories; I hope, however, to justify both of these decisions by hewing to a single, pervasive question throughout. If the passions are daemonic, Mann asks, how can we account for their creative potential without also exposing the mind to their potential for political and psychological devastation? How can the mind rightly esteem its rational faculties—faculties which, for Mann, grow increasingly important in their role as defenses against political aggression—without reducing the passions to arbiters of shame, corruption, or degradation? In the attempt to respond to these questions, he develops an idiosyncratic narrative strategy, one that uses techniques of delay and disabuse to re-create the belated discovery of passion's "invasion." Understanding this strategy is the first step in gauging Mann's ambivalence toward passion and its alternately creative and destructive potential.

The final step is attending to his mature portrayals of passion as a catalyst for substantive artistic creation, for the embodiment of its mundane and clairvoyant energies in concrete and enduring aesthetic forms.

DELAYED IN VENICE

According to Mann's comments in "On Myself," *Death in Venice* is not about the breakdown of the elderly philosopher Gustave Aschenbach's aura of control and serenity but about the revelation of its hollowness; that is, it is not a narrative of tragic descent but one of disabuse. We should not underestimate the implications of this distinction. The novella seems to begin in control and containment and slowly, almost imperceptibly, progress toward frenzy and contagion, a descent which leads most scholars to postulate a turning point or "hinge" upon which Aschenbach's tragic deformation turns.[3] In the terms with which Mann outlines the trajectory in his working notes, the question we apparently face is this: at what point does the "temporary disturbance of psychological balance" that afflicts Gustave Aschenbach upon his arrival in Venice (or perhaps before then) transform into "a state of the overwhelming of the self-conscious spirit, a state of possession by foreign powers?" (*Venice* 72).[4] Is it the bizarre "horror" and "passion" that Aschenbach feels after his chance encounter with the red-haired stranger at the outset of the story (5)? The uncontrollable shiver of disgust (a detail that returns with vehemence in the later novels as well) with which he reacts to the drunken fop aboard the ferry and which he experiences as a sickening mental distortion that "would spread if he did not put a stop to it" (15)? Or is it rather the moment when, after the young boy Tadzio smiles at him directly—offering him a salutation not altogether unlike those that feature prominently in troubadour love lyrics— Aschenbach suffers a physical collapse under the immense pressure of his frenzied desire and longing, a state of delirious exhaustion that returns later in the story with sinister literality once the Asiatic cholera has invaded his blood and begun to corrupt him from within?

> He who had been the recipient of this smile rushed away with it as if it were a gift heavy with destiny. He was so thoroughly shaken that he was forced to flee the light of the terrace and the front garden and to seek with hasty tread the darkness of the park in the rear. Strangely indignant and tender exhortations broke forth from him: "You must not smile so! Listen, no one is allowed to smile that way at anyone!" He threw himself on a bench; he breathed in the nocturnal fragrance of the plants, beside himself. Leaning back with his arms hanging at his sides, overpowered and shivering uncontrollably, he whispered the eternal formula of longing—impossible under these conditions, absurd, reviled, ridiculous, and yet holy and venerable even under these conditions— "I love you!" (44)

In the terms with which I have explored modernist passion thus far, Aschenbach is the recipient, the acted upon, the patient; he spirals into helplessness and paralysis, seemingly propelled by a force outside of himself and not at his command. The uncharacteristic proclamation of love breaks forth from his lips involuntarily, as if the words themselves hastened to expose the intensely shame-filled mental state that they would otherwise zealously keep hidden. Immediately after his collapse—the timing is essential—the narrator reveals the first, vague hints of the imminent epidemic, which has by this time (like Aschenbach's own worsening state) already silently and imperceptibly begun its invasion of the city: "In the fourth week of his stay on the Lido Gustav Aschenbach made a number of disturbing discoveries regarding the events in the outside world. . . . The German papers mentioned rumors, cited highly varying figures, quoted official denials" (*Venice* 44–5).

We are accustomed to understanding this transition as the moment when the novella's allegorical dual-focus snaps into alignment, bringing together the slow degradation of the protagonist with the gradual spread of Asiatic cholera through Venice. The city and the man, that is, begin to reveal their oneness. What interests me, however, is the mechanism of the delay itself, its psychological effects in *Death in Venice,* and its implications for Mann's later work. In the words of one critic: "As with so much surrounding the question of irony, everything depends on what we know and when we know it."[5] If Mann had wanted to invoke the classical model of tragedy, even in the name of parody, he could easily have allowed us to watch knowingly as the epidemic first entered and slowly ravaged the city; he could even have remarked upon Aschenbach's ignorance of it. That he chose not to, that the cholera is irreversible and widespread by the time we discover (alongside the protagonist) its presence, tells us something important about Aschenbach's earliest state, and about the affective purposes that prompted Mann to make this narrative decision. From the evidence in his preparatory notes—which include page upon page of detailed information about the Asiatic cholera transcribed from a medical manual—we know that Mann was obsessed with the specific ways in which the body harbors the disease unknowingly. Frightening enough is the fact that the initial symptoms may resemble little more than a case of food poisoning. But after detailing the ghastly physical breakdown that eventually follows, he notes with the detachment of a physician that "often, however, the warning signals don't appear; it begins in a flash" (*Venice* 84). In the novella he translates this informal observation with a characteristically quick stroke: "It sometimes happened that a few lucky ones suffered only a mild discomfort followed by a loss of consciousness from which they would never again, or only rarely, awaken" (54).

None of Mann's protagonists recognize what he himself clearly knew and meditated upon at length: the absence of warning signals does not mean the absence of disease. What caught his attention while he was composing *Death in*

Venice—and what holds sway over his imagination for the many years that pass before the composition of "The Black Swan" (1953), in which a strikingly similar scenario unfolds—is the fact that the "microscopic agitators" of disease may grow and thrive unsuspected, having discovered the ideal, fertile conditions for infection.[6] For Aschenbach, as later for Leverkühn's harrowing narrative of delay and disabuse in *Doctor Faustus*, the discovery is always too late. The most seemingly healthy person, even he who secretly rejoices at the total absence of symptoms or physical hints, may fall victim suddenly to this quick, fatal affliction. Even if Mann himself was not prey to hypochondria (and all accounts indicate that he was), this is a remarkably piercing analysis of the hypochondriac's worst fears. Thus he describes, with an eye toward his protagonist, the city's intrinsic vulnerability to the illness: "The early arrival of summer's heat made a lukewarm broth of water in the canals and thus made conditions for the disease's spread particularly favorable. It seemed as though the pestilence had been reinvigorated, as if the tenacity and fecundity of the microscopic agitators had been redoubled" (*Venice* 54).

The cholera may infect any city that its microscopic agitators choose to invade, but some cities, it seems, demonstrate a more fragile vulnerability to it than others. According to the psychological allegory of the novella, this means that some minds "invite" the degradation and corruption of passion more than others. Or, more accurately, it means that Mann always holds open the possibility of this natural invitation to disease and decay; he repeatedly dramatizes the intense, crippling shame of a mind that suspects itself somehow intrinsically corrupt and more prone to degradation than others. And it means that despite the apparent self-control and possession that Aschenbach displays at the story's beginning, and despite his seemingly *gradual* descent into illness and depravity, he is in some way the "unnerved, shattered, a powerless victim of the demon" even from the time the novella opens (57).[7] It is precisely this knowledge—hidden by the speaker under a veil of impenetrable fear, self-doubt, and self-disgust—that helps to account for the aura of ominous, symbolic portent that surrounds his early encounters.

The "demon" to whom Aschenbach falls victim not only harkens forward to the daemonic possession of the composer Adrian Leverkühn in *Doctor Faustus* but also recalls the Platonic arbiter of inspiration and creativity that so captured Yeats's imagination, the Daemon. In fact, the working notes for *Death in Venice* reveal that the relationship between Plato's daemonic inspiration and Aschenbach's debilitating sickness were a conscious part of Mann's original plan for the novel.[8] But, in Mann's early novella, this kind of demonic visitation, so rich with creative energy and potential that Yeats was compelled time and again to envision it as the primal origin of his art, issues in no realization of artistic form for its visitant. The protagonist writes no treatise on the subject, no poem to memorialize it, and no musical composition to transfigure it. The only issue of his erotically inspired state, we are told, is "a page and a half of choice prose," which (although apparently laden with feeling and nobility of style) does not capture its object at all but merely speculates on "a certain great and burning problem of culture and taste" (*Venice* 38). The irony here implies not sublimation but mere extravagant overstatement of the topic's importance and the writer's grandiosity. The "possession" of Aschenbach—and thus, Mann implies, of all artists who wait upon the whims of inspiration—is but a fraud, an agent for the destruction of the very mental faculties that it promises to exalt and enlighten. Surrender to this demon brings no artistic virtue; it is merely the body's inevitable fall before the microscopic agitators that have already long since overtaken it. In *The Magic Mountain*, Mann will allow a similar possession to enact upon its victim a "heightening" or "enhancement" of the creative mind. But the ironic, classicist momentum of *Death in Venice*, what the author himself called its "beautiful severity," will tolerate no such illusions of progress (*Venice* 72).[9] The novella implies that if there exists a way to avoid the terrors that beset Aschenbach (and at this stage, Mann is not certain that there does); a way to be certain that the body is safe from the repulsive diseases that it might otherwise secretly harbor; and a way to transfigure painful human experiences into lasting creative form; if such a way exists, it does not lead the artist through the contagious and uncontainable energies of passion.

"FAVORABLE CONDITIONS": *THE MAGIC MOUNTAIN*

The Magic Mountain began as a companion piece to *Death in Venice*, a philosophical satire that would turn Aschenbach's tragedy on its head. Its elaborate, Renaissance verbosity stands in stark contrast to the classical austerity of the earlier story, and its protagonist lingers at length in a contained, controlled version of the disastrous, cholera-swept Venetian setting: a mountainous rest cure for tubercular patients. But as Mann relates in his English account of the origins of the story, "The Making of *The Magic Mountain*" (1953), the novel soon began to take a direction of its own.[10] One particular aspect of the story that maintains a close resemblance to its tragic predecessor is the author's lengthy digressions on the biological details and etiology of disease, which possess the same microscopic intensity (if not the horrid urgency) of the previous narrator's accounts of the Asiatic cholera. In the section of chapter 5 titled "Research," the protagonist Hans Castorp lounges on his balcony late into the night, absorbed in a medical textbook:

> He held a volume of pathological anatomy in the red ray from his table-lamp, and conned its text and numerous reproductions. He read of the existence of parasitic cell-juncture and of infectious tumours. These were forms of tissue —and very luxuriant forms too—produced by foreign cell-bodies *in an organism which had proved receptive to them, and in some way or another—one must probably say perversely—had offered them peculiarly favourable conditions.* It was not so much that the parasite took away nourishment from the surrounding

tissues, as that, in the process of building up and breaking down which went on in it as in every other cell, it produced organic combinations which were extraordinarily toxic—undeniably destructive—to the cells where it had been entertained. They had found out how to isolate the toxin from a number of microorganisms and produce it in concentrated form; and it was amazing to see what small doses of this substance . . . could, when introduced into the circulation of an animal, produce symptoms of acute poisoning and rapid degeneration. (*Mountain* 285; emphasis added)

If we dismiss this passage too quickly as another dramatization of hypochondriac obsession, we will miss the subtle but distinct changes that it reflects in the author's thinking since the publication of *Death in Venice*. As before, Mann's attention focuses on the unique vulnerability of certain organisms to pathogens. And as before, his imagination conjures a "foreign" agent introduced into the bloodstream itself, one with effects as rapid and unsuspected as the cholera. But these microorganisms are no longer merely destructive or negative; instead they demonstrate a creative or at least combinative tendency. Although its effects on the body are equally toxic, the growth process of this disease creates new combinations in the body; it is not merely invasive, it is transformative, crafting new organic amalgams. If the psychological allegory of *Death in Venice* still holds in *The Magic Mountain,* and I believe that it does, this means that the formerly devastating passions now possess a creative aspect, one which undergoes transformation and issues in the realization of new forms, albeit in the absence of the mind's awareness or intention. The fact that this creative tendency evades consciousness will assume a singular importance in the later works. But to claim, as some scholars do, that "in the world of *The Magic Mountain* . . . there is no possibility of healthy passion—either morally or physically healthy—because passion is aroused only in disease," is to miss Mann's conceptual advances since *Death in Venice* in terms of the novel's subtle yet profound conclusions about the potential creativity of passion.[11] And it is to ignore his gradual recognition that the passions are not merely corruptive, destructive, or disruptive but that they may create, concentrate, and build anew. In biological terms, this may be indeed merely "unhealthy," but the allegorical import that it holds for the artist's craft is certainly otherwise. In *The Magic Mountain,* this toxic creativity remains, as before, hidden deep within the inscrutable circulatory paths of the body, but now Mann regards the clandestine process with an ambivalence that reflects both the shame of internal corruption and the anticipation of artistic creation.

One of the ways that he dramatizes this ambivalence (which was so severely undercut by the irony of Aschenbach's demise in *Death in Venice*) is through Castorp's intellectual guide, Naphta, who repeatedly reminds his student of the proximity between disease and genius. We err to regard disease as unnatural or inhuman, he argues: "the genius of disease [is] more human than the genius of health" (*Mountain* 466). Artists consciously descend into the terrors of disease and affliction to bring genius to the "healthy" masses, and Naphta concludes, in this sacrificial gesture lies the true meaning of Christian atonement.[12] But in the allegorical economy of the novel, Naphta represents only one side of the dialectic. After Aschenbach's horrendous disaster, Mann realized that equating disease with genius would not suffice without some account of the creative forms that the artist must, if he is to be an artist and not merely a mute thinker, bring to realization.

Mann ventures another alternative in the extraordinary vision that Castorp experiences in the section of chapter 6 titled "Snow," which he later identifies as a crucial passage for understanding the protagonist's intellectual development.[13] Trapped in the mountains in the midst of a raging snowstorm, Castorp begins to sense the same physical lethargy and overwhelming energies that afflicted Aschenbach on the bench in Venice. He is "irresistibly drawn" in one direction and then another; he follows "an inner compulsion" that is beyond his power to alter or control (*Mountain* 473; 494). When he finally sits down to rest, he finds his facial muscles unresponsive and paralyzed by the cold. As Castorp begins to drift into a sleep, Mann makes certain that his readers recognize the wider significance of this threatening state, its relationship to the disease carriers of his earlier work. "Here," Castorp says to himself, "we have the typical reaction of a man who loses himself in the mountains in a snowstorm. Whoever hears about it afterwards, imagines it as horrible; but he forgets that disease—and the state I am in is, in a way of speaking, disease—so adjusts its man that it and he can come to terms; there are sensory appeasements, short circuits, a merciful narcosis—yes, oh yes, yes. But one must fight against them, after all, for they are two-faced, they are in the highest degree equivocal" (*Mountain* 484).

Like Aschenbach, who dreaded the results of revealing his shameful, corrupt organs (which include his thoughts, the "organs" of the mind), Castorp fears what may overtake him once he is no longer in control. But the imaginative dream vision that eventually does overtake him is not merely the horrific, orgiastic nightmare to which Aschenbach succumbs. Instead it combines both "faces" of passion, that is, both of passion's affective valences: first, a pastoral scene featuring a young mother suckling her child and an older version of the child as a noble youth; then, a horrific scene of cannibalism wherein two witchlike crones dismember a child and gorge themselves on its flesh. In essence, the protagonist's dream vision holds in suspension both the creative and the destructive aspects of passion; it refuses to dismiss either the Dionysian frenzy of shame and self-destruction or the invigorating, life-giving creativity of inspiration. Castorp is overwhelmed by emotion, first by "something very closely akin to ecstasy" and then by the sensation of disgust that makes him "sick, sick as never before" (*Mountain* 493; 494).

When the dreamer awakes, Mann allows him to articulate the most significant theoretical discovery and advance that *The Magic Mountain* makes over its tragic forerunner:

> "I felt it was a dream, all along," he rambled, "a lovely and horrible dream. I knew all the time that I was making it myself—the park with the trees, the delicious moisture in the air, and all the rest, both dreadful and dear. . . . But how is it a man can know all that and call it up to bring him bliss and terror at once? Where did I get the beautiful bay with the islands, where the temple precincts, whither the eyes of that charming boy pointed me, as he stood there alone? Now I know that it is not out of our single souls we dream. We dream anonymously and communally, if each after his fashion. The great soul of which we are a part may dream through us, in our manner of dreaming, its own secret dreams, of its youth, its hope, its joy and peace—and its blood sacrifice. Here I lie at my column and still feel in my body the actual remnant of my dream—the icy horror of human sacrifice, but also the joy that had filled my heart to its very depths, . . . Ah yes, it is well and truly dreamed. I have taken stock. I will remember." (*Mountain* 495–96)

What first strikes Castorp is not the deeply conflicted content of the dream but its uncanny autonomy, the fact that it so forcefully compels him between the emotional extremes of joy and terror.[14] Just as elsewhere Mann had envisioned the body transformed unwittingly into a host organism for an invasive, malignant infection, here Castorp has been a vehicle, a medium invaded by a "foreign god" (whom the author now calls by its traditional Neoplatonic name that Yeats also knew as the *anima mundi,* the "world soul") and moved against his will into an imaginative state of creativity both toxic and benevolent in its symptoms. Like the microorganic pathogens that he so arduously studied earlier in the novel—and in fact, very much like Yeats's protean Daemon, or his shape-changing Druid—Castorp's vision is shifting, volatile, and metamorphic; "the scene before him," Mann clarifies, is not static but rather "constantly transformed and transfigured . . . before his eyes" (*Mountain* 490). The dream sequence is, in many ways, a vivid psychological echo of the physiological process that Mann lays out earlier in the chapter.

Castorp's confident declaration also marks a significant advance—and I mean "advance" in terms of both emotional complexity and artistic potential—over Aschenbach's confusion and delirium. Not entirely unlike the artist Lily Briscoe's final proclamation in Woolf's *To the Lighthouse* ("Yes, she thought, laying down her brush in extreme fatigue, I have had my vision" [*Lighthouse* 209]), the protagonist's avowal of the dream's value and finality sets it apart from a casual or random vision. His gesture intimates the kind of conscious stylistic decision with which an artist begins to shape his material. Although not yet fully realized in the verbal, plastic, or musical form of art, Castorp's vision is cemented (albeit temporarily) in the storehouse of the imagination, rather than dissipated and diffused in drunken ecstasy as Aschenbach's was in his last days. In short, *The Magic Mountain* finds a way to recuperate the microscopic passions of *Death in Venice* and account for them in a way that elides neither their threatening, deathly contagiousness nor their potential for unexpected and unintentional creative discoveries and combinations.

POLITICS, MAGIC, AND PSYCHOANALYSIS

Between *The Magic Mountain* and *Doctor Faustus,* Mann watched with growing dejection and fear as Germany suffered extreme economic hardship and rose in defiance of the international community and the peace accord. The rise of the National Socialist Party, Mann believed, depended upon a vehement denunciation of human liberty, a political and philosophical censure of intellectual freedom and rational inquiry. In the April 1931 issue of the *Criterion,* T. S. Eliot published Lowe-Porter's translation of the famous speech that Mann had delivered in Berlin the year before, "An Appeal to Reason." There Mann condemns the modern cultural and intellectual obsession with the daemonic and what he the calls "the darkly creative" as a harbinger of the escalating political crisis in Europe.[15] He describes the devastating effect of this repudiation of reason in terms almost identical to those that he had formerly used to portray Aschenbach stricken by the torments of passion after Tadzio's smile: a "mighty wave . . . that sweeps over the world to-day, assailing the nerves of mankind with wild, bewildering, stimulating, intoxicating sensations" (*Order* 55).[16] Mann's essay is, on the surface, a grand refutation of what had become known as the Romantic aesthetic, the mode of thought that derogates "bourgeois" ideals of optimism, progress, and reason, and that values "the unconscious, the dynamic, the darkly creative" over the intellect, which it views as mechanistic and self-destructive (*Order* 54). But the essay is also a conflicted and self-reflexive meditation on these very elements of his own earlier work, on the ways in which he had played ambiguously, creatively, even dangerously with the idea of "an ecstatic nervous collapse" as an arbiter of artistic insight rather than solely a shameful product of political fanaticism (*Order* 58). In a way "An Appeal to Reason" is Mann's attempt to banish his own passion scene, to turn aside and brood no more on its bitter, seductive mysteries.

Not long before "An Appeal to Reason," Mann had published "Mario and the Magician" (1930), a narrative that vividly reflects his growing, politically motivated mistrust of the passions but, once again, registers his ongoing ambivalence about their role in artistic creation or performance. The "magician" of the story's title, Cipolla, is actually no magician at all but an expert in mind control and hypnosis. His tantalizing performance (whose eloquent verbosity prefigures Mephistopheles' monologues in *Doctor Faustus,* and whose power to captivate distinctly recalls the antics of the street performer in *Death in Venice*) consists of compelling his audience members, one by one, to perform acts against their will, ranging from the comic and absurd to the shameful and degrading. This seemingly magical show is, the narrator realizes belatedly and describes in militaristic terms, "one long series of attacks upon the will-power, the loss or compulsion of volition" (*Stories* 637). It is quite likely that, in Cipolla's violent and merciless psychological attack on his rapt audience, Mann intends to offer his readers an analogue of Mussolini and the rise of Fascism. But to dismiss the narrative as political satire or allegory alone would be to elide the very tension that likely compelled Mann to compose it: Cipolla is also an artist, one who broods and suffers over his craft in ways that recall the intense suffering and grandiose ambitions of the artist in the early story, "A Weary Hour," whose chosen vocation subjects him to "the struggle and compulsion, the passion and pain" of the conventional Romantic artist (*Stories* 359). In light of the fact that even Mann's family referred to him in letters as "the Magician," we cannot help but think that he saw more of himself than he may have liked in the elegant, silver-tongued enchanter.[17]

Although seemingly not in alignment with Mann's other microscopic materializations of the passions, "Mario and the Magician" nonetheless marks an important moment for us, both for what it tells us about the artist's passions and for what it reveals about his own uncomfortable proximity to the motives and origins of Fascism. Cipolla embodies not only the shameful, elusive disease that preys upon its victim's willpower (underneath his elaborate, nineteenth-century suit and hat, the hypnotist is crippled, his back malformed and his teeth decaying), but also the menace, deceit, and intentional malevolence that Mann's political convictions compelled him to associate with passion. And once again, he preys upon those who, unknowingly and without volition, seem predisposed and particularly susceptible to his charms. When late into the performance he finally summons Mario, a waiter from the local restaurant, to the stage, Cipolla admits that his irresistible power over the young man has already been long under way: "Well, ragazzo mio, how comes it we make acquaintance so late in the day? But believe me, I made yours long ago. Yes, yes, I've had you in my eye this long while and known what good stuff you were made of. How could I go and forget you again?" (*Stories* 645).

Mario's public degradation—under the sway of a malicious spell, he kisses Cipolla, persuaded that the magician is his beloved—results at least in part from his simplicity, the weakness of mind that makes him so willing to serve. "It was only too easy to see why he obeyed," the narrator adds, "After all, obedience was his calling in life; and then, how should a simple lad like him . . . refuse compliance with a man so throned and crowned as Cipolla at that hour" (*Stories* 644)? Mario's susceptibility to Cipolla's charms—the "good stuff" that the magician says he is made of—is unmistakably similar to the conditions that make Venice "particularly favorable" to the cholera, the predisposition that makes Aschenbach so vulnerable to Tadzio's beauty, and likewise to the "receptive" and "peculiarly favourable conditions" of some bodies for the growth of infectious tumors that Hans Castorp reads about from his sickbed (*Venice* 54; *Mountain* 288).

The public degradation is also the catalyst for Mario's murder of the magician, the quick and definite annihilation of the dark forces that threaten his volition. Insofar as he suggests that the hypnotist suffers twofold every violence that he inflicts upon his victims—that he is both victim and attacker—Mann allows his ambivalent depiction of Cipolla to achieve a degree of sympathy. But the abrupt, unexpected conclusion of the narrative after the shooting allows for little further equivocation. Whatever the artistic "merit" of the performance, whatever admiration Cipolla commands by means of his eloquence and ominous mastery of the occult, is subordinated to the sensation of relief that the narrator and the audience feel at his violent death. It is as if Mann allows himself to entertain the possibility that Cipolla might be right, that passion is both the artist's curse and his creative blessing, but finally and suddenly turns against this threatening insight, against his own potentially dangerous speculation. The narrative structure implies that freedom and self-mastery—the rational, deliberate judgments of the sovereign intellect—however illusory they may seem at times, must finally trump ambivalence and equivocation. The other blade of passion's double edge is too sharp, and so Cipolla must fall.

In the following years, the urgency of addressing and opposing Germany's growing political momentum continued to outweigh the difficult ambivalence that Mann had cultivated while writing *The Magic Mountain*. It no longer seemed possible to entertain the creative potential of the passions without embracing what he viewed as the political tyranny to which they gave rise. "The moment has long since come," he wrote in his diary on 16 March 1935, "for us to fight for rationality with every ounce of strength we have" (*Diaries* 235). The evening before, however, Mann had read an article on psychoanalysis in the German periodical *Europäische Hefte* that addressed Carl Jung's opposition to the "soulless rationality" which, Jung feared, aimed to make the eradication of all human neurosis the primary goal of psychoanalytic therapy. Despite his distaste for what he believes to be Jung's implicit sympathies with Nazism, Mann enthusiastically agrees: "Jung is correct when he insists that only a kind of 'soulless rationality' could overlook the fact that there is something positive about neurosis, that it is a precious part of the soul, and that the patient should not have to learn how to get rid of it, but how to live with it. 'For he is the illness himself. . . . To lose a neurosis means virtually to lose the ground one stands on. . . . ' That is entirely true, and it would be mean to respond by saying that it would be a fine doctor indeed who would refuse to cure a tubercular patient on the grounds that the tuberculosis was 'precious' to him" (*Diaries* 235).

Despite the speculative defense that concludes this passage, Mann seems to realize here that the kind of eradication that he dramatized at the end of "Mario and the Magician" preserves not a freedom of the will but only a "soulless rationality," determined to defend itself at the cost of the neuroses so peculiar to art and imagination. As he writes in *The Magic Mountain* in the guise of Naphta: "he who would destroy passion, that man desires nothing less than pure nothingness" (525). His abortive rebuttal of Jung relies upon the undeniably positive effects of Hans Castorp's "precious" affliction and his prolonged stay at a rest cure for tubercular patients. Strangely enough, in the midst of his own most stringent misgivings, Mann seems more convinced than ever that passion (as either physical illness or mental neurosis) constitutes a fundamental element of human personality, that it is not an obstacle to be overcome but a crucial element of the psyche for which we must account. He makes a similar claim in his essay on Freud, the English version of which Eliot also published in a 1933 issue of the *Criterion*. Freud peered into the mind's "dark precincts," Mann writes, and it is essential that we too allow ourselves to "know very much of them, be very thoroughly at home therein."[18] But in light of what he viewed as Nazism's wholesale denigration of reason and intellectual freedom, he also feared that the attempts to elevate and mystify the passions "tend to glorify nazism and its 'neurosis'"(*Diaries* 235).[19]

In the eyes of many of his contemporaries, the choice between a dry rationality and the Nazis' ideological scorn for rationalism should be supremely clear; but for Mann, who had spent the better part of his career calibrating the rational mind's relationship to that which extends beyond its control, it poses a significant problem. Is there a way, he must have asked, to account for the creative potential of passion, illness, or neurosis without reducing the rational mind to impotence and sterility? And perhaps more important, given Mann's ongoing attention to the human body's predisposition to disease and illness, is there a way of relating to the passions, specifically to how they affect the hidden and autonomous mechanisms of the body and the mind, that will do justice to both the debilitating shame and the creative joy with which the human organism so often regards itself? It is with a sense of intellectual urgency intensified by political turmoil that Mann attempts to formulate answers to these questions—or rather to embody the tensions of the questions themselves—in the sinister account of Adrian Leverkühn.

LATE AND BELATED PASSIONS: *DOCTOR FAUSTUS*

Mann was fond of remarking that an author's new work never breaks entirely new ground nor abandons the well-tilled soil of his previous works, old and barren as they may seem. Instead his advances are always "the result of the old already containing elements of the new" and "the new taking up elements of the old again and leading them forth. This is the relationship," he concludes, "of *Death in Venice* to *The Magic Mountain*" (*Venice* 111–12). It is also the relationship of the two earlier works to Mann's tragic masterpiece, *Doctor Faustus,* which circles back to reexamine the deeply ambivalent conclusions about passion and creativity that he had reached in the process of moving from the catastrophe of Gustave Aschenbach to the bildungsroman of Hans Castorp's "heightening."[20] Although I cannot do justice to the full complexity of the novel's treatment of passion in these few pages, my aim in concluding with *Faustus* is to demonstrate succinctly its conceptual achievements vis-à-vis the trajectory that I have traced thus far in Mann's career.

As one might expect, *Doctor Faustus* returns to the strategies that Mann had employed successfully in *Death in Venice* and *The Magic Mountain:* the intense, detailed descriptions of pathogenic agents and the narrative technique of delayed revelation. Only now it is no longer the narrator who peers with the intensity of the X-ray machine into the organic inner processes of the body, but the *demonic* embodiment of the *daemonic* muse, the unconscious, the dark passions, that is, the devil whom Adrian Leverkühn encounters in the novel's haunting twenty-fifth chapter. Like Aschenbach, who discovers the truth about the cholera only after it has already grown rampant, Leverkühn learns the true nature of his affliction long after he has slept with the woman from whom he contracts syphilis. The physicians whom he halfheartedly tries to visit avail him nothing; the symptoms are already the source of excruciating pain. In this surprising twist on both the Faust legend and Mann's own delay technique, then, the devil comes only to confirm Leverkühn's disease and to reveal the minute processes whereby the agents of infection have already long since begun their invasion: "You have there the spinal sac with the pulsating column of fluid therein, reaching to the cerebrum, to the meninges, in whose tissues the furtive venereal meningitis is at its soundless stealthy work. But our little ones could not reach into the inside, into the parenchyma, however much they are drawn, however much they longingly draw thither —without fluid diffusion, osmosis, with the cell-fluid of the pia watering it, dissolving the tissue, and paving a way inside for the scourges" (*Faustus* 235).

As before, these microscopic agitators—which Mann now christens "the little ones," a modification that both likens them to "precious" children and endows them with an even more anthropomorphic agency—are already soundlessly, invisibly at work, although now with a "stealth" that hints toward an intentional deceit and malevolence absent from their earlier incarnations. The pathogenic process is no longer either natural or neutral, an impassive and indifferent invasion of foreign agents; its self-destructive vehemence parallels the hatred with which Leverkühn regards his own body and mind. Mann also returns to the idea that this host organism is particularly vulnerable to infection, that it invites the disease and provides a fertile soil for its growth. Leverkühn's response—"Slanderer, I have no connection with you. I did not invite you"—reveals the familiarity with which he recognizes this distasteful proposal; the devil's mocking retort—"La, la, sweet innocence!"—shows us precisely what is at stake in the accusation, namely, the disabuse of Leverkühn's seeming innocence and the shame that follows upon the revelation of a self-inflicted bodily and spiritual corruption (*Faustus* 233). From Leverkühn's point of view, neither syphilis nor this demonic visitor could have appeared if his own body had not been so weak and corrupt as to "invite" them. "Don't, I beg of you, pretend you're put on," Mephistopheles concludes, "I also have my self-respect, and know that I am no unbidden guest" (233). And like Cipolla in "Mario and the Magician," who had discerned from afar his vulnerable victim long before he acted upon him, so Mephistopheles tells Leverkühn: "Really gifted. That is why we recognized betimes and why from early on we had an eye on you— we saw your case was quite definitely worth the trouble, that it was a case of the most favorable situation"(232). Like Mann's other protagonists—including one whom I have not addressed, Felix Krull, the deviously compelling protagonist who repeatedly insists upon his innate superiority, whence originates, fittingly, his pro-clivity for dissimulation and criminality—Leverkühn's apparently intrinsic cor-ruption makes him solely responsible, at least in his own mind, for the disaster that befalls him.

The intensification of this sense of shame and self-disgust in *Doctor Faustus* is matched by Mann's refusal to grant Leverkühn any of the joyful realizations that the protagonist of *The Magic Mountain* had enjoyed in the midst of his disease.[21] By this time, Mann had declared his allegiance to the cause of "Reason" and de-plored the ideological consequences attendant upon the dark, diseaselike passions. Gone entirely is Hans Castorp's snowstorm vision of birth and regeneration; now, there remains only the raw fact of "repulsive, individual, private disease," and the "uncontrollable disgust" that overwhelms the protagonist repeatedly in the pres-ence of his guest, just as Castorp was disgusted by the scene of cannibalism and dismemberment in the mountains (*Faustus* 232; 249). Even the emotional richness of the creative potential inherent in passion threatens to become, in Mann's late vision, an index of shame and another mode of self-immolation and destruction. The syphilitic inspiration (the apt phrase is Albright's) that the devil promises to Leverkühn seems not a celebration of the creative spirit and the shaping imagi-nation but rather a militant and unforgiving coercion of the artistic faculties:[22] "A genuine inspiration, immediate, absolute, unquestioned, ravishing, where there is no choice, no tinkering, no possible improvement; where all is as sacred mandate, a visitation received by the possessed one with faltering and stumbling step, with shudders of awe from head to foot" (*Faustus* 237). This state of radical passion— at least the one that the devil promises, which is not necessarily identical to the one that the novel as a whole implies—is the obverse of the self-dispersing rapture that both Rhoda and Jinny experience in *The Waves*. Though equally violent and fright-ening, theirs is the kind of *kenotic* (self-emptying) impersonality that lends itself to imaginative empathy. Leverkühn's leads only further away from the despised, corrupt self. Woolf's protagonists become streaming, rippling elements of nature, vibrantly alive in their receptivity; Mann's Leverkühn is in danger of becoming a robot, an empty shell, stumbling about and shuddering in its metallic frame.

There are, however, several striking conceptual differences between *Doctor Faustus* and its predecessors, and those differences mark a significant change in the way that Mann regards the relationship between passion and creativity. First: unlike Gustave Aschenbach, whose visions dissipated into madness and delirium; and unlike Hans Castorp, who memorialized his dream vision only by marking its place in his imagination, a place which ultimately proves (only a few pages later) almost as ephemeral as the vision itself; unlike these, Adrian Leverkühn brings the inchoate imaginative passions to fruition as fully realized works of art.[23] Despite the emotional and physical degradations that he suffers, and despite the devil's promise that his artistic faculties will devolve into automatism, Leverkühn's compositions represent, in fact, the epitome of artistic structure and formal design. They are shocking, disturbing works of dissonance and symphonic chaos, but their consummate craftsmanship—along with the author's own admission of their derivation from the revolutionary work of his contemporary Arnold Schönberg—seems to indicate Mann's increased confidence in the passions as a viable source of real artistic creation. If as Mann suggests in *Reflections of a Nonpolitical Man* (1918), "the most intimately difficult and fruitful experience" of his youth was "learning that passion is clairvoyant," then one of the most significant aesthetic achievements of *Doctor Faustus* is the discovery that this clairvoyance may find realization in durable artistic form.[24] Despite his immense spiritual failure, and despite the disastrous emotional and physical consequences of his genius, Leverkühn is the only protagonist whom we have examined in this chapter whose works remain influential after his death and whose creative innovations go on to be widely respected and admired. Of course Mann's novel itself shares much with Leverkühn's musical oeuvre: the masterful parody, the stylistic innovation, the imitative fluency, and the subtle modulations of motifs. One cannot, standing safely in the shade of an ambiguous irony, refuse to see that Leverkühn's final composition is a metaphor for *Doctor Faustus* itself, and therefore that the fundamentals of Leverkühn's imaginative process (if not the ghastly details) bear directly upon our understanding of Mann's thinking about his own creativity.

The second difference, with which I conclude my reflections on Mann, also involves the relationship between passion-as-disease and creativity. In *Doctor Faustus*, Mann recuperates the delay mechanism that he had used to such terrifying and negative ends in *Death in Venice* and turns it into an asset for the artistic vocation. What had most insistently occupied his imagination in the two previous novels—and what provoked the devil's description of Adrian's disease as "stealthy" and "soundless"—was the possibility that one may seem healthy outwardly but be inwardly, invisibly diseased, that the infectious agents may be operating without betraying themselves through bodily symptoms. Mann now asks himself, in effect:

if disease is akin to artistic creativity, might not the creative processes also be invisibly at work, even when the mind remains unaware of them? This possibility does not find fulfillment solely in the moment of creative visitation, when the mind's active faculties are dispersed and annihilated by the "absolute, unquestioned" mandate of demonic inspiration; rather, it accumulates during the mundane stretches of time when the creative mind seems impotent, during what Eliot referred to as "the waste sad time / Stretching before and after" the moment of vision (*CPP* 122). If the mind can suffer invasion unknowingly, might not this invasion have creative results at times?

Thus the narrator explains the origins of Leverkühn's *Apocalypse,* finally bringing to realization the implicit parallels between the hidden growth of infection and the earliest stirrings of the creative act: "This was the work which he was mastering, the while it mastered him; for which his powers were slowly gathering head while they lay stretched in torments. Was I not right to say that the depressive and exalted states of the artist, illness and health, are by no means sharply divided from each other? That rather in illness, as it were under the lee of it, elements of health are at work, and elements of illness, working geniuslike, are carried over into health. . . . Genius is a form of vital power deeply experienced in illness, creating out of illness, through illness creative" (*Faustus* 355).

Although we must be cautious of the narrator's speculative declarations, which are frequently undercut by way of irony and understatement, this particular passage is the first full statement of the theory of imagination with which Mann had been experimenting since *Death in Venice.* It is the artistic correlative to what he had called, in a 1925 letter to Julius Bab, "the mysticism of the body, the organic mystery."[25] Despite the devastating tragedy that Leverkühn undergoes, and despite the vehemence with which the novel treats passion-as-inspiration, this passage promises to rescue for Mann the long, maddening periods of frustration that he experienced between his own creative projects. In essence it implies that the origin of a work of art extends backward to a time before the artist is aware of it. Invisibly making its way through the circulatory system of the imagination, it takes possession of the artist and compels him, without or against his intention, to bring it into being. This reversal of artistic agency also implies that, for Mann, the creative act is always necessarily belated, that the act of writing itself is the paradigm for the delayed revelation technique that he had so successfully learned to deploy as a narrative strategy in *Death in Venice* and *The Magic Mountain.* And like these other delayed revelations, once the work itself has begun to appear, it has already (in the narrator's appropriate phrase) "mastered" he who believes that he is mastering it.

CONCLUSION

Modernist Compensations

I have tried to keep my generalizations about modernism to a healthy minimum, but I would be remiss to conclude without briefly addressing the implications of this project for contemporary scholarship on modernist literature and art. I believe that shifting our attention to the increasing emphasis on passion and to modes of emotional intensity in the first half of the twentieth century will point us toward an alternative model of modernist aesthetics and psychology that will, in turn, challenge a number of dominant critical paradigms, foremost among them the idea that modern art is a compensatory response to threatening and chaotic external stimuli. I suspect that this subtle but surprisingly pervasive paradigm underlies many of the misunderstandings about modernism that I have addressed briefly in the preceding chapters and that I recapitulate here. Drawing on Woolf's ideas about the modern artist's shock-absorbing capacity, and on Eliot's about the imagination's immense passive strength, I have argued that modernist passion involves a heightened and intensified degree of receptivity, so I begin these concluding reflections by taking a fresh look at German sociologist Georg Simmel's widely influential diagnosis of the changes in mental receptivity that were taking place, according to an array of other thinkers as well, in the early twentieth century.

In his seminal "The Metropolis and Mental Life" (1903) Simmel argues that life in modern cities generates new types of mental experience, and that these new types of experience fundamentally change the way that the mind responds to external forces. For him, the most significant effect of the metropolis on the individual mind involves an excess of stimulation from both external and internal sources, an intensification and multiplication of movement suffered passively by the mind and body. Our senses are bombarded with changing, varying, and conflicting stimuli, Simmel argues, and our emotions respond in kind, provoked into an equal number of changing, varying, and conflicting sentiments. Our emotional lives, in other words, vibrate to the frequency dictated by our sensory receptivity, and that frequency reaches its highest levels in the modern city. Simmel describes the flood of stimuli with such vividness and metaphorical depth that one is almost uncertain at times whether he is lamenting or celebrating it: "the rapid crowding of changing images," "the sharp discontinuity in the grasp of a single glance," "the unexpected-ness of onrushing impressions."[1] Yeats's self-begetting images, Woolf's subatomic storm, and even the assault of Pater's sharp and importunate reality all seem to belong to the mental weather of Simmel's modern metropolis. His diagnosis is an exemplary instance of that "sense of being swept along or assailed by raw, un-leashed energy" that, as Richard Sheppard has recently suggested, was one of the affective poles around which modernism would soon take form.[2]

Simmel's well-known conclusion is that the paradoxical result of this storm of passions—in his words, the "intensification of nervous stimulation which results from the swift and uninterrupted change of outer and inner stimuli"—is neither a heightened capacity to feel nor an increasingly acute sense of differentiated recep-tivity.[3] Instead the result is the formation of a protective mental covering, a calcu-lating, objective intellectuality meant to quell the mind's emotional upheaval and internal turbulence. This covering may eventually manifest itself in what he calls the blasé attitude—an incapacity to respond to stimuli with appropriate energy—or it may simply translate into a hypervigilance of the rational mind, an instinctive and reactive mode of self-preservation: "Thus the metropolitan type of man—which, of course, exists in a thousand individual variants—develops an organ protecting him against the threatening currents and discrepancies of his external environment which would uproot him. . . . Intellectuality is thus seen to preserve subjective life against the overwhelming power of metropolitan life, and intellec-tuality branches out in many directions."[4]

The mind's response to normal sensations is part of its vitality, of how it senses itself to be alive and how it navigates the world. But as the sensations grow wild and overwhelming, this potentially vital response, Simmel suggests, "is shifted to an organ [the intellect] which is least sensitive and quite remote from the depth of the personality."[5] The psychological energies that might reconfigure or otherwise creatively modify the receptivity of the mind are channeled away from receptiv-ity entirely in order to avoid further mental harm. In effect, the mind is like a sub-marine with a ruptured hull: it responds to the damage by systematically closing off and sealing the flooded compartments while simultaneously shifting the crew to its few remaining safe areas, far away from the threatening external environ-ment. Simmel implies that the necessary result of feeling too much is feeling too little, or more accurately, that the only way for the mind to handle excessive feel-ing is by reverting to a kind of involuntary *askesis*, a deflection of feeling by means of calculation, objectivity, and abstraction.

Simmel's diagnosis is important for my argument in two ways. First, it dis-cerns a deepening and intensification of passion (as sensation, emotion, and per-ception) at the root of a distinctly modern psychological crisis. Just as Stephen Spender would later define the "modern I" in terms of its unparalleled capacity for suffering, passivity, and receptivity, so Simmel detects a historical and cultural uniqueness to the way the modern mind absorbs and receives stimuli.[6] I think that Tim Armstrong is right to align Simmel's prognosis with a number of other contemporaneous conceptual developments that reflect this uniqueness, including physician George M. Beard's description of neurasthenia, Freud's concept of the "protective shield" in *Beyond the Pleasure Principle* (1920; 1922), and later, Walter Benjamin's essay on Baudelaire's *flâneur*. "Heightened sensitivity," Armstrong concludes, is not only "central to modern experience" but is "part of the psychopathology of modernism."[7] But Simmel's conclusions are also important because the paradigm that he uses to describe how the mind counteracts excessive emotion with excessive rationality—what one could call the essay's compensatory logic—anticipates and rehearses in miniature a critical approach to modernist aesthetics that became increasingly dominant in the mid-twentieth century and, in fact, still pervades much contemporary scholarship. It was, I believe, one of the factors underlying Harry Levin's early claim in his well-known "What Was Modernism?" (1960) that the "ultimate quality" of modernist art "is its uncompromising intellectuality."[8] Though few scholars now agree with Levin's assessment, a surprising number still adhere to his implicit assumption about the compensations of modernist art. I do not think that one needs to argue in favor of a direct causal link between Simmel's conclusions and contemporary scholarship on modernism in order to begin to appreciate how his essay illuminates and anticipates a particular way of thinking about modernist aesthetics with which I shall take issue.

Before demonstrating how this model maps onto contemporary scholarly debate, I want to consider another of its influential forerunners: the one-time student of Simmel, Wilhelm Worringer, whose *Abstraction and Empathy* (1908) was to have such a significant impact on early modernist aesthetic theories via the art criticism of T. E. Hulme. It is Worringer who adapts Simmel's sociological prognosis to the sphere of modern art (though he denies drawing his theory from his former teacher). For him, all art answers a psychological need, and this need arises from the mind's disposition toward externality or its "feeling about the world."[9] He proposes that the "urge to abstraction" in any art—the movement away from naturalism or realism and toward geometric forms—registers a profound anxiety and unrest in our mental relation to the external world. The absolute necessity and fixedness of abstract forms, he argues, helps the human mind protect itself against "the extended, disconnected, bewildering world of phenomena" that would otherwise overwhelm it.[10] The use of straight, clear lines and severe geometrical shapes helps to reduce these potentially damaging and harmful stimuli to order and form. As Simmel had done, Worringer assumes that the modern mind risks being consumed by external and internal stimuli, that it desperately needs protection. Unlike Simmel, however, he postulates the deployment of this protection not as the result of a Darwinian-like instinct for self-preservation but as an exemplary imaginative decision, what he calls "the ultimate product of cognition."[11] Worringer transforms the unfortunate and damaging intellectualization of Simmel's metropolitan man into an ideal aesthetic strategy for managing the chaotic flux of external stimuli and internal sensation.

Despite his celebration of cognition's apparent triumph, however, Worringer reserves his most vivid, compelling language not for the succor that abstraction promises but for the threatening state of mental affairs against which it protects. We are "tormented by the entangled inter-relationship and flux"; "lost and spiritually helpless amidst the things of the external world"; wracked by "anguish and disquiet."[12] And he makes it clear that this anguished, powerless state is not merely a bygone stage of historical development but, in fact, a cycle that modernity has very recently reentered: "man is now just as lost and helpless vis-à-vis the world-picture as primitive man."[13] Like Simmel's, Worringer's vivid metaphors and insistence on modern man's passive condition—a condition remarkably similar to those that Eliot, Yeats, Woolf, and Mann envision as central to the creative process —betray a fascination with helplessness and powerlessness, an allure that would seem to align him with the other figures in this book, were it not for his emphasis on the imaginative need to counteract and elide this powerlessness with order and self-mastery. In his well-known and widely influential essay on Worringer's theories of abstraction, "Modern Art and Its Philosophy" (1914; 1924), T. E. Hulme attempts to diminish the urgency of the psychological threat by referring to it mildly as the "disharmony or separation between man and nature."[14] But in other essays, Hulme's own aesthetic and epistemological theories convey an equally threatening sense of the undifferentiated flux and chaos against which the modern classicist must pose discipline, severity, and abstract order. At a fundamental level, Worringer's abstraction and Hulme's classicism arise from the same intense concern and engagement with powerlessness and loss of control that I have remarked throughout the preceding chapters. The difference, of course, lies in their reluctance to admit a creative and spiritual potential that inheres in the mind's actual experience of powerlessness rather than in its imaginative defense against it or recovery from it. Although she overstates the case, Helen Carr offers a penetrating diagnosis of the lesson that Hulme learned from Worringer—and of the emotional implications of the compensatory paradigm more generally—when she asserts that Hulme was "an extreme example of those with a horror of the abject, of anything that threatens the borders of the ego, that evades control."[15]

If this paradigm of modernist aesthetics sounds particularly familiar, it is because a good deal of contemporary criticism still operates in tacit accordance with the assumptions embedded in it. According to the contemporary critical version, modernist formal innovations, aesthetic theories, and philosophies of language are all articulated in direct response to a set of potentially destabilizing and threatening forces—affective, cultural, political, or otherwise—and are aimed at defending against or deflecting those forces away from the individual subject or the autonomous work of art. Like the overstimulated inhabitants of Simmel's metropolis, modern artists sense the threat of heightened receptivity and respond with formal and stylistic structures aimed at negating that threat, even if in order to do so they must produce an imitative fragmentation or disruptiveness. In light of this paradigm, for instance, modernism's ostensible commitment to aesthetic autonomy arises from the desire to shield and protect the artist from the invasion of threatening and chaotic historical and cultural forces. This seems to me one of the implicit yet foundational assumptions that underwrites the now well-known assessments of modernism's ambivalent commitment to aesthetic autonomy by Peter Bürger, Andreas Huyssen, and Richard Murphy, each of whom uses a similar tactic to distinguish modernism's "institutional" sympathies and "anxiety of contamination" from the avant-garde's liberating iconoclasms.[16] Likewise, the emphasis of certain schools of modernism on formal experiment, of others on irony and ambivalence, or still others on abstraction and objectivity—according to this model—all derive from a nearly involuntary, compensatory response to excessive feeling, the formation of a mental shell that protects against (in Simmel's words) "threatening currents" and "discrepancies" of the external world.[17]

Thus Peter Nicholls, in his tremendously influential investigation of the various schools and writers often eclipsed by modernism's dominant narratives, applies a version of the compensatory paradigm to the "Men of 1914" when he claims that writers such as Pound, Joyce, Lewis, and Eliot all pursued experimental methods with the ultimate goal of "stablising the self, closing it to the turbulent movements of desire."[18] Nicholls maintains that the formal and conceptual innovations of these writers aim at diffusing or deflecting the threatening "flux of sensation," that they reflect a "privileging of intellect above emotion," and that they protect not only the human mind but, more important, a reactionary politics: "a set of political views is not only inscribed within [this] aesthetic but protected and legitimated by it."[19] As Nicholls reveals, the signal tropes of the compensatory model of criticism are "protection," "closing," "deflection," and the like, and they typically occupy the negative pole of a binary that favors postmodernism, the avant-garde, or an alternate, "non-mainstream" strand of modernist experiment. Though he avoids overstating the political implications of modernist form, Tim Armstrong agrees with Nicholls in his recent cultural history of modernism. Armstrong offers a compelling account of the ways in which the "theoretical preoccupation with defence against stimuli" manifests itself in discussions of trauma and shock.[20] Freud's "protective covering," for instance, shields the fragile psyche by filtering the influx of stimuli into more manageable samples.[21] When Armstrong turns his attention from Simmel, Freud, and Beard to modernist literary projects, however, he errs by simply attempting to transfer the compensatory model. He neglects to ask, that is, whether the literary text might complicate the model's logic and assumptions, and he concludes that "a defence of the self is . . . central to the aesthetics of 'high' modernism."[22]

A cursory survey of how contemporary critics continue to write about impersonality and other modernist methods of depersonalization (a wider-ranging term that is less directly tied to Eliot) will help to demonstrate just how entrenched the assumptions of this paradigm are. In an essay on alternative modes of impersonality, for instance, David James is willing to grant exceptional status for formerly marginalized modernist writers, but only after agreeing that conventional modernist depersonalization amounts to "a sort of inoculation: a means of immunizing the creative self against the disruptive vagaries of modern social life."[23] Gregory Jay agrees that such defensive inoculation is "decidedly modernist" and that it always aims to protect "an embattled Self," "to shore up an anxious personal and cultural identity by casting the Other" in negative terms.[24] Lisa Low quips, "Impersonality can be boring . . . part of the preserve of the canon in which men with very long white beards and white togas balance on marble plinths in the sky."[25] Despite her good humor, however, Low still discerns in impersonality "a terrifying coldness and remove" that is motivated by a "male Modernist" devotion to detachment and abstraction.[26] Even Eve Sorum, whose work on modernism's masochistic aspects resonates with mine on many levels, persists in claiming that the "modernist aesthetic depends on a dynamics of suffering and compensation."[27] Despite the exemplary expansions of the modernist canon and the invaluable correctives offered by cultural and historicist criticism in the recent decades, scholarship of canonical modernism often seems determined to preserve this outworn paradigm, which prevents us from realizing a richer, more complex understanding of writers such as Eliot and Yeats. It has become an implicit component of what Fredric Jameson calls "the ideology of modernism," the set of dominant, widely accepted characterizations of modernism—always "first and foremost" committed to "the autonomy of the aesthetic"—that derive primarily from post–World War II aesthetics and art criticism and which have assumed the calcified appearance of historical fact.[28] Like the other components of the ideology of modernism, this one is neither wholly misleading nor categorically wrong, but its critical dominance eclipses other equally valid and perhaps more conceptually challenging interpretations. It is the product of what Raymond Williams calls "selective appropriation" in modernist criticism, insofar as it yields "a highly selected version of the modern which then offers to appropriate the whole of modernity."[29]

As I hope to have shown by aligning this contemporary critical tendency with the model operative in Simmel, Worringer, and elsewhere, I believe that the compensatory paradigm is an accurate and useful way of describing certain elements of certain modernisms. It cannot, however, adequately account for literary modernism *en tout,* and it falls particularly short for the authors whom I have discussed in this book. Proponents of this paradigm frequently rely upon Eliot's much-quoted remarks in "Tradition and the Individual Talent" about poetry as an escape from emotion, and they use this formulation to make claims about modernism more broadly. But the same scholars invariably overlook the ways in which his hundreds of other essays and reviews complicate and even contest that early perspective. Do Eliot's experiments with the etherized patient reflect a desire to escape suffering or to protect himself from emotional upheaval? Do Yeats's abnormal restlessness and fascination with daemonic psychology aim to defend against stimuli or, conversely, to intensify his receptivity to psychological energies from both within and without?

A brief and selective glance beyond the limited scope of this book will reveal other well-known modernists whose commitment to passion and receptivity further helps to demonstrate the shortcomings of the compensatory model. Can we claim, for instance, that H.D.'s theories of imaginative vision and creative experiment aim at defending the self against threats and violence? Her most striking and memorable trope for artistic vision and creativity—what she calls in *Notes on Thought and Vision* (1919; 1982) the "jelly-fish" experience—involves the externalization of a psychic organ of sorts, as if a kidney or a lung were not tucked away safely inside the body but attached at the hip or clavicle, receptive, exposed, and vulnerable to external stimuli. As the intensity of the receptive experience grows, she explains, the jellyfish substance expands from simply enveloping the artist's head to covering her entire body, extending outward like tentacles. Much like Woolf's horrendously vulnerable eyeball, H.D.'s metaphor—alongside the complementary lexicon of her poems, especially the early *Sea Garden* (1916) lyrics with their depictions of ocean flora that are "slashed and torn / but doubly rich"—does not involve an attempt to compensate for an excess of feeling; rather, it describes an intensification of feeling and receptivity to the point of actual physical pain and violence.[30] The visionary experience, she argues, "is accompanied by grinding discomfort of mental agony."[31] In H.D.'s psychosomatic theory of creativity, the body "assumes its highest function when it is being consumed," and the imagination is like the skin turned inside out.[32] In contrast to the inhabitants of Simmel's metropolis, who develop additional layers of mental skin to deflect the amplification of stimuli, her artist is determined to remove anything that might blunt her receptivity.

Wallace Stevens seems, at first, an ideal countercase. His best-known and widely quoted essay appears to embrace the very model that I have been critiquing, postulating a subjective force that attempts to counteract and deflect the pressure of reality, "a violence within that protects us from a violence without."[33] But even here, the compensatory model falls sorely short of capturing Steven's subtle theories of the imagination and productive anxieties about passion and receptivity.

His "imagination" is not the same as Simmel's "intellect" or Worringer's abstract-ing "cognition"; it protects not by sheltering or sealing the mind but by provoking a parallel mental violence. Additionally the imagination operates not according to logic but according to sensation, Stevens argues, and is most exciting when stretched and extended into what he calls "abnormal" and "extreme ranges of sensibility."[34] Frank Lentricchia has persuasively argued that "Sunday Morning" — and particularly lines like "she makes the willow shiver in the sun"—might be seen as a condensation of Stevens's lifelong concerns with the delicacy and fragility of perceptual pleasure.[35] I believe that the shivering willow also speaks to the ways in which a dramatic and acute sensitivity usually reserved for the "feminine"— especially in the sentimental genre, where it is de rigueur—becomes, in Stevens's hands, a crucible of aesthetic creation. Similar claims have been made for Robert Frost, as well as for his most original reader of the postwar generation, Randall Jarrell.[36]

D. H. Lawrence offers perhaps the most compelling antithesis to the paradigm of psychic compensation, not least because his metaphors so strikingly recall and reverse those that Simmel and Worringer use. In his review of Harry Crosby's *Chariot of the Sun*—an essay that became well-known under the title "Chaos in Poetry" (1929)—Lawrence reimagines the protective, intellectualized shield of the compensatory model as a vast umbrella, sheltering the mind from the raging storm of experience. In the midst of chaos, it provides "a house of apparent form and sta-bility, fixity."[37] Over time the umbrella expands and grows increasingly stifling; it swells in proportions from a wire birdcage into a mausoleum, a dome, a vault. The task of the artist, Lawrence argues vehemently, is not to adorn the umbrella nor give it form—whether that form is realistic or abstract makes no difference—but to pierce it entirely, to expose the mind to the ravaging but transformative ener-gies of external stimuli and sensations. The soul opening itself to what he calls the "roving, uncaring" and "untamed" chaos constitutes the ultimate creative and poetic activity—"the essential poetic and vital act"—which he calls simply "atten-tion."[38] As Lawrence dramatizes repeatedly in his poetry and prose—especially in volumes like *Look! We Have Come Through!* (1917) and *Psychoanalysis and the Unconscious* (1921)—the most vital imaginative process depends entirely upon the rending of the mental veil that Worringer's alienated artist would interpose be-tween himself and the threatening world of experience.

Shifting our emphasis toward passion reveals the compensatory model's short-comings and suggests alternate models, at least one of which involves not the deflection of receptivity but its absorption and amplification. However, even more important than reversing the model's polarity—from less feeling to more feeling, or from the mitigation of emotion to its amplification—is the challenge that Eliot, Yeats, Woolf, Mann, and others pose to the structural logic of the conventional model in the first place. As we have seen, the compensatory paradigm involves a rational intervention aimed at defending and protecting the mind from violent stimuli and the emotional upheavals that attend them. But this description implies that the normative life of the mind consists of intellectual activity; that is, it posits a preexisting state of equilibrium and self-possession which some foreign force temporarily interrupts and which the intellect subsequently attempts to restore. If we imagine the interruption occurring on the level of individual consciousness, then this idyllic state of mental equilibrium is a retroactive fiction of psychology; if it occurs on an epochal scale, as in Simmel and Worringer, then it swells to a fiction of history. In this way, the modernist renderings of passion that we have examined actively resist the kind of nostalgia for psychological wholeness —once upon a time, before the twentieth century and its excess of stimulation— that is implicit in the compensatory paradigm and that admittedly pervades a number of other areas of modernist aesthetic and cultural theory.[39] Woolf's revision of her myth of the origins of personality, her desire to situate passion prior to all action or consciousness, as I have argued, is the direct result of this anti-nostalgia, on both the level of the individual life and that of the epoch.

The modernist models of passion also challenge the assumption, implicit in the compensatory paradigm, that the two mental states—the active and the passive —are mutually exclusive, that they are contiguous rather than continuous, and that we can clearly distinguish between them. Each of the modernists considered here goes to great lengths to avoid relegating passion to the secondary status of an aberrance or a departure from the norm. That is, each writer refuses to grant the viability of an intellectual and self-possessed stability that would somehow exclude and safeguard against the unruly and unpredictable energies of passion. If passion is a structural, consistent part of our mental processes—if it is constitutive and not accidental—then any attempt to "compensate" will be, itself, underwritten by the very passive energies that it aims to quell. If, as Yeats concludes, passion and action are ultimately simultaneous, if they imperceptibly coincide and if consciousness cannot adequately distinguish between them, then we cannot claim that one interrupts or supersedes the other. In Mann's case, for instance, the assertion of rational, conscious self-control and self-possession always coincides with (and at times even attempts to hide or obscure) a more pervasive passivity, a hidden passion whose movements the poet suffers without awareness and upon whose energies his creativity depends.

Eliot's mature renderings of the recognition scene characterize recognition as an upheaval or intrusion only insofar as it is a catalyst for disabuse, not a "stimulus" that must be quelled or deflected. For Eliot, recognition offers the opportunity to grasp the ways in which the mind *was already* intruded upon, that is, the ways in which this psychological openness or vulnerability to intrusion is neither weakness nor aberration but a structural part of how we experience the world and a constitutive part of the creative process. To "protect" against recognition—to defend, via art or intellect, against its manifold emotional ramifications—would mean to deny its transformative potential, to choose the illusion of human unity and completeness. Likewise, even though Yeats remains committed to an ideal of the relentless activity of the will—what he calls "abnormal restlessness"—he recognizes that this activity is driven by a more fundamental passion, a state that underwrites and makes possible both the activity of the heroic and the passivity of the ascetic. To varying degrees and with varying consistency, all four writers emphasize the ways in which passion—in its broadest sense, being moved, suffering movement—is not a mental state from which we can recover or for which we must compensate by somehow reestablishing the sovereignty of the intellect. In this way, the modernists gathered in these pages offer a rich and illuminating counterweight to the conventional view of passion as "a sign of the contingent in human beings, that is to say, that which they wish to master."[40]

At every turn the passions of modernism seem to lead toward a critique of intellectual self-possession and self-transparency. They demand that we situate paradox (the simultaneity of action and passion) rather than logic and causality at the foundation of psychology and aesthetics and thus seem to belong to the critique or "diagnosis" of Modernity by which modernism defined itself and with which postmodernism continues to identify.[41] In addition to the centrality of passion to several fundamental modernist projects, however, I hope also to have demonstrated the remarkable stubbornness and tenacity with which intellectual inquiry continues to participate in and complicate those same projects. Eliot, for instance, concludes his longtime engagement with the etherized patient scene by valorizing the spiritual and emotional virtue of surrender, the "awful daring" of abandon. And yet he reaches this conclusion only by means of an excruciatingly conscious, self-aware, and self-determined capacity to dwell within and negotiate his own passivity. Eliot's nuanced, detailed dramatizations of this process in *East Coker* testify to the ways that the supposedly Enlightenment values of intellect and rationality can not only coexist with but actually become catalysts for innovative and experimental ways of engaging with passion and passivity. Mann's Leverkühn in *Faustus;* Yeats's soldiers of "The Black Tower"; Woolf's Rhoda in *The Waves;* in each of these instances we can clearly discern modernism's obdurate refusal to devalue or dismiss the active mind. Even as it struggles to relinquish its claims to mastery and control, in other words, the "modernist mind" finds itself repeatedly confronted with the ways in which action promises to deepen and intensify passion, and likewise, the ways in which passion guides consciousness toward a recognition of its own range and limitations.

NOTES

INTRODUCTION

1. Arthur Clutton-Brock, "Not Here, O Apollo," 322.

2. T. S. Eliot, *The Waste Land: A Facsimile and Transcript*, 1.

3. For instance, see Peter Nicholls's suggestion that the scene rehearses "Eliot's characteristically contemptuous view of love among the lower classes" and that its irony depends upon an "absolute moral perspective" in order to critique "the contemporary world's more blatant reduction of passion to mechanism." *Modernisms: A Literary Guide*, 257. See also Grover Smith, *T. S. Eliot's Poetry and Plays*, 88–90; Hugh Kenner, *The Pound Era*, 369; F. O. Matthiessen, *The Achievement of T. S. Eliot*, 30–33; Cleanth Brooks, "*The Waste Land*: An Analysis," 106–36.

4. With a degree of overstatement that few contemporary scholars would share, Kenner pronounced it "the great *tour de force*" of *The Waste Land* as a whole. *The Invisible Poet*, 166. More recently, Lawrence Rainey allotted it "exemplary status" in the poem, though his revisionary historicist reading of the void and vacancy at the center of the scene's non-relationship comes strangely close to the earlier, more heavy-handed moralistic treatments that interpreted it as symptomatic of Eliot's disgust with modern sexuality and relationships in general. Rainey helpfully emphasizes the strangeness of the typist's "automatic hand," which, he claims, draws our attention to the "helplessness of automatism." *Revisiting "The Waste Land,"* 68. This sensation of powerlessness is also central to Tim Dean's reading of the scene, especially insofar as its result is, in other sections as well, the music of lyric itself. "T. S. Eliot, Famous Clairvoyante," 61. For Jason Harding's suggestion that the scene is "not 'void and vacant' but intimate with suffering," see "Eliot without Tears," 921.

5. Nicholls, *Modernisms*, 4, 289.

6. Ibid., 203, 193.

7. Ibid., 251, 194, 200.

8. Sandra M. Gilbert and Susan Gubar, "Tradition and the Female Talent," 154.

9. Ophir, "Toward a Pitiless Fiction," 95; Charles Altieri, *The Art of Twentieth-Century American Poetry*; Richard Sheppard, *Modernism—Dada—Postmodernism*; Tim Dean, "T. S. Eliot, Famous Clairvoyante."

10. See Timothy Clark's *The Theory of Inspiration*; Helen Sword's *Engendering Inspiration* and her *Ghostwriting Modernism*; and Devin Johnston, *Precipitations: Contemporary American Poetry as Occult Practice*.

11. For instance Lisa Rado offers this reading of the concept's conventions: "The imagination and its processes assume forms that reflect particular cultural anxieties and demands. Central to my argument is the premise that the greatest of these imperatives is not so much the artist's need to be inspired as to be empowered or authorized by the culture within which he or she creates." *The Modern Androgyne Imagination*, 2.

12. Michel Meyer, *Philosophy and the Passions,* translated by Robert F. Barsky, 5–6.

13. For the "erotics of the image" and the ways that it attempts to elide emotional ambivalence, see Anita Sokolsky, "The Resistance to Sentimentality: Yeats, de Man, and the Aesthetic Education."

14. Those most germane to my work include Leo Bersani, *The Freudian Body;* Judith Ryan, *The Vanishing Subject;* Kylie Valentine, *Psychoanalysis, Psychiatry and Modernist Literature;* and Michael Cotsell, *The Theater of Trauma.*

15. Susan James, "Explaining the Passions," 19.

16. Meyer, *Philosophy and the Passions,* 6.

17. René Descartes, *The Passions of the Soul,* pt. 1, para. 1, p. 329.

18. Ibid., 1.20, 336.

19. Ibid., 1.28, 339.

20. Ibid., 1.21, 336.

21. Ibid., 1.46, 345.

22. *The Nicomachean Ethics of Aristotle,* translated by F. H. Peters, bk. 7, sec. 3, 220; Descartes, *Passions of the Soul,* 1.46, 345.

23. See Richard Strier's "Against the Rule of Reason: Praise of Passion from Luther to Shakespeare to Herbert."

24. Mann, *"On Myself" and Other Princeton Lectures,* 51.

25. Descartes, *Passions of the Soul,* 1.50, 348.

26. Scholars of the last decade have demonstrated the importance of the sentimental tradition to the modernist enterprise, especially its influence on modern women writers and the modern novel of sensibility. See especially Suzanne Clark's *Sentimental Modernism;* Karen Kilcup's *Robert Frost and Feminine Literary Tradition;* and Laura Jane Ress's *Tender Consciousness.*

27. Edmund Burke, *Philosophical Enquiry,* 36.

28. Burke, *Philosophical Enquiry,* 67; Wordsworth, *The Prelude,* 14.245–46.

29. Burke, *Philosophical Enquiry,* 53.

30. Ibid., 79.

31. Preceding three citations from Wordsworth, *The Prelude,* 1.59–60; 2.545–46; and 3.40–41.

32. Ezra Pound, "A Retrospect," *Literary Essays* 12; T. E. Hulme, *Speculations,* 127. In particular, see Hulme's "Romanticism and Classicism": "There is a general tendency to think that verse means little else than the expression of an unsatisfied emotion. People say 'But how can you have verse without sentiment?' You see what it is: the prospect alarms them. A classical revival to them would mean the prospect of an arid desert and the death of poetry as they understand it" (127).

33. Suzanne Clark suggests that sentimentalism as a discourse has been "defined by opprobrium" since it began to acquire negative connotations in the late eighteenth century (*Sentimental Modernism,* 19). Rado's discussion of Yeatsian sentimentality in "Among School Children" is an exception here insofar as it discerns the relationship between sentiment (which she understands in its contemporary sense) and "the heterogeneous configuration of investments which is the self" (*Modern Androgyne,* 83).

34. Kilcup goes a long way toward reevaluating the place of sentimental discourse in modernism with respect to Robert Frost yet seems to deny the possibility for figures such as Eliot (*Robert Frost and Feminine Literary Tradition,* 17). Suzanne Clark explicitly suggests that Eliot's "conservative propriety" remains intact despite intimations of the sentimental in his early poetry (*Sentimental Modernism,* 31). Robert Langbaum sketches a more inclusive paradigm in proposing that the modern dramatic monologue derives from sentimentalism

and its attempt to "heal the breach" between thought and feeling that Eliot described as the dissociation of sensibility (*The Poetry of Experience*, 38).

35. Attempts to measure these influential pressures frequently focus on the rhetorical means that modernism adopts from Victorian poets to oppose the Romantic emphasis on sincerity and expressivity. "Despite their anti-Victorianism," Carol Christ suggests, "Modernist poets explore ways of objectifying poetry that show striking continuities with Victorian poetics . . . . Departures from Romanticism," she concludes, "lead the Victorians and the Modernists to similar poetry strategies" (*Victorian and Modern Poetics*, 3). See also Christ's "T. S. Eliot and the Victorians." Altieri offers a valuable distinction in claiming that while Victorian poetics experimented with objectivity and irony, modern poets such as Eliot were committed instead to "staging *the desire for objectivity* as a conflicted stance" (*Art of Twentieth-Century American Poetry*, 59). The most influential critical assessments of the continuities and oppositions between Victorian and modern poetics remain Frank Kermode's *Romantic Image;* Louis Menand, *Discovering Modernism: T. S. Eliot and His Context;* and George Bornstein, *Transformations of Romanticism in Yeats, Eliot, and Stevens.*

36. Adela Pinch, *Strange Fits of Passion*, 3, 10.

37. Gesa Stedman, *Stemming the Torrent*, 63.

38. Matthew Arnold, *The Poetical Works*, xix.

39. Ibid., xviii.

40. Ibid., 415.

41. Ibid., 241.

42. Matthew Arnold, *Essays in Criticism: Second Series*, 154–55.

43. Ibid., 158–59.

44. Walter Pater, *Appreciations: With an Essay on Style*, 41.

45. Ibid., 19.

46. Ibid., 24.

47. Ibid., 24.

48. Ibid., 209.

49. Walter Pater, *Marius the Epicurean*, 1:143. Cf. Eliot's well-known formulation in 1919 that the mind of the poet must become a "finely perfected medium" for emotional combinations and that it must confine itself to dealing primarily with "the passions which are its material" (*SE* 18).

50. Walter Pater, *The Renaissance*, 190.

51. John Ruskin, *Modern Painters*, 3:207.

52. Ibid., 3:207.

53. T. S. Eliot, *The Use of Poetry and the Use of Criticism*, 103.

54. Ibid., 108.

55. Stephen Spender, *The Struggle of the Modern*, 71–72.

56. Ibid., 72.

57. Quoted in Margaret Mills Harper, *Wisdom of Two*, 22.

CHAPTER 1: PASSION AND SURRENDER

1. "If I died, this money would be most important for Vivien," Eliot wrote to his mother on 31 October 1920. "I have to plan for the contingency of Vivien and one of her parents surviving me. . . . Therefore I should not for a moment consider letting the insurance drop" (*Letters* 419–20).

2. For John of the Cross, see Eliot's remarks in *Varieties of Metaphysical Poetry*, 104–5 and "Thinking in Verse: A Survey of Early Seventeenth-century Poetry"; he quotes at length from the *Benjamin Major* by the twelfth-century theologian Richard of St. Victor in *The*

Varieties of Metaphysical Poetry, 102–3. See also Grover Smith's *T. S. Eliot's Poetry and Plays,* 99, and Ronald Schuchard's *Eliot's Dark Angel,* 176–77.

3. Eliot praises Henry Treece as "a poet of plan and construction rather than of fitful lyric inspiration." An excerpt from the unpublished blurb Eliot intended for the dust wrapper of Treece's *The Exiles* (1951) is included in Sackton's *The T. S. Eliot Collection of the University of Texas at Austin,* 173. For Eliot's distrust of the "Inner Voice" and "intuition," see especially his remarks in "The Function of Criticism," 37, and "Mr. Read and M. Fernandez," 756.

4. Eliot, introduction, *The Art of Poetry,* by Paul Valéry, xviii.

5. Eliot, "A Commentary" (October 1932), 77. See also Eliot's "A Commentary" (April 1932), "Man must have something to which to he is ready to sacrifice himself; he must, if necessary, sacrifice himself, but he must not be sacrificed" (470). In an address to the Women's Alliance less than a year after "The *Pensées* of Pascal," Eliot admitted his own utter dependence, in matters both spiritual and aesthetic, on those moments of passivity that allow the mind to crystallize and which come but seldom and unexpectedly. See the unpublished lecture entitled "The Bible as Scripture and as Literature" (Harvard). In "The Hawthorne Aspect," he suggests that "Hawthorne and James have a kind of sense, a receptive medium, which is not of sight. . . . They perceive by antennae; and the 'deeper psychology' is here" (50–51). And in his "Critical Note" to Harold Monro's *Collected Poems,* he contends that a poet must be original and unique "only so far as is dictated . . . by the nature of that dark embryo within him which gradually takes on the form and speech of a poem" (xiii).

6. Eliot, "Modern Tendencies in Poetry," 10.

7. Eliot, introduction, *A Choice of Kipling's Verse,* 20n. (Hereafter cited as *A Choice.*) Cf. also Eliot's "Critical Note" to the *Collected Poems* of Harold Monro, in which he claims that "the external world, as it appears in [Monro's] poetry, is manifestly but the mirror of a darker world within" (xvi).

8. Eliot, "London Letter," 331.

9. Eliot, "The Relationship between Politics and Metaphysics" (Houghton Library, Harvard University).

10. For example, see Thomas Aquinas's *Summa Theologica* (Ia-IIae, q. 22, a. 3, ad. 2): "Intensity of passion depends not only on the power of the agent, but also upon the passibility of the patient." Eliot encountered Aquinas primarily through the eminent medievalist Étienne Gilson, whose *La Philosophie au Moyen-Âge* and *St. Thomas D'Aquin* (1925) he owned in his personal library. He abstracts his knowledge of Aquinas in "Mr. Middleton Murry's Synthesis": "It is limited to the accounts of Gilson and de Wulf, to two volumes of extracts, one prepared by Gilson and the other by M. Truc, to two or three books by M. Maritain and modern Dominicans, and to the new edition of the *Summa* published by Desclée" (340).

11. Ted Hughes, "The Poetic Self: A Centenary Tribute to T. S. Eliot," 281.

12. Eliot suggests in 1920 that the most "direct" approach to emotion is that which passes through the objects immediately associated with it: "The poet's 'emotion' must always be in such close relation to objects that when he sets the objects before you, you 'get' the emotion. He must appeal to your senses. The emotion is the resultant activity of the combination of what are ultimately sense-data. . . . You will find that many of the second rate poets are second rate because of their attempt to deal with the emotions direct instead of through the senses." "Modern Tendencies in Poetry," 15–16.

13. Eliot may have adopted and transposed this scene from John Davidson's "The Testament of a Vivisector," in which the narrator (who likens himself to "a pale inquisitor, / Beholding pangs of stubborn heresy / A-sweat upon the rack") performs a brutal surgical dissection upon a paralyzed man who comes to him in a state of extreme vulnerability and weakness. *The Poems of John Davidson,* 2:327.

14. "This scene of Philomel's rape recurs throughout the poem," Tim Dean observes, "in episodes of sexual aggression and degradation—such as that of the typist and the 'young man carbuncular'—that end with images of music or song." The radical (and Dean adds, emasculating) violence that Philomel suffers is "the precondition for poetic voice." "T. S. Eliot, Famous Clairvoyante," 61.

15. In "Modern Tendencies in Poetry," Eliot himself doubts even the possibility of a state of such radical passivity: "If you imagine yourselves suddenly deprived of your personal present, of all possibility of action, reduced in consciousness to the memories of everything up to the present, these memories, this existence which would be merely the totality of memories, would be meaningless and flat, even if it could continue to exist" (12).

16. Eliot, "The Literature of Fascism," 288.

17. William James, *The Varieties of Religious Experience*, 309. On one of the sixty index cards that Eliot annotated during his studies at Harvard, he transcribed James's accounts in *The Varieties of Religious Experience* of his acquaintance's ether dream and of B. P. Blood's investigation into "anesthetic revelation" (Harvard). See Robert Crawford, *The Savage and the City in the Work of T. S. Eliot*, 72–81, and Ricks's note to "Do I know how I feel? Do I know what I think?" (*IMH* 80).

18. Hervey Allen, *Israfel: The Life and Times of Edgar Allan Poe*, 2:755. Eliot reviewed Hervey Allen's biography of Poe along with an edition of Poe's stories in "Israfel," 219. See also "'A Dream within a Dream': T. S. Eliot on Edgar Allan Poe," 243–44, and *From Poe to Valéry*, 327–42.

19. Edgar Allan Poe, *Works*, 2:261.

20. Ibid., 2:268.

21. Ibid., 2:278.

22. Eliot, "Beyle and Balzac," 393.

23. Charles Baudelaire, *Intimate Journals*, trans. Christopher Isherwood, 23–24.

24. For Eliot as the "savage comedian," see Schuchard, *Eliot's Dark Angel*, 88–9. The two Baudelaire essays appear in succession in the edition of Baudelaire's works that Eliot likely owned, *Oeuvres Complètes de Charles Baudelaire*, vol. 2, *Curiosités Esthétiques*, ed. M. Jacques Crépet (Paris: Louis Conard, 1903). Seven volumes of Baudelaire's *Oeuvres* are listed in the inventory of Eliot's personal library performed in January 1936 (Bodleian Library, Oxford University).

25. Charles Baudelaire, "Some Foreign Caricaturists," in *The Painter of Modern Life*, 187.

26. For a detailed account of Vivienne's ether addiction, see Anthony Fathman, "Viv and Tom: The Eliots as Ether Addict and Co-Dependent," 33–37. For several contemporaneous accounts of Vivienne's addiction, see Carole Seymour-Jones's *Painted Shadow*: "From 1930, stories of Vivienne's bizarre behaviour were legion in literary London, many centering around her abuse of ether, then used as an anaesthetic, which could be inhaled or rubbed on the body. . . . According to his relatives, Dr. Miller, Vivienne's doctor, who practiced at 110 Harley Street, prescribed paraldehyde for her as a massaging gel, which smelt strongly of ether" (474).

27. Seymour-Jones, *Painted Shadow*, 474.

28. Blake Morrison, "The Two Mrs. Eliots," 144.

29. Robert Craft, *Stravinsky: Chronicle of a Friendship*, 32.

30. Eliot to Richard Cobden-Sanderson, autograph letter undated but marked received on 21 September 1925 (Harry Ransom Center, University of Texas at Austin).

31. Virginia Woolf, *The Diary of Virginia Woolf. Vol. 1: 1915–1919*, 240.

32. Ibid., 250. Woolf relates that Eliot and his wife dined with her on 6 April 1919 (262). In a diary entry from the previous month, she relates: "Yesterday I had a tooth out. . . . The

queer little excursion into the dark world of gas always interests me. I came home in the Tube wondering whether any of the people there suspected its existence. I wake from it, or sccm rather to step out of it & leave and go on hurtling through space while the world of Harrison and Dr Trueby engages my attention—'Open your mouth, Mrs. Woolf—Now let me take out this little bit of wood.' Suppose one woke instead to find the deity himself by one's side!" (250).

33. For instance, see Eliot's laudatory review of L. C. Martin's recently published essay ("A Forgotten Poet of the Seventeenth Century") on the devotional poet Nathaniel Wanley, "Wanley and Chapman," 907. For more on Wanley's influence on Eliot, see my "T. S. Eliot's Forgotten 'Poet of Lines,' Nathaniel Wanley." In his essay on John Ford (1932), Eliot quotes an equally apposite passage from *The Broken Heart* (1633), IV. ii.: "'tis a fine deceit / To pass away in a dream; indeed, I've slept / With mine eyes open a great while" (*SE* 199).

34. Eliot to John Hayward, 2 February 1931 (Hayward Bequest, King's College Archive Centre, Cambridge).

35. Roger Vittoz, *Treatment of Neurasthenia by Means of Brain Control,* 5 (hereafter cited in text as Vittoz).

36. For the similarities between Vittoz's text and the final section of *The Waste Land,* see especially Peter Ackroyd, *T. S. Eliot: A Life,* 115; Adam Piette, "Eliot's Breakdown and Dr. Vittoz," 38; and Matthew Gold, "The Expert Hand and the Obedient Heart," 519–33.

37. Donald Gallup attributes the translation of "Poetry and Religion" to Eliot, although it was originally credited to F. S. Flint. *T. S. Eliot: A Bibliography,* 214. For Eliot's phrase "the leader of the Catholic rationalists," see "The Idealism of Julien Benda," 299, reprinted from a contribution originally published on 12 December 1928. For "the most conspicuous figure," see "A Commentary" (January 1927), 3.

38. Eliot, trans., "Poetry and Religion," by Jacques Maritain, 18–19.

39. Ibid., 22.

40. "As it was, Dorothy Pound said she and Ezra always felt Eliot was 'wrestling with a devil or an angel,' which they found most uncomfortable." Humphrey Carpenter, *A Serious Character: The Life of Ezra Pound,* 261. Carpenter quotes from the unpublished notebooks of Noel Stock.

41. Eliot, trans., "Poetry and Religion," 22n.

42. In the Clark Lectures (1926), Eliot suggests that John Donne's poems and sermons, in contrast to Dante's *Commedia,* "always give me the impression of an incomplete concentration, of a direction of forces more by a strong will than by surrender and assent" (*Varieties of Metaphysical Poetry,* 117). In "The *Pensées* of Pascal," he identifies personally with Pascal's variety of "mystical experience" during which "a piece of writing meditated, apparently without progress, for months or years, may suddenly take shape and word; . . . He to whom this happens assuredly has the sensation of being a vehicle rather than a maker" (*SE* 405). And elsewhere he claims that Rudyard Kipling "is not merely possessed of penetration, but almost 'possessed' of a kind of second sight" and that his verse betrays "something which has the true prophetic inspiration" (*A Choice* 19; 16).

43. "Personality and Demonic Possession," 98. When first published in the *Virginia Quarterly* in 1934, the essay that would eventually become part III of *After Strange Gods* (1934) bore this conspicuous title. Eliot explains that the essay is concerned with "the intrusion of the *diabolic* into modern literature" and the dynamic whereby "a positive power for evil [works] through human agency" ("Personality" 98). However, he also implies that this mode of artistic "possession" is not limited to "the *diabolic*." D. H. Lawrence, for example, "with his acute sensibility, violent prejudices and passions, and lack of intellectual and social train-

ing, is admirably fitted to be an instrument for forces of good or forces of evil; or as we might expect, partly for one and partly for the other" (100–101).

44. Helen Gardner, *The Composition of "Four Quartets,"* 67.

45. Ibid., 42.

46. Eliot, "Whether Rostand Had Something about Him," 665.

47. Gardner, *The Composition of "Four Quartets,"* 105.

48. The speaker of "Usk" (1935) prefigures, to a lesser extreme, the renunciatory gestures performed by the narrator of *East Coker* as he sinks into the ether: "Glance aside, not for lance, do not spell / Old enchantments. Let them sleep" (*CPP* 94). And the "children's voices in the orchard" in "New Hampshire" (1934) are of course also forerunners of this stanza; in the earlier lyric, we hear their whispers "between the blossom- and the fruit-time," while *East Coker* sets them among the "wild thyme" and "wild strawberry" (93).

49. Charles Baudelaire, *Intimate Journals,* 23–24.

50. Eliot, "Modern Tendencies in Poetry," 14.

51. E. Martin Browne, *The Making of T. S. Eliot's Plays,* 191.

52. Gardner, *The Composition of "Four Quartets,"* 189.

53. William James, *The Varieties of Religious Experience,* 309.

54. Eliot, introduction, *Revelation,* 24.

55. Eliot, introduction, *Nightwood* by Djuna Barnes, xiii.

56. For Eliot's description of inspiration as the "dark embryo within," see his "Critical Note" to Harold Monro's *Collected Poems* (xiii).

57. Eliot, *Knowledge and Experience in the Philosophy of F. H. Bradley,* 28.

58. In actuality, Eliot's unpublished 1909 essay on Kipling, "The Defects of Kipling," written while he was an undergraduate at Harvard, condemns Kipling for his intellectual immaturity and his dated fascination with the exotic. In Eliot's 1919 review of Kipling's *The Years Between,* he repeats the charge of immaturity but adds, "Mr. Kipling is very nearly a great writer. There is an unconsciousness about him which, while it is one of the reasons why he is not an artist, is a kind of salvation." "Kipling Redivivus," 298.

59. Eliot, introduction, *The Art of Poetry,* by Paul Valéry, xviii.

60. Eliot, *Varieties of Metaphysical Poetry,* 117.

61. Valéry, *The Art of Poetry,* 60.

62. Ibid., 60.

63. Ibid., 63.

64. "This demand for a premature denouement is the principle of figuration: it engenders the image, or, if you will, the idol, and the curse which attaches to it is that which attaches to idolatry. Man wants unity right away." Maurice Blanchot, *The Space of Literature,* trans. Ann Smock, 79. See Timothy Clark's "Contradictory Passion: Inspiration in Blanchot's *The Space of Literature,*" in *The Theory of Inspiration,* 238–58.

65. Eliot, "Scylla and Charybdis," 5.

66. Ibid., 5.

67. Ibid., 9.

68. Eliot, preface, *John Davidson: A Selection of His Poems.* Eliot had first encountered Davidson as early as 1917, when he included his name among Dowden, Johnson, and other "nineties" poets in the syllabus for the second year of his tutorial course on modern English literature at Southall, Middlesex. Schuchard, *Eliot's Dark Angel,* 43. In a review written in the same year for the *Egoist,* he applauds Davidson for attaining "an occasional flash of exact vision." "Reflections on Contemporary Poetry," 134.

69. Eliot, preface, *John Davidson: A Selection,* xi.

70. Davidson, *Poems,* 2:328; Eliot, preface, *John Davidson: A Selection,* xii.

71. Davidson, *Poems,* 2:327.

72. Eliot, preface, *John Davidson: A Selection,* xii.

73. Davidson, *Poems,* 1:129.

74. Ibid.

75. Ibid.

CHAPTER 2: WHO STOOD OVER ELIOT'S SHOULDER?

1. Eliot, "A Fable for Feasters," published in the *Smith Academy Record* in February 1905 (*PWEY* 7).

2. Scholarly attention to the recognition scene has been limited to Eliot's explicit statements about his intentions in "Marina." See Grover Smith, *T. S. Eliot's Poetry and Plays,* 130–34; Ronald Bush, *T. S. Eliot: A Study in Character and Style,* 166–69; William Empson, *Argufying: Essays on Literature and Culture,* 356–59; Denis Donoghue, *Words Alone: The Poet T. S. Eliot,* 164–80. See also Kristian Smidt's much more abstract exploration of recognition in *The Importance of Recognition: Six Chapters on T. S. Eliot,* 5–7, 76–79.

3. Eliot, review of *Religion and Science: A Philosophical Essay,* by John Theodore Merz, 126.

4. William Melaney recapitulates the conventional formulation succinctly in suggesting that the aesthetic projects of modernism involve challenges "to the strictly cognitive claims of rationalist epistemology" and reflect a further "movement away from the centrality of the subject." *After Ontology: Literary Theory and Modernist Poetics,* 4–5. For Kalaidjian's robustly historicist account of these challenges in terms of trauma, see his *The Edge of Modernism: American Poetry and the Traumatic Past;* Jean-Michel Rabaté, *The Ghosts of Modernity;* see also Steve Giles: "The notion that modernism involves a critique of the self-understanding of modernity construed in terms of the Enlightenment project is, of course, essential to any theoretical understanding of modernism." *Theorizing Modernism: Essays in Critical Theory,* 178.

5. D. H. Lawrence, *Psychoanalysis and the Unconscious,* 15.

6. Eliot to F. R. Leavis, 16 December 1935 (Harry Ransom Center, University of Texas at Austin).

7. Eliot, "Personality and Demonic Possession," 101.

8. Eliot is still thinking about the irreducible plurality of these units four years later in "Tradition and the Individual Talent" when he offers his brief critique of "the metaphysical theory of the substantial unity of the soul" (*SE* 19).

9. "The soul is so far from being a monad that we not only have to interpret other souls to ourself but to interpret ourself to ourself" (*KE* 148).

10. Eliot encountered Leibniz's notion of "unconscious perceptions"—the soul's many hidden responses to phenomena in the world and itself—in 1916 when he published two articles on the *Monadology* (1714) : "The Development of Leibniz's Monadism" and "Leibniz's Monads and Bradley's Finite Centers." The element of the theory that most significantly influenced him was Leibniz's association of the totality of such unconscious responses with the Absolute: "It may even be said that in consequence of these petite perceptions, the present is big with the future and laden with the past . . . and that in the least of substances eyes as penetrating as those of a God might read the whole succession of things in the universe." Gottfried Wilhelm Leibniz, *The Monadology and Other Philosophical Writings,* trans. Robert Latta, 370.

11. In the dissertation, Eliot disparages the "unconscious" as a concept "of very doubtful value" (*KE* 28). Though not the preferred coinage among his philosophy professors at Harvard, the unconscious was a familiar psychological category well before the early twentieth century. See Lancelot Law Whyte's *The Unconscious before Freud* and Kylie Valentine's *Psychoanalysis, Psychiatry and Modernist Literature*.

12. Eliot, "The Significance of Charles Williams," 895.

13. Eliot to William Turner Levy, 21 August 1954 (Harry Ransom Center, University of Texas at Austin).

14. Eliot, *The Use of Poetry and the Use of Criticism*, 155.

15. F. H. Bradley, "In what sense are psychical states extended?" *Collected Essays*, 2:358. The original version appeared in *Mind* 4 (April 1895): 225–35.

16. Ibid., 358.

17. Ibid., 357. Not long after finishing the dissertation, Eliot would revisit this concept via the similar assumptions embedded in German psychologist Johann Friedrich Herbart's concept of "apperception mass," to which he refers in "The Education of Taste," 521.

18. In an unpublished letter to Paul Elmer More written on 10 August 1930, Eliot not only admitted to being a Bradleian at heart but also to the distinct likelihood that his own mature thoughts and beliefs were more profoundly influenced by Bradley's philosophy than even he could tell (Harvey S. Firestone Library, Princeton University).

19. Eliot, *On Poetry and Poets*, 93; for "penumbral consciousness," see *The Waste Land: A Facsimile and Transcript*, 37.

20. Eliot, "In Memory," 46.

21. Eliot, introduction to *The Wheel of Fire*, by G. Wilson Knight, xv.

22. Eliot, introduction to *Shakespeare & the Popular Dramatic Tradition*, by S. L. Bethell, 8–9.

23. Eliot, *For Lancelot Andrewes: Essays on Style and Order*, 21.

24. According to Knight, Eliot was much impressed by "Myth and Miracle"; he not only composed the introduction for Knight's *The Wheel of Fire* (1930) but also referred to him in "John Ford" (1932) and in an unpublished lecture delivered at the University of Edinburgh in 1937, "Shakespeare as Poet and Dramatist." See "T. S. Eliot and Pericles," Knight's appendix to *Neglected Powers*, 489–90. B. C. Southam quotes from Eliot's July 1930 letter to E. McKnight Kauffer in *A Guide to the Selected Poems of T. S. Eliot*, 247.

25. The sea vessels in "Marina" draw from Knight's contention that "the individual soul is the 'bark' putting out to sea in a 'tempest,'" and Knight's "shaft of light penetrating into the very heart of death" reappears six years later in *Burnt Norton*, when "sudden in a shaft of sunlight / Even while the dust moves" the narrator hears the joyous whispers of rebirth (*CPP* 72–73, 122). G. Wilson Knight, "Myth and Miracle," *The Crown of Life: Essays in Interpretation of Shakespeare's Final Plays*, 17–18.

26. G. Wilson Knight, "T. S. Eliot: Some Literary Impressions," 247. See also Knight's *Crown of Life*, 57, 66. In his assessment of the poem, Denis Donoghue seems to agree with Knight: "its content, its story, is Eliot's conversion to Christianity, his waking up to find himself a Christian and wondering what to make of it all." *Words Alone*, 180.

27. Eliot explains that "the theme is paternity; with a crisscross between the text and the quotation." Quoted in Southam, *A Guide to the Selected Poems of T. S. Eliot*, 247.

28. Eliot, "In Memory," 46.

29. Eliot hints at the metaphysical aspect of this discovery when he applauds the Shakespearean recognition scene, claiming that its characters appear "more than human" and

seem to move in "a light more than that of day." From "Shakespeare as Poet and Dramatist," an unpublished lecture given at Edinburgh University in 1937; quoted in Elizabeth Drew, *T. S. Eliot: The Design of His Poetry,* 127.

30. With regard to the balance between the Senecan epigraph and the monologue itself, Grover Smith contends: "The underlying parallel to the Hercules recognition serves to qualify for the reader the flash of pure delight felt by Pericles. There is an irony superior to the poem, and even if inadequately transferred from the epigraph into the monologue, it works an effect." *T. S. Eliot's Poetry and Plays,* 133.

31. Eliot, "The Idea of a Literary Review," 5–6.

32. Eliot, *After Strange Gods,* 55

33. Ibid., 55.

34. Ottoline Morrell, *Ottoline at Garsington: Memoirs of Lady Ottoline Morrell, 1915–1918,* ed. Robert Gathorne-Hardy, 101.

35. Djuna Barnes, *Nightwood,* 62. In his introduction, Eliot reveals that he had already "read *Nightwood* a number of times, in manuscript, in proof, and after publication" (xi). See also his review of *Nightwood,* which appeared the following year in the *Criterion* (April 1937).

36. Drawn to "the mystery and the attraction" of Narcissus, Eliot had experimented with him in an early poem, and he later applauded, with some hesitation, "the aloofness and frigidity of that spiritual celibate." See "The Death of Saint Narcissus" (*PWEY* 34–35) and Eliot's introduction to *The Art of Poetry,* by Paul Valéry, xxiii.

37. See Dante's revision of the Narcissus myth in *Purgatorio* XXX, 76–79; for an account of this passage and the medieval allegorical interpretations of the Ovidian myth, see Kevin Brownlee, "Dante and Narcissus (Purg. XXX, 76–99)," 201–6. Eliot was also familiar with the contemporary medievalist Étienne Gilson, in whose work he would have found an apposite account of the necessity that the soul "pass through" its own reflection by recognizing, in itself, the *Imago Dei:* "The soul, passing in a way through itself, avails itself of the factual resemblance in order to attain to God. . . . It remains imperfect so long as it is merely shut down on itself, and only becomes fully itself when it explicitly refers itself to its model." *The Spirit of Medieval Philosophy (Gifford Lectures 1931–1932),* trans. A. H. C. Downes, 213.

38. "No dying figure in Shakespeare looks *forward;* they all look backward; none thirst for the otherness of God; they all enjoy, or suffer in, and with, and for, the visible, or at least, the immanent alone." Eliot, "An Emotional Unity," 112.

39. Eliot, preface to *The Little Book of Modern Verse,* ed. Anne Ridler, 8.

40. After quoting Murry's distrustful opinion of "a completely achieved mental consciousness of our own natures," Eliot writes in agreement: "This seems to me important, sound and well put." Review of *Son of a Woman: The Story of D. H. Lawrence,* by John Middleton Murry, 774.

41. David Mayer, "The Family Reunion," 29.

42. Cleanth Brooks, "Sin and Expiation," 114.

43. Eliot to George Barker, 24 January 1938 (Harry Ransom Center, University of Texas at Austin).

44. Eliot, *Christianity and Culture,* 49.

45. For the most incisive treatments of the problem of dramatic motivation among the play's contemporary reviewers, see Philip Horton, "Speculations on Sin"; Frederick A. Pottle, "A Modern Verse Play"; anonymous, "Mr. Eliot in Search of the Present"; Phoebe Fenwick Gaye, "Expiation Becomes Orestes"; and Delmore Schwartz, "Orestes in England."

46. Brooks Atkinson, "Theatre: Eliot's *The Family Reunion,*" 39.

47. Eliot, "Critical Note," in *The Collected Poems of Harold Monro*, xvi.

48. In *The Family Reunion*, Eliot associates the garden with the psyche: "We do not like the maze in the garden, because it too closely resembles the maze in the brain" (*CPP* 290). And in *The Cocktail Party* (1950), Henry Harcourt-Reilly quotes another doubling, ghostly "garden scene" from Shelley's *Prometheus Unbound* to preface his description of another recognition scenario: "*Ere Babylon was dust / The magus Zoroaster . . . / Met his own image walking in the garden. / That apparition, sole of men, he saw*" (*CPP* 383). Immediately afterward, he offers a familiar description: "When I first met Miss Coplestone, in this room, / I saw the image, standing behind her chair, / Of a Celia Coplestone whose face showed the astonishment / Of the first five minutes after a violent death" (*CPP* 384).

49. "There are moments, perhaps not known to everyone, when a man may be nearly crushed by the terrible awareness of his isolation from every other human being; and I pity him if he finds himself only alone with himself and his meanness and futility, alone without God." Eliot, "Literature and the Modern World," 20.

50. Eliot, "Critical Note," in *The Collected Poems of Harold Monro*, xvi.

51. In a letter to George Russell (AE) written in November 1896, Yeats suggests that the gift of vision can only occur when the "shining candelabra" of civilization do not prevent us from looking into the darkness of the soul, and he is certain that "when one looks into the darkness there is always something there." *The Collected Letters of W. B. Yeats, II: 1896–1900*, 60.

52. Augustine, *Confessions*, trans. John K. Ryan, 124 (*V*, 9:16); citations for the *Confessions* include page number from this edition, followed by standard book, chapter, and paragraph numbers.

53. Ibid., 171 (VII, 10:16).

54. Ibid., 238 (X, 8:15).

55. Ibid., 260 (X, 32:48).

56. Ibid., 245 (X,16:25).

57. Eliot, "The Literature of Fascism," 288.

58. Donald Hall, *Remembering Poets: Reminiscences and Opinions*, 86.

59. Ibid., 85–86.

60. See Lord Claverton's question in *The Elder Statesman*: "What is this self inside us, this silent observer, / Severe and speechless critic [?]" (*Plays* 317). See also Mary's remark in *The Family Reunion*: "A curse is written / On the under side of things / Behind the smiling mirror" (*CPP* 292).

61. E. Martin Browne, "T. S. Eliot in the Theatre," 122.

CHAPTER 3: YEATS'S ABNORMAL RESTLESSNESS

1. Yeats to Lady Gregory, 8 September 1917, Unpublished letter, *CL InteLex* #3320.

2. Yeats to Lady Gregory, 13 October 1917, Unpublished letter, *CL InteLex* #3340.

3. Ibid.

4. See "The Symbolism of Poetry," wherein he identifies emotion with "the power, the god it calls among us": "All sounds, all colours, all forms, either because of their preordained energies or because of long association, evoke indefinable and yet precise emotions, or, as I prefer to think, call down among us certain disembodied powers, whose footsteps over our hearts we call emotions" (*E&I* 157).

5. In a letter to Cornelius Weygandt, the American journalist and critic, written as early as 30 May 1897, Yeats reveals that "the chief influence" on his work (second only to Irish folklore) has been "certain mystics of the middle ages" (*CL2* 106).

6. See Alex Zwerdling's *Yeats and the Heroic Ideal*; John Byars, *Yeats's Introduction of the Heroic Type*. The copy of Thomas Common's *Nietzsche as Critic, Philosopher, Poet, and Prophet: Choice Selections from his Works* (London: G. Richard, 1901) that Yeats annotated was given to him in 1902 by his friend and lawyer, John Quinn (Charles Deering Library, Northwestern University).

7. Edmund Dulac, "Without the Twilight," in *W. B. Yeats: Interviews and Recollections*, vol. 2, ed. E. H. Mikhail, 290; published originally in *Scattering Branches: Tributes to the Memory of W. B. Yeats*.

8. Larry Brunner, *Tragic Victory: The Doctrine of Subjective Salvation in the Poetry of W. B. Yeats*, 102–3; Richard Ellmann, *The Identity of Yeats*, 117; Phillip L. Marcus, *Yeats and Artistic Power*.

9. Daniel Albright, *Quantum Poetics*, 52.

10. Margaret Mills Harper shows persuasively that contemporary guides for mediumship did not, in fact, posit the need for such a passive, involuntary surrender. As a counterweight to Yeats's understanding of the "old order," she offers the following from M. H. Wallis's *A Guide to Mediumship and Psychical Unfoldment*: "we unhesitatingly affirm that it is not necessary that mediums should regard themselves as mere 'conduits' through which the spirits are to pour just whatever they choose. . . mediums must study their own powers." Quoted in *Wisdom of Two*, 12.

11. For instance, in *The Stirring of the Bones*: "Lady Gregory and I had heard many tales of changelings, grown men and women as well as children, who, as the people believe, are taken by the faeries, some spirit or inanimate object bewitched into their likeness remaining in their stead, and I constantly asked myself what reality there could be in these tales, often supported by such testimonies" (*Au* 284). See also "Irish Fairies, Ghosts, Witches, Etc.," included in January 1889 issue of the theosophical magazine *Lucifer* in *Early Articles and Reviews*, 78; and Deirdre Toomey's "Away" in *Yeats and Women*, 151–55.

12. Yeats also recalls thinking immediately about Balzac's reluctance to take opium "because he dreaded the surrender of his will" (*Au* 106). Katharine Tynan recalls Yeats's violent reaction during and after the séance in *Twenty-five Years: Reminiscences*: "Willie Yeats was banging his head on the table. . . . He explained to me afterwards that the spirits were evil. To keep them off he had been saying the nearest approach to a prayer he could remember" (209).

13. Yeats, *The Speckled Bird*, 44.

14. In *The Stirring of the Bones*, he recounts a mystical feeling of surrender that he experienced in Sligo, after which he awakened to discover himself speaking: "The next morning I awoke near dawn to hear a voice saying, 'The love of God is infinite for every soul'" (*Au* 284). He gives the account in a more familiar form in *Memoirs* (126) and in *Per Amica Silentia Lunae*: "Once, twenty years ago, I seemed to awake from sleep to find my body rigid, and to hear a strange voice speaking these words through my lips as through lips of stone: 'We make an image of him who sleeps'" (*LE* 32). Albright suggests, "It was perhaps the eeriest of Yeats's experiences, this sensation that he was only a surrogate for himself" (*Quantum Poetics*, 46).

15. *Yeats's Vision Papers*, vol. 3, ed. Robert Anthony Martinich and Margaret Mills Harper, 9. According to Harper, "This 'new method' involved a number of methods, all involving a sleep-like state, during or after which she would speak." *Wisdom of Two*, 8. See also "The Gates of Pluto" in the 1925 edition of *A Vision*: "In sleep we enter upon the same life as that we enter between death and birth." Yeats, *A Vision (1925)*, ed. Catherine E. Paul and Margaret Mills Harper, 201.

16. R. F. Foster, *W. B. Yeats: A Life*, vol. 1, *The Apprentice Mage*, 464.

17. Ibid., 464.

18. In the first version of his "Autobiography" (1916–17), Yeats recounts the admonitory effects of his experiences with MacGregor Mathers and his wife—both practicing spiritualists—during his stay in Paris in 1894, remembering that Mathers's psychic evocations "were a dangerous strain" and that the older man would often spit blood afterward from exhaustion (*Mem* 73). And regarding the loss of self-possession that often accompanies such experiments, he contends fiercely: "It is always inexcusable to lose one's self-possession. It always comes from impatience, from a kind of spiritual fright at someone who is here and now more powerful" (*Mem* 138).

19. Daniel Albright, "Yeats and Modernism," *Cambridge Companion to W. B. Yeats*, ed. Marjorie Elizabeth Howes and John Kelly, 73.

20. For critical accounts of the relationship between Yeats's occult and spiritualist pursuits and his theories of poetics, symbolism, and artistic impersonality, see Timothy Materer, *Modernist Alchemy: Poetry and the Occult*, 25–48; Helen Sword, *Ghostwriting Modernism*, 103–18; and Leon Surette, *The Birth of Modernism: Ezra Pound, T. S. Eliot, W. B. Yeats, and the Occult*.

21. See his remarks in a February 1909 journal entry: "Surely the idea of culture expressed by Pater can only create feminine souls. The soul becomes a mirror not a brazier" (*Mem* 159). Yeats goes on to propose a culture founded not on the Victorian model of "wise receptivity" but on the active "imitative energy" that thrived during the Renaissance (160). Albright agrees that "wherever Yeats looked among the official masterpieces of Victorian England, Yeats saw passivity, suspension, impotence." *Quantum Poetics*, 57.

22. Yeats to Katharine Tynan, 25 August 1888: "Did I ever tell you that a clairvoyant told me months ago that I had made too many thoughts and that for a long time I should have to become passive[?] . . . Most passive I have been this long while, feeling as though my brain had been rolled about for centuries in the sea, and as I look on my piles of MSS, as though I had built a useless city in my sleep. Indeed I have grown more and more passive ever since I finished Oisin and what an eater up of ideals is passivity for every things [*sic*] seems a vision and nothing worth seeking after" (*CL1* 92).

23. See his autograph inscription to Mabel Dickinson, dated March 1908, in her copy of *Stories of Red Hanrahan* (Dundrum: Dun Emer Press, 1904), in the Manuscript, Archives, and Rare Book Library, Emory University. The inscription appears almost one year later, verbatim but for corrected spelling, in his private journal (*Mem* 155).

24. Yeats to Mohini Chatterjee, 29 September 1935 (*CL InteLex* #27). See also *EE* 292.

25. Yeats did not, as he apparently planned, include "The Way of Wisdom" in his 1903 collection, *Ideas of Good and Evil*, nor did he consider it appropriate for inclusion in *The Cutting of an Agate* (1912); it did not see print again after the 1908 *Collected Works*. His autograph revisions and corrections to his personal copy of the original *Spectator* article, preliminary to inclusion in *Collected Works*, vol. 8, are in the Manuscript, Archives, and Rare Book Library, Emory University, MS 600, Box 1, folder 59. See also *EE*, appendix B, 291–92.

26. In Yeats's schema of the twenty-eight lunar phases, the saint occupies the twenty-seventh, the penultimate phase before the closure of what he calls the subjective or "antithetical tincture." True to Yeats's earliest visions of the saint's passivity and renunciation, "his joy is to be nothing, to do nothing, to think nothing; but to permit the total life, expressed in its humanity, to flow in upon him and express itself through his acts and thoughts" (*A Vision* 180). Though the hero is not named as such, his phase is most likely the

tenth, characterized by "more desire of action and of command," "brutal violence," and a calculated "subjective fury" (123).

27. In a revealing note to *The Wind Among the Reeds*, Yeats explains that Aedh, Hanrahan, and Michael Robartes "are personages in 'The Secret Rose;' but . . . I have used them in this book more as principles of the mind than as actual personages" (*VP* 803).

28. Yeats, *John Sherman & Dhoya*, 121.

29. Yeats, *Later Articles and Reviews*, 297.

30. Yeats, *Early Articles and Reviews*, 439.

31. For Yeats's assertion of this transformation and mutability as a structural feature of the creative mind, see *Memoirs*: "The nature of the man seems to prepare for a continual change, a phantasmagoria. One day one god and the next another" (138).

32. Yeats, *Early Articles and Reviews*, 252.

33. Yeats records Chatterjee as concluding his advice on surrender and acquiescence thus: "I have lived many lives. I have been a slave and a prince. Many a beloved has sat upon my knees, and I have sat upon the knees of many a beloved" (*EE* 290). He later reworked the saying in the lyric "Mohini Chatterjee": "I have been a king / I have been a slave / Nor is there anything / Fool, rascal, knave, / That I have not been" (*VP* 496).

34. Margaret Mills Harper quotes from Yeats's "Remarks" delivered to the Ghost Club on 7 June 1911. *Wisdom of Two*, 22.

35. I agree with Zwerdling that "Yeats's visionary . . . like all his other heroic men, is not a success but a failure," but I believe that he underestimates the danger and psychological complexity of Yeatsian vision in claiming that its attainment depends upon "transcendence of that failure" and that "the failure which Yeats's hero experiences is primarily external. His defeat in the world of circumstance prepares for his triumph in the internal world of the self." *Yeats and the Heroic Ideal*, 9.

36. Cf. Yeats's interview in March 1955, originally published in *London Magazine*: "We went on from [*Othello*] to definitions of tragedy, which Yeats defined as the struggle of the soul with an obstacle which can be escaped only in death. 'In farce, the soul is struggling against a ridiculous object: in comedy, with a removable object: in tragedy, with an irremovable object.'" *W. B. Yeats: Interviews and Recollections*, 2:152.

37. Yeats, *Mythologies*, 337.

38. Vendler's suggestion remains relevant: "It is as a stylistic arrangement of experience—a poet's experience—that *A Vision* must be seen if it is to shed light on Yeats's poetry and plays." *Yeats's Vision and the Later Plays*, 2. See also Ellmann: "The soul may be said to pass through all the phases within a single lifetime." *Yeats: The Man and the Masks*, 226. Yeats himself claims that the great wheel represents "every completed movement of thought or life, twenty-eight incarnations, a single incarnation, a single judgment or act of thought" (*Vision* 81).

39. Yeats frequently describes this moment of complete self-realization with a (misattributed) quote from Thomas Aquinas. See "Swedenborg, Mediums, and the Desolate Places": "All has been kneaded up anew, arrayed in order and made one piece . . . for Villiers de l'Isle-Adam quotes Thomas Aquinas as having said, 'Eternity is the possession of one's self, as in a single moment'" (*Ex* 37). For the relationship between "Unity of Being" and personality, see Ellmann, *Yeats: The Man and the Masks*, 239–242.

40. Oliver Hennessey, "'I shall find the dark grow luminous . . . ,'" 7–8.

41. In her introduction to the Cornell manuscript edition of *The Hour-Glass*, Catherine Phillips calls the play "a dramatized debate about the comparative value Yeats saw in learned wisdom and simple faith." *The Hour-Glass: Manuscript Materials*, ed. Catherine Phillips, xxix.

42. Yeats, *The Hour-Glass: Manuscript Materials*, xxii.

43. For Yeats's remarks on the symbolic mental paradigms of the wise man and the fool here and in *On Baille's Strand*, see his letter to Gordon Craig (3 November 1910), reproduced in part in *The Hour-Glass: Manuscript Materials*, xxix. Elsewhere Yeats explains that the fool "wears a mask designed by Mr. Gordon Craig which makes him seem less a human being than a principle of the mind" (*VP* 645).

44. See, for instance, Yeats's doubts and incredulities regarding the "spirit" known as Leo Africanus in "The Manuscript of 'Leo Africanus,'" ed. Steve L. Adams and George Mills Harper. He describes himself there as "doubting, conscientious and timid" (13). And elsewhere, in an unpublished letter to Lady Gregory on 17 December 1913, he again confesses that "my mind is too scientific, too restless. I make communication difficult by disturbing the stream as it were" (*CL InteLex* #2328).

45. For the differences between the early draft and the first published version, see *The Hour-Glass: Manuscript Materials*, 40, 60. In a letter to Frank Fay, Yeats says that he drew upon Dante's *Paradiso* for his cosmological allusions to the fixed and moving stars (*CL3* 225–26).

46. Yeats, *Early Articles and Reviews*, 137.

47. Albright, *Quantum Poetics*, 32.

48. See Yeats's note to the 1914 version of *The Hour-Glass*: "I have for years struggled with something which is charming in the naïve legend but a platitude on the stage. I did not discover till a year ago that if the wise man humbled himself to the fool and received salvation as his reward, so much more powerful are pictures than words, no explanatory dialogue could set the matter right" (*VPl* 646). Apparently his dissatisfaction with the play's ending had begun as early as 1903, when he wrote to Lady Gregory: "I propose to put certain parts of 'The Hour-Glass' into verse. . . . I have got to think this necessary to lift the 'wise man's' part out of a slight element of platitude" (*CL3* 294–95).

49. Cf. *Pages from a Diary Written in Nineteen Hundred and Thirty*, in which Yeats discusses the creative implications of "dying into the freedom of God and then coming to birth again" (*Ex* 306).

50. Yeats, *The Hour-Glass: Manuscript Materials*, 139.

51. Ibid., 247, 296, 330.

52. "My father once said to me that contemplative men had been for centuries in conspiracy to exalt their form of life, and I think I remember his denying that painter and poet were contemplative." Yeats continues, "I think I assert [the same as my father] when I assert that we hold down as it were on a sword's point what would, if undefeated, grow into the counter-truth" (*Ex* 307).

53. For the most recent of these, see Vendler's *Our Secret Discipline: Yeats and Lyric Form*, 370–75.

54. As Vendler, Bloom, and others point out, Yeats's "Shiftings" is a state that involves an emptying of personality akin to what the wise man describes as the self's "perishing" into nothingness in *The Hour-Glass* (*VPl* 636). See Vendler, *Yeats's Vision* (249), and Bloom: " In terms of Yeats's system, the Shrouds are moving through the last moments of the state called 'The Shiftings.' . . . In this shifting of your whole morality as a man, you are emptied out, and are made ready for the Shrouds' transfiguration into complete equilibrium or wholeness." "Death and the Native Strain in American Poetry," 456–57.

55. Helen Vendler, "The Later Poetry," *The Cambridge Companion to W. B. Yeats*, 97.

56. Though he declared himself "incompetent to expound Indian philosophy," Yeats composed a number of introductions and essays on the subject during the last decade of his life, paying particular attention to the mystical " 'deep sleep,' where man 'feels no desire, creates

no dream'" and to the "dreamless sleep of the soul" wherein the mind knows itself "an instrument of that other Will" (*LE* 171; 157; 150). See his introductions to *An Indian Monk* (1932), *The Holy Mountain* (1934), the "Mandukya Upanishad" (1935), and *Aphorisms of Yôga* (1938), as well as his preface to *The Ten Principal Upanishads* (1937), all undertaken in cooperation with Shri Purohit Swami, whom Yeats had met in June 1931 at the home of T. Sturge Moore.

57. Yeats to Dorothy Wellesley, 6 April 1936, *CL InteLex* #6531.

58. Hazard Adams, *The Book of Yeats's Poems*, 240.

59. Foster, *W. B. Yeats: A Life*, vol. 2, 84.

60. Yeats moved temporarily into the partially renovated tower in the summer of 1922, just when the smoldering political conflict over the Anglo-Irish Treaty of January 1922 began to escalate into actual violence. The nearby countryside was prey to roving bands of disguised dissidents, and the Yeatses actually were awakened by a similar knocking upon their door when local rebels politely alerted them, on 19 August 1922, that the bridge adjacent to their tower would be detonated in less than an hour. See Foster, *W. B. Yeats: A Life*, vol. 2, 205–23.

61. Yeats's rhetoric in the letter is aimed at the practical purpose of dissuading the members of the Hermetic Order of the Golden Dawn from continuing to allow separate fringe "groups" to operate within it for fear that, disclaiming their obligations to the society's general rule, they will "be free to misuse that knowledge in the Rooms of the Order itself" (*CL3* 43). What frightens Yeats about the "groups," and what allows him to align them with the "foreign element" in the individual mind, is that they bear no allegiance to the Order's governing body and instead demand control for themselves.

62. Hazard Adams suggests that "the speaker [of "The Black Tower"] is very suspicious of foreign influences," but I believe he mistakes Yeats's piercing psychological allegory for mere nationalistic sentiment in claiming that the poem encourages young poets to be faithful to "ancient Irish heroes." Hazard Adams, *The Book of Yeats's Poems*, 241. The psychological trope—"sometimes the sphere of an individual man is broken"—was still on Yeats's mind in 1915 when, fearing the influence of a multiplying, foreign energy within his own mind, he asked himself urgently, "Is your own mind broken & your will doubled?" Steve L. Adams and George Mills Harper, "The Manuscript of 'Leo Africanus,'" 29.

63. Only three years before "The Black Tower," Yeats reflects upon this sort of sudden, imminent revelation in his introduction to Shri Purohit Swami's translation of the "Mandukya Upanishad": in the ancient texts, he suggests, it is only after the holy pilgrim "strained his heroic will to the utmost" that he arrives at "the event, the supreme drama," and, Yeats concludes, "this revelation has been sudden" (*LE* 160).

64. *The Gonne-Yeats Letters: 1893–1938*, ed. Anna MacBride White and A. Norman Jeffares, 450.

65. Ibid., 451.

CHAPTER 4: THE TURBULENT LIVES OF PAINTED HORSES

1. W. B. Yeats to John Quinn, 31 December 1919, *CL InteLex* #3696.

2. Shotaro Oshima, *Yeats and Japan*, 5 n. 2, 21.

3. Yeats informed his wife of the offer in a letter written on 10 July 1919 (*CL InteLex* #3629). In a session on 17 November 1919, George's new "Instructor," Ameritus, was remarkably unambiguous in his advice: "Tower this year—I said before no Japan next year." George Mills Harper, *The Making of Yeats's 'A Vision': A Study of the Automatic Script*, 2:359.

4. Oshima, *Yeats and Japan*, 21.

5. Yeats added the legend of the Japanese painter to his memoirs only after he had received and declined the offer to lecture in Tokyo. It is absent from the early version, "First

Draft" (wr. circa 1915–16), even though the other material that he includes in section 4 of that manuscript corresponds roughly to the contents of section 20 of "Four Years" (in the 1922 edition), where the fable eventually appears. For the dating of "First Draft" and the structural correspondences between it and "Four Years," see Curtis B. Bradford, *Yeats at Work*, 348–51.

6. Though Yeats shifts its position in the early publications of *Four Years*, the account of the painted horses remains largely unaltered from 1921 to 1955, aside from minor punctuation changes and the (most likely accidental) omission of a word ("dark") in the Cuala edition. The only significant change occurs in the edition of *The Trembling of the Veil* published privately by T. Werner Laurie in December 1922, wherein Yeats substitutes "slipped down after dark" (1922 and after) for the earlier "stepped down after dark" (1921). The painted horses appear in sections 18 and 22 of "Four Years" in the *London Mercury* (August 1921), 371, 376; in 17 and 21 of the Cuala edition (December 1921), 78–79, 90; and in 20 and 23 of *The Trembling of the Veil* (T. Werner Laurie, 1922), 72, 79; *Autobiographies: Reveries Over Childhood and Youth* and *The Trembling of the Veil* (London: Macmillan, 1926), 230–31, 240; and *Au* 186, 194.

7. See Yeats's letters to Ezra Pound (8 December 1920) and Lady Gregory (12 December 1920) containing reports of the progress and completion of *Four Years*. R. F. Foster, *W. B. Yeats: A Life*, vol. 2, 177, 701 n. 33.

8. See especially Ronald Schuchard's discussion of Yeats's "spiritual democracy" in *The Last Minstrels: Yeats and the Revival of the Bardic Arts*, 191–218; Rob Doggett's *Deep-Rooted Things: Empire and Nation in the Poetry and Drama of William Butler Yeats*; *W. B. Yeats and Postcolonialism*, ed. Deborah Fleming; and Michael McAteer's *Standish O'Grady, AE and Yeats: History, Politics, Culture*.

9. W. H. Auden, *Collected Poems*, ed. Edward Mendelson, 247.

10. Ernest Hart (1835–1898), *Lectures on Japanese Art Work*, 27–28.

11. In "The Tragic Theatre," he describes "that beauty which seems unearthly because the individual woman is lost amid the labyrinth of its lines as though life were trembling into stillness and silence" (*E&I* 243–44). The phrase appears again in "The Phases of the Moon" (1919) : "Under the frenzy of the fourteenth moon, / The soul begins to tremble into stillness" (*VP* 374).

12. "KOSE NO KANAOKA, who lived in the ninth century, is said to have painted a horse for the temple of Ninnaji, near Kyoto, which left its canvas to browse in the neighbouring fields, until one of the monks added a tether and a peg to the picture." Henri L. Joly, *Legend in Japanese Art*, 299. Binyon had recommended Joly's book to Yeats, who wrote on 29 January 1924 of his intention to borrow it from the London Library; see *CL InteLex* #4465. See also Siegfried Bing's essay "The Origin of Painting Gathered from History," in vol. 3 of *Artistic Japan*. In Bing's version, "the animal disappears through a temple door, his hunters follow him, they search everywhere around and cannot find him, until on the wall in a celebrated picture which hangs in its accustomed place, they see the fiery beast, who has just re-entered his frame, entirely covered with foam, and still panting from his frantic race" (176). Though Bing's account includes the trampled rice fields that Yeats mentions in *Four Years* and is chronologically viable as a source, it makes no mention of the "drops of moisture" in Hart's account (28) that so distinctly resemble Yeats's "shower of water-drops" (*Au* 186).

13. In *The Flight of the Dragon*, Laurence Binyon relates a similar, albeit less detailed, fable about "horses so charged with life that they galloped out of the picture" (20). For Yeats's familiarity with Binyon's works on Eastern painting, see his remarks in "The Bounty of Sweden" (*Au* 547) and his letter to Binyon written on 11 September [1919] (*CL InteLex* #3651). In "The Story of Kwashin Koji," Lafcadio Hearn suggests that "there are many stories to prove

that really great pictures have souls. . . . It is well known that a horse, painted upon a certain kakemono, used to go out at night to eat grass." *Shadowings and A Japanese Miscellany,* 218. See also Hearn's "The Boy Who Drew Cats," in *Japanese Fairy Tales,* 37–45. For Yeats's familiarity with Hearn's work and the brief, ungainly correspondence that the two shared in the summer of 1901, see *CL3* 101–2. Joe Earl discusses the history of the late-nineteenth-century popularization of Japanese art in "The Taxonomic Obsession: British Collectors and Japanese Objects, 1852–1986."

14. Hearn quotes this phrase in a passage that he attributes to the collection of tales in the *Otogi-Hyaku-Monogatari* by "the old Japanese author, Hakubai-En Rosui." "The Screen-Maiden," *Shadowings and a Japanese Miscellany,* 13.

15. For Yeats's reports on the completion of *Dhoya,* see his letters to H. H. Sparling (10 September [1887]) and Katharine Tynan ([18 November 1887]), *CL1* 36 n. 5, 42.

16. Yeats, *John Sherman & Dhoya,* 81.

17. Yeats, *The Secret Rose, Stories by W. B. Yeats: A Variorum Edition,* 12–13.

18. Yeats, *Mythologies,* 100.

19. Paul Muldoon, *Poems 1968–1998,* 178.

20. *The Senate Speeches of W. B. Yeats,* ed. Donald R. Pearce, 52.

21. *Inferno,* 16:121–22, *The Divine Comedy,* trans. Henry Cary.

22. In a long letter to his father written on 14 March 1916, Yeats returns to a similar criterion, substituting Chinese for Japanese art: "I think Keats perhaps greater than Shelley and beyond words greater than Swinburne because he makes pictures one cannot forget & sees them as full of rhythm as a Chinese painting. Swinburne's poetry all but some early poems is as abstract as a Cubist picture" (*Wade* 608).

23. Discussing the value of anti-naturalist dramatic scenery in the 1904 issue of *Samhain,* Yeats proposes that although "we can only find the right decoration for different types of play by experiment," the range of experimentation must fall upon a spectrum that includes both Byzantine mosaic and Kanaoka's type of design: "it will probably range between, on the one hand, woodlands made out of recurring pattern, or painted like old religious pictures upon gold background, and upon the other the comparative realism of a Japanese print" (*IDM* 78).

24. Steve L. Adams and George Mills Harper, eds., "The Manuscript of 'Leo Africanus,'" 29. See also Yeats's nostalgic claim in a 1904 issue of *Samhain:* "An old writer saw his hero, if it was a play of character . . . moving before him, living with a life he did not endeavor to control" (*IDM* 68).

25. For Yeats's well-known note on unexpected transformations that occurred during the composition of "Leda and the Swan," see *VP* 828.

26. Richard Londraville, "Four Lectures by W. B. Yeats," 115.

27. Frank Kermode, *Romantic Image,* 52–58.

28. Yeats, *Interviews and Recollections,* vol. 2, ed. E. H. Mikhail, 329.

29. Thomas Carlyle, *On Heroes, Hero-Worship, and the Heroic in History,* 136–37.

30. Ibid., 149.

31. Ibid., 150.

32. Ibid.

33. Walter Pater, *Appreciations: With an Essay on Style,* 79.

34. Ibid., 80.

35. Ibid., 81, 55. According to Pater, Wordsworth was the poet "who thought that in all creative work the larger part was given passively, to the recipient mind, who waited so dutifully upon the gift, to whom so large a measure was sometimes given. Pater, *Appreciations,*

39. Of course his own protagonist in *Marius the Epicurean* cultivates a strikingly similar receptivity: "From that maxim of *Life as the end of life,* followed, as a practical consequence, the desirableness of refining all the instruments of inward and outward intuition, of developing all their capacities, of testing and exercising one's self in them, till one's whole nature became one complex medium of reception, toward the vision—the 'beatific vision.'" *Marius the Epicurean,* 1.143.

36. Pater, *Appreciations,* 24.

37. See Pater: "There are some to whom nothing has any real interest, or real meaning, except as operative in a given person; and it is they who best appreciate the quality of soul in literary art. They seem to know a *person,* in a book, and make way by intuition." *Appreciations,* 24.

38. Oscar Wilde, *Intentions,* 202.

39. Ibid., 175–76.

40. Ibid., 164, 161.

41. Ibid., 158–59.

42. Kermode, *Romantic Image,* 56.

43. Ibid., 79.

44. Ibid., 111.

45. Arthur Symons, *The Symbolist Movement in Literature,* 14.

46. Kermode, *Romantic Image,* 80. Oliver Hennessey also places Yeats at the modern end of this tradition in claiming that "the Yeatsian linguistic symbol is set up as more than metaphor or representation. It becomes alive, existing as both a form of literary artifice and as the tool by which the spirit world can act upon the mundane." "'I shall find the dark grow luminous . . . ,'" 6.

47. John Keats, "Ode on Melancholy," in *A Critical Edition of the Major Works,* ed. Elizabeth Cook, 290.

48. See for instance Bernard Gendron's *Between Montmartre and the Mudd Club* (2002) and David Chinitz's *T. S. Eliot and the Cultural Divide* (2003), both of which offer useful correctives to more recent and sympathetic readings of Bürger and Huyssen, such as Richard Murphy's *Theorizing the Avant-Garde* (1999).

49. Yeats to Laurence Binyon, 11 September [1919] (*CL InteLex* #3651). In his *Lectures on Japanese Art Work,* Hart relates that "the very few pictures which remain known to us as the authentic works of Kanaoka are entirely Buddhistic portraitures of deities, and although there are extant traditions deeply implanted in Japanese literature of his surpassing skill in the portraiture of animals . . . there are no existing examples" (27). By the time Binyon was writing *Painting in the Far East,* art historians had disputed the authenticity of even the few that remained: "Kanaoka, one of the greatest names in all the art of Japan, if we are to accept the unvarying voice of tradition, but alas! a name only. . . . Not a single picture now existing is allowed to be by his brush" (104–6).

50. Even if he did not remember Kanaoka's name when he was writing *Four Years,* Yeats had encountered it not only in Hart's *Lectures* but in Binyon's *Painting in the Far East* as well: "With the ninth century, too, we come to the first pre-eminent name in Japanese painting—Kanaoka. . . . He painted figures, landscapes, animals, birds, and flowers. He was noted, like Han Kan, for his horses" (104). See Yeats's "Estrangement": "I have been talking of the literary element in painting with Miss E— G— and turning over the leaves of Binyon's book on Eastern Painting" (*Au* 489).

51. Around the same time, Yeats also wrote to a professor at the Taihoku Imperial University, Formosa, "expressing a great temptation to visit Japan" and assuring him that the

"best things that he wanted to see with his own eyes were all in Japan." Oshima, *Yeats and Japan*, 23.

CHAPTER 5: VIRGINIA WOOLF

1. T. S. Eliot to Virginia Woolf, unpublished letter, 2 September 1925 (Berg Collection of English and American Literature, New York Public Library).

2. Eliot wrote to her in eager anticipation of the essay again on 28 October 1925, promising publication in the January 1926 issue of the *Criterion* (Harry Ransom Center, University of Texas at Austin). Woolf records his earliest entreaties in a diary entry on 14 September 1925, and she relates her disappointment at his "unenthusiastic response" on 7 December (*Diary* 3.41, 49).

3. T. S. Eliot to Virginia Woolf, unpublished letter, 3 May 1925 (Harry Ransom Center, University of Texas at Austin).

4. I believe that claims such as Elena Gualtieri's—that art possesses, for Woolf, "a therapeutic function that is both a liberation and a relief"—underestimate the psychological dangers that Woolf envisioned as inseparable from creativity. *Virginia Woolf's Essays*, 104. See also Patricia Moran, *Virginia Woolf, Jean Rhys, and the Aesthetics of Trauma;* Elizabeth Abel, *Virginia Woolf and the Fictions of Psychoanalysis;* Tammy Clewell, "Consolation Refused: Virginia Woolf, the Great War, and Modernist Mourning"; and Karen DeMeester, "Trauma and Recovery in Virginia Woolf's *Mrs. Dalloway.*"

5. Louise Poresky, *The Elusive Self: Psyche and Spirit in Virginia Woolf's Novels,* 16. In fairness to her argument, I must point out that Poresky does view the eventual psychic dissolution in *The Waves* as a necessary dialectical descent away from the fully achieved Self, but this descent nonetheless relies upon similar models of self-recovery and self-unity.

6. Eve Sorum suggests that Woolf's passively absorbed "shocks" of experience are "integral to the act of writing": "The writer . . . must place herself in a position of vulnerability and receptivity to suffering in order to derive pleasure from the production of art, as well as to experience an empowering sense of control over the world at large." I am doubtful, however, that Woolf's ideal writer actually benefits from this sense of control or that she views suffering as an exchange through which "pain becomes pleasure and helplessness is rewritten as power." "Masochistic Modernisms," 35. Charles Bernheimer also emphasizes "the reparatory and sublimatory functions of art" and argues that, for Woolf, "the shattering of the self's boundaries may serve to dramatize the existence of those boundaries." "A Shattered Globe: Narcissism and Masochism in Virginia Woolf's Life-Writing," 203, 194. Makiko Minow-Pinkney focuses upon the linguistic nature of Woolf's "precarious dialectic between identity and its loss" that nonetheless results in a new, "healed" model of subjectivity grounded in the semiotic. *Virginia Woolf and the Problem of the Subject,* 155. See also Louise DeSalvo's *Virginia Woolf: The Impact of Childhood Sexual Abuse on Her Life and Work.*

7. Most germane to this argument are Richter's reading of the atomic shower as a metaphor for "the synthesized responses of mind and body . . . to outside influences" in *Virginia Woolf: The Inward Voyage,* 30, and Albright's explanation of the "red hot" experiences that "destroy different patches of our insulation, leave us mottled, figured, articulated, regrettably human" in *Personality and Impersonality,* 98.

8. I am indebted to Albright's keen discussion of this trope and of Woolf's "myth of personality" in *Personality and Impersonality,* 96–100.

9. Woolf would have encountered Emerson's famous metaphor in October 1909 when, as we know from her reading notebooks, she was reading John Morley's edition of his *Works*

(Macmillan, 1883) along with James Cabot's two-volume biography (*A Memoir of Ralph Waldo Emerson,* Boston: Houghton Mifflin, 1887) in preparation for her review of his *Journals,* which appeared in the *TLS,* 3 March 1910, 69–70. See Brenda R. Silver, *Virginia Woolf's Reading Notebooks,* 147; *Essays* 1.335–40.

10. Regarding Eliot's aversion to Emerson and the transcendentalism that he associated with American Unitarianism, Schuchard suggests, "To Eliot he was the romantic embodiment of everything he wanted to exile himself from in America—religious liberalism, individualism, optimism, sentimentalism. . . . Emerson's Unitarian virus, working on a weakened strain of New England Puritanism, had transformed itself into Transcendentalism, and a young Eliot found the blanched, dissolvent morality abhorrent." "Burbank with a Baedeker, Eliot with a Cigar: American Intellectuals, Anti-Semitism, and the Idea of Culture," 2.

11. Woolf records Eliot's recitation—"He sang it & chanted it rhythmed it" in her sitting room on the previous Sunday—in a journal entry on 23 June 1922 (*Diary* 2.178).

12. Albright, *Personality and Impersonality,* 100.

13. Cf. James Naremore's pertinent claim: "Mrs. Woolf suggests that beneath the surface of civilization there runs a current of emotion, a general truth that unites all men who submit to it. To make oneself truly aware of this current is to subordinate reason to feeling, and to lose awareness of the self." *The World without a Self: Virginia Woolf and the Novel,* 26. Naremore recognizes the necessary possibility of this creative dissolution but frequently elides its more dangerous and threatening aspects by discussing it in terms of a transcendent potential: "The individual personality is continually being dissolved by intimations of eternity" (245).

14. Harvena Richter claims that the novel's main characters "suggest various facets of the imagination, its diverse processes, its conscious and unconscious areas" and finally "the individuation of the creative self." *Virginia Woolf: The Inward Voyage,* 22. Cf. Lisa Rado's contention that such a claim "ignores the validity of Rhoda's historical situation as a creative, unmarried woman in a man's world . . . it functions to disembody her." *The Modern Androgyne Imagination: A Failed Sublime,* 201 n. 12.

15. For a thorough examination of this *topos* in Woolf's work, see J. Hillis Miller's "Mr. Carmichael and Lily Briscoe: The Rhythm of Creativity in *To the Lighthouse.*" Minow-Pinkney also speculates on its epistemological implications in *Virginia Woolf and the Problem of the Subject,* 161.

16. Woolf reiterates this impression much later in *A Sketch of the Past,* when she recalls—still with great surprise and disbelief—how she "made up, as I sometimes make up my books, *To the Lighthouse;* in a great, apparently involuntary, rush. One thing burst into another" (*Moments* 81).

17. Makiko Minow-Pinkney, *Virginia Woolf and the Problem of the Subject,* 183. Louise Poresky recognizes the Neoplatonic origins of this psychological and artistic dissolution when she claims that the "composite personality" of *The Waves*—that abstract entity composed of all of the characters combined—must eventually and painfully "descend from the realm of Selfhood and drop back into the world of psychic dissolution." *The Elusive Self,* 185. The "transcendental ego . . . threatened with dissolution" is central to Minow-Pinkney's argument as well, though I believe that her generalization of the phenomenon dilutes the urgent and crucial significance it holds for Woolf's theories of the imaginative process in particular. *Virginia Woolf and the Problem of the Subject,* 170.

18. Naremore, *The World without a Self: Virginia Woolf and the Novel,* 55.

CHAPTER 6: THOMAS MANN

1. Thomas Mann, *"On Myself" and Other Princeton Lectures,* ed. James H. Bade, 51. See also Mann's letter to Carl Maria Weber, 4 July 1920: "On a more serious note: passion as confusion and as a stripping of dignity was really the subject of my tale" (*Letters* 103). Here and throughout this chapter I have given the titles of Mann's works in English translation, but for purposes of maintaining an accurate chronology, the dates of publication refer to the German originals.

2. "Secondly there was his personal mistrust of passion as such, a Protestant and puritanical burgher trait which he shares with Aschenbach, and which counteracted any 'Greek' view of homosexual love." T. J. Reed, *Thomas Mann: The Uses of Tradition,* 153.

3. See especially Gary Johnson, "*Death in Venice* and the Aesthetic Correlative": "This unhinging marks the beginning of the end for Aschenbach, for now he abjures self-criticism and devotes himself to the pursuit of Tadzio. In a sense, Aschenbach has abandoned his original character—the one described as leading a tense but controlled existence, like a tightly balled fist—and has relaxed into a licentious old man. To borrow a phrase from the plastic arts, Aschenbach has failed to hold his pose" (92). The ongoing critical debate regarding the story's tragic elements revolves around whether one sees Aschenbach's demise as a "fall from high estate" or, as I propose, merely a delayed revelation of his already fallen condition. See Edgar Rosenberg's "Mann's *Death in Venice,*" 154; Rita Bergenholtz, "Mann's *Death in Venice,*" 146; Peter Heller, "Thomas Mann's Conception of the Creative Writer," passim; and Martin Travers, *Thomas Mann,* 57–58.

4. Mann's working notes, originally published in T. J. Reed's *"Der Tod in Venedig": Text, Materialen, Kommentar* (Munich: Hanswer, 1983), appear in English for the first time in Koelb's Norton Critical edition, 70–92.

5. Jean-Pierre Mileur, "Revisionism, Irony, and the Mask of Sentiment," 203.

6. "The Black Swan" (1953) revisits *Death in Venice* from the perspective of an aged woman. The aristocratic widow Rosalie von Tümmler becomes erotically obsessed with an adolescent boy, only to discover shortly thereafter that a cancerous uteran tumor (composed of what Mann calls "murderous cell groups" and a "voracious brood") has fatally spread throughout her body. As with Aschenbach's malignant psychological disease, we cannot say precisely when this cancer began; the "murderous brood" (as Mann calls it) was literally lying in wait for decades (*Stories* 896).

7. Though he will make this continuity painfully clear in the later novels—and I believe that we are thus justified in recognizing its incipient patterns here—Mann resists the possibility of it in his notes for *Death in Venice,* which initially sketch out a progression from dignity and self-possession into humiliation and loss of self-control: "Ascent from problems to dignity. And now! The conflict is: beginning from "dignity," from an enmity to knowledge and a second state of ease, from an antianalytical state he falls into *this* passion" (*Venice* 71).

8. From the working notes: "*Plato says there is a kind of madness that does not arise without divine influence,* a rapture and inversion of reason and judgment [this condition is referred to as enthusiasm], whose origin and movement is derived from a higher power" (*Venice* 78, italics and brackets in original).

9. I believe that Reed underestimates Mann's ambivalent but severely ironic treatment of passion in *Death in Venice* when he claims that: "In Venice, [Mann] has an intense emotional experience. It inspires him to treat it in a form which is far from his usual literary stock-in-trade and is thereby a kind of creative rebirth. . . . Tadzio is celebrated hymnically,

the passion he inspires is affirmed because it is fruitful . . . indispensable for great art." Reed, *Thomas Mann: The Uses of Tradition*, 155.

10. "The Making of *The Magic Mountain*" first appeared in *The Atlantic Monthly* in January 1953; it is included as an appendix to the 1966 Knopf edition used here.

11. T. E. Apter, *Thomas Mann: The Devil's Advocate*, 75.

12. See Naphta's account in the section of chapter 6 of *The Magic Mountain* subtitled "Operationes Spirituales": "Men consciously and voluntarily descended into disease and madness, in search of knowledge which, acquired by fanaticism, would lead back to health; after the possession and use of it had ceased to be conditioned by that heroic and abnormal act of sacrifice. That was the true death on the cross, the true Atonement" (466). To Settembrini's one-word denunciation of this proposal—"The Reason"—Naphta replies in kind: "The Passion" (466).

13. See Mann's letter to Josef Ponten, 5 February 1925 (*Letters* 136).

14. If we mistake the passion scene (here and elsewhere) as merely a manifestation of the death drive, we overlook the tensions that allow Mann to entertain the possibility of a creative, aesthetic passion that is not restricted solely to decay and disintegration. See, for instance, T. E. Apter: "This tender release from consciousness and from the pressures of organic life is only one face of the death-wish; its other aspect is violent and destructive." *Thomas Mann: The Devil's Advocate*, 66.

15. Mann, "An Appeal to Reason," 400; reprinted in *Order of the Day: Political Essays and Speeches of Two Decades*, 46–68.

16. Regarding the connection between National Socialism's recent rise to power and the sympathy for passion in the intellectual sphere, Mann admits, "It may seem daring to associate the radical nationalism of our day with these conceptions from a romanticizing philosophy. Yet the association is there, and it must be recognized" (*Order* 55). See also his letter to Ferdinand Lion dated 13 March 1952: "My democratic attitude is not really genuine, it is merely an irritable reaction to German 'irrationalism' and the swindle of its profundity . . . and to any form of fascism, which I really and honestly cannot endure." See Paul Bishop and Ritchie Robertson's "The Intellectual World of Thomas Mann," 36.

17. Jeffrey B. Berlin, "On the Nature of Letters," 62.

18. Mann, "Freud's Position in the History of Modern Thought," 557; reprinted in *Past Masters and Other Papers*, 178.

19. See T. E. Apter's formulation in *Thomas Mann: The Devil's Advocate:* "Psychoanalytic theory might be a forward looking, healing, humanising science, but Mann nevertheless felt that it was not secure from the darker, backward tendencies within Romanticism" (5).

20. Mann describes the inverse relationship between the hero's path in the later novel and in *Death in Venice:* "Its pretensions are even more far-reaching, for the book deals with yet another fundamental theme, that of 'heightening,' enhancement (*Steigerung*). . . . in the hermetic, feverish atmosphere of the enchanted mountain, the ordinary stuff of which [Hans Castorp] is made undergoes a heightening process . . . His story is the story of the heightening process, but also as a narrative it is the heightening process itself" (*Mountain* 725–26).

21. In this way, *Doctor Faustus* may seem to represent a partial abrogation of the ambivalence that *The Magic Mountain* had proposed and that, according to many scholars, constitutes Mann's most fundamental artistic strategy. See Heller: "The structure of Mann's ideology is determined by his need for emotional oscillation. Mann's ambivalence is balanced. . . . Torn between opposing emotions directed toward the same object, he desires mediation; yet the partial resolution of the conflict immediately reactivates his ambivalence." "Thomas Mann's Conception of the Creative Writer," 144. For the classical case for

Mann's dedication to "the art of ambivalence," see Reed's *Thomas Mann: The Uses of Tradition*, 144–78.

22. For "syphilitic inspiration," see Albright, *Personality and Impersonality*, 283. Although he does not emphasize the implicit connection between Leverkühn's self-damaging tendencies and his outbursts of shame and self-disgust, Albright suggests that the artistic consequences of the devil's proposal are merely (as the devil himself admits) an extension of the protagonist's momentum toward self-destruction: "Leverkühn, in his struggles to escape from the grip of evil . . . must eradicate his own character, exterminate himself. . . . This can be considered a breakthrough, but it is also a logical extension of the intellectual self-destruction that had led Leverkühn into miniaturism" (283).

23. Mann briefly remarks the ephemerality of Castorp's vision in the conclusion of "Snow": "What he had dreamed was already fading from his mind. What he had thought—even that selfsame evening it was no longer so clear as it had been at first" (*Mountain* 498). See also Mann's letter to Josef Ponten on 5 February 1925, in which he asserts that instead of triumphantly bearing away the "insight" of his vision, "Hans promptly forgets it again; in general he is not personally able to cope with his higher thoughts" (*Letters* 137).

24. Mann, *Reflections of a Nonpolitical Man*, 50.

25. Mann to Julius Bab, 22 February 1925. Writing shortly after the publication of *The Magic Mountain*, Mann justifies the novel's preoccupation with the occult by claiming that it fits with the "design of the book, which refers repeatedly back to the mysticism of the body, the organic mystery" (*Letters* 139).

CONCLUSION

1. *The Sociology of Georg Simmel*, 410.

2. Sheppard, *Modernism—Dada—Postmodernism*, 13.

3. *The Sociology of Georg Simmel*, 410.

4. Ibid., 411.

5. Ibid.

6. Stephen Spender, *The Struggle of the Modern*, 71–72.

7. Tim Armstrong, *Modernism: A Cultural History*, 90, 93.

8. Harry Levin, "What Was Modernism?" 628.

9. Wilhelm Worringer, *Abstraction and Empathy*, trans. Michael Bullock, 13.

10. Ibid., 16.

11. Worringer initially denies that abstraction is primarily an intellectual response. The urge to abstraction "emanates not from the observer's intellect," he argues, "but from the deepest roots of his somato-psychic constitution" (35). This denial, however, seems to be motivated primarily by his desire to account for the presence of abstract art in primitive cultures. Elsewhere he admits that "that which was previously instinct is now the ultimate product of cognition" (18).

12. Ibid., 16, 18, 23.

13. Ibid., 18.

14. T. E. Hulme, *Speculations*, 87; see, however, Alun R. Jones, who argues that Hulme's position eventually reversed Worringer's, in "T. E. Hulme, Wilhelm Worringer, and the Urge to Abstraction," 1–7.

15. Helen Carr, "T. E. Hulme and the 'Spiritual Dread of Space,'" 110.

16. Andreas Huyssen, *After the Great Divide*, vii; Peter Bürger, *Theory of the Avant-Garde*; Richard Murphy, *Theorizing the Avant-Garde*. See, however, Bernard Gendron's *Between Montmartre and the Mudd Club* as well as David Chinitz's *T. S. Eliot and the Cultural Divide*,

which argues persuasively that modernists "adopted a variety of positions with respect to popular culture that cannot be reduced to either of the poles codified and popularized by Huyssen" (4).

17. *The Sociology of Georg Simmel,* 411.

18. Nicholls, *Modernisms,* 194.

19. Ibid., 196.

20. Armstrong, *Modernism: A Cultural History,* 93.

21. See Armstrong's "Two Types of Shock in Modernity."

22. Armstrong, *Modernism: A Cultural History,* 93.

23. David James, "Realism, Late Modernist Abstraction, and Sylvia Townsend Warner's Fictions of Impersonality," 112. James explicitly aligns himself with Tamar Katz's similar claims in *Impressionist Subjects,* 12.

24. Gregory S. Jay, "Postmodernism in *The Waste Land,*" 223, 235.

25. Lisa Low, "Refusing to Hit Back: Virginia Woolf and the Impersonality Question," 269.

26. Ibid.

27. Eve Sorum, "Masochistic Modernisms," 25.

28. Fredric Jameson, *A Singular Modernity: Essay on the Ontology of the Present,* 161.

29. See Fred Inglis's reconstruction of the lecture that Williams delivered in 1987 at the University of Bristol, published as "When Was Modernism?" (1989).

30. H.D., *Collected Poems, 1912–1944,* 14.

31. H.D., *Notes on Thought and Vision & The Wise Sappho,* 19.

32. Ibid., 47.

33. Wallace Stevens, *The Necessary Angel,* 36.

34. Ibid., 66.

35. Frank Lentricchia, *Ariel and the Police,* 171.

36. See Karen Kilcup's *Robert Frost and Feminine Literary Tradition* and James Longenbach's "Randall Jarrell's Semifeminine Mind" in *Modern Poetry after Modernism,* 49–64.

37. D. H. Lawrence, *Phoenix: The Posthumous Papers,* 255.

38. Ibid., 259–61.

39. While I will not deny that modernist poetry has its share of nostalgic mythologies—Eliot's theory of dissociated sensibility, for instance, or Lawrence's dialectic of illusion and disabuse in "Chaos in Poetry"—I would suggest that these are typically formulated in the service of literary history and criticism rather than as an integral part of a psychological model. I agree, however, with Michael Levenson's suggestion that modernist novels often "pursue their formal disruption of character even as they so often sustain nostalgic longing for a whole self." *Modernism and the Fate of Individuality,* xiii.

40. Contemporary philosopher Michel Meyer argues in opposition to this perspective in *Philosophy and the Passions,* 6.

41. See Richard Sheppard's account in *Modernism—Dada—Postmodernism,* 31–70.

BIBLIOGRAPHY

Abel, Elizabeth. *Virginia Woolf and the Fictions of Psychoanalysis.* Chicago: University of Chicago Press, 1989.

Ackroyd, Peter. *T. S. Eliot: A Life.* New York: Simon and Schuster, 1984.

Adams, Hazard. *The Book of Yeats's Poems.* Tallahassee: Florida State University Press, 1990.

Adams, Steve L., and George Mills Harper, eds. "The Manuscript of 'Leo Africanus.'" *Yeats Annual* 1 (1982): 3–47.

Albright, Daniel. *Lyricality in English Literature.* Lincoln: University of Nebraska Press, 1985.

———. *Personality and Impersonality: Lawrence, Woolf, and Mann.* Chicago: University of Chicago Press, 1978.

———. *Quantum Poetics: Yeats, Pound, Eliot, and the Science of Modernism.* Cambridge: Cambridge University Press, 1997.

———. "Yeats and Modernism." In *Cambridge Companion to W. B. Yeats,* edited by Marjorie Elizabeth Howes and John Kelly, 59–76. New York: Cambridge University Press, 2006.

Alighieri, Dante. *The Divine Comedy.* Translated by Henry Cary. 1908. Reprint, London: Dent, 1994.

Allen, Hervey. *Israfel: The Life and Times of Edgar Allan Poe.* 2 vols. New York: Doran, 1926.

Altieri, Charles. *The Art of Twentieth-Century American Poetry: Modernism and After.* Malden, MA: Blackwell, 2006.

Anonymous. "Mr. Eliot in Search of the Present." *Times Literary Supplement,* 25 March 1939, 176.

Apter, T. E. *Thomas Mann: The Devil's Advocate.* New York: New York University Press, 1979.

Aquinas, Thomas. *The Summa Theologica of Saint Thomas Aquinas.* Translated by Fathers of the English Dominican Province. New York: Benziger Bros., 1947–48.

Aristotle. *The Nicomachean Ethics of Aristotle.* Translated by F. H. Peters. London: Kegan Paul, Trench, Trübner & Company, 1891.

Armstrong, Tim. *Modernism: A Cultural History.* Cambridge: Polity, 2005.

———. "Two Types of Shock in Modernity." *Critical Quarterly* 42 (April 2000): 60–73.

Arnold, Matthew. *Essays in Criticism: First Series.* London: Macmillan, 1865.

———. *Essays in Criticism: Second Series.* London: Macmillan, 1888.

———. *The Poetical Works of Matthew Arnold.* Edited by C. B. Tinker and H. F. Lowry. London: Oxford University Press, 1950.

Atkinson, Brooks. "Theatre: Eliot's *The Family Reunion.*" *New York Times,* 21 October 1958, 39.

Auden, W. H. *Collected Poems.* Edited by Edward Mendelson. New York: Vintage, 1991.

Augustine. *Confessions.* Translated by John K. Ryan. New York: Doubleday, 1960.

Barnes, Djuna. *Nightwood.* 1936. New York: New Directions, 1961.

Baudelaire, Charles. *Intimate Journals.* Translated by Christopher Isherwood. 1930. Reprint, San Francisco: City Lights, 1983.

————. *The Painter of Modern Life and Other Essays*. Translated by Jonathan Mayne. New York: Da Capo, 1986.

Bergenholtz, Rita A. "Mann's *Death in Venice*." *Explicator* 55 (1997): 145–47.

Berlin, Jeffrey B. "On the Nature of Letters: Thomas Mann's Unpublished Correspondence with His American Publisher and Translator, and Unpublished Letters about the Writing of *Doctor Faustus*." *European Journal of English Studies* 9 (April 2005): 61–73.

Bernheimer, Charles. "A Shattered Globe: Narcissism and Masochism in Virginia Woolf's Life-Writing." In *Psychoanalysis And . . .* , edited by Richard Feldstein and Henry Sussman, 187–206. New York: Routledge, 1990.

Bersani, Leo. *The Freudian Body: Psychoanalysis and Art*. New York: Columbia University Press, 1986.

Bing, Siegfried, ed. *Artistic Japan: Illustrations and Essays*. 6 vols. London: Sampsom Low, Marston, Searle & Rivington, 1889.

Binyon, Laurence. *The Flight of the Dragon: An Essay on the Theory and Practice of Art in China and Japan, Based on Original Sources*. London: John Murray, 1911.

————. *Painting in the Far East: An Introduction to the History of Pictorial Art in Asia, Especially China and Japan*. 1908. Reprint, London: Edward Arnold, 1923.

Bishop, Paul. "The Intellectual World of Thomas Mann." In *The Cambridge Companion to Thomas Mann*, edited by Ritchie Robertson, 22–42. Cambridge: Cambridge University Press, 2002.

Blanchot, Maurice. *The Space of Literature*. Translated by Ann Smock. Lincoln: University of Nebraska Press, 1982.

Bloom, Harold. "Death and the Native Strain in American Poetry." *Social Research: An International Quarterly of the Social Sciences* 39 (1972): 449–62.

Bornstein, George. *Transformations of Romanticism in Yeats, Eliot, and Stevens*. Chicago: University of Chicago Press, 1976.

Bradford, Curtis Baker. *Yeats at Work*. Carbondale: Southern Illinois University Press, 1965.

Bradley, F. H. *Collected Essays*. 2 vols. Oxford: Clarendon Press, 1935.

Breton, André. *Manifestoes of Surrealism*. Ann Arbor: University of Michigan Press, 1972.

Brooker, Jewel Spears. *T. S. Eliot: The Contemporary Reviews*. New York: Cambridge University Press, 2004.

Brooks, Cleanth. "Sin and Expiation." *Partisan Review* 6 (Summer 1939): 114–16.

————. "*The Waste Land*: An Analysis." *Southern Review* 3 (Summer 1937): 106–36.

Browne, E. Martin. *The Making of T. S. Eliot's Plays*. Cambridge: Cambridge University Press, 1969.

————. "T. S. Eliot in the Theatre: The Director's Memories." In *T. S. Eliot: The Man and His Work; A Critical Evaluation by 26 Distinguished Writers*, edited by Allen Tate, 116–32. New York: Dell, 1966.

Brownlee, Kevin. "Dante and Narcissus (Purg. XXX, 76–99)." *Dante Studies* 96 (1978): 201–6.

Brunner, Larry. *Tragic Victory: The Doctrine of Subjective Salvation in the Poetry of W. B. Yeats*. Troy, N.Y.: Whitston, 1987.

Bürger, Peter. *Theory of the Avant-Garde*. Translated by Michael Shaw. Minneapolis: University of Minnesota Press, 1984.

Burke, Edmund. *A Philosophical Enquiry into the Origin of Our Ideas of the Sublime and Beautiful*. Edited by Adam Phillips. Oxford: Oxford University Press, 1998.

Bush, Ronald. *T. S. Eliot: A Study in Character and Style*. Oxford: Oxford University Press, 1983.

Byars, John A. *Yeats's Introduction of the Heroic Type*. Toronto: Hakkert, 1966.

Carlyle, Thomas. *On Heroes, Hero-Worship, and the Heroic in History.* Edited by H. D. Traill. New York: Scribner's, 1901.

———. *Sartor Resartus & Selected Prose.* New York: Holt, Rinehart and Winston, 1970.

Carpenter, Humphrey. *A Serious Character: The Life of Ezra Pound.* Boston: Houghton Mifflin, 1988.

Carr, Helen. "T. E. Hulme and the 'Spiritual Dread of Space.'" In *T. E. Hulme and the Question of Modernism,* edited by Edward Comentale and Andrzej Gasiorek, 93–112. Aldershot, England: Ashgate, 2006.

Chinitz, David E. *T. S. Eliot and the Cultural Divide.* Chicago: University of Chicago Press, 2003.

Christ, Carol. "T. S. Eliot and the Victorians." *Modern Philology* 79 (1981): 157–65.

———. *Victorian and Modern Poetics.* Chicago: University of Chicago Press, 1984.

Clark, Suzanne. *Sentimental Modernism: Women Writers and the Revolution of the Word.* Bloomington: Indiana University Press, 1991.

Clark, Timothy. *The Theory of Inspiration: Composition as a Crisis of Subjectivity in Romantic and Post-Romantic Writing.* New York: St. Martin's Press, 1997.

Clewell, Tammy. "Consolation Refused: Virginia Woolf, the Great War, and Modernist Mourning." *Modern Fiction Studies* 50 (Spring 2004): 197–223.

Clutton-Brock, Arthur. "Not Here, O Apollo." *Times Literary Supplement,* 12 June 1919, 322.

Comentale, Edward, and Andrzej Gasiorek, eds. *T. E. Hulme and the Question of Modernism.* Aldershot, England: Ashgate, 2006.

Cotsell, Michael. *The Theater of Trauma: American Modernist Drama and the Psychological Struggle for the American Mind.* New York: Peter Lang, 2005.

Craft, Robert. *Stravinsky: Chronicle of a Friendship.* New York: Knopf, 1972.

Crawford, Robert. *The Savage and the City in the Work of T. S. Eliot.* Oxford: Clarendon, 1987.

Cuda, Anthony. "T. S. Eliot's Forgotten 'Poet of Lines,' Nathaniel Wanley." *ANQ: A Quarterly Journal of Short Articles, Notes, and Reviews* 19 (Spring 2006): 56–61.

Davidson, John. *The Poems of John Davidson.* 2 vols. Edinburgh: Scottish Academic Press, 1973.

Dean, Tim. "T. S. Eliot, Famous Clairvoyante." In *Gender, Desire, and Sexuality in T. S. Eliot,* edited by Cassandra Laity and Nancy K. Gish, 43–65. New York: Cambridge University Press, 2004.

DeMeester, Karen. "Trauma and Recovery in Virginia Woolf's *Mrs. Dalloway.*" *Modern Fiction Studies* 44 (Fall 1998): 649–73.

DeSalvo, Louise A. *Virginia Woolf: The Impact of Childhood Sexual Abuse on Her Life and Work.* Boston: Beacon Press, 1989.

Descartes, René. *The Passions of the Soul.* In *The Philosophical Writings of Descartes,* vol. 1. Translated by John Cottingham, Robert Stoothoff, and Dugald Murdoch, 325–404. Cambridge: Cambridge University Press, 1984.

Dettmar, Kevin J. H., and Stephen Watt. *Marketing Modernisms: Self-Promotion, Canonization, Rereading.* Ann Arbor: University of Michigan Press, 1996.

Doggett, Rob. *Deep-Rooted Things: Empire and Nation in the Poetry and Drama of William Butler Yeats.* Notre Dame, Ind.: University of Notre Dame Press, 2006.

Donoghue, Denis. *Words Alone: The Poet T. S. Eliot.* New Haven, Conn.: Yale University Press, 2000.

Doolittle, Hilda (H.D.). *Collected Poems, 1912–1944.* Edited by Louis L. Martz. New York: New Directions, 1983.

————. *Notes on Thought and Vision & the Wise Sappho.* San Francisco: City Lights Books, 1982.

Drew, Elizabeth A. *T. S. Eliot: The Design of His Poetry.* New York: Scribner's, 1949.

Dulac, Edmund. "Without the Twilight." In *Scattering Branches: Tributes to the Memory of W. B. Yeats,* edited by Stephen Gwynn, 135–44. London: Macmillan, 1940.

Earl, Joe. "The Taxonomic Obsession: British Collectors and Japanese Objects, 1852–1986." *Burlington Magazine* 128 (December 1986): 864–73.

Eliot, T. S. *After Strange Gods: A Primer of Modern Heresy.* New York: Harcourt, Brace, 1934.

————. "Beyle and Balzac." *Athenaeum,* 30 May 1919, 392–93.

————. "The Bible as Scripture and as Literature." Unpublished address read before the Women's Alliance, King's Chapel, Boston, 1 December 1932. Houghton Library, Harvard University.

————. *Christianity and Culture: The Idea of a Christian Society and Notes toward the Definition of Culture.* New York: Harcourt, 1960.

————. "A Commentary." *Criterion* 5 (January 1927): 1–6.

————. "A Commentary." *Criterion* 11 (April 1932): 467–73.

————. "A Commentary." *Criterion* 12 (October 1932): 73–79.

————. *The Complete Plays of T. S. Eliot.* New York: Harcourt, Brace & World, 1967.

————. *The Complete Poems and Plays, 1909–1950.* New York: Harcourt, Brace, 1952.

————. "Critical Note." In *The Collected Poems of Harold Monro,* edited by Alida Monro, xiii–xvi. London: Cobden-Sanderson, 1933.

————. "The Development of Leibniz's Monadism." *Monist* 26 (October 1916): 534–56.

————. "A Dream within a Dream: T. S. Eliot on Edgar Allan Poe." *Listener,* 25 February 1943, 243–44.

————. "The Education of Taste." *Athenaeum,* 27 June 1919, 520–21.

————. "An Emotional Unity." *Dial* 84 (February 1928): 109–12.

————. *Essays Ancient & Modern.* 1936. Reprint, London: Faber and Faber, 1949.

————. *For Lancelot Andrewes: Essays on Style and Order.* Garden City, N.J.: Doubleday, Doran and Company, 1929.

————. *From Poe to Valéry.* New York: Harcourt, Brace, 1948.

————. "The Function of Criticism." *Criterion* 2 (October 1923): 31–42.

————. "The Hawthorne Aspect." *Little Review* 5 (August 1918): 47–53.

————. "The Idea of a Literary Review." *Criterion* 4 (January 1926): 1–6.

————. "The Idealism of Julien Benda." In *The New Republic Anthology, 1915–1935,* edited by Groff Conklin, 293–300. New York: Dodge Publishing, 1936.

————. "In Memory." *Little Review* 5 (August 1918): 44–47.

————. Introduction to *The Art of Poetry,* by Paul Valéry, translated by Denise Folliot, vii–xxiv. New York: Pantheon, 1958.

————. Introduction to *A Choice of Kipling's Verse,* edited by T. S. Eliot, 5–36. London: Faber and Faber, 1941

————. Introduction to *Nightwood,* by Djuna Barnes, xi–xvii. 1936. Reprint, New York: New Directions, 1961.

————. Introduction to *Revelation,* edited by John Baillie and Hugh Martin, 1–40. London: Faber, 1937.

————. Introduction to *Shakespeare & the Popular Dramatic Tradition,* by S. L. Bethell, 7–9. London: Staples Press, 1944.

————. Introduction to *The Wheel of Fire,* by G. Wilson Knight, xi–xix. 1930. Reprint, London: Methuen, 1972.

———. *Inventions of the March Hare: Poems 1909–1917.* Edited by Christopher B. Ricks. New York: Harcourt, Brace, 1996.

———. "Israfel." *Nation & Athenaeum,* 21 May 1927, 219.

———. "Kipling Redivivus." *Athenaeum,* 9 May 1919, 297–98.

———. *Knowledge and Experience in the Philosophy of F. H. Bradley.* New York: Farrar, Straus, 1964.

———. "Leibniz's Monads and Bradley's Finite Centers." *Monist* 26 (October 1916): 566–76.

———. *The Letters of T. S. Eliot. Vol. 1: 1898–1922.* Edited by Valerie Eliot. New York: Harcourt Brace Jovanovich, 1988.

———. "Literature and the Modern World." *American Prefaces* 1 (November 1935): 19–22.

———. "The Literature of Fascism." *Criterion* 8 (December 1928): 280–90.

———. "London Letter." *Dial* 73 (September 1922): 329–31.

———. "Modern Tendencies in Poetry." *Shama'a* 1 (April 1920): 9–18.

———. "Mr. Middleton Murry's Synthesis." *Criterion* 6 (October 1927): 340–47.

———. "Mr. Read and M. Fernandez." *Criterion* 4 (October 1926): 751–57.

———. "The Mysticism of Blake." *The Nation & Athenaeum,* 17 September 1927, 779.

———. *On Poetry and Poets.* New York: Farrar, Straus and Cudahy, 1957.

———. "Personality and Demonic Possession." *Virginia Quarterly Review* (January 1934): 94–103.

———. *Poems Written in Early Youth.* New York: Farrar, Straus and Giroux, 1967.

———, trans. "Poetry and Religion," by Jacques Maritain. *Criterion* 5 (January 1927): 7–22.

———. "Poets' Borrowings." *Times Literary Supplement,* 5 April 1928, 255.

———. Preface to *John Davidson: A Selection of His Poems,* edited by Maurice Lindsay, xi–xii. London: Hutchinson, 1961.

———. Preface to *The Little Book of Modern Verse,* edited by Anne Ridler, 5–9. London: Faber, 1942.

———. Preface to *Thoughts for Meditation: A Way to Recovery from Within,* edited by N. Gangulee, 11–14. London: Faber, 1951.

———. "Reflections on Contemporary Poetry." *Egoist,* October 1917, 133–34.

———. Review of *Nightwood,* by Djuna Barnes. *Criterion* 16 (April 1937): 560–64.

———. Review of *Religion and Science: A Philosophical Essay,* by John Theodore Merz. *International Journal of Ethics* 27 (October 1916): 125–26.

———. Review of *Son of a Woman: The Story of D. H. Lawrence,* by John Middleton Murry. *Criterion* 10 (July 1931): 768–74.

———. *The Sacred Wood.* 1920. Reprint, London: Methuen, 1967.

———. "Scylla and Charybdis." *Agenda* 23 (Spring–Summer 1985): 5–21.

———. *Selected Essays.* 3rd ed. London: Faber and Faber, 1972.

———. "The Significance of Charles Williams." *Listener,* 19 December 1946, 894–95.

———. "The Silver Bough." *Times,* 6 April 1958, 4.

———. "Thinking in Verse: A Survey of Early Seventeenth-Century Poetry." *Listener,* 12 March 1930, 441–43.

———. *The Three Voices of Poetry.* New York: Cambridge University Press, 1954.

———. *To Criticize the Critic: And Other Writings.* New York: Farrar, Straus and Giroux, 1965.

———. *The Use of Poetry and the Use of Criticism: Studies in the Relation of Criticism to Poetry in England.* 1933. Reprint, London: Faber and Faber, 1970.

———. *The Varieties of Metaphysical Poetry.* Edited by Ronald Schuchard. New York: Harcourt, Brace, 1994.

———. "Wanley and Chapman." *Times Literary Supplement,* 31 December 1925, 907.

————. *The Waste Land: A Facsimile and Transcript of the Original Drafts Including the Annotations of Ezra Pound*. Edited by Valerie Eliot. New York: Harcourt Brace Jovanovich, 1971.

————. "Whether Rostand Had Something about Him." *Athenaeum*, 25 July 1919, 665–66.

Ellmann, Maud. *The Poetics of Impersonality: T. S. Eliot and Ezra Pound*. Brighton, England: Harvester, 1987.

Ellmann, Richard. *The Identity of Yeats*. New York: Oxford University Press, 1964.

————. *Yeats: The Man and the Masks*. New York: Norton, 1978.

Empson, William. *Argufying: Essays on Literature and Culture*. Edited by John Haffenden. Iowa City: University of Iowa Press, 1987.

Evans, Martyn. "Madness, Medicine, and Creativity in Thomas Mann's *The Magic Mountain*." In *Madness and Creativity in Literature and Culture*, edited by Corinne Saunders and Jane Macnaughton, 159–76. New York: Palgrave Macmillan, 2005.

Fathman, Anthony. "Viv and Tom: The Eliots as Ether Addict and Co-Dependent." *Yeats Eliot Review* 11 (Fall 1991): 33–36.

Fleming, Deborah, ed. *W. B. Yeats and Postcolonialism*. West Cornwall, Conn.: Locust Hill Press, 2001.

Foster, R. F. *W. B. Yeats: A Life*, vol. 1: *The Apprentice Mage*. 2 vols. Oxford: Oxford University Press, 1997.

————. *W. B. Yeats: A Life*, vol. 2: *The Arch Poet*. 2 vols. Oxford: Oxford University Press, 2003.

Gallup, Donald. *T. S. Eliot: A Bibliography*. New York: Harcourt, 1969.

Gardner, Helen. *The Composition of "Four Quartets."* New York: Oxford University Press, 1978.

Gaye, Phoebe Fenwick. "Expiation Becomes Orestes." *Time and Tide* 20 (25 March 1939): 388–89.

Gendron, Bernard. *Between Montmartre and the Mudd Club: Popular Music and the Avant-Garde*. Chicago: University of Chicago Press, 2002.

Gilbert, Sandra M., and Susan Gubar. "Tradition and the Female Talent." In *No Man's Land: The Place of the Woman Writer in the Twentieth Century*, vol. 1, *The War of the Words*, 125–64. New Haven, Conn.: Yale University Press, 1988.

Giles, Steve. *Theorizing Modernism: Essays in Critical Theory*. New York: Routledge, 1993.

Gilson, Étienne. *The Spirit of Medieval Philosophy (Gifford Lectures 1931–1932)*. Translated by A. H. C. Downes. 1936. Reprint, Notre Dame, Ind.: University of Notre Dame Press, 1991.

Gold, Matthew K. "The Expert Hand and the Obedient Heart: Dr. Vittoz, T. S. Eliot, and the Therapeutic Possibilities of *The Waste Land*." *Journal of Modern Literature* 23 (Summer 2000): 519–33.

Gordon, Lyndall. *T. S. Eliot: An Imperfect Life*. New York: Norton, 1999.

Gualtieri, Elena. *Virginia Woolf's Essays: Sketching the Past*. New York: St. Martin's Press, 2000.

Hall, Donald. *Remembering Poets: Reminiscences and Opinions*. New York: Harper & Row, 1978.

Harding, Jason. *The Criterion: Cultural Politics and Periodical Networks in Inter-War Britain*. Oxford: Oxford University Press, 2002.

————. "Eliot without Tears." *Modernism/modernity* 13 (2006): 917–24.

Harper, George Mills. *The Making of Yeats's 'A Vision': A Study of the Automatic Script*. 2 vols. London: Macmillan, 1987.

Harper, Margaret Mills. *Wisdom of Two: The Spiritual and Literary Collaboration of George and W. B. Yeats*. Oxford: Oxford University Press, 2006.

Hart, Ernest. *Lectures on Japanese Art Work, Delivered before the Society, May 4, 11, and 18, 1886, with a Catalogue of Objects Exhibited, and an Index of Japanese Artists.* London: W. Trounce, 1887.

Hearn, Lafcadio. "The Boy Who Drew Cats." In *Japanese Fairy Tales.* Mount Vernon, N.Y.: Peter Pauper, 1936.

———. *Shadowings and a Japanese Miscellany,* vol. 10, *The Writings of Lafcadio Hearn.* Boston: Houghton Mifflin, 1922.

Heller, Erich. *The Ironic German: A Study of Thomas Mann.* Boston: Little, Brown, 1958.

Heller, Peter. "Thomas Mann's Conception of the Creative Writer." In *Critical Essays on Thomas Mann,* edited by Inta M. Ezergailis, 143–75. Boston: Hall, 1988.

Hennessey, Oliver. "'I Shall Find the Dark Grow Luminous When I Understand I Have Nothing': Yeats's Failing Vision." *Yeats Eliot Review* 21 (Summer 2004): 2–19.

Hickman, Miranda B. *The Geometry of Modernism: The Vorticist Idiom in Lewis, Pound, H.D., and Yeats.* Austin: University of Texas Press, 2005.

Hite, Molly. "Virginia Woolf's Two Bodies." *Genders* 31 (2000).

Horton, Philip. "Speculations on Sin." *Kenyon Review* 1 (Summer 1939): 330–33.

Howes, Marjorie Elizabeth, and John Kelly, eds. *The Cambridge Companion to W. B. Yeats.* New York: Cambridge University Press, 2006.

Hughes, Ted. "The Poetic Self: A Centenary Tribute to T. S. Eliot." In *Winter Pollen,* edited by William Scammell, 268–93. New York: Picador, 1994.

Hulme, T. E. *Speculations: Essays on Humanism and the Philosophy of Art,* edited by Herbert Read. 1924. Reprint, New York: Routledge & Kegan Paul, 1987.

Huyssen, Andreas. *After the Great Divide: Modernism, Mass Culture, Postmodernism.* Bloomington: Indiana University Press, 1986.

James, David. "Realism, Late Modernist Abstraction, and Sylvia Townsend Warner's Fictions of Impersonality." *Modernism/modernity* 12 (2005): 111–31.

James, Susan. "Explaining the Passions: Passions, Desires, and the Explanation of Action." In *The Soft Underbelly of Reason: The Passions in the Seventeenth Century,* edited by Stephen Gaukroger, 17–33. London: Routledge, 1998.

———. *Passion and Action: The Emotions in Seventeenth-Century Philosophy.* Oxford: Clarendon Press, 1997.

James, William. *The Varieties of Religious Experience.* 1902. Reprint, New York: Collier, 1961.

Jameson, Fredric. *A Singular Modernity: Essay on the Ontology of the Present.* New York: Verso, 2002.

Jay, Gregory S. "Postmodernism in *The Waste Land:* Women, Mass Culture, and Others." In *Rereading the New: A Backward Glance at Modernism,* edited by Kevin J. H. Dettmar, 221–48. Ann Arbor: University of Michigan Press, 1992.

John, Brian. "Yeats and Carlyle." *Notes and Queries* 215 (December 1970): 455.

Johnson, Gary. "*Death in Venice* and the Aesthetic Correlative." *Journal of Modern Literature* 27 (Winter 2004): 83–96.

Johnston, Devin. *Precipitations: Contemporary American Poetry as Occult Practice.* Middletown, Conn.: Wesleyan University Press, 2002.

Joly, Henri L. *Legend in Japanese Art: A Description of Historical Episodes, Legendary Characters, Folk-Lore Myths, Religious Symbolism, Illustrated in the Arts of Old Japan.* 1908. Reprint, Rutland, VT: Tuttle, 1967.

Jones, Alun R. "T. E. Hulme, Wilhelm Worringer, and the Urge to Abstraction." *British Journal of Aesthetics* 1 (1960): 1–7.

Jones, David. *The Plays of T. S. Eliot.* London: Routledge & Kegan Paul, 1960.

Kadlec, David. *Mosaic Modernism: Anarchism, Pragmatism, Culture.* Baltimore: Johns Hopkins University Press, 2000.

Kalaidjian, Walter B. *The Edge of Modernism: American Poetry and the Traumatic Past.* Baltimore: Johns Hopkins University Press, 2006.

Katz, Tamar. *Impressionist Subjects: Gender, Interiority, and Modernist Fiction in England.* Urbana: University of Illinois Press, 2000.

Keats, John. *A Critical Edition of the Major Works.* Edited by Elizabeth Cook. Oxford: Oxford University Press, 1990.

Kenner, Hugh. *The Invisible Poet: T. S. Eliot.* New York: McDowell Obolensky, 1959.

———. *The Pound Era.* Berkeley: University of California Press, 1971.

Kermode, Frank. *Romantic Image.* 1957. Reprint, New York: Routledge, 2002.

Kilcup, Karen. *Robert Frost and Feminine Literary Tradition.* Ann Arbor: University of Michigan Press, 1998.

Knight, George Wilson. *The Crown of Life: Essays in Interpretation of Shakespeare's Final Plays.* London: Methuen, 1965.

———. *Neglected Powers: Essays on Nineteenth and Twentieth Century Literature.* New York: Barnes & Noble, 1971.

———. "T. S. Eliot: Some Literary Impressions." In *T. S. Eliot: The Man and His Work,* edited by Allen Tate, 245–61. New York: Dell, 1966.

———. *The Wheel of Fire: Interpretations of Shakespearian Tragedy with Three New Essays.* 1930. London: Methuen,1972.

Laity, Cassandra, and Nancy K. Gish, eds. *Gender, Desire, and Sexuality in T. S. Eliot.* Cambridge: Cambridge University Press, 2004.

Langbaum, Robert Woodrow. *The Poetry of Experience: The Dramatic Monologue in Modern Literary Tradition.* New York: Random House, 1957.

Lawrence, D. H. *Phoenix: The Posthumous Papers of D. H. Lawrence.* Edited by Edward McDonald. 1936. Reprint, New York: Viking, 1972.

———. *Psychoanalysis and the Unconscious.* New York: Viking, 1960.

Lawrence, D. H. *Selected Literary Criticism.* Edited by Anthony Beal. New York: Viking, 1966.

Leibniz, Gottfried Wilhelm. *The Monadology and Other Philosophical Writings.* Translated by Robert Latta. Oxford: Clarendon Press, 1898.

Lentricchia, Frank. *Ariel and the Police: Michel Foucault, William James, Wallace Stevens.* Madison: University of Wisconsin Press, 1988.

Levenson, Michael H. *Modernism and the Fate of Individuality: Character and Novelistic Form from Conrad to Woolf.* Cambridge: Cambridge University Press, 1991.

Levin, Harry. "What Was Modernism?" *Massachusetts Review* 1 (August 1960): 609–30.

Londraville, Richard. "Four Lectures by W. B. Yeats, 1902–4." *Yeats Annual* 8 (1991): 78–122.

Longenbach, James. *Modern Poetry after Modernism.* New York: Oxford University Press, 1997.

Low, Lisa. "Refusing to Hit Back: Virginia Woolf and the Impersonality Question." In *Virginia Woolf and the Essay,* edited by Beth Carol Rosenberg and Jeanne Dubino, 257–74. New York: St. Martin's Press, 1997.

MacBride White, Anna, and A. Norman Jeffares, eds. *The Gonne-Yeats Letters: 1893–1938.* New York: Norton, 1993.

Mann, Thomas. "An Appeal to Reason." Translated by H. T. Lowe-Porter. *Criterion* 10 (April 1931): 393–411.

———. *Collected Stories.* Translated by H. T. Lowe-Porter. London: Everyman's Library, 2001.

———. *Death in Venice: A New Translation, Backgrounds and Contexts, Criticism.* Edited by Clayton Koelb. New York: W. W. Norton, 1994.

———. *Diaries, 1918–1939.* Translated by Richard and Clara Winston. Edited by Hermann Kesten. London: A. Deutsch, 1983.

———. *Doctor Faustus: The Life of the German Composer Adrian Leverkühn as Told by a Friend.* Translated by H. T. Lowe-Porter. New York: Knopf, 1992.

———. *Essays of Three Decades.* Translated by H. T. Lowe-Porter. New York: A. A. Knopf, 1947.

———. "Freud's Position in the History of Modern Thought." Translated by H. T. Lowe-Porter. *Criterion* 12 (July 1933): 549–70.

———. *Letters of Thomas Mann, 1889–1955.* Translated by H. T. Lowe-Porter. New York: A. A. Knopf, 1971.

———. *The Magic Mountain.* Translated by H. T. Lowe-Porter. New York: A. A. Knopf, 1966.

———. *"On Myself" and Other Princeton Lectures: An Annotated Edition Based on Mann's Lecture Typescripts.* Edited by James N. Bade. Frankfurt: Lang, 1996.

———. *Order of the Day: Political Essays and Speeches of Two Decades.* Translated by H. T. Lowe-Porter. New York: A. A. Knopf, 1942.

———. *Past Masters and Other Papers.* Translated by H. T. Lowe-Porter. New York: Knopf, 1933.

———. *Reflections of a Nonpolitical Man.* New York: F. Ungar, 1983.

Marcus, Phillip L. *Yeats and Artistic Power.* New York: New York University Press, 1992.

Materer, Timothy. *Modernist Alchemy: Poetry and the Occult.* Ithaca, N.Y.: Cornell University Press, 1995.

Matthiessen, F. O. *The Achievement of T. S. Eliot: An Essay on the Nature of Poetry.* New York: Oxford University Press, 1947.

Mayer, David. "The Family Reunion." *Plays and Players* 26 (May 1979): 29.

McAteer, Michael. *Standish O'Grady, AE and Yeats: History, Politics, Culture.* Dublin: Irish Academic Press, 2002.

Melaney, William. *After Ontology: Literary Theory and Modernist Poetics.* New York: State University of New York Press, 2001.

Menand, Louis. *Discovering Modernism: T. S. Eliot and His Context.* New York: Oxford University Press, 1987.

Meyer, Michel. *Philosophy and the Passions: Toward a History of Human Nature.* Translated by Robert F. Barsky. University Park: Pennsylvania State University Press, 2000.

Mileur, Jean-Pierre. "Revisionism, Irony, and the Mask of Sentiment." *New Literary History* 29 (Spring 1998): 197–233.

Miller, J. Hillis. "Mr. Carmichael and Lily Briscoe: The Rhythm of Creativity in *To the Lighthouse.*" In *Modernism Reconsidered,* edited by Robert Kiely and John Hildebidle, 167–89. Cambridge, Mass.: Harvard University Press, 1983.

Minow-Pinkney, Makiko. *Virginia Woolf and the Problem of the Subject.* New Brunswick, NJ: Rutgers University Press, 1987.

Montgomery, Marion. *Eliot's Reflective Journey to the Garden.* Troy, N.Y.: Whitston, 1979.

Moran, Patricia. *Virginia Woolf, Jean Rhys and the Aesthetics of Trauma.* New York: Palgrave Macmillan, 2007.

Morrell, Ottoline. *Ottoline at Garsington: Memoirs of Lady Ottoline Morrell, 1915–1918.* Edited by Robert Gathorne-Hardy. London: Faber, 1974.

Morrison, Blake. "The Two Mrs. Eliots." In *Too True,* 135–56. London: Granta Books, 1998.

Muldoon, Paul. *Poems 1968–1998.* New York: Farrar, Straus and Giroux, 2001.

Murphy, Richard. *Theorizing the Avant-Garde: Modernism, Expressionism, and the Problem of Postmodernity.* New York: Cambridge University Press, 1999.

Naremore, James. *The World without a Self: Virginia Woolf and the Novel.* New Haven, Conn.: Yale University Press, 1973.

Nicholls, Peter. *Modernisms: A Literary Guide.* Berkeley: University of California Press, 1995.

Ophir, Ella Zohar. "Toward a Pitiless Fiction: Abstraction, Comedy, and Modernist Anti-humanism." *MFS: Modern Fiction Studies* 52 (2006): 92–120.

Oshima, Shotaro. *W. B. Yeats and Japan.* Tokyo: Hokuseido Press, 1965.

Pater, Walter. *Appreciations: With an Essay on Style.* London: Macmillan, 1895.

———. *Marius the Epicurean, His Sensations and Ideas.* 2 vols. London: Macmillan, 1913.

———. *The Renaissance: Studies in Art and Poetry: The 1893 Text.* Edited by Donald L. Hill. Berkeley: University of California Press, 1980.

Piette, Adam. "Eliot's Breakdown and Dr. Vittoz." *English Language Notes* 33 (September 1995): 35–39.

Pinch, Adela. *Strange Fits of Passion: Epistemologies of Emotion, Hume to Austen.* Stanford: Stanford University Press, 1996.

Poe, Edgar Allan. *The Works of Edgar Allan Poe.* Raven edition. 5 vols. New York: Collier, 1903.

Poresky, Louise A. *The Elusive Self: Psyche and Spirit in Virginia Woolf's Novels.* Newark: University of Delaware Press, 1981.

Pottle, Frederick A. "A Modern Verse Play." *Yale Review* 28 (June 1939): 836–39.

Pound, Ezra. *Literary Essays.* New York: New Directions, 1968.

Rabaté, Jean-Michel. *The Ghosts of Modernity.* Gainesville: University Press of Florida, 1996.

Rado, Lisa. *The Modern Androgyne Imagination: A Failed Sublime.* Charlottesville: University Press of Virginia, 2000.

Rainey, Lawrence S., ed. *The Annotated Waste Land with Eliot's Contemporary Prose.* New Haven, Conn.: Yale University Press, 2005.

———. *Revisiting "The Waste Land."* New Haven, Conn.: Yale University Press, 2005.

Reed, T. J. *"Der Tod in Venedig": Text, Materialen, Kommentar.* Munich: Hanswer, 1983.

———. *Thomas Mann: The Uses of Tradition.* Oxford: Clarendon Press, 1974.

Ress, Laura Jane. *Tender Consciousness: Sentimental Sensibility in the Emerging Artist—Sterne, Yeats, Joyce, and Proust.* New York: P. Lang, 2002.

Richter, Harvena. *Virginia Woolf: The Inward Voyage.* Princeton, N.J.: Princeton University Press, 1970.

Rosenberg, Beth Carole, and Jeanne Dubino. *Virginia Woolf and the Essay.* New York: St. Martin's Press, 1997.

Rosenberg, Edgar. "Mann's *Death in Venice*." *Explicator* 62 (2004): 154–59.

Ruskin, John. *Modern Painters,* vol. 3. New York: Thomas Y. Crowell, 1873.

Ryan, Judith. *The Vanishing Subject: Early Psychology and Literary Modernism.* Chicago: University of Chicago Press, 1991.

Sackton, Alexander H. *The T. S. Eliot Collection of the University of Texas at Austin.* Austin: University of Texas, Humanities Research Center, 1975.

Schuchard, Ronald. "Burbank with a Baedeker, Eliot with a Cigar: American Intellectuals, Anti-Semitism, and the Idea of Culture." *Modernism/modernity* 10 (2003): 1–26.

———. *Eliot's Dark Angel: Intersections of Life and Art.* New York: Oxford University Press, 1999.

———. *The Last Minstrels: Yeats and the Revival of the Bardic Arts.* Oxford: Oxford University Press, 2008.

Schwartz, Delmore. "Orestes in England." *Nation,* 10 June 1939, 767–77.

Seymour-Jones, Carole. *Painted Shadow: The Life of Vivienne Eliot, First Wife of T. S. Eliot.* New York: Random House, 2001.

Sheppard, Richard. *Modernism—Dada—Postmodernism.* Evanston, Ill.: Northwestern University Press, 2000.

Silver, Brenda R. *Virginia Woolf's Reading Notebooks.* Princeton, N.J.: Princeton University Press, 1983.

Simmel, Georg. *The Sociology of Georg Simmel.* Translated by Kurt H. Wolf. Glencoe, Ill.: Free Press, 1950.

Smidt, Kristian. *The Importance of Recognition: Six Chapters on T. S. Eliot.* Tromsø, Norway: Norbye, 1973.

Smith, Grover Cleveland. *T. S. Eliot's Poetry and Plays: A Study in Sources and Meaning.* Chicago: University of Chicago Press, 1956.

Sokolsky, Anita. "The Resistance to Sentimentality: Yeats, de Man, and the Aesthetic Education." *Yale Journal of Criticism* 1 (1987): 67–86.

Sorum, Eve. "Masochistic Modernisms: A Reading of Eliot and Woolf." *Journal of Modern Literature* 28 (2005): 25–43.

Southam, B. C. *A Guide to the Selected Poems of T. S. Eliot.* 6th ed. New York: Harcourt, 1996.

Spender, Stephen. *The Struggle of the Modern.* London: Hamish Hamilton, 1963.

Stedman, Gesa. *Stemming the Torrent: Expression and Control in the Victorian Discourses on Emotions, 1830–1872.* Burlington, Vt.: Ashgate, 2002.

Stevens, Wallace. *The Necessary Angel: Essays on Reality and the Imagination.* New York: Vintage Books, 1965.

Strier, Richard. "Against the Rule of Reason: Praise of Passion from Luther to Shakespeare to Herbert." In *Reading the Early Modern Passions: Essays in the Cultural History of Emotion,* edited by Gail Kern Paster et al., 23–42. Philadelphia: University of Pennsylvania Press, 2004.

Surette, Leon. *The Birth of Modernism: Ezra Pound, T. S. Eliot, W. B. Yeats, and the Occult.* Montreal: McGill-Queen's University Press, 1993.

Sword, Helen. *Engendering Inspiration: Visionary Strategies in Rilke, Lawrence, and H.D.* Ann Arbor: University of Michigan Press, 1995.

———. *Ghostwriting Modernism.* Ithaca, N.J.: Cornell University Press, 2002.

Symons, Arthur. *The Symbolist Movement in Literature.* New York: E. P. Dutton, 1908.

Tate, Allen, ed. *T. S. Eliot: The Man and His Work; A Critical Evaluation by 26 Distinguished Writers.* New York: Dell, 1966.

Toomey, Deirdre, ed. *Yeats and Women.* New York: St. Martin's Press, 1997.

Travers, Martin. *Thomas Mann.* Houndsmill, U.K.: Macmillan, 1992.

Tynan, Katharine. *Twenty-five Years: Reminiscences.* London: John Murray, 1913.

Unger, Leonard, ed. *T. S. Eliot: A Selected Critique.* New York: Rinehart, 1948.

Valentine, Kylie. *Psychoanalysis, Psychiatry and Modernist Literature.* New York: Palgrave Macmillan, 2003.

Valéry, Paul. *The Art of Poetry.* Translated by Denise Folliot. New York: Pantheon, 1958.

Vendler, Helen. "The Later Poetry." In *The Cambridge Companion to W. B. Yeats,* edited by Marjorie Elizabeth Howes, 77–100. New York: Cambridge University Press, 2006.

———. *Our Secret Discipline: Yeats and Lyric Form.* Cambridge, Mass.: Harvard University Press, Belknap Press, 2007.

———. *Yeats's Vision and the Later Plays.* Cambridge, Mass.: Harvard University Press, 1963.

Vittoz, Roger. *Treatment of Neurasthenia by Means of Brain Control.* 2nd ed. London: Longmans, Green, 1913.

Wallis, M. H. *A Guide to Mediumship and Psychical Unfoldment.* London: Friars Printing Association, 1903.

Whyte, Lancelot Law. *The Unconscious before Freud.* New York: Basic Books, 1960.

Wilde, Oscar. *Intentions,* vol. 10, *Works of Oscar Wilde.* New York: AMS Press, 1980.

Williams, Raymond. "When Was Modernism?" *New Left Review* 1, no. 175 (May–June 1989): 48–52.

Woolf, Virginia. *Collected Essays.* Edited by Leonard Woolf. 4 vols. London: Hogarth Press, 1966–67.

———. *The Death of the Moth, and Other Essays.* New York: Harcourt, Brace, 1942.

———. *The Diary of Virginia Woolf.* Edited by Anne Oliver Bell. 5 vols. New York: Harcourt Brace Jovanovich, 1977–1984.

———. *The Essays of Virginia Woolf.* Edited by Andrew McNeillie. 4 vols. London: Hogarth Press, 1986–1994.

———. *The Moment, and Other Essays.* Ed. Leonard Woolf. New York: Harcourt, Brace, 1948.

———. *Moments of Being.* Edited by Jeanne Schulkind. New York: Harcourt Brace Jovanovich, 1985.

———. *The Second Common Reader, Annotated Edition.* Edited by Andrew McNeillie. 1932. Reprint, New York: Harcourt Brace Jovanovich, 1986.

———. *To the Lighthouse.* New York: Harcourt Brace Jovanovich, 1981.

———. *The Waves.* New York: Harcourt, Brace, 1931.

Wordsworth, William. *The Prelude, or Growth of a Poet's Mind; an Autobiographical Poem.* Edited by Ernest de Selincourt. London: Oxford University Press, 1947.

Worringer, Wilhelm. *Abstraction and Empathy: A Contribution to the Psychology of Style.* Translated by Michael Bullock. Chicago: Ivan R. Dee, 1997.

Wylie, Elinor. "Mr. Eliot's Slug-Horn." *New York Evening Post Literary Review,* 20 January 1923, 396.

Yeats, W. B. *Autobiographies.* Edited by William H. O'Donnell and Douglas N. Archibald. New York: Scribner, 1999.

———. *The Collected Letters of W. B. Yeats.* Edited by John Kelly. Oxford: Oxford University Press (InteLex Electronic edition), 2002.

———. *The Collected Letters of W. B. Yeats, Vols. 1–4.* Edited by John Kelly, Warwick Gould, Deirdre Toomey, Eric Domville, and Ronald Schuchard. Oxford: Clarendon Press, 1986–2005.

———. *Early Articles and Reviews: Uncollected Articles and Reviews Written between 1886 and 1900.* Edited by John P. Frayne and Madeleine Marchaterre. New York: Scribner, 2004.

———. *Early Essays.* Edited by Richard J. Finneran and George Bornstein. New York: Scribner, 2007.

———. *Essays and Introductions.* New York: Macmillan, 1968.

———. *Explorations.* New York: Macmillan, 1962.

———. *Four Years.* Churchtown, Dundrum, Ireland: Cuala Press, 1921.

———. "Four Years." *London Mercury* (August 1921): 364–77.

———. *The Hour-Glass: Manuscript Materials.* Edited by Catherine Phillips. Ithaca, N.Y.: Cornell University Press, 1994.

————. *Interviews and Recollections.* 2 vols. Edited by E. H. Mikhail. New York: Harper and Row, 1977.

————. *The Irish Dramatic Movement.* Edited by Mary FitzGerald and Richard J. Finneran. New York: Scribner, 2003.

————. *John Sherman & Dhoya.* Edited by Richard J. Finneran. Detroit, Mich.: Wayne State University Press, 1969.

————. *Later Articles and Reviews: Uncollected Articles, Reviews, and Radio Broadcasts Written after 1900.* Edited by Colton Johnson. New York: Scribner, 2000.

————. *Later Essays.* Edited by William H. O'Donnell. New York: Charles Scribner's Sons, 1994.

————. *The Letters of W. B. Yeats.* Edited by Allan Wade. New York: Macmillan, 1955.

————. *Letters to the New Island.* Edited by George Bornstein and Hugh Witemeyer. Basingstoke, U.K.: Macmillan, 1989.

————. *Memoirs.* Edited by Denis Donoghue. New York: Macmillan, 1972.

————. *Mythologies.* New York: Touchstone, 1959.

————. *Prefaces and Introductions: Uncollected Prefaces and Introductions by Yeats to Works by Other Authors and to Anthologies Edited by Yeats.* Edited by William H. O'Donnell. New York: Macmillan, 1988.

————. *The Secret Rose: Stories by W. B. Yeats. A Variorum Edition.* Edited by Phillip L. Marcus et al. Ithaca, N.Y.: Cornell University Press, 1981.

————. *The Senate Speeches of W. B. Yeats.* Edited by Donald R. Pearce. Bloomington: Indiana University Press, 1960.

————. *The Speckled Bird: An Autobiographical Novel with Variant Versions.* Edited by William H. O'Donnell. Basingstoke, U.K.: Palgrave Macmillan, 2003.

————. *Stories of Red Hanrahan.* Dundrum, Ireland: Dun Emer Press, 1904.

————. *The Trembling of the Veil.* London: Privately printed by T. Werner Laurie, 1921.

————. *The Trembling of the Veil.* London: Macmillan, 1926.

————. *The Variorum Edition of the Plays of W. B. Yeats.* Edited by Russell Alspach and Catharine Alspach. New York: Macmillan, 1966.

————. *The Variorum Edition of the Poems of W. B. Yeats.* Edited by Peter Allt and Russell Alspach. New York: Macmillan, 1977.

————. *A Vision.* London: Macmillan, 1937.

————. *A Vision (1925).* Edited by Catherine E. Paul and Margaret Mills Harper. New York: Scribner's, 2008.

————. *W. B. Yeats: Interviews and Recollections.* Edited by E. H. Mikhail. 2 vols. New York: Barnes & Noble Books, 1977.

————. *Yeats's Vision Papers,* vol. 3: *Sleep and Dream Notebooks, Vision Notebooks 1 and 2, Card File.* Edited by Robert Anthony Martinich and Margaret Mills Harper. London: Macmillan, 1992.

Zwerdling, Alex. *Yeats and the Heroic Ideal.* New York: New York University Press, 1965.

INDEX

References to endnotes followed by parenthetical citations are used to indicate titles and authors that are quoted or discussed in the body of the text but identified only in the endnotes.

ABOUT THE AUTHOR

Anthony Cuda is an assistant professor at the University of North Carolina at Greensboro, where he teaches
courses in American literature and
twentieth-century poetry. He is the
coeditor of the *Complete Prose of T. S.
Eliot: Volume II, 1919–1925.*